Contents at a Glance

Table of Contents

About the Author

Jeffrey Zeldman has been designing websites since the Crimean War. His personal website at www.zeldman.com has been visited by millions. Jeffrey is the publisher and creative director of *A List Apart* (www.alistapart.com), a weekly magazine "For People Who Make Websites"; cofounder and leader of the advocacy group, The Web Standards Project (www.webstandards.org); and founder of Happy Cog (www.happycog.com), a web design agency. He is a featured columnist for publications including Adobe Web Center, *PDN-Pix* Magazine, and *Crain's Creativity* Magazine and speaks at web and design conferences around the world. But what he really wants to do is direct.

About the Technical Editor

Steve Champeon is the CTO of hesketh.com, a web services firm in Raleigh, NC, that specializes in distinctive B2B and corporate sites, vibrant online communities, and high impact applications. He has provided technical editing on the topics of XML, XHTML, and other web-related topics and was the development editor for Jeff Veen's recent bestseller, *The Art and Science of Web Design*, published by New Riders. In addition to his work as an editor, Champeon is a frequent contributor to online and print magazines for web professionals and is the author of *Building Dynamic HTML GUIs* (published by IDG Books Worldwide).

A highly sought-after speaker at trade conferences, Champeon regularly participates in CMP's Web conference circuit and Cool Site in a Day competition, Thunder Lizard, South by Southwest (SxSW), and others, often speaking on DHTML and how to grow successful online communities.

Dedication

To Joan, whose love makes me feel happy and safe.

To my Dad, who taught me to be independent.

To my Mom, who loved books. I wish she could have seen this one.

Acknowledgments

I cannot possibly name all the people whose creativity has inspired me, or those I've been lucky enough to collaborate with over the years. It would take hundreds of pages to properly thank those I've worked with this year alone.

In childhood, I attended a wedding where the bride and groom thanked the special people in their lives. In the flush of the moment, they forgot to name one friend. He harbored a resentment that deepened over the years. Ultimately, a tragedy ensued, in which innocent bystanders lost their lives. But I digress.

Rather than make a similar mistake, I'm going to deliberately omit the names of many special people who contributed to my knowledge of the Web and thus, however unwittingly, to this book. Even if you are not named below, I love you and am grateful to you, and you should buy this book regardless.

To Steve Crozier of Populi, who envisioned an intelligent method of teaching web design, and to Margaret Alston and Cheryl Stockton, who collaborated with me on the development of the Populi Curriculum, my sincere and endless thanks.

My deep gratitude to Michael Nolan for asking me to write this book. To Michael and Karen Whitehouse for shepherding it safely through the minefields of the publishing industry. To development editor Victoria Elzey for keeping it real. And to my friend and this book's technical editor Steven Champeon for finding all the mistakes and not telling anyone but me.

To my beloved friends Fred Gates, Leigh and TJ Baker-Foley, and Katherine Sullivan: thank you for sharing your lives, keeping me sane, and forgiving the disappearances, hibernation, and mood swings that accompanied the writing of this book.

To Jim, who asked only an occasional phone call and got nothing but months of silence: I wrote this book for you, I owe you more than these words express, and I promise to start calling again, really.

To Don Buckley, my friend and first web client, and to my first web design partners, Steve McCarron and Alec Pollak, sincere thanks and respect.

All web designers owe thanks to Glenn Davis for contributions too numerous to describe here. Similarly, respect and thanks to George Olsen, Teresa Martin, and Michael Sweeney. You know what you did.

Love, thanks, and respect to Brian M. Platz, co-founder of A List Apart back when it was a mailing list for web designers. To Bruce Livingstone, Nick Finck, Webchick, and Erin Kissane, who help keep ALA going. And to the fine writers who make it worth reading, including Joe Clark, J. David Eisenberg, Curt

Cloninger, Alan Herrell, Scott Kramer, Jeffrey Veen, John Allsopp, Robin Miller, Denice Warren, Jason Kottke, Lance Arthur, Glenn Davis, Alyce McPartland, Ryan Holsten, Julia Hayden, Peter-Paul Koch, Wayne Bremser, D.K. Robinson, L. Michelle Johnson, Mattias Konradsson, Steven Champeon (again), Chris Schmitt, Marlene Bruce, Lee Moyer, Bob Stein, Dave Linabury, Mark Newhouse, Bob Jacobson, Erika Meyer, Ross Olson, Rich Robinson, Bill Humphries, Scott Cohen, Peter Balogh, Robert Miller, Shoshannah L. Forbes, Pär Almqvist, Simon St. Laurent, Jennifer Lindner, Nick Finck (again), Jim Byrne, Makiko Itoh, Ben Henick, George Olsen (again), and Chris MacGregor.

Thanks to everyone who's ever looked at any site I've had a hand in creating, and especially to those who've written (even if you wrote to say it stank). Thanks to all the web designers and developers who joined The Web Standards Project.

Hello? Thanks to Tim Berners-Lee for inventing the Web. Thanks to the Web's first teachers: Jeffrey Veen (again), Glenn Davis (again), Dan Shafer, David Siegel, and Lynda Weinman. Thanks to Jim Heid and Steve Broback of Thunder Lizard for support, encouragement, great programs, and fine hotel accommodations.

Thanks to Michael Schmidt and Toke Nygaard for the secret work you did on this book, for the incredible work you do on the Web, and for your friendship. Similar thanks to the incredible Carlos Segura.

Thanks to Todd Fahrner and Tantek Çelik for contributing to my knowledge and (more importantly) to the sane advancement of the Web. Likewise, each in their own way: Tim Bray, Steven Champeon (again), Rachel Cox, B.K. DeLong, Sally Khudairi, Tom Negrino, Dori Smith, Simon St. Laurent, Eric Meyer, Eric Costello, J. David Eisenberg (again), Dave Winer, Stewart Butterfield, Carl Malamud, Joe Jenett, Evan Williams, Robert Scoble, and Peter-Paul Koch (again).

Huge shout-outs to my supremely talented web designer pals. I value your friendship and love your work. You know who you are, and if you didn't know you might get a clue from the fact that I am always linking to you or referring obliquely to you, and if that's not enough, you'll find yourselves in the Exit Gallery at zeldman.com.

The paragraph above and the one you're now reading constitute the toughest part of writing this book. In the six years I've spent designing websites, I've met or corresponded with tens of thousands of talented people, worked with or gotten close to hundreds. I can't list you all. This is so painful I feel like canceling the book, but my publisher insists otherwise. Please accept these tragically empty paragraphs as my attempt to embrace you all in love and gratitude.

Love and thanks to Peyo Almqvist, Derek Powazek, Josh Davis, Heather Champ, Daniel Bogan, Craig Hockenberry, Lance Arthur, Michael Cina, Heather Hesketh, Dave Linabury, Dan Licht, Brian Alvey, Shauna Wright, Halcyon, Hasan, Matt, Jason, Big Dave, Lmichelle, Fish Sauce, Toke, Michael, Leigh, and Uncle Joe.

Foreword

I wrote this book for four people:

For Jim, a print designer who's tired of sending his clients to someone else when they need a website.

For Sandi, a gifted art director, who's hit a wall in her advertising career, and is eager to move into full-time interactive design.

For Billy, whose spare-time personal site has gotten so good, he'd like to become a professional web designer—but is unsure about what is expected or how to proceed.

And for Caroline, a professional web designer who wants to better understand how the medium works and where it is going.

I did not make up these names or descriptions: These are real people. I knew the book was finished when it had covered everything they needed to know.

An entire curriculum, a year of work and thought, and 100 years of professional experience (mine, my editors', and my collaborators') have gone into this book.

Enjoy.

Jeffrey Zeldman
1 April 2001
New York City

Web vs. Print: A Note About URLs

The Web is an ever-changing flow of ideas, designs, and redesigns. Sites evolve and decay. Some move to new locations. Others disappear. By the time you read this book, some of the sites it describes will surely have changed, while others may have vanished altogether.

This flow and flux is natural to the Web, and in some ways it is even healthy. It's good when mediocre sites improve, and it's inevitable that pointless sites (like pointless products) eventually fade away.

But healthy and natural or not, the medium's constant dynamism can wreak havoc with books about the Web, and thus with those books' readers. You read about an interesting design or technological decision, fire up your web browser, and discover that the site no longer demonstrates what was discussed in the book.

Fortunately, dear reader, you can minimize the damage by bearing these things in mind:

1. Most of the concepts and techniques discussed here are fairly widespread. If Site A no longer sports a nifty rollover technique we've described, you'll probably find it at Site B or Site C. The principles are more important than the specific examples.

2. Sites should not arbitrarily change page locations, but unfortunately, many do. If a particular web page seems to have disappeared, try factoring the URL to a simpler version. For instance, if www.yahoo.com/games/thrills/ no longer works, go back to its purest form, www.yahoo.com/, and see if you can navigate to the page's new location that way.

3. Finally, if a site we've hailed as an example of creative excellence or touted as a superb resource for further learning seems to have disappeared, try visiting the zeldman.com Exit Gallery at www.zeldman.com/exit.html. If the site is truly special and has moved to a new location on the Web, you'll find that new address in our Exit Gallery. If the site has actually changed its name, we'll mention the former name to help you get your bearings.

Now go forth, design, and conquer.

Introduction

WHEN WE FIRST MET STEVE CROZIER, president of Populi, we liked what he had to say.

He said, "I want to buy you lunch."

When he told us his company's vision, we liked that even more.

It was a simple solution to a complex problem. On one side, thousands of designers and art directors are eager to take their talents to the Web but aren't sure how. On the other, web agencies could not find enough good web designers to get their work done.

The Populi program was designed to close the web talent gap by training traditional designers in the ways of the Web. Until ithe Populi program comes to your town, this little book can teach you what you need to know.

This is not one of your "Learn HTML in 24 Hours" books, nor is it one of the many introductory books on web graphics. It won't teach you how to imitate the stylistic tricks of famous web designers, turn ugly typography into ugly 3-D typography, or build online shopping carts by bouncing databases from one cryptic programming environment to another. This is a book for working designers who seek to understand the Web as a medium and learn how they can move to a career in web design. It's also suited to designers who wish to add web design to their repertoire of client services.

Populi (www.populi.com), the Web Talent Incubator, turns traditional designers and programmers into web builders.

Why did we base this book on the Populi curriculum? For one thing, it's one of the only programs we know that actually works. For another, we wrote the curriculum. (To be honest, we wrote the curriculum in cooperation with courseware developer Margaret Alston, and designer-instructor Cheryl Stockton, of the Pratt Institute. The cranky opinions are ours; the thoroughness and good sense—theirs.)

The concepts contained in the Populi curriculum and this book have been field-tested on working designers. They've been reviewed by web agency consultants and Pratt faculty members, spoken aloud to tens of thousands of web conference attendees, rolled in flour, and slow-baked at 450 degrees.

This book will teach you how web design compares to and differs from the job you know and love. It will explain the medium's challenges, such as bandwidth, navigation, and browser compatibility. And it will teach you enough of the technical details to work with your peers on the production end and to pinch-hit as needed.

The *Populi Curriculum in Web Communication Design*, created in cooperation with Pratt Institute, was launched in Dallas in 2000 and will eventually come to your town.

On the other hand, the book you are holding is available now, at a modest price.

You know what to do.

Part I

WHY: Understanding the Web

chapter 1

Splash Screen

WHAT DO DESIGNERS DO? Designers organize information, shape identities, and create memorable experiences that entertain while communicating. Increasingly, designers are performing these tasks on the World Wide Web (*the Web*, to its friends). If you've picked up this book, you're either doing the work already, thinking of migrating to the field, or considering adding web design to your repertoire of existing services.

Whether you design websites full-time or just occasionally, you'll be helping to shape what may be the most inherently profound medium since the printing press. The Web is vast, intrinsically democratic, and dripping with creative, personal, and business potential. Oddly enough, for something that gets used and talked about every day by hundreds of millions, it is also quite often misunderstood by practitioners as well as users.

Before you do anything drastic, such as buying "web software," changing your career, or leaving that louse who is only pretending to love you, it makes sense to find out where you are going and what you will be dealing with. So let's start by examining what the Web is—exactly.

Meet the Medium

The Web is a part of *the Internet*, a group of interconnected computer networks that spans the globe. Web servers deliver content of many kinds, much of it connected to other content via *hyperlinks* and therefore referred to as *hypertext*. Most of these documents are written in a simple markup language called HTML, about which we will have much more to say. But web servers aren't limited to publishing HTML documents; they can deliver almost any digital content you care to envision.

Put another way, the Web is a medium, like print or television. It is available worldwide to anyone with an Internet connection. Unlike with print or television, though, the Web is a two-way street. Not only can anyone with an Internet connection view and interact with websites, he or she also can create or contribute to such sites.

At this moment in history, the Web is usually experienced on a desktop computer. This is changing rapidly, though, as web-enabled cell phones and Palm Pilots become Yuppie accessories that make you just want to slap them. (The Yuppies, not the accessories.)

Desktop *web browsers*, such as Netscape Navigator, Microsoft Internet Explorer, and Opera Software's Opera, are used to view and interact with the content on websites. These "sites" are collections of web documents published online at specific virtual locations. They're called *sites*, not *books*, because the Web is not print and because the founders of the Web were obsessed with solving basic problems such as that of location. Where do web documents go? Where can people be assured of retrieving them? The founders of the Web developed a system of Uniform Resource Locators (URLs), affording every web document the luxury of a permanent address—hence, a *site* collection, not a *book* collection.

By the way, while URLs make possible a permanent address for every web document, such permanence is not guaranteed. Companies go out of business and take down their sites; products are replaced by newer models, and the old web pages go offline; news and information sites hampered by limited server space kill old stories to make room for new ones; or a new publishing system comes online, and old web addresses such as www.url.com/issues/01/03/story.html are replaced by new robot-generated URLs such as www.url.com/content.cgi?date=2001-03-21/article.cgi?id=46&page=1.

Outside the corporate web sphere, personal sites go offline when their creators get bored or they move to a new location, and the creator neglects to leave a forwarding address. There are as many scenarios as there are web pages that have disappeared. This is a problem for web users who bookmark certain pages in hopes of revisiting them and for directories such as Yahoo.com or search engines such as Google.com whose business is to connect seekers of specific information with sites that meet their needs.

Expanding Horizons

Searches and similar activities underscore the fact that the web experience is interactive—another difference between it and print and TV. Visitors not only link from page to page at their discretion, they also can post their own content to some sites, shop at others, play games, or alter the design elements to suit their tastes at still others.

Needless to say, these interactive aspects of the Web present incredible design challenges and opportunities, which grow more interesting and more sophisticated as the Web's capabilities expand. And they are expanding every minute. While we wrote this book, Microsoft came out with IE5.5, Opera unveiled Opera 5, Netscape produced Navigator 6, and Macromedia premiered Flash 5. To varying degrees, all four products have changed profoundly what the Web can be—the three browsers by offering increased support for powerful web standards such as CSS, XML, and the DOM and Flash 5 by providing richer (though proprietary) design and programming tools.

Note

We will discuss CSS, XML, and the DOM in due course. If you're nervous or simply curious, skip ahead to Chapter 5, "The Obligatory Glossary," then come on back.

In terms of technological acceptance, the Web has grown faster than any medium in history. In 1990, there were two "wired persons" (people connected to the Web): Tim Berners-Lee, the physicist who invented the Web, and his friend and colleague Robert Caillou. By 1993, there were 90,000 web users. Two years later, there were three million. By early 1999, that number had grown to over 200 million, 80 million of them in the U.S. alone. Six months later, estimates were well over 300 million. Soon there will be more web users than McDonald's burgers sold. Fortunately, no animals were harmed in the making of the Web.

Computers will always be unaffordable for some folks, and others simply dislike technology. How will the Web keep growing after everyone with the means and desire has bought a computer and a modem (or whatever high-speed connectivity that replaces the modem)?

It will grow by slipping past its existing borders. Drivers will receive directions from devices in their cars without realizing that the data is stored on a site you may have designed. Technophobes will interact with sites while finding out local movie times over the phone. They won't know they're getting information from the Web; for them this will simply be a conventional telephone experience. You won't be responsible for porting the data (geekspeak for translating web content into something a web-enabled phone can understand), but your sites will undoubtedly reach people who have never touched a "traditional" web browser.

Within the next five to ten years, it's fair to say that "everyone" will use the Web, just as "everyone" uses the telephone. Of course, there are human beings who don't use the phone (and many who don't answer it, especially if they owe you money), but we're speaking in generalities to emphasize a simple point:

> *You are about to begin designing for a medium that will eventually reach practically every home and office in every corner of the world. Your work will potentially affect the lives of billions. You will never be lonely or go hungry again. But on the flip side of that joyous news, you will face new challenges and will need to learn new skills throughout your web career.*

"Billions" sounds like a pretty daunting audience. But as with all design, remember that you're not trying to reach or please everyone. If you design to communicate ideas and if your clients are focused enough to have products or causes worth sharing with specific people, then the right hundreds, thousands, or millions of people will visit and be enriched by your sites. "Your sites." It sounds nice, doesn't it?

Working the Net...Without a Net

Given this vast, worldwide audience, you will no longer be able to assume certain things—for instance, that everyone who visits the site speaks English. Or that every visitor has an equally powerful computer, an equally up-to-date browser, or an equally glorious monitor with which to view your work. You can't even assume that all your visitors can view your work at all, in the conventional sense of that word. Millions of people with visual (and other) disabilities use the Web every day; believe it or not, your designs can accommodate them. (We'll talk about how that's done throughout the book.)

In art direction and graphic design, before you even begin conceptualizing your approach, you must target your audience and learn the size of the medium you'll be working with (magazine spread, quarter-page newspaper, or outdoor billboard). On the Web, audience projection is an imperfect science at best, and there are no absolute sizes, or absolute anything else. But don't reach for the Absolut vodka—there's nothing to fear. Your design vocabulary is simply going to enlarge. In fact, your whole conception of what it means to design will expand.

While it broadens in its reach, the Web also is constantly increasing its capabilities—from the early, text-only Web, to text plus images, to streaming media (audio, video, and multimedia environments created in Flash, Shockwave, and Java). From static pages, to dynamically generated pages, to sites to which the word "page" does not apply at all. (For a taste, visit www.eneri.net, www.photomontage.com, or www.once-upon-a-forest.com.)

Most of the time in this book, we'll be discussing the Web as we know it and as your clients understand it: an interactive digital medium accessed via a desktop computer with an Internet connection and viewed by means of a web browser such as Internet Explorer, Netscape Navigator, or Opera.

We also will assume that you've used the Web yourself. Maybe you while away the hours in a chat room where you're known as HotBuns32 or you spend half your life checking other people's bleeding edge site designs. Perhaps you just check your email once a week (and pretend you haven't read it when it's from a relative) or log on once a year to save $5 on a Mother's Day bouquet. If you haven't done any of this, go online now, and we'll talk later.

Though we'll focus on the Web you know, we also will talk about the ways the Web is changing—because those changes will have as profound an impact on your career as they will on our civilization. What you'll learn in this book is only the beginning. (If you're not comfortable with the idea that a career in web design necessitates continual learning, put this book down now and back slowly away.)

On the other hand, you might like the idea that the Web is steadily expanding its borders. That people can already access some web content via handheld devices such as Palm Pilots. That there are web phones out there and browsers for the blind. That web-based navigation systems are finding their way into the cars and trucks we drive. That there is actually a prototype web refrigerator, and that before we get much older almost every device imaginable will be accessing the Web in some way or other—whether it needs to or not.

All these applications will require the skills of talented designers (and programmers, of course). So congratulations on making an absolutely brilliant career move. Now buy this book so you can actually start doing something about all this.

If you're curious about how the heck this Web thing got started, see Chapter 4, "How This Web Thing Got Started." If you're unsure of your terminology, see Chapter 5, "The Obligatory Glossary." You'll find both chapters in Part 2, "WHO," in the middle of this book, along with useful material on the project life cycle and a detailed definition of the web designer's role. If you'd like to hear more about how smart you are for deciding to learn about web design, phone your Mom—that is, if she's forgiven you for that cheap floral bouquet you got her.

On the other hand, if you're ready to plunge into the most interesting aspects of web design, Chapter 2, "Designing for the Medium," has your name on it, baby. But before you dive into it, we need to make one more prefatory point.

Smash Your Altars

With the exception of a few facts, everything in this book is subject to debate. Web design, like the medium, is too new to be bound by fusty rules. When we explain general principles and accepted practices, our goals are to clarify how the medium functions and to ground you in the thinking and methods of most working web practitioners. You will need to know this in order to do your job. But it is only the beginning, and you are encouraged to constantly think beyond everything we tell you here.

For every ten sites that fail because they've ignored a certain web verity (for instance, that navigation should be clear and streamlined), there is at least one site that succeeds precisely because it violates this "rule" in a unique and brilliant way. For every hundred sites that fundamentally misunderstand the medium by behaving like static Illustrator layouts, there is one that achieves greatness by doing so.

Most web designers begin each project by considering the end-user. But we know of at least one certifiable web design genius who starts every job by inventing dynamic behaviors he has never seen on anyone else's sites and then following those behaviors wherever they lead. Remarkably enough, they lead to professional and usable sites whose uniqueness delights precisely the users they were intended to serve. This should not work at all, but it not only does work, it enlarges what the Web can be.

There is stupidity (and there is a lot of it). And then there is innovation and creative rule-breaking that sometimes leads to greatness.

If your boss or client dictates or forbids a certain web design practice because of some rule in an old web book (or, sadly, in a new book full of bad ideas), we won't mind you citing this book to counter the argument. But please don't invoke this book as an authoritative set of web design commandments. This is not a book of rules, and any web book that pretends to be is full of it. Take what we say seriously but stay flexible. Musicians learn scales before writing melodies. These are the scales; you'll write the tunes.

chapter 2

Designing for the Medium

THE WEB IS LIKE EVERY OTHER MEDIUM to which you've applied your talents and like no other medium you've ever grappled with. Everything you know as a designer will help you tremendously, yet nearly everything you know must be rethought. Sounds like a sales pitch—until you've actually tried your hand at web design.

The Web is different because websites must function as both documents and databases. It's different again because the medium is somewhat ephemeral in nature, never looking or functioning exactly the same way for each person who encounters it. Prove this to yourself by visiting any sophisticated site using IE5 on an iMac, Netscape 6 in Linux, and IE4 on a Windows PC. If it looks and works exactly the same in all three settings, we'll eat our Aunt Miriam's crepe de chine hat. And these are just three of thousands of possible combinations.

The Web is both more and less capable than print. On the one hand, it provides near-instant access to information, offers rich multimedia experiences, and responds dynamically to the visitor's actions. On the other, it defeats the designer's desire to completely control the visual experience.

The Web is different because anybody can make a website, but not everybody can do it well.

Finally, the Web is different because it works best when it's lean and mean. Looking at a full-bleed, two-page spread places no strain on magazine readers, but viewing sites that make extensive use of images, sounds, and other "heavy" media can put a serious crimp in the web user's experience—particularly if the designer has not taken pains to optimize the site. File sizes must be kept small if web pages are to download quickly and efficiently over slow, dialup modem connections (or even fast connections). Include too many images or other files per page, and the fastest connection will slow to a crawl due to limitations in the number of files that can be served simultaneously.

This conflict between size and speed is known as *bandwidth*, and we will have much to say about it later in this chapter. For now, the following disturbingly technical definition will either give you your bearings or send you screaming back to the safety of print design.

A Definition of Bandwidth

According to Whatis.com (www.whatis.com):

"Bandwidth (the width of a band of electromagnetic frequencies) is used to mean... how fast data flows on a given transmission path.... It takes more bandwidth to download a photograph in one second than it takes to download a page of text in one second. Large sound files, computer programs, and animated videos require still more bandwidth for acceptable system performance."

Designing for the medium is a joy—once you understand the Web's limitations and opportunities.

Breath Mint? Or Candy Mint?

If you know your web history (or if you've skipped ahead to Chapter 5, "The Obligatory Glossary"), you'll recall that the Web was conceived as an open platform for distributing structured text documents. When physicists Tim Berners-Lee and Robert Caillou created Hypertext Markup Language (HTML) as a limited subset of a much more complex open standard for document publishing, graphic design was the last thing on their minds.

HTML was as simple as rain. It was built in that way so scientists could learn it quickly and use it to publish their physics papers online. Documents published in HTML were "styled" by the default settings of early Web browsers (the familiar Times New Roman on a gray background). Early web pages looked exactly like physics papers, which was pretty darned great if you were a physicist.

But clients don't buy physics papers. After designers and their clients grasped the Web's commercial potential, they began seeking ways to make web pages look as good as other professional publications. Today, web standards such as Cascading Style Sheets (CSS) allow us to do just that. But in 1994 and 1995, these standards did not exist, so web designers and browser makers such as Netscape began "extending" the behavior of HTML in nonstandard ways.

What happened to HTML was not unlike what happens to legislation introduced in the U.S. Congress. A legislator wants to change the speed limit in his home state. By the time it gets out of committee, the bill includes taxes on liquor and tobacco, gun licensing restrictions, subsidies for farmers, mandatory parental warnings on CDs and cassettes, and an impassioned plea for school prayer. Over the years, HTML was similarly amended, extended, and tacked onto by a thousand hands. Many of those amendments were intended to facilitate the needs of designers. A few were just plain wacky. We've been coping with the damage ever since. Take the following example:

HTML in the "Good Old Days":

```
<a href="index.html"><IMG SRC="image.gif" alt="Return to the home page."></a>
```

HTML Today:

```
<tr><td valign="top"><a HREF="index.html" target="elchico" onMouseOver="
window.status='Home again, home again, jiggity jig.'; changeImages('toc', 'omen2/
coreover.gif'); return true;" onMouseOut="window.status=''; changeImages('toc',
'omen2/core.gif'); return true;"><img name="toc" src="omen2/core.gif" width="49"
height="25" border="0" alt="Return to the core page." Title="Home again, home again,
jiggity jig."></a></td></tr>
```

Later in this chapter, we'll talk about HTML and web standards in more detail. For now, it's important to realize that the impulse behind the Web's creation was logical, structured, and intended to address a basic need: the simple sharing of data. It was never about marketing or design.

Despite all that has befallen since those early days, many people continue to view the Web as an archive or database of searchable information. And some of these folks have espoused a set of "rules" to ensure that web pages yield their information with a minimum of fuss and confusion. Let's call this group the *Usability People*. Jakob Nielsen is one of their foremost exponents, and you can read what he has to say at www.useit.com. To Usability fans, anything that impedes access to the data is bad; anything that momentarily confuses even a single user is bad; and thus, pretty much anything out of the ordinary is viewed with suspicion or banned outright. This view of the Web is straightforward and can serve as a touchstone for web designers, though the guidelines espoused by Usability gurus should not be confused with Commandments. (Last time we checked, the Commandments were written by Someone else.)

Usability basically reminds designers to think about the needs of their audience. On many commercial and informational sites, web users simply hope to find things or do things as quickly as possible. When checking sports scores or seeking low airfares, they do not wish to be creatively challenged by a complex multimedia experience. They merely want to find what they seek and get on with their lives.

This does not mean that web design is a cold, calculating science. Far from it: Like all good design, web design is aesthetic, emotional, and largely unquantifiable. The value in the Usability perspective is that it reminds web designers to create sites that people can actually use.

This ought to go without saying, but you'll find that in web design almost nothing goes without saying. Perhaps in print you've known designers who become so carried away with graphic design for its own sake that they forget to communicate. The synergy between headline and visual gets lost in a haze of technique; typography advances toward illegibility; subtleties of lighting completely obscure the subject, and so on. When web designers make the same mistake, potential readers and customers are thwarted in their desire to use the site. The folks in suits start beating the designers over the head with Jakob Nielsen's latest book, and a good time is had by no one. Don't let this happen to you. It's easy to avoid if you keep the intended user and usages in mind.

Magazine and ad layouts may be wild or restrained as long as they are legible. Web design must be much more than legible, though many sites fail to achieve even basic readability, and few indeed are a pleasure to read. (To say nothing of the fact that most ad layouts are intended to convey simple messages, while websites often perform numerous, complex functions.) In his widely read 1996 treatise, *Creating Killer Websites*, David Siegel listed three cardinal virtues of web design: "Clarity, Brevity, Bandwidth." Though Siegel was a graphic designer and not a Usability Person (and though he did not always achieve these goals in his own work), there's likely not a Usability Person on the planet who would disapprove of that trinity.

But many designers and artists saw something quite different in the Web: the chance to create and publish creative works that plunge the viewer into a unique world of imagery, exploration, and cinematic or personal narrative. This view, implicit in sites such as Photomontage (www.photomontage.com) and Presstube (www.presstube.com), is as vital to the health of the medium as the contrasting Usability perspective. We'll call its exponents the *web artists*, though this label is somewhat misleading. For while it's true that many web artists are motivated by the urge toward pure creative expression, the trails they blaze are invariably followed by marketers in search of deep online branding opportunities. The innovations delivered by pioneering multimedia artists quickly become the basis for sites touting Motown, Madonna, or Barney's New York.

Web artists do not believe in holding the visitor's hand. They judge that websites can be as challenging as paintings, music, literature, or Swedish movies. They further hold that there is an audience for sites that raise bars and test boundaries. They are, of course, correct. Challenging sites can reward patient viewers. They don't please everyone but neither does modern painting. Writer Curt Cloninger summed up the conflict between those who view the Web as an informational database and those who see it as a wide-open aesthetic frontier when he shrugged, "Usability Experts are from Mars, Graphic Designers are from Venus" (www.alistapart.com/stories/marsvenus/).

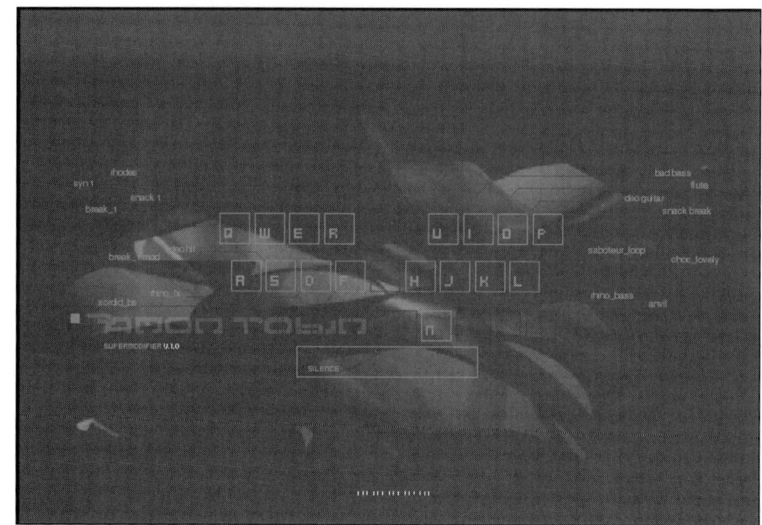

Figure 2.1

Supermodified looks like (and is) a work of multimedia art. Yet it serves a commercial purpose. Visitors can trigger loops of music by typing on the keyboard. A strictly informational approach to site design, such as the Google Search Engine (Figure 2.2), would be far less effective at creating excitement about the composer's work (www.amontobin.com).

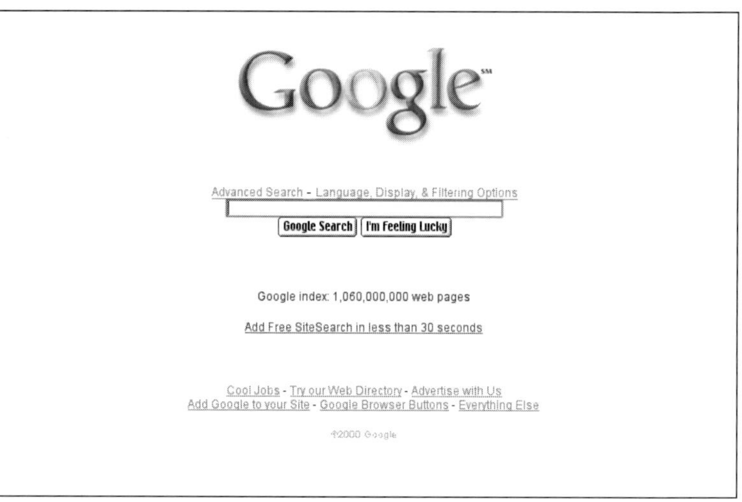

Figure 2.2

The Google Search Engine. A classic example of function driving form (with the possible exception of the logo). Google's search engine delivers solid results, and hardcore geeks love it because it strips away the clots that clog the arteries of most commercial search engines. Both Google and amontobin.com are successful at doing what they set out to do, yet they are clearly different in their approach to the user experience (www.google.com).

Mars and Venus, left and right brain, utility and artistry. On one side stands a set of Usability Commandments based on roughly a decade of trial and error and a heaping teaspoon of pseudo-science. On the other lies the indefinable essence of art and a horde of marketers who stand ready to exploit it.

Somewhere between these two extremes you will find the appropriate balance for each site. The ideal balance for most sites will not be found in the stone tablets of Mars or the sensual abandon of Venus. Rather, it will come from each project's intended audience. Your visitors' needs set the parameters; your taste, inspiration, and expertise do the rest.

That tension between structure and style, function and aesthetics, is key to understanding web design and web technology. Users have needs; technology sets limitations. The conflict will resurface throughout this book and your career—and it is only the beginning. Web design is different in fascinating ways. Following are a few key points of difference.

Where's the Map?

Books, magazines, CDs, and videocassettes do not need to explain themselves. Most of us read from left to right and top to bottom; we turn the page. We insert the disc or tape and press Play. Websites are not so self-explanatory. Consequently, web designers spend a great deal of effort creating contextual and navigational cues to guide readers, viewers, and "users" through the site.

Visitors take their cues from non-web experiences. From a lifetime of newspaper reading, they know that headlines carry more weight than subheads and body copy. They intuitively grasp that right-pointing arrows mean "more" or "continue." (This intuitive grasp is, of course, the result of previously absorbed social conventions. Red, green, and yellow buttons suggest traffic lights to an American web user; they may mean something different or nothing at all in Papua, New Guinea.) Web users also take their cues from other sites they've seen. Soon after figuring out how the modem works, users learn that underlined text is almost always a link, and they know that when the cursor changes shape they are hovering over an "active" link or image.

Mars and Venus

Adept web designers take care to follow some familiar contextual conventions while breaking or reinventing others. On one site you might use CSS to turn off link underlining; on another, you preserve link underlining because the site is intended for neophyte users who need to be led by the hand. One site requires idiot-proof icons with text labels; another cries out for subtle, dynamic navigational menus. Usability People lecture sternly about the "sins" of web design, but designers don't sin—they make decisions. A good web designer may break as many rules as she follows. Visitors determine whether the site succeeds as a piece of communication or is merely a failed, cryptic experiment. This book explores issues of navigation and interface in Chapter 3, "Where Am I? Navigation & Interface." You'll be exploring them for the rest of your career.

That we devote an entire chapter to navigation and interface should be indication enough that graphic design alone does not equal web design—a point we'll restate several times in case some of you haven't had your coffee yet. Choosing and setting type, crafting pretty buttons, and developing a grid are all well and good but not good enough. Above all, web designers are the architects of user experience.

You might feel that your training and experience have not prepared you to build such architecture, but you'll soon see that it's the web equivalent of what a designer always does: guide viewers toward an understanding.

Web Physics: Action and Interaction

Design for the Web is different. It's different because web pages don't just sit there; they do things. More importantly, they allow visitors to do things. Magazine pages may be beautiful (or not) but the reader's interactivity consists of reading the page (or not), dog-earing it (or not), and rereading it (or not). At most, the reader might cut it out and mail it to a friend. Strictly speaking, none of this can truly be called interactivity. Beautiful magazine layouts do not change in response to the viewer's actions. Newspaper ads do not sprout additional body copy if the reader shows genuine interest. The Web invites depth of exploration in ways traditional media cannot. For a designer, the creative possibilities are tantalizing and practically limitless.

On the Web, linear motion gives way to user emotion. Site visitors link randomly as they choose. Set up as many careful hierarchies and navigational cues as you want; visitors will still do what they like on most sites. Not only may visitors move up, down, and sideways, they also can bookmark any page they fancy; download it to their hard drives; save the images from it; and even study the HTML markup with which it was produced.

Readers can order books on the Web by typing in HTML form fields supported by scripts written in Perl, Java, or other programming languages (www.amazon.com). They can post their opinions to message boards (www.metafilter.com). If the designer has given them the option, they may change the background colors to suit their mood (www.camworld.com). On fancy *Dynamic HTML* (DHTML) sites, they can drag images from place to place (www.dhtml-guis.com/game/). On fancier ones, they can do much more (www.assembler.org). On a corporate intranet site, employees may spend hours updating a group calendar or adding phone numbers to a contact database. (Anything to avoid working.)

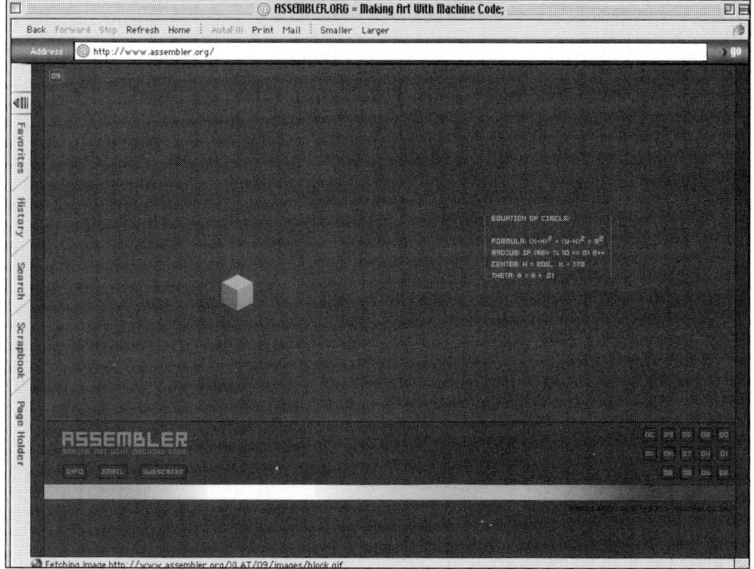

Figure 2.3

Non-commercial interactivity: Assembler.org was created with DHTML (here it is done well). As of this writing, the site was optimized for Netscape and Microsoft's 4.0 browsers, which rely on proprietary coding techniques. Thus the site's marvels would be invisible to users of recent browsers that avoid proprietary, old-school DHTML. By the time you buy this book, the site should function well in standards-compliant browsers such as Netscape 6 (www.assembler.org).

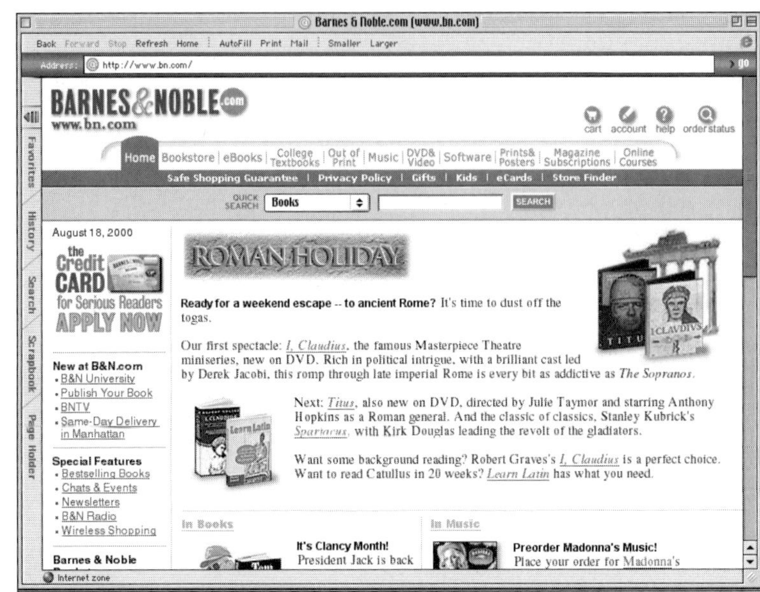

Figure 2.4

Commercial interactivity: Barnes & Noble, a functional and attractive shopping site. Successful e-commerce sites work in as many browsers as possible and add value to the commercial transaction by providing content and artificially intelligent "shopping tips." Though Barnes & Noble has a real-world heritage, Amazon.com dominates the online market because Amazon came first. When web brands are effective, users can be incredibly loyal (www.bn.com).

There is obvious commercial value to commercial interactivity; novelty or "proof of concept" value to dynamic artwork and games; branding value to interactive multimedia (www.barneys.com); and hidden value to still other types of interactivity. (Changing the background color may seem trivial to you or me, but it could be vitally important for a color-blind web user.) Overall, interactivity is a defining characteristic of the Web and thus of web design. Lesbian poetry and physics papers did not drive the rapid expansion of the medium. Commerce did that, and commerce depends on interactivity: the visitor clicks, the sale is made.

No offense to the lesbian poetry sites. In fact, no offense to the hundreds of thousands of noncommercial sites that bring richness, depth, and meaning to the Web. Without these noncommercial sites, the medium would be nothing more than a dialup variation on the infomercial. But without all the commercial sites, the Web's infrastructure, services, and rate of adoption might never have grown so quickly.

At least, that's what the marketers tell us. Consider this another Mars/Venus variation for your pleasure. The Internet grew in popularity for at least two years before any commercial sites were allowed on the Net, much less the Web. And many defining characteristics of the modern Web ($20 unlimited access dialups, 56K modems, free browsers) were established by 1995-96, a time when most web users were also web designers, and the word "commerce" did not begin with the letter "e." Still, the Web has expanded like nobody's business since business came online. And if you ask most normal humans who've gone online in the past few years why they bought a computer and signed up for an Internet account, "shopping" seems to top the list.

Different Purposes, Different Methodologies

It is still possible for a lone web designer or small team to create personal, artistic, and corporate sites using an image editor, HTML, style sheets, and JavaScript. But the "lone rider" approach is increasingly rare in the corporate web development space. Today, teams of specialists with odd-sounding job titles develop most sites collaboratively. (See Chapter 5, "The Obligatory Glossary" and Chapter 7, "Riding the Project Life Cycle," for the funky titles and the typical web project life cycle.) It is not your job to program a shopping cart or develop a database. It *is* your job to understand where your work fits into the bigger picture.

As a professional web designer, you will work closely with programmers to implement the appropriate interactivity in every site. You also might be called upon to execute rudimentary interactivity yourself—for instance, writing JavaScript to swap images on navigational menus.

Web Agnosticism

Design for the Web is also different because the Web is not a fixed medium. It has no size, no inks, no paper stock. Even your typographic choices may end up as mere suggestions. That's because the Web is *platform-agnostic* and *device-independent.* Good web design adapts to different browsers, monitors, and computing systems. What's sauce for the goose may not be sauce for the gander. More literally, what's Geneva for the Mac may be Arial for Windows; what's VBScript for Windows may be error messages for Mac and Linux users. (So don't use VBScript to build websites.)

Looking at poorly implemented sites, you could come away with the impression that the Web is a Windows application or even an extension of the Windows desktop. And there are certainly marketers who'd like you to believe that. But it just ain't so.

Berners-Lee and Caillou invented the Web on a NeXT computer. The first browser ever released was for UNIX, the second for Mac OS. Berners-Lee envisioned the Web as a completely *portable* medium—one that could be accessed not only by every computer operating system (including dumb terminals), but also by all kinds of devices from hand-held Personal Digital Assistants (PDAs) to telephones and other common appliances. Slowly and sometimes painfully, everything Berners-Lee envisioned in 1990 has been coming true.

To help the Web evolve in an orderly fashion, Berners-Lee founded the World Wide Web Consortium, or W3C (www.w3.org). It's a place where university professors join engineers from companies such as Sun, Microsoft, AOL/Netscape, IBM, Compaq, and Apple to hammer out common technological standards, such as HTML and CSS...and more recently, Extensible Markup Language (XML) and the Document Object Model (DOM). For a complete listing of W3C member organizations, see the following web page: www.w3.org/Consortium/Member/List.

Don't worry about what the acronyms stand for at the moment. Just dig the concept: If everyone supports the same standards (or "Recommendations," in W3C parlance), then designers and programmers will have the tools they need to deliver a dynamic and attractive Web that works for any human being, on any platform or device. Sweet, smart, simple.

Sadly, due to competitive pressures, the desire to innovate, and sheer cussedness, the companies that make web browsers have not always done a superb job of implementing commonly shared standards. In fact, until quite recently, you could argue that their support for these standards was sometimes downright shoddy. You might even be forgiven for suspecting that browser makers deliberately avoided fully implementing any standard for fear that supporting common standards would hurt business.

In the beginning of this chapter, we mentioned that the Web was spawned as a beautiful medium for the delivery of physics papers. And that to deliver commercially viable sites—sites with some semblance of visual appeal—web designers felt they had no choice but to "hack" HTML, forcing the deliberately primitive markup language to serve their aesthetic needs. Netscape (now AOL) joined web designers in extending HTML beyond its creators' intentions.

Initially, the Web was a one-horse town. If you wanted to design a commercial site, you wrote nonstandard HTML that was "optimized" for Netscape's browser. Once Microsoft's browser entered the picture, all hell broke loose, as two powerful software companies began deforming HTML in mutually exclusive ways.

Browser development was originally viewed as just another genre of software development. Adobe Illustrator competes with Macromedia Freehand by offering features Freehand lacks. Freehand does the same to Illustrator. God Bless America.

Similarly, Netscape competed with Microsoft (and vice versa) by offering functionality not supported by the competitor's product. Each company hoped these unique features would seduce web developers into creating sites optimized for its browser alone.

Eventually, the market split in two. Though a tiny percentage of web users sported alternative browsers including Lynx, Mosaic, Opera, and Amaya, basically 50% of the market was using Netscape's browser; the other 50% was using Microsoft's. To create "technologically advanced" sites for their clients without alienating half the potential visitors, designers and developers felt obliged to create Netscape-specific and Microsoft-specific versions of their sites. Clients then paid more than they should have to support the development of these incompatible site versions. Thanks in part to protests from groups such as The Web Standards Project (www.webstandards.org) and mainly to the hard work of browser company engineers, support for common standards is constantly improving—though not without occasional backsliding.

Complicating the issue, many of today's web standards were yesterday's proprietary innovations: things that worked only in one browser or another. You can't blame Wendy's for not offering McDonald's secret sauce, and you can't fault browser companies for failing to implement technology invented by their competitors.

When Netscape unveiled <FRAMES> (the ability to place one web page inside another), the technology was widely adopted by designers and developers. Refer back to Figure 2.3, Assembler.org, for an example of the way frames work. The bottom frame contains a menu; the top frame contains the content. Clicking the menu changes the content by loading a new content frame. Both frames are controlled by yet a third document, called the <FRAMESET>, which links to the frames, establishes their size and positioning relative to one another, and determines such niceties as whether or not the user can resize a given frame.

Eventually Netscape brought its invention to the W3C. Much later, it ended up as part of a temporary standard: the HTML 4 Transitional Recommendation. It took Microsoft a while to support frames, because Microsoft's browser developers had to reverse-engineer Netscape's invention to figure out how it worked. Ironically enough, Microsoft's 4.0 browser eventually supported frames better than Netscape's.

In 1995, Netscape came up with a programming language initially called LiveScript and eventually renamed JavaScript. Besides being easy to learn (at least, as far as programming languages go), JavaScript made web pages far more dynamic. And it did this without straining the computers used to serve web pages (*servers*), because the technology worked in the user's browser instead of having to be processed by the server itself—the way Perl scripts and other traditional programming languages had been. With less strain on the server, more web pages could be served faster. Thus, JavaScript was bandwidth-friendly.

JavaScript eventually became a standard, but not before putting Microsoft at a competitive disadvantage for several years. The latest, "standard" version of JavaScript is referred to as ECMAScript, which sounds like the noise our Uncle Carl used to make in the morning. Don't worry—'most everybody still calls it JavaScript, which isn't exactly Yeatsian poetry either, come to think of it. (ECMAScript is so named because the European Computer Manufacturers Association [ECMA] supervised the standardization process.) While Netscape and Microsoft invented competitive new technologies, the W3C worked to develop recommendations that looked beyond the "Browser Wars." At times, the W3C seemed to be out of touch with what was actually taking place in the market. Back then, the browser companies seemed to be ignoring the W3C. (The irony is that both AOL/Netscape and Microsoft participate in the W3C and play a vital role in developing the web standards they have sometimes gone on to ignore.) Today it appears that the W3C is ahead of what browser companies can realistically deliver in the next year or two. Indeed, even hardened web designers with years of experience can feel their innards turn to jelly when reading about upcoming standards proposed by the W3C. (XML Namespaces, anybody?)

The important thing is that there is now a road map for browser companies, developers, and designers. If you took your talent to the Web in the 1990s, you had no way of knowing what new technologies might come down the pike, what new skills you would have to learn, and how quickly what you learned (and designed) would become obsolete. Today we know which standards have been fully or partially implemented in browsers and which ones we can expect to work with in the next year or two. As opposed to the past when Netscape could surprise us by inventing JavaScript and frames or Microsoft could spring VBScript and ActiveX on us and expect us to quickly learn and use those technologies, today we know what to anticipate and what to learn to prepare for the future.

Open Standards—They're Not Just for Geeks Anymore

We'll bore you with the details in Part III of this book. For now, it is enough that you understand three fundamentals of web agnosticism.

Point #1: The Web Is Platform-Agnostic

The Web owes no special fealty to any particular operating system. It is designed to work in Windows, Mac OS, Linux, UNIX, BeOS, FreeBSD, OS2, DOS, and any other platform that comes along. This presents web designers with special challenges in terms of gamma, screen resolution, color palettes, and typography—all of which we'll explore a bit later in this chapter. This is one heck of a chapter—we hope you realize that. If you get tired and want to take breaks, we'll understand.

At first blush, the programmers on your team would seem to have a tougher job than you do. How on earth are they supposed to accommodate all those different operating systems? The answer is, they don't have to. Browser companies are stuck with the tough job of supporting all those platforms (or a limited subset thereof). Web standards do the rest. JavaScript is JavaScript whether it's running in Linux or Mac OS. Style sheets are style sheets whether they're running on Windows 2000 or BeOS. The more web standards the browsers support and the more completely they support those standards, the fewer migraines programmers (and web users) will have to endure.

You, on the other hand, will continually test your designs for cross-platform feasibility. You will have to cope with the fact that your favorite Mac system font is not available on the PC (or vice versa). That those tawny PC colors look pale as Christina Ricci on the Mac. That the large, bold sans serif headline that looks so dapper on systems with scalable type and built-in anti-aliasing (such as Mac OS and Windows 98) may look hillbilly-homely on platforms lacking those niceties (such as Linux).

What You See Is What You Get (WYSIWYG) programs, such as Macromedia Dreamweaver and Adobe GoLive, attempt to give designers the sensation of retaining complete visual control over web layouts. It is an illusion. A vast majority of professional web designers *still* hand-code their pages. At the very least, they hand-tweak Dreamweaver- or GoLive-generated code to accommodate the reality of browser and platform differences.

Browser and platform differences mean that the precise control you've come to expect from publishing programs such as Quark XPress and Adobe InDesign simply does not exist on the Web. You can bemoan this fact or learn to create beautiful work that exploits the medium's changeable nature and facilitates the needs of millions—perhaps even entertaining them in the process. Not such a bad trade-off, when you come right down to it.

Point #2: The Web Is Device-Independent

Your work not only has to remain usable on a terrifying variety of computer desktops, it also may be accessed via Palm Pilots, web phones, and other instruments of Satan. A year ago it appeared that web designers and programmers would have to continually learn new and incompatible markup languages to accommodate this plethora of web-enabled devices. Instead, the W3C is guiding us toward using Extensible Hypertext Markup Language (XHTML) and CSS to get the job done. (Don't panic! XHTML is, more or less, simply a newer and cleaner version of HTML.)

From www.w3.org/Mobile/Activity:

"Mobile devices are unlikely to be able to use exactly the same markup as a normal page for a PC. Instead they will use a subset of HTML tags. The expectation is that different devices will make use of different modules of XHTML; similarly they will support different modules of style sheets. For example, one mobile device might use the basic XHTML text module and the style sheet voice module. Another device with a large screen might also allow the XHTML tables module."

The W3C website is visually lackluster, unmanageably immense, and written in language only a Stanford professor could love. Nevertheless, the W3C is frequently the voice of sanity in the chaos and frenzy of an ever-changing, commerce-driven Web. Learn to overlook the site's lack of visual panache, and the W3C will be your best friend as the Web and your career move forward. Which brings us to Point #3.

Point #3: The Web Is Held Together by Standards

To design websites, you will have to learn technologies such as HTML, JavaScript, and CSS, which really isn't that hard. As you grow more adept, you will become aware of wonderful features offered in only one browser or another. We advise you to avoid these nonstandard technologies and stick, as much as possible, to what is supported in all browsers.

You might find yourself working for companies or clients who demand special features that only work in one browser. Just say no. On an intranet site (see Chapter 5), it might be feasible to design a site that only works in IE5,

Netscape 4, or what have you, because those who commission the site control the browsers used to access it. But we've heard of plenty of companies that decided to go public with part of their intranet site—only to discover that its nonstandard features locked out millions of web users. We also know an agency that designed an intranet site to take advantage of Netscape 4's proprietary DHTML Layers technology. When Netscape abandoned this technology in favor of web standards, the company's IT department was unable to upgrade its users to the latest version of Netscape's browser, which would have made the site nonfunctional. Who took the blame for this fiasco: the client who had insisted on using proprietary, nonstandard technology or the web agency that had argued against it? If you've had any real experience as a designer, you'll understand that the question is rhetorical.

You can often get away with taking the moral high ground simply by explaining to your clients that delivering what they request will cost them 25% or more of their potential audience. The disabled are almost always among the first to be locked out of a site that relies on proprietary technology. Excluding millions of people from a public site is not exactly a brilliant business decision, and ethically speaking, it stinks. Excluding the disabled is also illegal in many instances, at least in the United States. Court cases have been fought over it, and the client usually loses. The Australian Olympics website was one legal casualty; the cost to the site's owners would have wiped out poverty in three small South American nations. If legal and ethical arguments don't work with your clients, show them the money.

Technologies such as HTML, JavaScript, and CSS are the building blocks of web design. In theory, all browsers fully support these standards, delivering on the promise of browser and platform-agnosticism and offering us a Web where we can "write once, publish everywhere." Theory and reality often diverge. In fact, the divergence between them is more or less the story of the Web. The good news is that built-in browser incompatibilities are gradually going the way of the Dodo bird as more standards-compliant browsers become available.

The 18-Month Pregnancy

In early 2000, Microsoft released IE5 Macintosh edition, a browser that delivers top-notch support for HTML 4, CSS, and JavaScript, three immensely important web standards. Soon afterward, Opera Software released its 4.0 browser, whose principal purpose is to deliver superior support for web standards. And a month before Christmas 2000, Netscape delivered Navigator 6, the most standards-compliant browser yet.

To read the preceding three sentences not only induces coma, it also suggests that designers are now free to use nothing but W3C standards in the sites they and their colleagues create.

Alas, this is not the case. IE5 for Windows currently offers excellent but incomplete support for standards. IE4, currently the most-used browser on the Web, has good but still less complete support for standards, and Netscape 4, still used by millions, offers even less. Sure, users can upgrade, and eventually they will—but at their own pace.

We call this upgrade period the *18-month pregnancy*, based on the time it usually takes before web users feel compelled to switch to an updated browser. Web designers and enthusiasts download new browsers immediately—not so your Uncle Nigel. While you beta-test next year's browser, your client sticks with AOL 3. Clients and other normal human beings tend to use the browser that came preinstalled on their computers. They upgrade when they buy a new PC. Computer manufacturers tend to install 3.0 browsers (considered stable) when 4.0 models are newly available; they offer 4.0 browsers when 5.0 models first come out; and so on. IT departments are equally conservative, tending to view new browsers the way cats regard changes to their litter. Those who use the Web primarily to shop, send email, or view pornography may not be aware for months that a new browser is available, and when they do find out they often don't care.

The browser upgrade path is slow, thus the transition to a Web built purely with standards could take 18 months or longer. Some say we will not see a fully standards-compliant Web before 2003. For the near future, you will likely find it necessary to employ nonstandard *workarounds* to address specific deficiencies in these older browsers. We'll explain these workarounds in the relevant chapters on HTML, CSS, and JavaScript.

Five years ago, the entire Web was a hack, held together with carpet tacks and lasagna. We are better off now than we were then. And soon the nightmare of browser incompatibilities will be a story we tell to bore our grandchildren.

Chocolatey Web Goodness

Having accepted that the Web varies from user to user and browser to browser, and that this will be true even when common standards enjoy universal support, let's move on to consider the medium's many unique strengths. If you already consider the Web the greatest thing since gender differentiation, feel free to skip ahead.

'Tis a Gift to Be Simple

Developing effective web architecture takes great skill. Setting type, designing images and elements, and laying out pages requires consistent vision and intelligence. Programming sites that will serve sophisticated and novice users alike is an art of the highest caliber. But anyone can make a website. A child of six can learn HTML and begin self-publishing in a matter of days. No other medium is as easy to learn and produce.

Millions of personal sites prove this point. Many are of interest mainly to their creator's immediate family and friends—and that's okay. But a surprising number offer valuable content and/or sophisticated design. You can view the vast outpouring of personal pages as proof that HTML is easy to learn. You also might see in it the unshakable human urge to reach out and connect with others. You can even view it as an extended experiment in democracy.

Democracy, What a Concept

Every medium in human history has presented a barrier to access. Writers have had to convince publishers that their books were worth distributing (or else build their own printing press, like poet William Blake). Screenwriters must convince studios to invest millions in their visions (and the writer is usually barred from the set once the script has been sold). Movie directors must argue with producers and bankers. Painters need galleries; musicians need concert halls and record deals.

But the Web presents few such barriers. Buy a computer and a modem, find a hosting provider, learn HTML and some UNIX filing conventions, and voila—you are a worldwide publisher! If you can't afford a computer and modem, most public libraries, universities, and schools offer free Internet access. If hosting fees are beyond your means, companies such as Geocities (www.geocities.com) provide free hosting in exchange for the privilege of running ad banners on your site. The Web places the virtual means of production in the hands of virtually every worker. What would Karl Marx think?

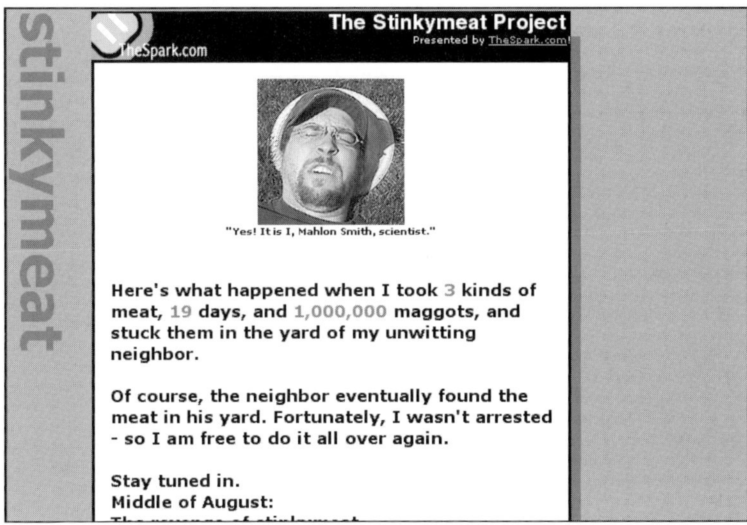

Figure 2.5

The Stinky Meat Project. On the Web, anyone can publish anything they like. Baby, that's democracy! (www.thespark.com/health/stinkymeat/)

Speaking of low access barriers, remember the days when you had to expensively laminate print proofs of your best work, slip them into a costly portfolio, and toss them out every six months as your new work made the old stuff obsolete? Well, forget all that. With a free or inexpensive Internet account, you can mount a web portfolio that's viewable anywhere in the world. Nothing to replace; nothing to bang into the knees of a Neanderthal seated across from you on the subway; nothing for your boss to see you lugging around when you look for a new job on your lunch hour.

Instant Karma

If the invention of the printing press brought humanity out of the Dark Ages, the building of the Internet and the growth of the Web have ushered in a new information age. It's an era where every voice can be heard and where truth can win out over lies—even when the liars have million dollar budgets. Say Detroit spews out a bad car (it happens) and decides to dump millions on advertising in the hope of selling it anyway. Message boards on the Web will quickly spread the word that the lemon gets five miles per gallon and spends more time in the shop than on the road. Angry owners may even start a protest site, garnering coverage in the traditional news media. The Web has changed the rules of the market. (See www.cluetrain.org for more on this.)

It also has changed publishing. Some of the Web's best-loved authors have never written a traditional book. Others have gotten traditional book deals based on the popularity of their online publications.

The Web has launched careers, CDs, and movies and brought together the globally scattered members of countless unnamed tribes. You might be the only Sufi in Piggott, Arkansas, but you can find thousands of fellow believers online. If the other kids attending Fredericksburg High don't share your passion for the music of Bernard Herrmann, you'll find folks more in tune with your interests online.

Social commentators sometimes worry that the Web is making us more isolated. In the picture these pundits paint, tortured introverts peck out desperate messages in dark, lonely chat rooms. We take a different view. In ordinary life, extraordinary people often feel terribly isolated because no one around them can understand them other than superficially. The Net and the Web offer real hope and true companionship for those willing to express themselves and seek out like-minded souls. This, we think, is a good thing.

The Whole World in Your Hands

They don't call it the *World Wide* Web for nothing. As individuals, we can not only email pen pals in Istanbul and Amsterdam, we can find out what people in those countries think by reading their personal sites or talking with them in online communities.

People living in nondemocratic nations can publish their protests anonymously without fear of government retaliation. In lands where all views are tolerated, everyone from amateur gemologists to alien conspiracy freaks can broadcast their theories to a global audience.

Free online services, such as Alta Vista's Babelfish (babelfish.altavista.com) translate text on the Web into a variety of languages. These translations may be awkward and even hilarious—after all, translation is an art best practiced by human beings. But the gist of the text survives the translation. If you publish the story of your child's first steps on your personal site, your tale may be accessible to families in Indonesia and Zimbabwe.

The Web not only reaches the world, it changes it. As a web designer, you will be an agent of change, which is a lot easier and much less dangerous than becoming an agent of the FBI. You'll also sleep better, and you won't have to wear a tie.

Just Do It: The Web as Human Activity

Unlike any other mass medium, the Web encourages human activity instead of passive consumption. This can have a transformative effect, as consumers become active participants, reinvent themselves as content producers, and launch political parties or small businesses without begging for third-party capital. Armed with nothing more than the Web, individuals or small groups can affect the way the world does business, call global attention to a regional injustice, or bring hope to a cancer patient (http://vanderwoning.com/living/blog.html).

Visit a web community, and you'll see people who used to channel-surf devoting their leisure hours to arguments, flirtations, and other classic forms of human interactivity. These communities can spill over from the virtual realm to the real world. The members of Redcricket, for example, visit each other's cities (www.redcricket.com). The readers and writers of Fray (www.fray.org) hold live personal storytelling events each year. The members of Dreamless (www.dreamless.org) participate in collaborative design projects (www.kubrick.org) and hold noncommercial "underground" design festivals in cities such as London and New York.

The Viewer Rules

On the Web, the viewer is in control. She can alter the size of your typography. She can turn off images. She can turn off JavaScript. She can force all pages to display her choice of fonts and background colors. In advanced browsers such as Netscape 6 and IE5/Mac, she can even use her own style sheet to disable or interact with the one you've designed. For designers, this can be either a nightmare or a new way of thinking about design. The open-minded may wish to read "A Dao of Web Design" for a positive approach to this aspect of the medium (www.alistapart.com/stories/dao/).

Designers can thwart the user's power if they insist—with mixed results. For instance, to force the viewer to see what you want her to see, you can deliver body text in an image instead of typing it in HTML. This is a classic mistake of the novice web designer. Why is it so wrong? Let us count the ways:

1. If the viewer has turned off images in her browser, she cannot read what you (or your client) have to say.
2. She cannot copy and paste your text into an email message she's sending to her family.
3. Search engines will not see the text because it is embedded in a graphic image, and as a result, fewer people will discover your page.
4. A near-sighted visitor might find it difficult or impossible to read your 9pt. Futura "graphic text."

5. As if those are not reasons enough to stick with HTML text, consider the fact that each image must be downloaded, translated, and displayed by the browser—a process that can take more time than the reader is willing to devote to your site.

Lest you run scared, bear in mind that most web users rarely, if ever, change their browsers' defaults. By default, images are turned on, JavaScript is turned on, and style sheets are turned on, which means that your typographic choices and other design decisions come through intact (albeit filtered by the visitor's browser and platform). Nevertheless, educated users do have the power to filter your work through their preferences, so it is important to think of web design as a partnership with the people who read and view your sites and to accept the fact that your layouts might be transformed by visitors with special needs or quirky preferences.

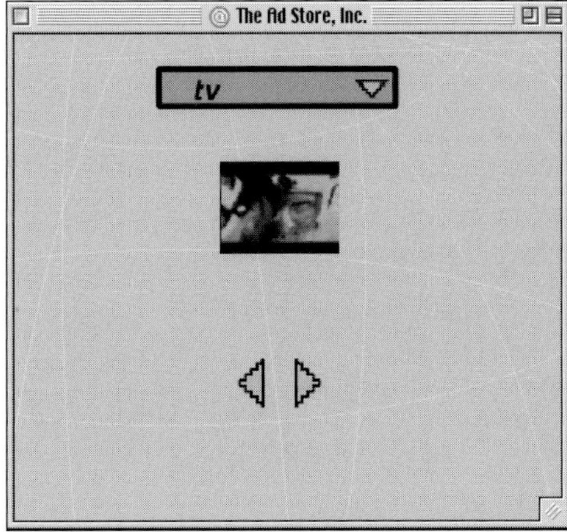

Figure 2.6

An embedded QuickTime video at The Ad Store's website. QuickTime *streams* the video, enabling it to begin playing before the file has fully downloaded. In this way, the needs of the low-bandwidth user are accommodated without impacting file quality (www.the-adstore.com).

Multimedia: All Talking! All Dancing!

The Web not only presents text and images, it also can present music, movies, and unique forms of interactive animation such as interactive vector animations created in Macromedia Flash (www.flash.com) and videos delivered in the QuickTime, Real, or Windows Media Player formats. Design benefits include the power to absolutely mesmerize viewers. Design challenges include creating the work itself; optimizing the work so that it streams quickly to the viewer's browser instead of taking half an hour to download; and developing alternative content for those who cannot view the multimedia file. Additional challenges include avoiding cliches and knowing when multimedia is inappropriate.

On the Web, multimedia is most often delivered through free players (such as RealPlayer) and free browser "plug-ins." These are much like the third-party plug-ins that add new capabilities to programs such as Adobe Photoshop, except that they're free. Browser plug-ins are downloadable mini-applications that handle specific types of multimedia (MIME) content. For instance, the QuickTime plug-in (www.apple.com/QuickTime/) allows Mac and Windows users to view digitized videos. It also plays MP3 audio files, Windows WAV audio files, Windows AVI movies, PNG images, BMP images, and other common media formats.

When the visitor encounters a web page with an embedded QuickTime movie (www.apple.com/trailers/), she can watch the movie with a click of the mouse. If she hasn't installed the plug-in yet, she can download it and then watch the movie. The QuickTime plug-in comes standard in both Netscape and Explorer's browsers, so the issue is moot for most web users, who usually use one or both of these browsers. Flash and RealPlayer also come standard with Netscape's browsers.

The Server Knows

The quality of the movie may vary depending on the visitor's access speed. With QuickTime 4 and higher, for instance, the faster the connection, the larger the movie and the higher its quality. This is accomplished through an ingenious scheme whereby QuickTime content is exported (saved) at a variety of quality levels and stored as a series of related files on the web server. When the visitor's browser requests the file, the server checks to determine the visitor's connection speed and responds with the appropriately optimized file.

How does the server "know" the user's connection speed? The plug-in "tells" the server. QuickTime includes a control panel, which asks the user to select her connection speed. This information is then conveyed to the plug-in. Ingenious.

The server actually knows quite a lot about each site visitor's setup. For instance, it knows what kind of browser is requesting each file on a given web page, which version of that browser (5.0, 5.5, and so on) is being used, and which operating system runs on the visitor's desktop. The ability to access this information can be quite useful when you're coping with browser and platform incompatibilities—as we'll discuss in Chapter 11, "The Joy of JavaScript."

Because the server finds out and records this information every time a web page file is requested, you also can find it out for yourself by checking your site's referrer logs. What are those? Glad you asked.

Referrer logs are a standard means of letting the site's builders or owners know how many people are visiting, what browser and platform they're using, and which third-party sites "referred" these visitors via links. They also track the national origin of each unique visitor, tell you which pages are the most visited, and much more. Referrer logs are cool.

You won't find your visitors' names, addresses, and telephone numbers, of course. That information is private, not because all site owners are decent human beings but because such information is unknowable unless the visitor has voluntarily supplied it.

On certain news sites (www.nytimes.com) and some database-driven sites, the visitor must enter this private data before accessing content. The data is then stored on a *cookie* on the visitor's hard drive, allowing the user to return to the site without having to undergo the tedious log-in process each time. Advertisers and site owners foam at the mouth over the possibility of procuring information like this. We've even had a client ask if there was any way to find out each user's business phone number "without telling them." (Answer: No, and if there were, we wouldn't tell *you*.)

Web users' privacy concerns make them unlikely to provide personal data without sufficient motivation. Reading *The New York Times* free of charge may constitute sufficient motivation. Finding out more about Widgets.com probably does not.

Many sites over the years have unwittingly erected barriers by forcing users to enter personal data without first giving a clear picture of what the user would gain by doing so. Many of these were sites flung together like so much moldy cheese by traditional media moguls. When users failed to register, the moguls would claim that "Web content doesn't work" (if the ill-conceived site was their own) or trumpet the failure far and wide (if the site belonged to a competitor). Some of these sites offered decent content, but few folks were willing to cross the privacy barrier to find out about it.

Though web users are understandably reluctant to reveal their salaries and sexual preferences merely to view content, the server's tracking of less sensitive information can still be incredibly useful to the design and development team. For instance, if you discover that a great many visitors are coming from Sweden, you might commission a Swedish translation of the site—thereby enticing still more Swedes to visit. If you learn that 90% of your audience is using a 5.0 browser or better, you can incorporate standards-based dynamic technologies with less fear of alienating your core user base. The combination of server user awareness and sophisticated plug-ins such as QuickTime allows you to craft the optimum experience for each visitor.

The server can always tell each user's connection speed, operating system, and browser. This allows sophisticated plug-ins like QuickTime to deliver the optimum experience for each user. As we'll see later, it also enables us to do clever and useful things with JavaScript.

Not every player or plug-in format accommodates user connection speed in precisely the same way that QuickTime does. A Flash movie, for instance, does not vary depending on the user's connection speed; it is always the same Flash movie. Flash, however, was designed specifically to couple rich multimedia experiences with compact file sizes. Why is this important?

IT'S THE BANDWIDTH, STUPID

Aside from corporate users and a few lucky folks with Digital Subscriber Line (DSL) or cable modem access, most people view the Web through dial-up connections, which are not exactly peppy. In every multimedia format, digital compression is used to compensate for the narrowness of the user's "pipe"—the limitations of her bandwidth. As mentioned earlier, bandwidth represents the rate at which web content may be downloaded to the end-user's computer. Remember David Siegel's cry of "Clarity, Brevity, Bandwidth?" Bandwidth is arguably the most important component of this trinity. Web users will spend more time with mediocre sites that load fast than they will waiting for beauty that takes forever to show up on their screens. (Q. What's the most popular button on the Web? A. The Back button.)

Dialup modems top out at 56K. That's 56 kilobits, or 6 kilobytes, per second. (Actually, it's even less than that: The FCC mandates a top speed of 53K. Read the fine print on your modem.) Due to modem overheads ranging from 1% to 15%, phone line noise, server traffic levels, Internet congestion, and the alignment of the planets, modems rarely if ever actually achieve their top speed. 33.6 modems can do no better than 4.2K per second and frequently do less. 28.8 modems typically deliver 3 to 3.5K per second.

In ideal conditions, under a blue moon, on the Twelfth of Never, a home user is downloading less than 6K per second. So a 600K movie will take *at least* 100 seconds to download to the user's computer. The greater a format's compression ratio, the fewer kilobytes (or megabytes) your visitors have to download and the sooner they can start enjoying what you have to offer.

Flash, RealPlayer, QuickTime, and Windows Media Player all stream their content (begin playing the file soon after downloading begins). But even streaming formats are limited by the bandwidth constrictions of the end-user's modem. Streaming or not, no multimedia format can pour its data faster than the user's modem can drink it.

As you might expect, the format that compresses best uses the least bandwidth and is therefore the most popular. The RealPlayer (www.real.com) is the "best-selling" free video player on the market because it compresses video and audio down to sizes that work well even over dialup modems (though 56K modems are strongly recommended). QuickTime files tend to be larger than Real files and have higher quality; again, as common sense would lead you to expect, QuickTime is not quite as popular as RealVideo. Windows Media Player is currently the third most popular streaming format. Though it's native to the Windows Operating System, an oddly named "Windows Media Player for Macintosh" is available also, and seems to work well enough.

When appropriate, these players and plug-ins enable designers to bring rich multimedia (and in the case of Flash, interactivity) to the Web. And of course, when used unwisely, they make the medium a virtual hell of ugly spinning logos, unwanted soundtracks, and other detritus that adds insult to injury by taking forever to download.

Web Pages Have No Secrets

Web pages are immodest. You can see what's under their clothes. You can't learn the design secrets of a print layout by looking, touching, or clicking; but you can easily do this on the Web.

To begin with, every browser since Mosaic, released in 1993, has a menu item called View Source. As you'd expect, this allows you to view the source code of any web page. How the heck did the designer pull off that intricate web layout? View the source and find out. How did they make the image change when you dragged your mouse across it? Click View Source and study their JavaScript code. It is, of course, possible to obfuscate JavaScript source code, making it difficult for source snoops to understand what is going on. It's also possible to write extremely ugly code, but that's usually not intentional. For an example of the former, use View Source and compare: http://dhtml-guis.com/game/poetry.opt.html versus http://dhtml-guis.com/game/poetry.html.

Naturally, you need to know enough about HTML or scripting languages to understand the code you're looking at. Conversely, the more source code you view, the more you'll learn about the code that makes web pages work. Most web designers learn their trade this way. In fact it's fair to say that for every HTML book sold, there are a thousand web pages whose source code has been studied for free. Well, perhaps it's not fair to say, but we've gone ahead and said it anyway, and since we get paid by the word, we're adding yet another irrelevant clause to the mess.

The ability to view source code is there for a reason: to teach HTML and other markup and scripting languages by example. Even sharp operators who know all the angles are constantly learning new tricks and techniques by studying their peers' sources.

Make a mental note never to steal someone else's source code outright. All you want to do is learn from it. This is an ethical and professional issue, not a legal one. Unlike text, artwork, and photography, HTML markup is not protected by copyright, even though some web designers claim otherwise.

Unscrupulous designers do steal each other's code, but this is a bad practice. If the moral issues do not concern you, imagine your embarrassment—and possible business difficulties—should your client receive an angry letter from a designer whose code you swiped. It's not worth the risk.

In Chapter 8, "HTML, the Building Blocks of Life Itself," we'll teach you how to View Source in your HTML editor of choice rather than inside the browser. Because many designers won't bother reading that chapter, we'll pad it out with poignant childhood reminiscences and jokes involving creamed corn.

In addition to View Source, Netscape Navigator's menu bar offers an option to View Document (or Page) Info. Choose it, and the entire page will be deconstructed for you in a new window, image by image. Beside each image's name you'll find its complete URL (its address on the Web), its file size, how many colors it contains, and whether or not it uses transparency. Click the link beside each image, and the image will load in the bottom of the window. By viewing page info, you may discover that a large image is actually composed of smaller pieces stuck together with a borderless HTML table or that what looks like one image is actually two: a transparent foreground GIF image file floating atop a separate background image. Or you'll discover invisible (transparent) images, used to control the spacing of elements on old-fashioned web pages. (Today, designers use CSS to accomplish the same thing without subverting the structural purpose of HTML. Throw out those old web design books. The tricks they teach are outdated and considered harmful to the future of the Web.)

Microsoft's Internet Explorer does not let you view page info the way Netscape's browser does. But both browsers are free, and as a designer you will be using both anyway. In fact, you'll regularly be checking your work in at least two generations of Netscape and Microsoft's browsers and then double-checking it in WebTV, Opera, iCab, and Lynx.

In all likelihood, even when all browsers fully support common standards, you will still have to check your work in multiple browsers to avoid browser bugs—and of course you will have to view your work on multiple platforms. Or at least ask people on web design mailing lists to check it for you.

The Web Is for Everyone!

The last version of HTML—HTML 4—goes out of its way to make sure that everyone can use the Web, from Palm Pilot owners to the blind and from English speakers to, uh, nonEnglish speakers. HTML 4 contains improved accessibility features that enable web designers to accommodate all potential users, thus better fulfilling the medium's mandate. Throughout this book we'll be talking about ways to make your content accessible to everyone.

Web design is different because websites must be compatible with many browsers, operating systems, and access speeds. The following sections discuss some of the challenges that make all the difference between designing and designing for the medium.

It's Still the Bandwidth, Stupid

In the preceding section on multimedia, we defined bandwidth in terms of bits and bytes per second. The key to bandwidth is realizing that there is never enough of it. Design with a few small files, and you remove the bandwidth obstacle for most of your potential audience. Design with large files, and your audience shrinks to a chosen few who enjoy fast access at all times. Design with many large files per page, and your audience shrinks to you and you alone.

Bandwidth issues are complicated by the amount of traffic clogging the network. A corporate T1 line is very fast—until 500 employees log on over their lunch hour. Then it can be as dreary as the slowest home dialup modem.

Similarly, 10 early adopters share a super-fast cable modem line. They brag to their friends who quickly subscribe to the service and tell their buddies about it. Soon 1,000 people are connected to the same cable modem line, and it is no longer reliably fast because the available upstream bandwidth has shrunk. The cable modem is still offering the same peppy connectivity, but the bandwidth is now shared across multiple users.

Likewise, an Internet Service Provider (ISP) brags in its advertising that it offers multiple, redundant T3 connectivity (very, very fast). The advertising campaign is so successful that a million new users subscribe to the service, and suddenly the bandwidth available to any given subscriber is low. ISPs are like airlines. Airlines overbook flights, causing you to miss connections. ISPs underestimate needed capacity, slowing down connections. Bandwidth never exceeds the speed of the weakest link. Your corporate T1 line does you little good if the site is being served from a home machine connected to the Internet via the owner's Integrated Digital Services Network (IDSN) line. Or the server may be fast and powerful, but if a connecting router goes down in Chicago, bandwidth will slow to a trickle.

Differences in national phone service contribute to the problem. Sites served from Japan, Australia, and France are almost always slow to reach the U.S. no matter how powerful the server and no matter how fast the connection on your end.

Bandwidth also may be negatively impacted if the server is overloaded due to temporary traffic at one of the sites it serves. In 1999, when Internet Channel (www.inch.com) in New York City hosted a live webcast by Steve Jobs of Apple Computer, demand for Jobs's address ran so high that all sites on that server ran slower than normal—even though those other sites were unaffiliated with the Apple broadcast.

So let us repeat: There is never enough bandwidth. Therefore, the best web design is that which conserves bandwidth.

Good web designers are constantly performing digital sleight of hand to conserve bandwidth. By contrast, beginning web slingers with a background in design will typically create a comp in Adobe Photoshop, cut it apart in Adobe ImageReady, and use Macromedia Dreamweaver or Adobe GoLive to put it together again as a working web page. The page may look divine, but it's almost guaranteed to hog bandwidth.

So how do we conserve bandwidth?

Swap text and code for images

For one thing, we conserve bandwidth by using HTML text instead of typographic images wherever we can. As mentioned earlier, images must be downloaded, decoded, and expanded in the browser —and that takes time. Text may be downloaded in a fraction of the time. HTML is text-based and is thus a bandwidth-friendly technology. ImageReady is a great tool, but don't expect it to make all your decisions for you. If you use ImageReady or Macromedia Fireworks to generate the pieces of a web page, be prepared to replace some of those pieces with bandwidth-friendly HTML.

Trim those image files

We also conserve bandwidth by reducing the file size of our images when exporting them (saving them in web-friendly formats) from Photoshop. All designers know that file sizes diminish as resolution decreases. A 1200ppi (pixels-per-inch) image takes up more megabytes than the same image at 72ppi. On the Web, all images are rendered at 72ppi, but that is only the beginning. Later in this chapter, we'll discuss techniques for squeezing high quality out of small image files, and (again) replacing images with HTML even when you use a tool like ImageReady to automate part of the process.

Do more with less

Slicing a large image into a dozen pieces may reduce the bandwidth required by each piece, but there is a trade-off. As the server responds to one image request after another, the cumulative bandwidth used might be higher than needed to serve a smaller number of larger images. Each design requires you to experiment with these trade-offs.

Prune redundancy

Another technique to conserve bandwidth is to remove redundancy from HTML code. If you're unfamiliar with HTML, you can scan Chapter 8 for a quick overview. But even if you don't, the following example will probably make sense to you. If not, just nod along and come back later.

In traditional web design, we use HTML tables to position text and images on the page. HTML tables are just like tables in a spreadsheet, except that the borders are usually turned off (border="0") to hide the underlying technology from viewers. By default, elements in a table cell are left-aligned unless the programmer has specified otherwise by typing something like <td align="center"> or <td align="right">. Therefore, in an HTML layout, it is unnecessary to type:

```
<td align="left">
```

In our code, when:

```
<td>
```

Will suffice. Now, <align="left"> does not eat much bandwidth on its own, but multiplied thousands of times throughout a site, that kind of unnecessary markup adds up to a significant waste of bandwidth per visitor. If the site wastes 10K of bandwidth on each visitor, and one million visitors access the site each week, the waste of bandwidth is multiplied to an astounding 10 gigabytes per week, and visitors may experience a decline in the overall responsiveness of the web server.

Strange as it seems, we can even conserve bandwidth by minimizing white space in our HTML documents. Users never see these documents unless they are utilizing View Source, and technically, the amount of white space makes no difference in the rendering of the site. For example, this HTML snippet:

```
<div align="Center">
<form>
<input
type="button" style="font-size: 12px; font-family: geneva, arial, sans-serif; background-
color: #ff6600; color: #ffffff;"
value="Previous Reports"
```

```
onClick="window.location='com0800a.html';"
onMouseOver="window.status='More of same.'; return true;"
onMouseOut="window.status='';return true;">
</form>
</div>


<p>
 <br>
</p>
```

Is functionally identical to this HTML snippet:

```
<div align="Center"><form><input type="button" style="font-size: 12px; font-family:
geneva, arial, sans-serif; background-color: #ff6600; color: #ffffff;" value="Previous
Reports" onClick="window.location='com0800a.html';" onMouseOver="window.status
='More of same.'; return true;" onMouseOut="window.status='';return true;"></form>
</div><p> <br></p>
```

Note that this technique cannot be applied to the entire web page. If you mess with the white space and line breaks in JavaScript, you can generate scripting errors that cause pages to fail. It is only safe to delete the extra white space in the HTML portion of each document. HTML does not care whether the white space is there or not. But extra white space adds to the character count, which in turn, beefs up the document's overall weight. An HTML document with plenty of white space can weigh in at 11K, while an identical document without white space may be as little as 9K. Certainly, 2K is a negligible amount of bandwidth, but multiplied by a million users a week as per the previous example, it once again becomes significant.

Before you rush off and start deleting all the white space from your HTML files, bear in mind that white space helps the eye make sense of the code. Because a site that never changes is a site that soon loses its traffic, you will frequently find yourself reopening documents you created months before to update the content and design. Just as often, a coworker will have to open and revise a document you created, or you'll be editing one of theirs. Moreover, web design is becoming more and more collaborative, which means more and more documents change hands throughout the process. For this reason, most web designers leave plenty of white space in their documents—along with a trail of comments which help the designer or her successors make sense of the markup.

Typical Comments in HTML

```
<! -- Begin the menu bar here. -->
<! -- This script is used to preload images. -->
<! -- Another pathetic hack. -->
```

Bandwidth is key but not at the price of sanity. Nevertheless, some web shops routinely save bandwidth by removing the white space from their HTML documents. To protect themselves from suicidal despair, these shops first save a legible copy of each document and preserve it offline. When a particular HTML document needs to be updated, the designer or producer opens the original document, not the one from which white space has been removed.

Because it can be problematic and because it requires keeping duplicate files, most shops don't bother with this level of bandwidth conservation.

Okay, we're sorry we mentioned the whole thing.

Cache as Cache Can

One of the best ways to minimize bandwidth is to employ the caching mechanism built into all web browsers. The caching mechanism, which lives on the end-user's hard drive, is like a warehouse where files that have already been downloaded are stored in case the user needs them again. For instance, if a visitor returns to a previously viewed web page, the images on that page are loaded from her cache instead of having to be downloaded from the Web a second time. Because the files are already sitting on the hard drive, they load almost instantly.

That's all well and good for the web user, but how does it apply to the web designer's job?

The answer is simple: The more we reuse graphic elements, the less strain we put on our visitors' bandwidth. If we reuse the same graphic menu bar elements from page to page, these elements only have to be downloaded once. From then on, whenever the visitor hits a new page, the familiar menu bar graphics are reloaded from the cache on her hard drive. By contrast, if we change the design of the menu bar on each page, the visitor must download new graphics with every page, thus slowing the site experience (and adding to the toll on the server).

Repetitive elements help visitors make sense of the site; ever-changing elements confuse and disorient visitors. (Ever-changing elements don't help reinforce branding, either.) The need to minimize bandwidth, reinforce branding, and present the user with a comprehensible and intuitive navigational system all point to the same moral here: Keep using the same stuff over and over, relying on the user's cache to serve as much of the site as possible.

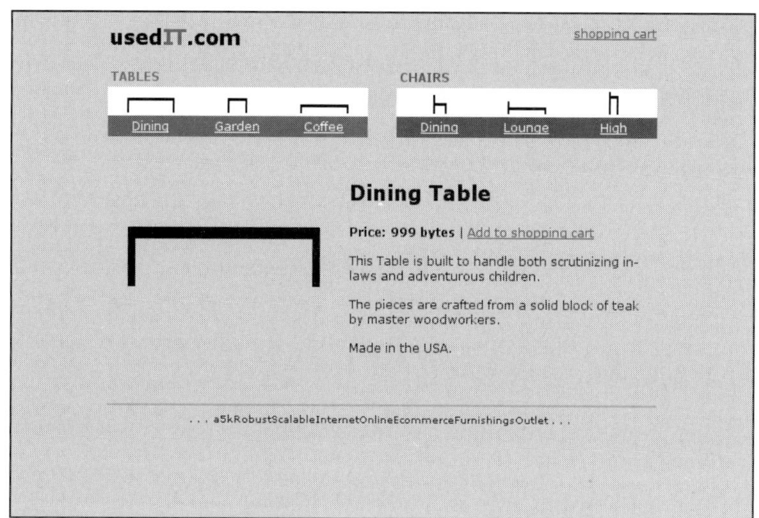

Figure 2.7

The title says it all: "a5kRobustScalableInternetOnlineEcommerceFurnishingsOutlet," the winning entry in the 5k Contest, is both a spoof and a functioning e-commerce site, created in less than 5K of bandwidth (www.the5k.org/). For those brand-new to the field, e-commerce was the Holy Grail of web design in 1999.

Much Ado About 5k

The need to conserve bandwidth is so essential that in 2000, Stewart Butterfield created a "5k Contest" challenging web designers to create some of the smallest sites in the world: complete websites that would weigh in at under 5 kilobytes. (To put this in perspective, 5K equals about seven or eight short paragraphs of plain text.)

To Butterfield's astonishment, thousands of web designers responded to the challenge. You can see the results at www.the5k.org. As you marvel at some of these creative solutions, bear in mind that the average web page is 32K (over 6 times as large as the 5k winners). (The average corporate web page is often much larger than that.) The 5k Contest proves that our pages do not have to be nearly so bloated. As a web design professional, you will always be seeking new ways to minimize bandwidth.

Screening Room

Luxuriating in your monitor's 21" screen, you design a site that looks sensational. How will it look on a 14" screen? Will it even fit? That is the challenge of screen resolution.

Screens range from 14" to 21" (and higher), with 15" and 17" currently the most popular. By the time this book is printed, 17" screens will dominate the home market, and ladies named Mistress Beatrice will dominate everywhere else. Laptops will continue to offer 14" and 15" screens along with the coveted 17-incher. Not only do screens vary, resolutions vary. Some folks view the web at 640 x 480; others at 1600 x 1200 (or even higher). This wild fluctuation in monitor size and screen resolution has a critical effect on page layout.

Are we saying that your site must be able to fit inside a 640 x 480 environment? No, you don't always have that much space. Consider that browsers do not make full use of the screen. In Windows, room is left at the bottom for the task bar, while the top of the screen is taken up with browser chrome (the buttons and text entry fields that allow users to navigate the Web). In Mac OS, the right-hand side of the screen is reserved for that little trail of icons representing the user's hard drive, saved files, and other work-related shortcuts, and the top of the screen is again given over to browser chrome.

Accounting for OS interface elements and browser chrome, the usable space may be less than 580 x 380. But if you design precisely to fit that small space as if it were a fixed newspaper ad size, your site may look forlorn or even ludicrous on a larger monitor running at 1600 x 1200. What's a mother to do?

Liquid Design

The solution is to embrace the fluid nature of the medium and, whenever possible, design in a resolution-independent manner. Glenn Davis, web critic and former Chief Technology Officer of Projectcool.com, uses the phrase *Liquid Design* to describe an approach to web design in which the content reflows as it is "poured" into any monitor size.

Narrow your browser window to 640 pixels or thereabouts, and visit www.jazzradio.net (see Figure 2.8). Now stretch your window as wide as it will go (Figure 2.9). Notice how the entire layout reflows to fill the screen. See also www.alistapart.com for another example of Liquid Design.

Figure 2.8

The original site design for jazzradio.net works well if the visitor's monitor is small...

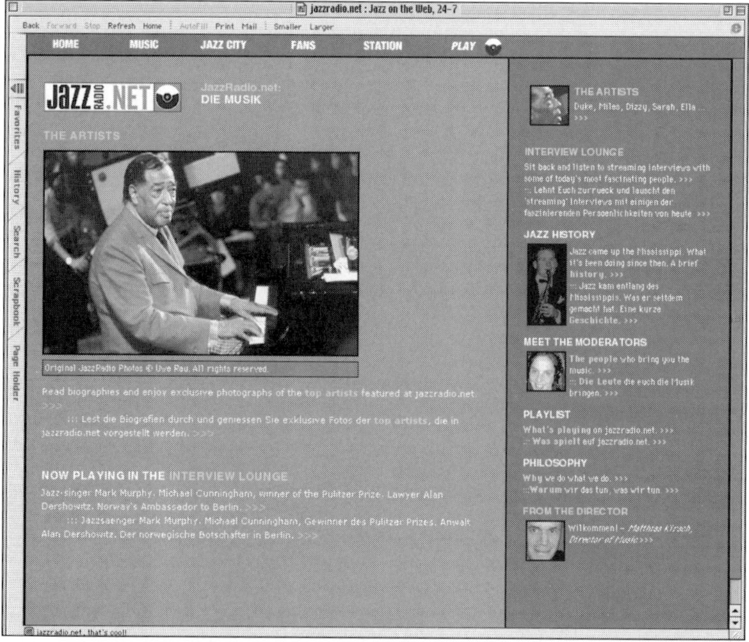

Figure 2.9

...and equally well if the monitor is large. Liquid Design makes users of any size monitor feel equally at home (www.jazzradio.net).

There are limits to how wide a web layout may be stretched before it begins to look ludicrous, but the goal is not to provide hours of "squash and stretch" fun for web users. (They're not going to perform this exercise anyway.) The goal is to provide a site that seems to naturally fit each visitor's monitor. This makes the visitor feel right at home, thereby encouraging her to spend more time on the site and drink milk right out of the carton when she thinks you're not looking.

By contrast, with a more rigid approach to web layout, your site might appear to be "shoved into the corner" of a user's large monitor. Or it might be too wide for the user's small monitor, forcing her to scroll left and right (or more probably, encouraging her to leave and never come back).

A great majority of websites are designed at 800 x 600 fixed resolution in the belief that most users have screens wide enough to accommodate this width and height. True, "most" users can accommodate it, but why not build something that fits every user like a glove?

With Liquid Design, you can do just that.

By contrast, Banana Republic (www.bananarepublic.com) (see Figure 2.10) and Three.oh (www.threeoh.com) offer fixed web layouts using absolute heights and widths. Banana Republic's site does this to fit inside small monitors. It certainly does that, but its attractiveness is marred on large monitors—where most of the screen lies empty and yearning.

Figure 2.10

Fixed web layouts can be attractive, but on larger monitors the design can suffer from that "shoved into the corner" feeling (www.bananarepublic.com). Sites must be designed to work on small monitors but need not be designed to look ludicrous on large ones. Liquid Design can solve this problem.

Where bananarepublic.com chooses a fixed layout approach to accommodate dinky screens, Three.oh's large, fixed layout requires the visitor to own a monitor big enough to take in the entire design at a glance. Three.oh is elegantly designed and serves an audience of graphic artists. Thus, the assumption that site visitors possess a large enough monitor to see the whole thing is reasonable enough. But by adhering to a print-like model of site design, using absolute widths and font sizes, Three.oh rules out visitors saddled with small monitors as well as the visually impaired. The site's designers no doubt feel justified in doing this because nondesigners and visually impaired folks could not possibly be interested in what the site has to offer. Most sites cannot make assumptions like this.

Liquid Design is accomplished through HTML tables that are built with percentages (rather than absolute widths), framesets that use percentages (rather than absolute widths), or CCS. Because 4.0 browsers are still in use at the time of this writing and will be for at least the next year, and because CSS support is less than perfect in 4.0 browsers, most designers choose tables or framesets to get the job done. We've created a simplified HTML example to show how Liquid Design differs from print-like, fixed design. Peek ahead to Chapter 8 if the markup confuses you.

Traditional versus Liquid Design

Here is a traditional, print-like approach to web design that uses table cells with absolute widths. All extraneous code has been deleted from this radically simplified example to focus on the points of difference between print-like and Liquid Design.

```
<html>
<table width="600">
<tr>
<td width="400">
<p>Content goes here.</p>
</td>
<td width="200">
<p>Navigation goes here. This column is half as wide as the content column.</p>
</td>
</tr>
</table>
</html>
```

Next, a similar web page, but this time it's liquid. Specifying percentages rather than absolute widths enables the page to fit any screen while preserving the relative proportions of the original layout.

```
<html>
<table width="100%">
<tr>
<td width="66%">
<p>Content goes here.</p>
</td>
<td width="34%"><p>Navigation goes here. As in the previous example, this column is
half as wide as the content column. However, this table will stretch or squash to fit any
monitor comfortably.</p>
</td>
</tr>
</table>
</html>
```

The liquid approach handles our horizontal problem, but what about the vertical? Simple: Remember that the first 380 pixels of vertical space is the only area that all your visitors are certain to see without scrolling. Make sure that your navigational menu (if any), logo (if any), headlines (if any), and other important content fits comfortably within that vertical area. Less important information can fall below the fold, and no harm done. Your client's advertisers will be clamoring for placement at the top of the screen for this very reason. Alas, if they get their wish, those with small monitors will see browser chrome, ad banners, and task bars to the exclusion of almost everything else. No wonder some people hate the Web the first time they see it.

Color My Web

As with the wide variety in screen resolutions, computers are far from uniform in their ability to display color. Designers work with machines that support millions of colors (24 or 32 bits). But many computer users are limited to thousands of colors (16 bits), and a significant minority is stuck with 256 colors (8 bits) or less.

Monitors that are limited to 256 colors face an additional problem in that up to 40 of these colors are "used up" in advance by the operating system itself. For instance, Windows reserves 40 Windows system colors for its own display purposes in lower-end color environments. That leaves exactly 216 colors at your disposal.

In 1994, the makers of Netscape Navigator mathematically subdivided the color spectrum into 216 *web-safe colors*, which are equidistant from each other along the color wheel. You will hear this mathematical arrangement of web-safe colors variously referred to as the Netscape Color Cube, the web-safe palette, and variations thereof, many of them unprintable in a family publication.

The Color Cube is the bane of many web designers' existence, but it need not be. Paper stocks have limitations; so do type families, and so does the Web. This is one of those limitations you can master upon accepting it as part of the discipline the medium imposes.

Know the Code

Photoshop 5 (and higher) includes a web-safe color palette, and the included VisiBone color palette is even more useful because it arranges the colors in ways with which designers can understand and work. But how can you tell in code alone if your colors are web-safe? Easy. Know the code. In HTML, all colors are indicated in three pairs (six digits) of hexadecimal code.

This, for instance, is red: #ff0000.

And this is a darker red: #cc0000.

What are these little characters? They are hexadecimal code for the Red, Green, and Blue channels of an RGB monitor. The first two digits indicate the amount of light pouring from the monitor's Red channel; the second pair tells how much Green appears; and the third tells how much Blue.

With #ff0000, the Red channel is going full blast (#ff is the highest possible two-digit value in hexadecimal), and the other two channels are "turned off" (#00). (Most of the time, you will be working with subtler color values.)

Web-safe colors are composed only of the following hexadecimal pairs:

00	33	66
99	cc	ff

Thus, #3399ff is a web-safe color, while #07ba42 is not.

Only the 216 web-safe colors (colors that can be described with the hexadecimal pairs indicated in the previous sidebar) are guaranteed to display correctly in both Windows and Mac OS in the 8-bit environment. Any other color will *dither* (be broken into dots) on a 256-color monitor and will *shift* (change to an unintended and subtly mismatched color) on a system with thousands of colors.

Thousands Weep

As of this writing, 56% of computer owners now have 16-bit color (thousands of colors), and this probably makes them happy because it makes the daily bikini models' flesh tones look more realistic. But for web designers, 16-bit color is a nightmare.

Sure, the dithering in 8-bit (256-color) systems is downright ugly and can make a web page unreadable, but you can avoid it by sticking to the web-safe Color Cube, which thus ends the problem. By contrast, the unavoidable color shifting that occurs on 16-bit systems springs from the dripping maws of Hell.

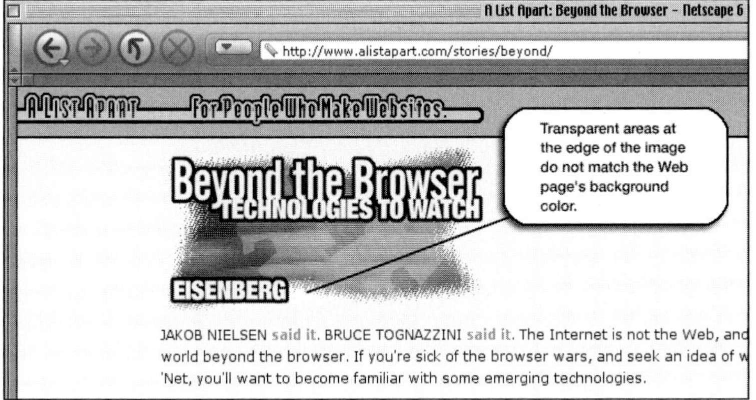

Figure 2.11

For reasons only a software company could explain, browsers and image editors round off 16-bit color calculations differently. As a result, for users of 16-bit color, image backgrounds and HTML (or CSS), backgrounds will never match (www.alistapart.com/stories/beyond/).

Say your web page has a web-safe, light brown background color. Say your client's product shot is supposed to sit on the page. Say the background color in that product shot is subtly "off" from the background of your web page. Say you're in big trouble, cowboy.

Due to differences between the way browsers calculate 16-bit color and the way image editors like Adobe Photoshop do it, in the 16-bit color space, browsers are off differently from the way GIF images are off. In other words, the background color of the image absolutely, mathematically cannot match the background color of the web page. All the web designer's careful illusions are revealed. There is nothing you can do about this except wait for 24-bit color to become cheaper so that more consumers will adopt it.

Some web designers work around this problem by using transparent backgrounds. This is fine as long as the image does not serve also as a link. (Most images these days do.) Why are links problematic? Today most web pages use the CSS hover property to make links light up (meaning change colors) when the visitor drags her mouse over them. As you'll see in Chapter 3, this kind of visual interactivity is helpful because it lets the user know that this particular set of words can take her somewhere else with a click of her mouse. When images serve as links and when links use the CSS hover property, the background color of a transparent image will change in response to the actions of the visitor's mouse. Freddie Kreuger has nothing on this unintentional visual effect. Web designers who wish to avoid this horror will either create incredibly complex style sheets or simply use solid, web-safe background colors in their images. And of course, these solid colors will be subtly mismatched on the screens of all 16-bit users. Welcome to the Web. Meantime, at least you can protect your 8-bit, 24-bit, and 32-bit using friends by sticking to the web-safe color palette as often as possible, particularly for large color fields, typography, and background colors.

At this point many designers scream: "These colors are ugly! This is not what I want." You will find, after you work with these colors, that it is possible to create pleasing combinations with them, and you will develop your own techniques for doing so. We promise.

When saving images, you do not need to worry about intermediate colors. If your type is web-safe orange, and your background is web-safe blue, the edges of the type will be filled in with intermediately shaded pixels that are probably not web-safe. They do not have to be. As long as the large areas of color are web-safe, a little dithering around the edges of type and images goes unnoticed by most users.

While GIFs are an appropriate format for logos, typography, and illustrations, the JPEG format is usually preferred for photography. It is impossible to shift colors to the web-safe palette in a JPEG. Again, this limitation of the medium is accepted or ignored by most users. But GIF images should generally be shifted as closely as possible toward the Color Cube. In the next sections, we will talk about ways of doing that.

Gamma Gamma Hey!

Gamma is a measurement of light, and different platforms come with different standard gamma settings. The Macintosh has a System Gamma setting of 1.8. Put simply, it looks bright and has a wide range of light-to-dark variance unless Mac users adjust their display to some other setting. Silicon Graphics Machines (SGI) have a System Gamma setting of 2.4. Their default output is darker than that of Mac OS.

The Windows, Linux, and Sun operating systems run on PCs. PCs and their components are built by a wide variety of manufacturers. While this keeps end-user costs down, it also means that PCs have no standard hardware gamma correction. Typically, their System Gamma is estimated at 2.4—darker than Macintosh. In practice, PC gamma can be all over the place, but it is always darker than that of Mac OS.

What does this mean to web designers? It means that if you do not compensate for this cross-platform gamma variance, the subtle "study in earth tones" that looks so moody and mysterious on your Mac will probably look like a "study in mud" on most PCs. Because PCs are used by at least 90% of your audience, a study in mud is not what you want.

In the late 1990s, Microsoft and Hewlett-Packard (www.w3.org/Graphics/Color/sRGB.html) came up with a gamma standard called standard RGB (sRGB) that gives Windows machines a common gamma setting of around 2.2—at least in theory. Of course, it doesn't work if users don't select it. And if they haven't calibrated their monitors, it still won't really work. But at least it gives us something to aim for. Windows-based web designers should calibrate their monitors, set their machines to sRGB, and find something else to worry about.

There are three ways for Mac-based web designers to compensate for gamma issues.

The simplest is to download and install *GammaToggle FKEY* (www.acts.org/roland/thanks/), a $5.00 shareware control panel created by Roland Gustafsson in the mid-1990s. After it's downloaded and installed in the System folder, this simple control panel allows you to toggle between your Mac gamma setting and a representative PC gamma setting at the touch of a command key. The software works flawlessly, the $5.00 shareware fee is optional (but how could you not pay the man?), and this tool has proved sufficient for hundreds of thousands of web designers since the earliest days of professional design on the Web. Another advantage to GammaToggle FKEY is that it is software-independent. In other words, you can toggle from Mac to PC gamma whether you're working in Photoshop, using a browser, or simply have the kooky urge to push a Command key in the middle of a slow day.

The second solution is to download the *Furbo Filters Webmaster* pack (www.furbo-filters.com), created by Iconfactory's brilliant Craig Hockenberry with kibitzing from your humble author. Unveiled in 1997, the Furbo Webmaster pack is a constellation of Photoshop plug-ins that (among other things) allows web designers to switch between Mac gamma and three kinds of PC gamma. The software also lets you preview the effects of various types of GIF and JPEG compression, and an included Web Scrubber (based on the pioneering efforts of user interface guru Todd Fahrner) lets you selectively shift your images toward the Color Cube. The shareware costs $40, and may be downloaded and used indefinitely for free. A nag screen helps your conscience decide when it's time to pay for the software.

In 1998, Adobe got wise to this whole cross-platform gamma issue (and related web design issues) and came out with ImageReady, a Photoshop-like application for creating and exporting web graphics. Like Furbo Filters, ImageReady lets you preview the effects of gamma differences and compression settings on your images, and it also lets you shift your colors closer to or further from the Color Cube.

In late 1998, with the release of Photoshop 5, Adobe made it possible to compensate for gamma differences between platforms using Photoshop alone. This is largely because Adobe supports the sRGB standard in Photoshop (even on Macs), and Apple supports it through the system's included ColorSync control panel.

Mac users, here's how to put sRGB to work:

1. Open the RGB Settings preference in Photoshop 5 or higher and select sRGB as your working environment.
2. Photoshop will prompt you to set up your System Gamma if you have not done so already. In Mac OS 8 and higher, you can set your Mac's System Gamma to sRGB using either the Mac's built-in ColorSync control panel or the Adobe Gamma control panel that comes with Photoshop.
3. Set your Mac to sRGB, and you will always be inside the Windows gamma space. If you prefer, leave it at typical Mac gamma (or some custom setting), and Photoshop will magically shift your images from the Mac to the Windows color space.

Choose Your Gamma

If you continue to design for print as well as the Web, stick with Apple's default settings and let Photoshop toggle you back and forth between Mac and sRGB gamma settings. If you're biting the bullet and plunging into full-time web design, by all means set your Mac to sRGB and be done with it. After you get used to working inside a slightly darker color space, it will look just fine to you, and you'll never have to worry about gamma compatibility again.

ImageReady 2.0 is included in Photoshop 5 and higher. Photoshop 5.5 is much more web-savvy than its predecessor, and Photoshop 6 is even more so. We heartily recommend these later versions of Photoshop. If you use an older version, by all means try GammaToggle FKEY or Furbo Filters.

Typography

Given what we've already discussed in terms of screen, color, and gamma differences, it should come as no surprise that there are vast differences in the way different platforms handle typography on the Web.

For one thing, different platforms offer different fonts. Two sans serif fonts, Geneva and Helvetica, come standard with Mac OS. Geneva is not found on any other platform, and while Helvetica is available in Linux, it may or may not be present on Windows systems. (Arial is the standard sans serif font that comes with Windows. There is also a version of Geneva that PC users can download, and we believe that three or four of them have done so.)

Confused, yet?

The 97% Solution

In 1997, Microsoft decided to do something about these typographic differences and commissioned a set of cross-platform *web fonts* for both Mac and Windows. These include Verdana, a lovely sans serif font designed by Matthew Carter; Georgia, also by Carter, a broad-in-the-beam serif font that can claim a distant kinship with Palatino; and Mac versions of the Windows fonts Arial, Impact, Times New Roman, Courier New, and so on.

The notion of cross-platform web fonts was a great idea. Unfortunately, not everyone bothered to download and install these fonts, so Microsoft included them in its Internet Explorer browser. (That took care of all the Windows users.) Microsoft then persuaded Apple to make IE the default browser that comes with the Macintosh Operating System. (That took care of the new Mac users and nearly took care of Netscape.)

This did nothing for Linux or UNIX users, but it did go a long way toward solving cross-platform font problems because Windows and Mac OS together make up about 97% of the market. (Depending on how you define the market, anyway.)

That still left a huge problem unsolved: the difference in typographic resolution between Mac OS and Windows.

Points of Distinction

By default in Mac OS, there are 72ppi, and a pixel is the same as a point. Thus 12pt. type is 12 pixels tall, 72pt. type is 72 pixels (or one inch) tall, and so on. Of course, most Mac users set their screens to higher resolutions, so this one-to-one equivalency between points and pixels soon becomes meaningless. But 72ppi is the starting point for Macs.

Windows users start off with 96ppi resolution; thus, 12pt. type in Windows is 16 pixels tall. Again, this varies according to the user's choice of screen resolutions, but 96ppi is the starting point.

In 4.0 (and older) browsers, what looks readable on a Mac looks big and horsey on a Windows PC. Conversely, what looks tasteful and discrete on a Windows box is often illegibly small on a Mac.

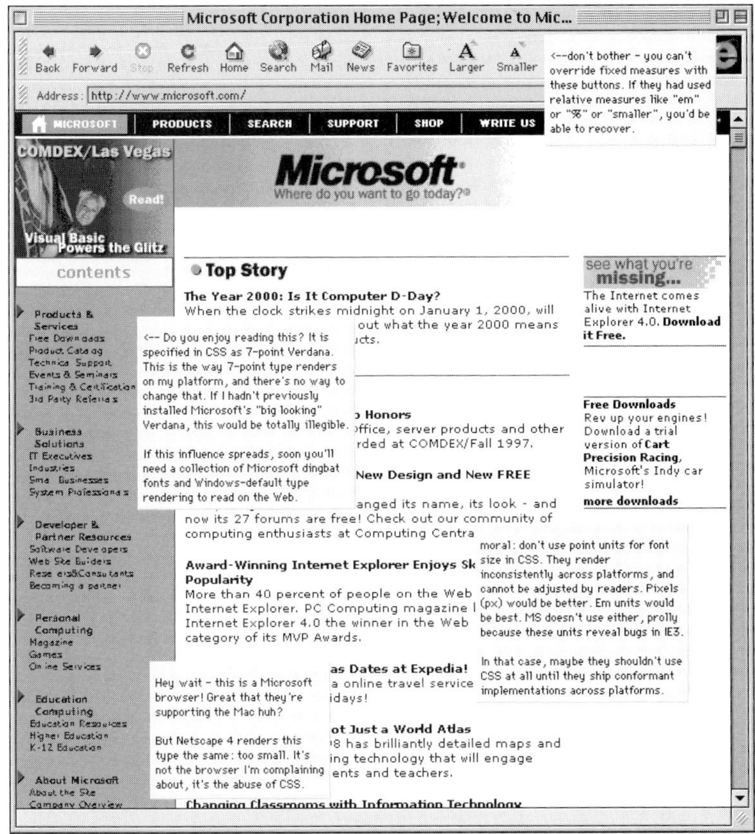

Figure 2.12

Font Wars: In 1997, CSS expert Todd Fahrner stuck this image in an obscure corner of the Web. It proved why using points was a brain-dead approach to CSS (too bad so few people listened). He sarcastically observed that if things got much worse, Macs would have to use Windows-size typographic defaults. Three and a half years later, Fahrner's sardonic prediction came true (http://style.metrius.com/font_size/points/font_wars.GIF).

Particularly since web designers began overcoming their fear of style sheets, Windows-based designers who do not check their work cross-platform have been giving Mac users type they could neither read nor enlarge in the browser. On a PC, 8pt. type looks swell. On a Mac, it looks like 8 pixels, which is at least 1 pixel shy of legibility.

Year 2000—Browsers to the Rescue

In 2000, browser makers figured out how to compensate for this long-standing problem. The first to do so was IE5 Macintosh Edition, released in March 2000. IE5/Mac's default setting is 16px type at 96ppi (Windows resolution). The Mac version of Netscape 6, released in November, followed suit.

In IE5/Mac and Netscape 6, users can change their preferences and restore the traditional "Mac" setting for text. By doing so, they risk continuing to be frustrated by the typographic resolution differences between their platform and the dominant Windows OS. But if they're smart enough to change their settings once, they're smart enough to change them back again when needed.

IE5/Mac also introduced *text zooming*, which enables users to enlarge (or shrink) HTML and CSS text on the page, no matter how the designer has formatted that text. This liberates web users from web designers' mistakes and makes the medium more accessible to the visually impaired. Netscape 6 offers similar functionality, though for some reason it was left out of the Macintosh version (at least in the initial Netscape 6 release).

Of course, 4.0 browsers are still very much among us, and the 18-Month Pregnancy period has only just begun. Consequently, cross-platform font size issues will continue to plague the Web for some time to come. In Chapter 10, "Style Sheets for Designers," we'll explain how to use style sheets to compensate for all these incompatibilities.

Touch Factor

When designing a book, your choice of materials and textures is limited only by the client's budget. When designing a website, you have no textures whatsoever. There is no "touch factor" in work designed for the digital screen. But this lack of sensory input does not mean that the site must be a cold, detached, clinical object. There are many tools to help you bring humanity and warmth to the Web.

Appropriate Graphic Design

Interactivity can go a long way toward simulating the effect of the "touch." For instance, when you move your mouse over or press the buttons at www.k10k.net, they seem to respond to your touch—like buttons in the real world. Intuitive, user-centered navigation helps as well. If the architecture is designed the way users think, navigating the site will be simple pleasure. There will be more on all that in Chapter 3. Smart, appropriate copywriting, which reads the way people talk, also can go a long way toward bringing warmth and humanity to the onscreen experience.

These approaches enable anyone to create a site that feels like a living entity. Failure to use these tools results in a site that feels cold and dead—high tech, but not high touch.

Accessibility, the Hidden Shame of the Web

The framers of the Web intended it to be a medium of universal access—a medium whose wealth of information would be accessible to anyone, regardless of physical, mental, or technological disability. Anything that stands in the way of that accessibility is contrary to the purpose of the Web. It is also inhumane, and, as we alluded to earlier, it is now against the law:

Section 508 of the Workforce Investment Act (www.usdoj.gov/crt/508/508law.html) requires all United States Federal Agencies with web-sites to make them accessible to individuals with disabilities. Inaccessible sites can be shut down by the government. In the private sector, inaccessible sites face lawsuits. In 1999, a group of blind citizens successfully sued America Online because its service was not accessible to them.

How do you design for the blind? It sounds like a paradox, but on the Web it is actually fairly easy.

The Web Content Accessibility Guidelines of the W3C (www.w3.org/TR/WAI-WEBCONTENT/) spell out everything designers must do to make their sites accessible to all.

Here are some of the things you can do to make your site accessible:

- Your <IMAGE> tags should include <ALT> text for the benefit of the visually impaired; adding <TITLE> attributes is a good idea as well. <ALT> and <TITLE> attributes can be spoken by audio browsers used by the blind, so they don't have to miss out on any content. For example, your web page on the wreck of the *Titanic* includes a photograph of that ill-fated ship. A bad <ALT> attribute reads "Image, 24K." Well, what good is that to the disabled user? So your site has an image, so what? A good <ALT> tag will read "S.S. Titanic." The <TITLE> attribute can provide additional description: "Photograph of the Titanic on her maiden voyage."
- If you use frames, include <NOFRAMES> content in the frameset document. <NOFRAMES> text shows up in browsers that cannot view frames. Old browsers fall into this category, but so do text browsers such as Lynx and special browsers for the blind. By copying your text and pasting it into the <NOFRAMES> area, you guarantee that anyone can access the information on your site, even if he or she cannot view your spectacular visual design efforts.
- Even if most users will be navigating via snazzy visual menu bars at the top of your site, be sure to include simple HTML links somewhere on the page so that the disabled—or folks with older, non-JavaScript-capable browsers—can still find their way around the site.

For more on accessibility and the law, see Alan Herrell's article in *A List Apart*, "Accessibility: The Clock is Ticking" (www.alistapart.com/stories/access/).

User Knowledge

A website must be designed so novice users can find their way through it without trouble. At the same time, a good site offers shortcuts and power tools for more experienced users. How do you serve these two very different audiences at the same time? We'll discuss that in the very next chapter.

chapter 3

Where Am I? Navigation & Interface

"I LEFT MY BABY DAUGHTER in the car while I went to buy dope. Then I drove away. I'd gone about five blocks when I realized my daughter wasn't in the car any more."

So begins a brief personal narrative that fills most of the screen of a web page. At the conclusion of this woeful tale, we see a link or button labeled More Stories. We are likely to click it.

Before doing so, we notice that a small Narcotics Anonymous logo appears in the upper left area of the screen and that four menu items appear in a column on the right. The Face of Addiction, reads one. There Is a Solution, reads another. Meetings, says a third, and Membership, reads the fourth.

Meetings takes us to a map of the United States. Clicking any city takes us to a schedule of Narcotics Anonymous meetings in that city. The Narcotics Anonymous logo, consistently placed at the upper left of every screen on the site, takes us back to the first page, with its riveting personal narrative and easily understood menu structure. Perhaps when we return to the home page we are served a different personal story. This story may be a bit longer than the first we encountered. After all, our attention is now engaged because we have committed at least a few minutes of our time to the site. At this point we are ready to involve ourselves with a slightly more elaborate narrative.

This is one possible interface for the home page of Narcotics Anonymous, a 12-Step program that helps addicts recover, one day at a time. Recovery begins by facing the problem and telling the truth about one's life—however painful that truth may be. The honesty of these stories enables the storyteller to get well and his listeners to identify with the problem his story demonstrates. The prototype web interface parallels this process because the designers have done their homework and found out how the "product" (Narcotics Anonymous) actually works.

What Color Is Your Concept?

Notice that we have not said a word about graphic design, typography, or technology. We are simply examining a prototype whose purpose is to immediately engage readers in the site's drama and promise. The site achieves this by plunging the reader into content (but not too much content) and by supporting that content with a quickly comprehensible menu structure, as well as a linear method of reading on (More Stories).

This simple site architecture, with its emphasis on human interest, provides an immediate way for addicts to identify with an anonymous speaker and thus begin to admit that they suffer from the same problem. It helps the loved ones of addicts to recognize their husbands and wives as addicts and start to understand why Harry or Sally is "that way." The site does not preach, nor does it overwhelm visitors with too much initial detail. Its careful structure engages the minds of a specific audience and allows them to get whatever level of support they need.

Every site should be this effective, whether it offers help for personal problems or half-price airfare. Every site should immediately engage its intended audience with compelling content that invites exploration. A web designer's first job is to find the heart of the matter: the concept. The second job is to ensure that readers understand it too. That is the purpose of architecture and navigation.

Business as (Cruel and) Usual

How would ineffective web designers and clients approach the Narcotics Anonymous project? It wouldn't be by providing immediately engaging content, nor by offering a streamlined menu with both global and linear functionality. They would likely present a standard menu bar with five to ten choices, a tedious welcome message, stock photos of smiling families implicitly representing addicts in recovery (at least, in the designer's mind), and overtly commercial tie-ins to an online retailer selling self-help books.

The interior of the site might offer similar content to that contained in our imaginary prototype, but the content would be buried several layers down in the site's hierarchy, where only the most dedicated would stand a chance of finding it. Instead of capturing and presenting the essence of the client's message, the site would merely mimic the boring "professional" surface appearance of thousands of other sites. Instead of potentially saving lives, the site would merely be one more roadblock in an addict's troubled life.

How would cutting-edge web shops approach the project? Possibly by creating a 250K introductory Flash movie featuring a spinning hypodermic needle. The needle might morph into a rotating navigational device. Or it might fill with blood that drips to form letters spelling out some horrific statistic on the mortality rate of drug addicts. Such a site might win awards in a graphic design showcase, but it would not help a soul.

In all probability, the Narcotics Anonymous organization would never commission a site like any of these, nor would we expect many drug addicts to go online in search of help. We've chosen this example because it quickly dramatizes the difference between effective and ineffective web design. In the case of Narcotics Anonymous, it could mean the difference between life and death. But this is equally true for any business or organization that requires an online identity—except that what's at stake is not the reader's life, but the survival of the business itself. Sites with strong concepts and solid, intuitive architecture will live. Sites lacking those things will die.

Web design is communication. It says specific things to specific people. It does this by offering meaningful content in the context of focused digital architecture. Navigation and interface are the doors to that architecture.

In a consumer society, communication is a function of time. Traditional designers and art directors are trained in the art of instant communication. They understand that consumers make split-second decisions based on emotional responses to visual information. Which toothpaste gets tossed into the shopping cart? A stripe of color may make one dentifrice appear more clinically effective than its competitor. Which paperback is bought in the airport bookstore? Color and typography make one book leap off the shelves while another is ignored. Which of a thousand billboard messages is remembered? The one with the smart line of copy and complementary image lingers in the mind.

When traditional designers and art directors take their talent to the Web, their consummate understanding of the power of the image would seem to position them as the ideal architects of the sites they design. After all, who knows better how to focus and deliver the appropriate message before the consumer has time to click the browser's Back button? In good shops, skilled web designers are empowered to do what they do best, but this is not the case in every web agency. Some shops constrict the designer's abilities by forcing her into a more limited role.

The Rise of the Interface Department

Traditional designers and art directors work in Design Departments and Creative Departments. The existence of these departments indicates the importance traditional media businesses place upon design—and rightly so. In such businesses, designers play an essential role in the formation of concepts and images that convey brand attributes and communicate meaningful intellectual and emotional propositions.

Sadly, many otherwise savvy web agencies do not have Creative or Design Departments at all. Nor do creative directors or lead designers show up often enough on some of these companies' organizational charts. What they frequently have instead are Interface Departments, implicitly or explicitly staffed by "interface designers." This departmental label trivializes and may even constrict the web designer's potential usefulness as brand steward, conceptualist, structural architect, and user advocate.

When a web designer is reduced to the handwork of graphic design, somebody else determines the overall focus and architecture of the site. Nevertheless, the rise of the Interface Department is telling because it underlines the supreme importance of interface design to web development.

Designing interfaces is only part of a web designer's job in the same way that working with actors is only part of a movie director's job. A director who can't work with actors will make a lousy movie, and a web designer who can't devise the most communicative interface for each particular site will serve up mediocrity. Websites provide content; interfaces provide context. Good interfaces support the visitor's (and client's) goals by visually and structurally answering two urgent questions:

1. **What is this?** What kind of site is this? What is its purpose? What messages are being conveyed or services offered? For whom is this site intended? If it's intended for me, does it offer the product or information I've been seeking, or is it all show and no substance?
2. **Where am I?** What kind of space is this? How does it work? Can I find what I need? If so, can I find it quickly? If I take a wrong turn, can I find my way back?

When a web designer fully understands the nature of the product or service, as in the example of the Narcotics Anonymous prototype above, then content and context, meaning and architecture, are one. Not only does the Narcotics Anonymous prototype quickly reveal the site's purpose by emphasizing appropriate text, it also understands and fulfills its potential viewer's gut-level needs by functioning simply and transparently. A wife who fears her husband is becoming an addict does not have time to waste. If the site confuses her, she's gone.

When a web designer does not fully understand the nature of the product or service—or understands but is not empowered to act upon that understanding—we get sites that excite and engage no one. Or we get potentially engaging sites that confuse and estrange the very people they worked so hard to attract.

There are too many such sites on the Web. What businesses must understand is that vague, non-engaging interfaces are a death sentence because they alienate potential readers, members, or customers rather than reassuring them that they've come to the right place. Good web design plunges the visitor into the exact content appropriate for the most efficient (and personal) use of the site and continues to guide him or her through each new interaction.

Movies immediately plunge a protagonist (and the audience) into conflict and action. Entertainment sites can work the same way.

Newspapers carry many stories but call the reader's attention to the most important ones. Content sites can work the same way.

Stores sell many products, but special displays on featured products arrest shoppers' attention as they enter. Commercial sites can work the same way.

Form and Function

Effective interfaces not only lead visitors to the content but also underscore its meaning, just as chapter divisions underscore the meaning of a book's content. Without usable, intuitive interfaces, websites might as well offer no content at all—because no visitor will be able to find it.

At their most basic level, web interfaces include navigational elements such as menu bars, feedback mechanisms such as interactive forms and buttons, and components that guide the visitor's interaction with the site such as magnifying glass icons and left or right arrows. Tired interfaces offer exhausted metaphors such as the ubiquitous folder tab and the heinous beveled push-button. Better interfaces are uniquely branded and help reinforce the site's thematic concerns (see Figure 3.1).

The Mary Quant site is a study in quick visitor orientation and structurally grounded design. the dominant but fast-loading photograph telegraphs "1960s" and "mini-skirt," which are the essence of fashion designer Mary Quant's legacy. The flower motif reinforces the 1960s theme as well as Quant's identity. A large flower fills in the space behind appropriately minimal text content; this is a fashion site, not a Ph.D. dissertation. Smaller flowers brand the five simple structural divisions: History, Makeup, Press Office, Shops, and Homepage.

Figure 3.1

The Mary Quant site—the perfect combination of solid design and ease of use (www.maryquant.co.uk).

The History label is faded to reinforce the visitor's position within the site's hierarchy. The Previous and Next buttons are placed left and right where a western audience would expect them and where even non-English speakers (at least those who read from left to right) will likely understand what these buttons do.

Although this is a fashion site, its structure is nearly identical to that sketched out in our imaginary Narcotics Anonymous prototype. The Previous and Next buttons provide linear navigation. Menu icons let the visitor jump from section to section. Engaging visual and text content match the desires of the intended audience.

Sophisticated interfaces work on multiple levels. On a well-made catalog site, not only will visitors find a main navigation bar, they also will be guided by contextual, user-driven navigational elements throughout the page. Both the photograph and the text description of a blue parka can serve as links to more detailed photographs and information or to an order form. The product photo caption may include a link to More Items Like This One, initiating a new and more focused search. Navigation does not live by menu bars alone.

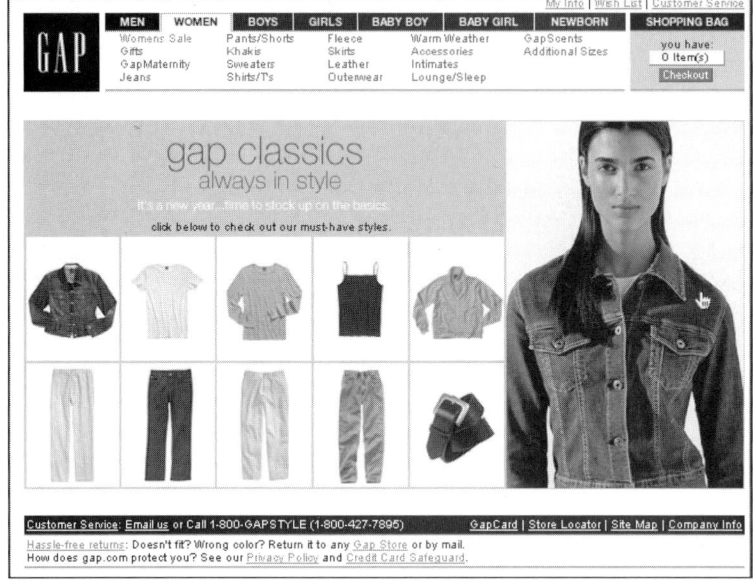

Figure 3.2

Multi-level navigation in action: the Gap site presents visitors with an overall menu bar but does not limit them to it. Clicking the model's photograph...

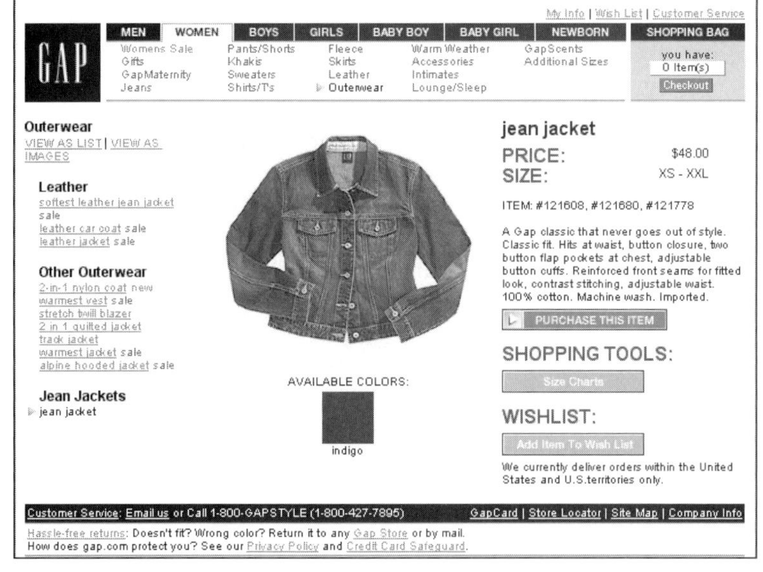

Figure 3.3

...links the visitor to a page displaying the jacket the model is wearing, along with relevant text information and the opportunity to buy the item (www.gap.com).

Copycats and Pseudo-Scientists

A site's navigational interface is the leading edge of the visitor's experience. It facilitates human needs or thwarts them. If it is not intuitive, it is useless. One reason we have so many unimaginative interfaces (visual Muzak) is because their familiarity makes them appear intuitive, and they therefore survive the pre-launch "user testing" phase.

For several years, nearly all sites offered left-hand navigation (menu items on the left side of the web page, content on the right). Was left-hand navigation easier to use or understand than any other configuration? No. In fact, some studies suggested that navigation worked better on the right. Navigation cropped up on the left because it was easier for web designers and developers to create HTML that way—and later, it was easier to control <FRAMES> that way.

Because it was easier to program, a few large sites such as CNET.com began offering left-hand navigation. Since CNET.com was a successful site, unimaginative web agencies copied its interface in hopes that CNET's success would somehow rub off on them. With so many sites engaging in this practice, consumers got used to it. Thus, in unsophisticated user acceptance testing, left-hand navigation was considered "intuitive" because consumers were accustomed to seeing it—not because it had any intuitive advantages on its own. The "folder tabs" metaphor used at Amazon.com has been copied for the same reasons. Every Nike spawns a thousand swooshes; every successful site with a particular stylistic flourish leaves a hundred thousand imitators in its wake. Bad processes encourage bad design.

There are good marketers and there are dolts in suits. Similarly, there is good user acceptance testing and there is worthless pseudo-science that promotes banality. Unfortunately, worthless pseudo-science is as easy to sell to web agency CEOs as it is to clients. It's hard to tell until you're actually working at a web agency whether its testing practices are informative or a shortcut to Hell. An engaged and thoughtful web designer will develop and fight for the best navigational structure for each site, knowing that each site is unique because its content and audience are unique.

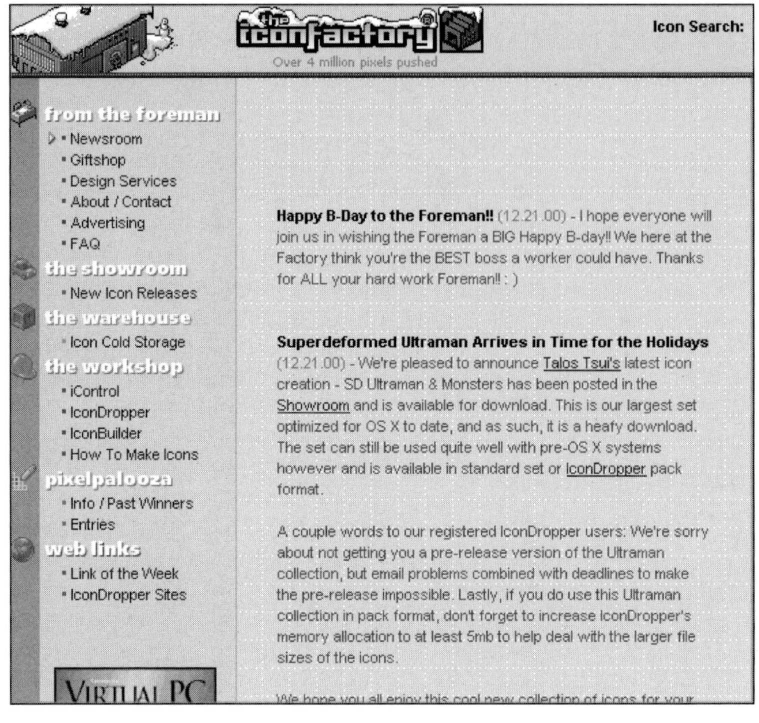

Figure 3.4

Ye Olde Left-Hand Nav Bar in action, seen here on the Winter 2000 edition of Icon Factory, creators of free, funky Mac desktop icons since 1995 (www.iconfactory.com). The left side is no better or worse than any other menu placement. But for several years, nearly all sites stuck their menus on the left because, well, nearly all sites stuck their menus on the left. Most left-hand navigation bars are nowhere near as cute 'n cuddly as Icon Factory's.

Chaos and Clarity

Beyond providing access to and subtly reinforcing a site's content, the interface also enables people to engage in interactive behaviors, such as shopping and searching. Or it frustrates them and sends them scurrying to a competitor's site, as in Figure 3.5, where clutter and lack of differentiation create chaos rather than a satisfying user experience. Sites of this nature, if they do not die immediately, persist in spite and not because of their architecture. They survive by offering something of value to those who are willing to overlook the experience's deficiencies. With better architecture they would attract more customers.

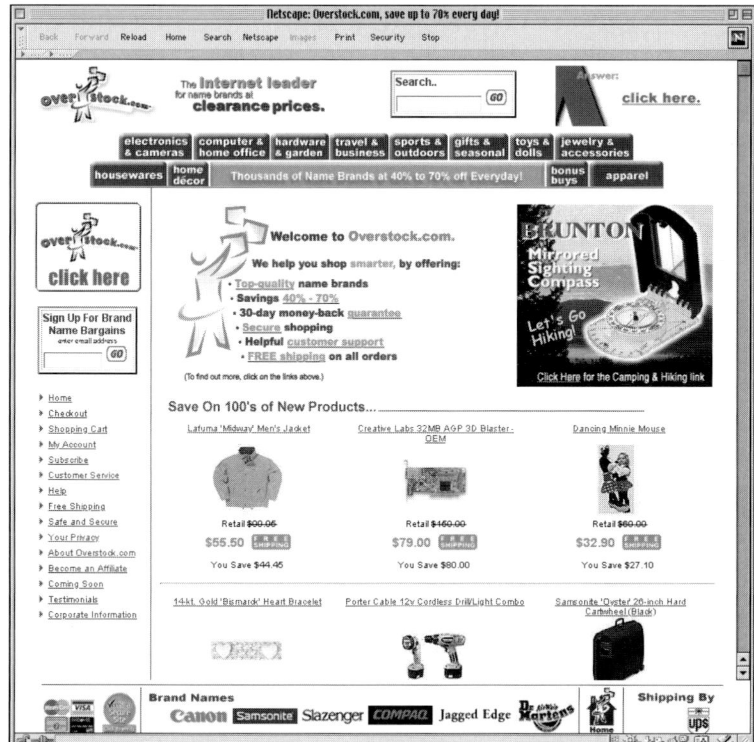

Figure 3.5

Where do I go from here? Most likely, my browser's Back button. Busy interfaces bore or confuse all but the most die-hard bargain seeker (www.overstock.com).

We once inherited an entertainment site that worked only on one platform and one browser (no names, please). Our client pointed out that he was getting four million visits a month. We replied that he was cheating himself out of an additional million visitors. Similarly, the owners of cluttered and confusing sites frequently mistake a profit margin for success. Better user experiences mean bigger profits, which is the best way to sell them to clients whose sole concern is money.

Clients are not alone in sometimes forgetting that sites are created to serve human needs. Web designers also can lose sight of their work's primary objective.

A Design Koan: Interfaces Are a Means too Often Mistaken for an End

As web designers become expert at crafting more and more sophisticated navigational structures, we sometimes forget that our interfaces do not come into being for their own sake. Interfaces are built to serve the user, not to demonstrate our cleverness and technical mastery (unless cleverness and technical mastery are an essential part of the brand). The best design may go unnoticed by users, but Heaven is watching and you will get your reward.

Universal Body Copy and Other Fictions

Good copy comes from the product; good interfaces come from considering the particular audience, content, and brand attributes of each site. When navigation anticipates the visitor's needs and guides her through the site, it succeeds at the baseline level. When it does this in a fresh and brand-appropriate manner, it succeeds as effective web design.

In this sense, web design is no different from advertising, print, or product design. At the lowest level, an advertisement's text must be grammatical, and its presentation must be legible. At the highest levels, design and concept are indistinguishable from the product experience. (Many would say they *are* the product experience.)

Impeccable graphic design does not necessarily equate to good interface design. As suggested by the design koan above, a site that looks drop-dead gorgeous but confuses visitors is a site that fails.

At the turn of the Millennium, several high-stakes web businesses went under because they forgot that their interfaces were supposed to be used by human beings. Looking at comps and demos, the board members said, "Oooo-Ahhh!" But when attempting to navigate the completed sites, the public went, "Huh?" The public is the final court of appeals.

There were other reasons a number of web businesses failed in late 1999 and early 2000. Some businesses that served no earthly purpose and appealed to no imaginable audience managed to suck up venture capital anyway—until the investors woke up. But many sites with legitimate business models bit the dust when it was discovered that nobody could navigate them except, perhaps, the designers.

Each site speaks to a particular demographic. A site that is "everybody's friend" is nobody's *best* friend. Focused, usable, brand-supportive interfaces are as particular as the taste of a fresh-picked plum on a summer's day.

While great web design, like all great design, is specific in nature, web design (like all design) has developed a series of guidelines and best practices that can aid you as you begin to shape your own sites. Some of these practices are rooted in common sense, others in human interface guidelines developed during the personal computer revolution of the 1980s. We will examine these guidelines in the following sections, bearing in mind that they are suggestions, not rules.

Interface as Architecture

Navigation is the experiential architecture of a site. Web designers use consistent visual cues to guide visitors through the site, as an architect guides a building's visitors from the lobby to the elevator bank. Subtle visual hints cue a building's visitors as to which areas of an office are open to the public, and which are private. Folks can find their way to a bathroom or a public telephone without asking for help. The goal of a navigational interface, like the goal of real-world architecture, is to enable people to do what they need to do.

As you develop web interfaces, ask yourself if you're helping people find the site's offices, elevators, and bathrooms or leaving them to fend for themselves. Poorly structured buildings win few tenants; poorly structured sites win few repeat visitors.

Ten (Okay, Three) Points of Light

In her book, *Web Navigation: Designing the User Experience* (available at www.oreilly.com/catalog/navigation/), Jennifer Fleming describes ten qualities shared by successful navigational interfaces. Fleming's ten points defy quick summarization, so we'll settle for three of them. In Fleming's view, good interfaces should:

1. Be easily learned
2. Remain consistent
3. Continually provide feedback

Be Easily Learned

A designer who buys Adobe Illustrator will accept the product's learning curve; an online shopper will not invest the same kind of energy into figuring out how www.halfpricefurniture.com works. Overly complex interfaces may please the designer who came up with them, but they rarely win favor with those trying to find their way through the site.

Why do most of us hate the remotes that come with our TVs and VCRs? Because there are too many buttons to push, and there is rarely an intuitive logic to the placement and size relationships of these buttons. We are always hunting for the button that resets the clock or programs the channels (and discovering that this function actually lies buried deep in a series of onscreen menus). We approach even the most basic tasks with the sense that we are somehow being forced to prove our mastery over a troublesome object.

Unless we wish to watch one TV channel for the rest of our lives, we have no choice but to click our way through the madness. But web users always have a choice—they can visit a website that is easier to use.

Remain Consistent

Each site presents the visitor with a unique interface. Compelling content or useful services are the only reason users bother learning how your site works. After they've gone to that trouble, they will not appreciate your changing the interface, misguidedly groping after "freshness."

Web users are not mind readers. After they've learned that flowers serve as visual links (as in Figure 3.1), you'd be foolish to switch to a folder tab metaphor. If there are five main menu items per page, suddenly adding a sixth and seventh at the same hierarchical level could make naïve web users think they've somehow linked to an unrelated site. Sophisticated users will think the site is being redesigned, and they've somehow caught you in mid-process.

Many times beginning web designers feel that each section of a site requires its own distinctive signature. It usually makes more sense to provide a consistent interface, acknowledging the new section (if at all) with a subtle color change or a simple section title.

Figure 3.6

Digital Web Magazine, a popular online resource for web designers, offers a consistent interface between sections...

Figure 3.7

...but differentiates each section with a subtle color change. Because you can't tell that the color is changing with the color scheme of this book, you'll have to visit the site and see for yourself (www.digital-web.com).

Continually Provide Feedback

In Chapter 2, "Designing for the Medium," we remarked on the "look and feel" issue and discussed a major difference between print and the Web. On the computer screen, there are no matte or glossy papers, no subtly textured finishes, no chance for the designer to emboss or overprint to achieve a richer look.

But what we lack in ink and paper choices, we make up for with an almost limitless variety of interactive options. On the Web, the images we create can respond to the visitor's virtual touch. This not only adds richness to our design; it helps the visitor comprehend the interface.

In the real world, buzzers buzz and doorknobs turn. Good web design mimics this kind of feedback, using techniques such as the JavaScript rollover (*image swap*) to create a sense that the site is responding to the visitor's actions.

Such digital responsiveness is nothing new. It began with the desktop computer revolution and specifically with the Apple Macintosh Graphical User Interface (GUI).

GUI, GUI, Chewy, Chewy

A website's GUI includes all its non-text visual elements. The GUI allows users to perform actions by interacting visually with the various graphical elements. Familiar GUI elements from the Macintosh Operating System include file and folder icons, scroll bars, and the Apple Menu. Windows has its own unique GUI with elements such as the Task Bar and Start Menu.

If you were still awake a few paragraphs above when we made the big stink about consistency, hold your nose 'cause here we go again. Logic and consistency are two reasons that Windows, Mac OS, and other UI-based computing systems are more popular than command-line interfaces. GUIs succeed by being clear (users don't wonder what a certain button does) and remaining consistent (if the File menu is on the left, it stays on the left). Because your visitors are using a computer to view your site, they expect such consistency.

It is worth studying existing GUIs (such as Mac OS and Windows) to figure out what their conventions are and why they work. If your GUI works in similar ways, you are that much less likely to baffle your audience.

Figure 3.8

The interface at panic.com not only suggests the Macintosh GUI, it actually emulates it. Because the site hawks Macintosh software, the emulation reinforces the site's themes and purposes. Mac users will think it's fun; Windows users will go somewhere else—appropriately, since there is nothing for them here (www.panic.com).

It's the Browser, Stupid

On the Web, the browser predetermines many elements of the GUI. For instance, in nearly all browsers, dragging a mouse cursor over a live link causes the cursor to change from an arrow to an upraised hand. These browser-based conventions help web users make sense of sites. Folks rely on these elements to understand what is happening without having to learn an entirely new set of conventions each time they load a new URL.

Web designers can change or override these conventions—for instance, by using Cascading Style Sheets (CSS) to place a hand cursor over plain text rather than live links—but it is rarely desirable to do so unless your goal is to confuse your visitors. There are sites, such as www.jodi.org and www.superbad.com, whose purpose is just that. These fall under the heading of fine art, and many web designers adore them. Even if they're not to your taste, you can learn a great deal about web users' expectations by studying the way these sites subvert them. On most sites, though, confusing visitors is usually not among the client's objectives.

Though the browser creates many GUI elements (underlined links, changes to the cursor state), the rest is up to the designer. Indeed, in a graphical browser, one could consider commercial sites custom GUIs whose purpose is to enable visitors to perform tasks while subliminally absorbing the client's brand.

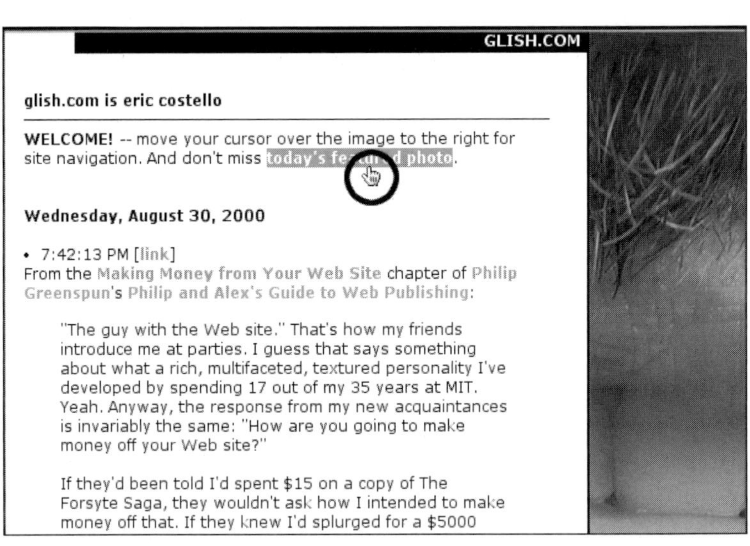

Figure 3.9

Visitors know what this cursor change means (www.glish.com).

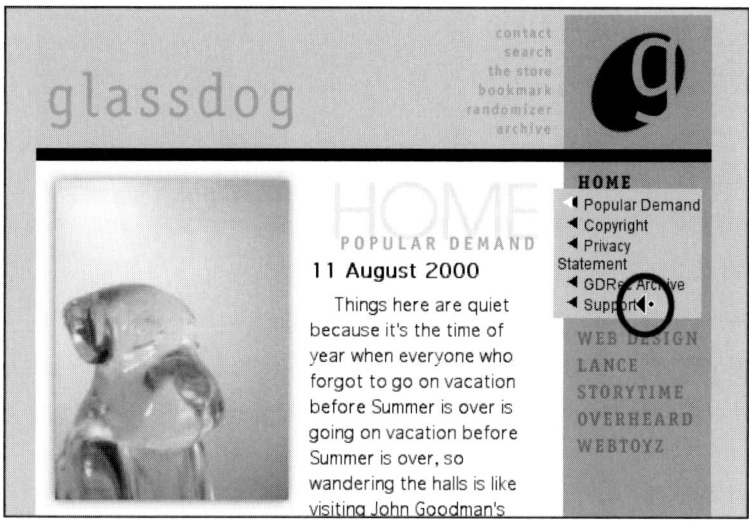

Figure 3.10

So why confuse them with *this* one? Changing familiar GUI elements "because you can" is a dog's rationale for licking himself. In this case, it's a Glassdog's rationale (www.glassdog.com).

Clarity Begins at Home (Page)

In developing GUI elements, web designers will frequently begin with the brand: funky elements for an entertainment site pitched at 20-somethings; somber, restrained elements for a news or medical site; and so on (more about branding in a moment). As each site presents a visitor with new GUI elements, those elements have the potential to brand the site while offering visitors a sense of identity and place. These elements also have the potential to confuse the heck out of people. As with the operating systems they mimic, GUI elements should be as clear and easy to use as possible. Clarity and ease of use are especially crucial factors in the development of iconic interface elements and site structure labels.

I Think Icon, I Think Icon

Graphical devices (icons) guide viewers through the site experience. Forward and reverse arrows are common ways of navigating from page to page. Graphical buttons are often used to trigger certain actions. For instance, a Play button may be used to trigger a recorded sound or an embedded, streaming QuickTime movie. A pen or pencil icon may link to a message board, or a book or newspaper icon can guide the visitor to a downloadable, printer-friendly version of the page's content.

Printing in the Browser Wars

Why aren't web pages themselves printer-friendly? It is because too often browsers are rushed into production as the latest assault in the "Browser Wars," instead of offering carefully considered and usable features. By the time this book is released, the worst of the Browser Wars will be behind us.

Icons, with or without text labels, frequently serve as quick, visual cues to the site's offerings. They also support international visitors for whom English is not a first language. Sites with massive amounts of content on their home pages, such as portals and magazine sites, can use icons to better organize and clarify sections (see Figures 3.11 and 3.12).

Figure 3.11

The icons seen here help draw the eye to the secondary menu, and some of them even communicate in ways a non-English speaking visitor might understand. Designing icons that communicate is difficult. Competing elements must fit within the narrow width of a lowest-common-denominator monitor, leaving little room in which to develop legible imagery (www.eloquent.com).

Figure 3.12

We are clearly in the land of the recreational website, as denoted by the tagline "professional martini consumer." Few sites would devote all that screen space to a menu structure. Indeed, this site recently went offline for a redesign (www.drymartini.com).

On the Web, as in talking to a policeman, clarity is a virtue. While it is tempting to get really creative with such elements, the most creative solutions are often the clearest.

Say you are designing a site for a chain of Wild West theme hotels. In visiting the hotels and studying the chain's promotional brochures and advertising, you can't miss the fact that Western paraphernalia is used to brand the franchise—from the bronze horse-head coat hooks in guest closets to the cowhide couches in the lobby. Thinking like a brand steward, you decide it might be fun to use lassos rather than arrows to indicate "previous page" and "next page" on the site. To you, as a visual person, it is readily apparent that the rope at the edge of the lasso "points" forward or backward.

Well, cowboy, test that design on some users before you fight for it. If users are confused by your branded iconic elements—if the lassos strike users as meaningless ornamentation rather than functional GUI elements—be prepared to rustle up some traditional left and right arrows, even if it chaps your spurs.

Adding "invisible" text labels to an icon via the <ALT> attribute of the HTML image tag or the <TITLE> attribute of a linked image can help explain the icon's purpose to inexperienced users. In modern graphical browsers, these <ALT> and <TITLE> attributes generate popup "tool tips" or help-balloon-style blurbs, enhancing the page's interactivity in a meaningful and user-friendly way.

Such tags also make the content more accessible to the visually disabled, to those using non-graphical browsers or Personal Digital Assistants (PDAs) such as the Palm Pilot, and to folks using conventional browsers who surf with images turned off. (As mentioned in Chapter 2, accessibility makes good business and moral sense. Besides, it's U.S. law.)

When invisible text labels are not enough, consider adding visible text.

Structural Labels: Folding the Director's Chair

In the early days of the Web, designers and copywriters frequently had fun coming up with creative labels for menu bar sections and other navigational items. For instance, the home page of a video editing company's site might be labeled "The Director's Chair," while downloadable video clips would be found in "The Screening Room."

Today, most web agencies find it better to err on the side of clear copy than cute copy. After all, if the visitor does not immediately grasp what "The Screening Room" means, she could leave the site without having discovered one of its most important content areas. While alternatives to traditional labeling may be appropriate for some types of sites (gaming sites, fun sites for kids), many corporate sites depend on such traditional labels as Home, About, and Clients to facilitate easy user navigation. Dull as dishwater, we know. *Be creative clearly,* and it need not be dull at all.

The Soul of Brevity

Back in Chapter 2 we recalled David Siegel's three hallmarks of good website design:

- Clarity
- Brevity
- Bandwidth

Because most web users have little time and less bandwidth to waste, good interfaces are rarely overwrought. Given the choice between a simple, functional design and one that is ornate, most folks prefer the simple web layout that loads quickly and is easy to understand. Web users don't tell you this by peering over your shoulder; they tell you this by visiting the site or neglecting it.

Even when bandwidth is not an issue, quick, clear communication always will be. Users lucky enough to have T3, cable modem, or DSL access may not be slowed down by a cluttered interface, but they will be just as baffled by it as dialup modem users are. Regardless of the user's access speed, your communication must be fast and clear, or users will retreat faster than you can say "failed dot com." It's a peanut butter and jelly scenario: By focusing on functionality, you will develop low bandwidth interfaces; by focusing on bandwidth, you will develop interfaces that speak quickly and clearly.

Many web designers initially feel constrained by this. Some feel they cannot truly express their vision unless every page sports a 128K background JPEG, an animated menu bar, and a series of spinning logos and pulsing photographs. We've all had that feeling. It passes as you discover the joy of communicating richly while using a few elements well, or it never passes, and you locate clients with tastes as baroque as yours. When citizens avoid visiting the resulting sites, your client and you can toast your superiority to the rest of humanity and then hurry on to the next failure.

When bad web designers die and go to Hell, they will spend eternity searching for the Heaven option on an endless menu bar of purgatories. (That is, if they're not simply stuck waiting for an infernal intro to finish downloading.)

Hypertext or Hapless Text

Brevity is just as important when putting text content on the Web. A book is easy to read. Hundreds of years of book design make it so. But on a glaring computer screen, at 72ppi (pixels per inch) or 96ppi, reading long passages is a chore. A reader will simply skip lengthy texts, whether they're providing valuable product information or explaining how to use some advanced feature of the site.

By breaking text down into usable sub-units of information, a web designer can help readers find critical information and more easily absorb content. White space, while useful in print, becomes even more crucial on a web page. The logical separation of chunks of information helps engage readers and maintain their interest. Designers can use paragraphs, section breaks, and links to new pages to chunk information.

The more white space, the greater the chance that readers will remain engaged. Use CSS by itself or in combination with table-based layouts to create pages that demand to be read.

Figure 3.13

Readable typography, an elegantly spare layout, and plenty of white space add up to a site that welcomes readers—a quality that is depressingly rare on the Web (www.harrumph.com). Contrast this with Figure 3.15.

In print, a designer might include ten sentences in a paragraph. On the Web, with its scrolling interface, ten sentences can feel like a life sentence. To enhance readability, web designers (or web designers in combination with web-savvy copywriters and editors) will separate one long paragraph into several shorter ones.

Learn when to stop one page and start another. Despite what some pundits tell you, readers *will* scroll to read an engaging story, but they will not scroll forever. After two or three screens, it may be time to present the reader with an arrow (or other page indicator) allowing them to move on to the next page of text. Doing so can relieve eye fatigue, enhance the drama of the presentation (www.fray.com), or simply give your client another page on which to sell ad banners.

Remember in Chapter 2 when we talked about the tradeoff between one large image that takes a long time to download and many small images that take a long time to display? (If this were a web page, we'd provide a link here.) Well, the same kind of tradeoff goes on with text. Jam too much of it on a single web page, and readers may be frightened away. Provide too little, forcing the reader to click to a new screen after every paragraph or two, and you practically guarantee that no one will read to the end of the article or story.

Working with client-supplied text is particularly tricky. If average citizens are bad writers, clients are bad writers with egos. Upper Middle Managers would rather *add value to cross-brand synergies while enhancing the functionality of strategically targeted product from the dairy side* than put milk in their coffee. Rare is the client who writes the way people talk; rarer still is the client who uses few words when many will suffice.

In brochures and catalogs, such copy is ineffective. On a web page, it's destructive on a nuclear scale. Consumers may ignore bad catalog copy if the layout and photography are compelling enough. But a site laden with vast blocks of ham-handed text is doomed. No visitor will stay long enough or scroll far enough to discover the million dollar photographs or compelling brand proposition buried on page three.

Laid out well (via text chunking and CSS), bad text can squeak by. Laid out badly, it kills websites dead. We cannot overemphasize the impact (and tragic rarity) of good writing on the Web nor the harm done by verbose and inexpressive texts, drizzled into layouts like so much phlegm. Learn web typography, practice text chunking, and work with good writers and editors. Do not let your clients or your project managers skimp on the writing budget unless you find failure exciting.

Figure 3.14

The front page of Sapient.com (www.sapient.com), a leading web agency, shows mastery and promise. Clean typography and high-quality photography, balanced as skillfully as in a classic Ogilvie print ad, direct the visitor's attention to the most important content. The carefully balanced page also makes use of Liquid Design (see Chapter 2) to accommodate variously sized monitors. So far, so good....

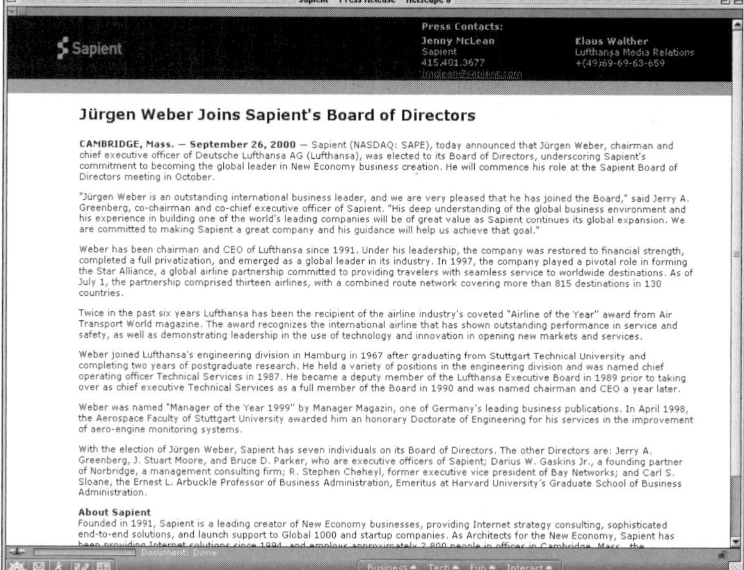

Sapient – Press Release – Netscape 6

Sapient

Press Contacts:

Jenny McLean
Sapient
415.401.3677

Klaus Walther
Lufthansa Media Relations
+(49)69-69-63-659

Jürgen Weber Joins Sapient's Board of Directors

CAMBRIDGE, Mass. — September 26, 2000 — Sapient (NASDAQ: SAPE), today announced that Jürgen Weber, chairman and chief executive officer of Deutsche Lufthansa AG (Lufthansa), was elected to its Board of Directors, underscoring Sapient's commitment to becoming the global leader in New Economy business creation. He will commence his role at the Sapient Board of Directors meeting in October.

"Jürgen Weber is an outstanding international business leader, and we are very pleased that he has joined the Board," said Jerry A. Greenberg, co-chairman and co-chief executive officer of Sapient. "His deep understanding of the global business environment and his experience in building one of the world's leading companies will be of great value as Sapient continues its global expansion. We are committed to making Sapient a great company and his guidance will help us achieve that goal."

Weber has been chairman and CEO of Lufthansa since 1991. Under his leadership, the company was restored to financial strength, completed a full privatization, and emerged as a global leader in its industry. In 1997, the company played a pivotal role in forming the Star Alliance, a global airline partnership committed to providing travelers with seamless service to worldwide destinations. As of July 1, the partnership comprised thirteen airlines, with a combined route network covering more than 815 destinations in 130 countries.

Twice in the past six years Lufthansa has been the recipient of the airline industry's coveted "Airline of the Year" award from Air Transport World magazine. The award recognizes the international airline that has shown outstanding performance in service and safety, as well as demonstrating leadership in the use of technology and innovation in opening new markets and services.

Weber joined Lufthansa's engineering division in Hamburg in 1967 after graduating from Stuttgart Technical University and completing two years of postgraduate research. He held a variety of positions in the engineering division and was named chief operating officer Technical Services in 1987. He became a deputy member of the Lufthansa Executive Board in 1989 prior to taking over as chief executive Technical Services as a full member of the Board in 1990 and was named chairman and CEO a year later.

Weber was named "Manager of the Year 1999" by Manager Magazin, one of Germany's leading business publications. In April 1998, the Aerospace Faculty of Stuttgart University awarded him an honorary Doctorate of Engineering for his services in the improvement of aero-engine monitoring systems.

With the election of Jürgen Weber, Sapient has seven individuals on its Board of Directors. The other Directors are: Jerry A. Greenberg, J. Stuart Moore, and Bruce D. Parker, who are executive officers of Sapient; Darius W. Gaskins Jr., a founding partner of Norbridge, a management consulting firm; R. Stephen Cheheyl, former executive vice president of Bay Networks; and Carl S. Sloane, the Ernest L. Arbuckle Professor of Business Administration, Emeritus at Harvard University's Graduate School of Business Administration.

About Sapient
Founded in 1991, Sapient is a leading creator of New Economy businesses, providing Internet strategy consulting, sophisticated end-to-end solutions, and launch support to Global 1000 and startup companies. As Architects for the New Economy, Sapient has

Document: Done

Business Tech Fun Interact

Figure 3.15

...Alas, once past the front page, visitors encounter too many pages like this one, where blocks of undifferentiated text, laid out with little care and no love, beg to be ignored rather than read. Since 99% of the Web consists of text that is intended to be read, the lack of attention to good textual presentation is tragic—hurting not only the site owner, but the would-be reader. Contrast this with Figure 3.13. (www.sapient.com).

Scrolling and Clicking Along

Some "experts" will inform you that users don't click. They also will inform you that users don't scroll. If users never clicked or scrolled, nobody would actually be using the Web. Of course users click. (How else would they link from page to page?) Of course users scroll. (How else would they, uh, scroll?)

Nobody clicks more than they *have to*—hence the so-called "Three-Click Rule," described later. And nobody scrolls for fun and profit. Visit an amateur home page and see how excessive scrolling drags its nails across the blackboard of the user's experience.

The previous section, "Hypertext or Hapless Text," discussed text chunking and offered methods to keep scrolling to a minimum, but this does not mean that every web page should be limited to one or two paragraphs of text. Particularly when presenting in-depth articles online, text chunking has its limits. Users would probably rather scroll through five longish pages of text than click through 25 short screens that present the same information. Develop a case-by-case, site-by-site sense for these nuances, and you will find your skills in demand.

Every newspaper is designed so that the most important headlines, photographs, and stories appear "above the fold" (where the paper naturally folds in half). As shown in Chapter 2, vital information is best served in this small space above the fold. When links to the site's most important content appear within the first 380 pixels of vertical space, even visitors saddled with small monitors can find what they seek without scrolling. Once enmeshed in a story that engages their interest, visitors *will* scroll down a few screens to continue reading.

How many screens of text will readers scroll before wearying of scrolling and seeking the blessed release of clicking to the next page? Three. Just kidding. Only a pseudo-scientist would pretend to know. As web designers, we use our best judgment on each site. That, after all, is what we're getting paid for.

One reason frames are popular is that they allow web designers to keep the interface onscreen in a consistent location, even when the user is scrolling up or down like a madman. For instance, a horizontal menu bar at the top (www.microsoft.com) or bottom (www.the-adstore.com) of the screen will stay in place no matter how long the page may run and no matter how much scrolling the user performs. Frames are on their way out (in W3C parlance, they have been "deprecated"), but you can achieve the same effects with CSS, a web standard.

Inexperienced designers sometimes create pages that require the user to scroll horizontally. This is almost always unwise. Except at certain "art gallery" sites, users will almost never scroll horizontally. Such interfaces are inconvenient and often appear to be mistakes rather than deliberate design decisions.

To understand why horizontal scrolling is an evil spawned from the festering loins of the incubus, imagine that you have to ... turn the page to finish reading this ... sentence and then fold the page back ... to read the next line of ... text, which bleeds ... backwards across the gatefold again, forcing you to ... turn the page, and then turn ... it back again in order to begin reading the next line.

No print designer would lay out book pages that way, but inexperienced web designers do so frequently, whether from misguided creative impulses or because they've made assumptions about their visitors' monitor sizes. This is another reason that Liquid Design (detailed in Chapter 2) comes highly recommended; it always fits neatly into any user's monitor.

It's also the reason that clients, designers, and IT departments that set "monitor baselines" of 800 x 600 are blockheads. If even 5% of the audience is expected to scroll horizontally simply to read marketing copy, the client or web agency is effectively sending millions of potential customers to a competitor's site.

Stock Options (Providing Alternatives)

Users employ a variety of means to access the Web, including modern browsers, older browsers, non-graphical browsers, audio browsers, and non-traditional devices such as cell phones and PDAs. If the goal of a site is to accommodate as many visitors as possible, then it is critical to provide alternative forms of navigation.

Imagine that you have designed a lovely, frames-based site and that your navigational menu exists in its own frame. A visitor using a text browser enters the site. He cannot see frames because his browser does not support them. You, however, have thoughtfully included a <NOFRAMES> tag in your HTML frameset. Inside the <NOFRAMES> tag you cut and paste the main content from the home page, along with an HTML-based text menu. The visitor can now use your content, even though he cannot see your frames-based layout. (Again, we remind you that frames are on their way out anyway.)

Options and alternatives increase the odds that someone will actually use what you've designed. Larger web agencies employ quality assurance (QA) staffs who spend all day hunting for online porn. Better QA staffers search for flaws in your design by testing it in a wide variety of old and new browsers on various platforms. Do not hate these site testers—they are your friends. Build alternatives into your navigational scheme, and you will win their admiration and more, importantly, that of your site's audience.

The mechanics of including alternate forms of navigation will be covered in Chapter 9, "Visual Tools."

Hierarchy and the So-Called Three Click Rule

To accommodate the need for rapid access to information, a web designer creates layouts that immediately reassure the visitor that she has "come to the right place." Brand-appropriate design accomplishes some of this purpose. A clear hierarchical structure does the rest.

It's widely agreed, even by people who are not idiots, that web users are driven by a desire for fast gratification. If they can't find what they're looking for within three clicks, they might move on to somebody else's site. Hence the so-called "Three-Click Rule," which, as you might expect, states that users should ideally be able to reach their intended destination within three mouse clicks.

With the average site offering hundreds if not thousands of items and options, the Three-Click Rule sounds preposterous. But it is actually fairly easy to achieve if you start by constructing user scenarios before you begin to design the site.

What will people who use this site want to do? Where will they want to go? Based on those scenarios, the site is structured into main areas of content. These are then organized into no more than five main areas. (See the next section, "The So-Called Rule of Five.") Submenus in each of the five main areas get the user close enough that he or she is *at least reassured* by the third click, even if it takes a fourth click to get to the final, desired page.

Let's play it out. You are designing a site for people who live with housecats. In the scenario portion of development, the team agrees that cat owners might want to read about Mister Tibbles' genetic heritage. In the top-level hierarchy, you create an item called Breeds. When Aunt Martha clicks Breeds, the site offers Long-Hair, Short-Hair, Tabby, and Exotic options. A second click takes her to Short-Hair, a third to Mister Tibbles' particular breed.

Like all so-called "laws" of web design, the Three-Click Rule is a suggestion, not an ironclad rule. It is, though, a suggestion based on the way people use the Web, and, particularly for informational and product sites, you will find that it works more often than not. If nothing else, the rule can help you create sites with intuitive, logical hierarchical structures—and that ain't bad.

The So-Called Rule of Five

The so-called "Rule of Five" sounds like a period out of Chinese history, but it's actually just another guideline most working web designers keep in mind—especially if they want to keep working.

The Rule of Five postulates that complex, multi-layered menus offering more than five main choices tend to confuse web users. A glance back at Figure 3.5 should confirm the common sense behind this "rule." The main menu at Overstock.com offers not five, not six, not seven, but a whopping twelve main categories to choose from. (And that's not even counting the strange tagline area that is inexplicably designed to resemble a clickable menu button.) Overstock.com is so busy offering *everything* that many users will be hard pressed to find *anything*.

By contrast, Sapient's main menu (back in Figure 3.14) offers four choices: Clients, Expertise, Company Info, and Careers. Giving users three, four, or five main choices makes it easier for them to decide where they want to go. Hitting them with ten or more choices makes their next move harder to predict—for them and for you. Confuse them enough, and it becomes easier to predict where they will go, namely: anywhere else.

As with the Three-Click Rule, evolving a site whose architecture can be navigated in five main areas or less is easier if you engage in scenario playing before you begin to design. Chapter 7, "Riding the Project Life Cycle," provides a detailed analysis of how you, your team, and your client can collaborate to develop logical site structures that facilitate the Three-Click Rule and the Rule of Five.

On multi-purpose sites (and there are many of those), several layers of navigation may peacefully coexist. Looking yet again at Sapient (Figure 3.14), four choices are enough to guide visitors to main areas of the site but not enough to help those seeking one-click access to various client/vendor success stories. The icon-driven menu on the right ignores the Rule of Five without incident.

On a shopping site, the main menu may offer three choices: Women's, Men's, and Kids'. But submenus can be far more extensive: the Women's section might offer Outerwear, Sportswear, Business Attire, Casual Wear, Accessories, Cosmetics, Health Aids, and sundry other stuff without confusing any shopper. As the shopper burrows deeper into the hierarchy, these submenus can sprout submenus of their own, for example Cosmetics could include Hair Products, Makeup, Toners, Cleansers, and beyond. Such submenus may run deep, as long as they appear when users expect them to appear and behave consistently from section to section.

Some site designers and architects distinguish between goal- and task-oriented navigation. With goal-oriented navigation, the user wants to go somewhere (Clients, Expertise, or Company Info, for example). With task-oriented navigation, the user wants to do something (apply for a job, log in, or read case studies). Combining the two types of user needs in the same navigational context can be more confusing than helpful. In such cases, task and goal-oriented navigation coexist separately (see Figure 3.16), and the Rule of Five pertains to each navigational stream rather than to the page as a whole.

Figure 3.16

Goal-oriented navigation (Expertise, Process, Proof) and task-oriented navigation (Hire Us, Work Here, Login) carefully separated and balanced. The user can quickly follow a desired activity path without becoming confused or overwhelmed. Such complex structures are hard to pull off (www.hesketh.com).

Highlights and Breadcrumbs

Drivers use road signs to track their location in space. Web users rely on navigation. Well-designed sites cue the visitor to her location within the site's hierarchy. For instance, if the visitor is within the Breeds section of the cat site, the Breeds item in the menu bar may be highlighted by a subtle change of color. This "you are here" indicator helps keep the visitor grounded, thus promoting lengthier visits (see Figure 3.17).

Figure 3.17

Subtle highlighting on the menu bar reminds you that you're on the Home Store page. Click to a different page, and a different menu item will be highlighted. Note, too, how much air the design team has managed to work into the page, in spite of the vast number of links and menu items the page must carry (www.bloomingdales.com). Compare with Figure 3.16 and contrast with Figure 3.5.

It's all about comfort. Better hotels offer fluffier pillows; better sites provide constant spatial and hierarchical reassurance. Breadcrumbs, called this because they resemble the trails left by Hansel and Gretel, not only serve as hierarchical location finders, but they also allow visitors to jump to any section further up in the hierarchy (see Figure 3.18).

Figure 3.18

Breadcrumbs remind you that you're on the Miles Davis page of the Artists section. Essential to complex directories, breadcrumbs can enhance branding, entertainment, and content sites by providing alternative navigation for those using less-capable browsers. They reassure beginners while enabling sophisticated users to skip tedious hierarchical layers and move quickly to the exact content they seek (www.jazzradio.net).

Consistent Placement

The location of the navigation in the digital nation permits much permutation without causing perturbation. Navigation can exist in a horizontal strip at the top or bottom of the site. It can live in a navigation bar on the left or right side of the page. It also can float in a JavaScript remote popup window (as long as alternatives are provided).

What matters most, aside from technological and user appropriateness (remote popup window navigation is probably not the best choice for the Happy Valley Retirement Home), is that the navigation stay in one place so the user knows where to find it when he or she is ready to move on. A handrail guides someone down a flight of stairs, and the guidance works because the handrail remains in the location where the user expects to find it. Good site navigation works the same way. With few exceptions, it doesn't really matter where you stick your navigation as long as you keep sticking it there throughout the site.

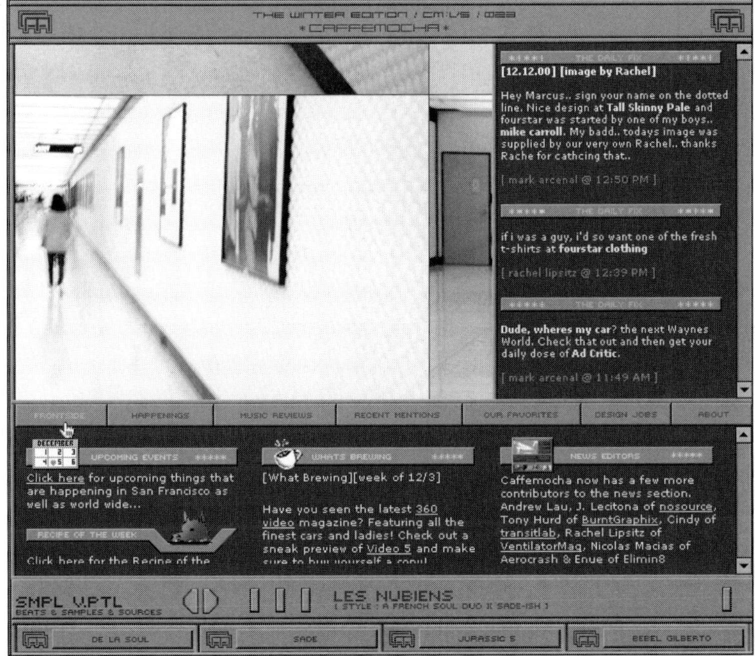

Figure 3.19

What's the "best" place for navigational menus? That's up to the web designer. Caffe Mocha runs its menu bar horizontally across the middle of the page (www.caffemocha.com).

Brand That Sucker!

We've discussed navigation and interface in terms of the user's needs, and they of course come first. But what of the client's needs? Meeting them is the role of branding.

A corporate website is the online expression of that company's brand identity. Making sure that the navigation fully supports the company's brand identity is crucial to the success of the site (and sometimes to the success of that company). Build the most navigable, information-filled site in the world, and if it lacks a coherent brand identity, nobody will remember it, nobody will tell their friends about it, and nobody will bother to bookmark it and return.

For over 100 years, advertisers have been working to build our joyful world of branding. When your stomach hurts, you reach for Alka-Seltzer (not an antacid). Sneeze, and you reach for Kleenex (not a disposable paper tissue).

Like millions, we may express our individuality through Levi's. You may choose Gap to show the world how different you are. Neither of us, as we don our separate uniforms, is likely thinking about the folks who picked the cotton, or groomed the silkworms, or trimmed the fleece from the sheep. Consciously or unconsciously, we're identifying ourselves with images created in small offices, thousands of miles from where the cotton grows and the silkworm arches toward the sun—images created by brand advertising.

Branding, branding, branding. McDonald's does not sell cereal mixed with the flesh of cows; it sells food, folks, and fun. Marlboro sells the myth of the freedom of the Wild West. Camels are not for everybody, but then, they don't try to be.

Branding is not limited to products. Although his verbal gymnastics, half-spoken vocal delivery, and angry social consciousness predate Rap, Bob Dylan can't perform Hip Hop; it would conflict with his brand image as the spokesman of the 1960s generation. But David Bowie can do hip-hop or drums-and-bass because his brand identity is that of an ever-changing, ever-current chameleon.

And how come Seinfeld can quip wisecracks about supermarket checkout lines but will never mine his personal sexual experiences for comic material? Hey, it's not part of the brand.

How does this relate to the task of web design? As a designer, you know the answer to this one already. Whether you're building a corporate site or a multimedia online funhouse, your first task is to understand and translate the existing brand to the web medium or to create a new brand from scratch.

Good interfaces reflect the brand. Sleek, high-tech graphics complement a sleek, high-tech company—or one that wants to be perceived that way. A "friendly" GUI is necessary for a "friendly" company such as AOL. (You in the back, keep your sarcastic observations to yourself.) It goes without saying that the company's color scheme, logo, and typographic style must be reflected in your web graphics and that existing print and other materials are often a guideline to what is appropriate for the site.

Smart web designers go far beyond the obvious. In addition to graphic design elements, savvy web folk craft interfaces whose very *functioning* reflects and extends the brand. A "fun" brand needs more than cute graphics. Its sectional titles should be fun to read and its menu fun to interact with. This may mean taking a cue from the world of gaming. It may mean building the interface in Macromedia Flash.

A movie studio's interface should not resemble that of a bank. A company that sells active wear should encourage active participation, through games, message boards, or contests. A literary site's interface should quietly promote reading, instead of busily distracting from it with funky dancing icons. (A literary site that avoids long copy belies its own brand identity.) The interface of a religious organization's site dare not resemble that of an e-commerce site, lest visitors along with moneylenders be driven from the temple.

IBM's brand image is that of a big-time solutions provider (www.ibm.com). If you're asked to design their site, it had better be technologically solid, visually impeccable, and easy to use. Anything less will send the wrong brand message.

- **Technologically solid,** in this brand context, doesn't mean a deluge of plug-ins or a reliance on safe, old 1990s web technologies; it means online forms that work, search functions that deliver usable results, and enhancements that shine in new browsers while degrading well in old ones.
- **Visually impeccable** means that imagery and typographic choices must play in the key of the brand. Type should be clean and readable—not fussy, not grungy, not softly feminine or boyishly abrasive. Photographic images need not be disgustingly corporate (two suits at a monitor will take you only so far), but images of crime, drugs, or bongo jams will obviously be inappropriate.
- **Easy to use** means easy to use. Why even mention it? Because if visitors find their way to content they seek on the IBM site, it reinforces *the overriding brand idea that IBM provides solutions.* If users get lost or don't know which button to push, it will send the opposite message. Sending the wrong brand message could harm a brand identity the company has carefully built up over generations.

Branding the WaSP

The Web Standards Project (WaSP), mentioned in Chapter 2, evolved from conversations between a number of frustrated web designers and developers. While some members brought high-level technological knowledge to the project and others brought "marquee value" (their names alone adding instant credibility to anything the WaSP might say or do), your humble author focused on creating a brand identity that would be both memorable and consistent with the task at hand.

Many names were bandied about; we pushed "The Web Standards Project" for a variety of reasons, not least of which was its ability to be referred to in shorthand by the acronym WaSP. Call us shallow, but we believed that this aggressive little insect was the perfect metaphor for our group. We also knew that a memorable identity was needed to keep the effort from becoming so technologically-focused as to confuse potential members.

After all, by agitating for compliance with web standards, we were taking on giant companies such as Netscape and Microsoft in spite of being a small grassroots effort. Which tiny creature has the power to disturb a giant? The wasp. It's a purposeful, productive beast with a powerful stinger, and while you may be able to swat away one wasp, you don't want to mess with an angry nest. The site's verbal tone and visual approach came straight out of this simple little brand image—from the color palette (wasp-yellow, gold, and black) to the tone of voice (www.webstandards.org).

When Kioken Inc. (www.kioken.com), a leading New York web shop, was charged with designing a site for the high-end retailer, Barney's, they carefully considered the client's brand identity as a provider of well-made, tasteful, and luxurious clothing. To put it bluntly, Barney's goods are well above the means of most of us working stiffs, and Barney's customers like it that way.

Kioken crafted a sophisticated, Flash-based interface like nothing else on the Web (www.barneys.com). If you were a savvy web user, owned a fairly powerful PC, had a fast connection, and were equipped with the latest Flash plug-in, you were treated to a unique showcase of Barney's clothing. Just navigating it made you feel smarter than the average web user.

If you were not an experienced web user, owned an old PC, had not downloaded the latest Flash plug-in, and were stuck with a slow dialup modem connection, Kioken (and their client) figured that you were not really a Barney's customer anyway. A certain elitism was as much as part of the interface as it is of the store. The Barney's site may not exemplify democratic humanism, but it is a perfect web translation of the client's brand.

Some critics faulted Barneys.com for failing to provide an e-commerce solution. You could look at Barney's clothing, but you could not buy it online. The criticism betrays a misunderstanding of the client's brand identity. You expect to be able to buy jeans from Sears' website, but to buy Barney's clothing online would be wrong for such a highfalutin' brand.

Interfaces that deeply and meaningfully reflect the brand will encourage repeat user visits and repeat assignments from your clients. As a web designer grounded in traditional art direction and design, you are better equipped than many working professionals to create brand-appropriate web interfaces: interfaces that don't just look like the brand, they behave like it.

Interfaces that look and act like the brand and that guide the right audience to the most important content or transactions form the foundation for the best sites on the Web—the ones you are about to design.

Part II

WHO: People, Parts, and Processes

chapter 4

How This Web Thing Got Started

1452

GUTENBERG CONCEIVES OF MOVEABLE TYPE based on a punch-and-mould system. Working with paper (brought to Europe from China in the twelfth century), oil-based ink, block print (brought to Europe by Marco Polo in the thirteenth century) and a wine press, he sets the stage for the mass production of books and the wide dissemination of learning.

1836

Cooke and Wheatstone patent the telegraph, thus bringing telecommunications to the world. For the first time in history, two people can carry on an argument even when they are miles apart.

1858

The first Atlantic cable is laid across the ocean floor, facilitating telecommunications between Europe and the United States. Unfortunately, the cable goes on the fritz after just a few days. (And you thought your cable service was bad.) A second attempt in 1866 succeeds. That cable will remain in service for close to a century.

1876

Alexander Graham Bell demonstrates the telephone. The first busy signal follows soon after.

Why We Mentioned These Things

The events we just mentioned set the stage for the Internet and thus eventually for the Web. Gutenberg's invention sets in motion the concept that information belongs to the people (at least, to those people with a few coins in the pockets of their funny fifteenth-century pants). The subsequent technological breakthroughs make possible the eventual sharing of data via telephone lines.

1945

Vannevar Bush, Science Advisor to U.S. President Roosevelt, proposes a "conceptual machine" that can store vast amounts of information linked by user-created associations. He calls these user-generated connections "trails and associations." Eventually they'll be called "hyperlinks." (*As We May Think*, www.theatlantic.com/unbound/flashbks/computer/bushf.htm).

1962

The Advanced Research Projects Agency Network (ARPANET) is established, which will eventually be known as the Internet. Dr. J.C.R. Licklider is assigned to lead ARPA's research into the military application of computer technology.

1965

Scientist Ted Nelson coins the word *hypertext* to describe "nonsequential writing—text that branches and allows choice to the reader, best read at an interactive screen." (See http://www.acclarke.co.uk/1960-1969.html and http://ei.cs.vt.edu/~wwwbtb/book/chap1/htx_hist.html for more information.)

Nelson dreams of a worldwide library of all human knowledge that can be read on a screen and based on links. Sound familiar? Nelson also dreams of micropayment-based royalty schemes, two-way links, and other features not found in the Web as we know it.

1966

ARPA scientist Robert Taylor, no doubt depressed when women find out he is not the movie star Robert Taylor, figures out a way for researchers at various locations to collaborate by means of electronic computer networks. Inexpensive terminals are linked to a few pricey mainframe computers. Scientists begin exchanging documents and email messages. The first public demonstration of what is now being called ARPANET will take place in 1972. The Internet is born.

1978

On January 3, Steve Jobs and friend, Woz, take Apple Computer public, thus launching the personal computer "revolution." As Gutenberg's invention brought human knowledge out of the monastery and into the hands of ordinary citizens, Jobs and Woz's invention takes the arcane business of data crunching out of the realm of Big Science and makes it available to folks like us. The subsequent Macintosh computer (1984) offers a Graphical User Interface (GUI), making it easier still for ordinary people to use a computer. The Graphical User Interface, based on work done in Xerox Parc in the 1970s, enables people to perform tasks by clicking onscreen icons and buttons. Most civilians find this easier than memorizing and typing cryptic commands. A Windows GUI follows in the PC realm. The point-and-click interface will be key to the eventual acceptance of the Web.

1981

The domain name server (DNS) is developed, thus making the future safe for web addresses (www.ietf.org/rfc/rfc0799.txt). At first these will have cryptic numerical "names" such as 191.37.4211, but eventually consumer-friendly domain names such as brandname.com will take their place. This is key because advertisers would see little value in adding "Visit us at 191.37.4211" to the end of their radio commercials but are perfectly happy asking us to visit brandname.com. When advertisers are happy, they spend money. When money is available, professionals arise to claim it. The rise of web design and development is thus partially made possible by the invention of consumer-friendly domain names.

1984

The Apple Macintosh ushers in an era of "desktop publishing," empowering designers to set their own type and place and color-correct their own images, rather than relying on the skills of third-party service professionals. Desktop publishing also empowers ordinary citizens to express themselves creatively, sometimes (though not always) with wonderful results. This too will be mirrored a decade later, when the Web empowers anyone with a computer and the willingness to learn HTML to become a "web designer."

As if all that was not enough, Apple makes use of Ted Nelson's hypertex concept in its HyperCard product, which enables creative folks to create link-based presentations.

1986

There are now 5,000 Internet *hosts* (computers connected to the Internet "backbone") and 241 newsgroups.

On the campaign trail, Al Gore makes frequent reference to the developing "Information Superhighway." The phrase actually refers to high-speed coaxial networks, but it is popularly understood to mean ARPANET or the Internet. Press confusion on the subject will later haunt Gore's 2000 bid for the U.S. presidency.

1988

The NSFNET backbone is upgraded to T1 (1.544 Mbps). We're not sure what this means either, except that stuff gets a lot faster.

Internet Relay Chat (IRC) is developed in Israel, thus paving the way for a future where office workers can complain about their jobs to friends in foreign lands, instead of simply boring their spouses with these petty grievances.

1989

Tim Bray and others cofound Open Text, an Internet search engine. Search engines cut through the chaos of the burgeoning Internet by enabling citizens to actually find things. This ability to find things brings value to the Net and will be an invaluable aspect of the coming Web. Search engines will eventually enable citizens to find half-price airline tickets or seek out information to help their children write school reports. The human and commercial potential built into that premise will empower the coming "revolution" of faster and faster networks, and larger and larger web agencies such as Scient, iXL, and Razorfish.

CERN is the biggest *Internet site* (location) in Europe. Working there is a young scientist, Tim Berners-Lee.

1990

On the twelfth of November at CERN, Tim Berners-Lee (with R. Cailliau) invents the World Wide Web, rooting the idea in hypertext:

"HyperText is a way to link and access information of various kinds as a web of nodes in which the user can browse at will... A program which provides access to the hypertext world we call a browser... World Wide Web (or W3) intends to cater for these services across the HEP [High Energy Physics] community." (See http://www.w3.org/Proposal.)

Not content with the profundity of this invention, Berners-Lee also develops a "web browser" on his NeXT machine. With Berners-Lee's browser, not only can you view web pages, you can also edit and *design* them. Fortunately, the "designing" part of the browser does not make it far out of Berners-Lee's lab, and thus the way is paved for professional designers and art directors, rather than scientists, to create the visual language of the Web. (The original CERN W3 package included a server, a browser, and a true WYSIWYG editor.)

1991

America Online (AOL) begins offering Internet access in addition to its proprietary content and newsgroup features. Millions of people begin "going online" thanks to AOL's easy-to-use point-and-click functionality and consumer-friendly brand imagery. This is important because if the Internet had remained the province of geeks, the Web would not have gained such ready acceptance, let alone exploded into public consciousness. You would not be thinking about a career in web design, and this book would be all about delicious low-fat recipes rather than the Web.

1993

January: Marc Andreessen and Eric Bina, young programmers working for the National Center for Supercomputing Applications (NCSA) invent a point-and-click graphical browser for the Web, designed to run on UNIX machines. It is called Mosaic because the name Pantaloons didn't do as well in testing. (Just kidding. Not kidding about Mosaic, they did indeed call it that. Just kidding about why they called it that because we frankly don't know and this paragraph felt a little "short" to us.)

August: Andreessen and his co-workers release free versions of Mosaic for Macintosh and Windows PCs.

December: Andreessen quits his day job.

There are two million Internet hosts and 600 websites.

The NCSA "What's New" page (www.ncsa.uiuc.edu/SDG/Software/Mosaic/Docs/whats-new.html) is both an early non-commercial web directory and one of the first *weblogs*. A weblog is a frequently updated, annotated directory of stuff on the Web. In 1998, weblogs (always quietly present) would "catch on" again thanks to sites such as Scripting News (scripting.com), Robot Wisdom (www.robotwisdom.com), and Memepool (www.memepool.com). By 1999 they would become downright trendy, as hundreds of web designers create personal weblogs to keep their friends abreast of the sites they like, while thousands of first-time web publishers use tools such as Blogger, Manila, and Pitas to produce their own personal "Blogs."

1994

Marc Andreessen hooks up with Jim Clark, founder of Silicon Graphics Inc. The two form a company called Mosaic Communications Corporation to promote their Netscape web browser. NCSA, holders of the Mosaic trademark, balk at this use of their trademark, eventually prompting the young browser company to rename itself Netscape Communications.

Two graduate students, Jerry Yang and David Filo, form Yahoo! (Yet Another Hierarchical Officious Oracle), a directory whose purpose is to keep track of the websites springing up everywhere (www.yahoo.com). The site is organized somewhat like a library's card catalog system. Other directories of lesser quality quickly spring up in imitation.

Wired Magazine's Hotwired site evangelizes the new medium and pioneers techniques of web design and web architecture.

Tim Berners-Lee founds the World Wide Web Consortium (W3C), an international non-profit think tank dedicated to providing a rational roadmap for the technological advancement of the Web.

People begin designing and producing personal sites *because they can.* "Justin's Links from the Underground" (www.links.com) is one of the first and most famous personal sites. Glenn Davis launches *Cool Site of the Day* (www.coolsiteoftheday.com) to keep track of interesting or funky content on the rapidly growing Web.

1995

Pushed into public consciousness and acceptance by the coolness of Netscape's Navigator graphical browser and by sites such as Cool Site of the Day, the Web mushrooms. There are now 6.5 million hosts and 100,000 websites.

The Web functions well, but its design potential is sadly underdeveloped. David Siegel, a typographer and early web designer, publishes "Web Wonk" (www.dsiegel.com/tips/), an online tutorial offering techniques with which designers can create pleasing, magazine-like page layouts on the Web by working around (hacking) the limitations of HTML—the language with which web pages are created. These techniques seriously conflict with the purpose of HTML as a simple, structured language for sharing documents. But they are all designers have to work with at this time. The rift between the W3C and graphic designers has begun. (In 1996, Siegel publishes the book, *Creating Killer Websites.* Though far from the first how-to guide, it will be one of the first books to treat web design as a serious issue.)

Netscape introduces the tiled background image in Navigator 1.1. Warner Brothers' "Batman Forever" site is among the first to make intelligent use of the feature, hacking it to create the illusion of full-screen images.

Batmanforever.com helps prove that the Web has tremendous potential for anyone wishing to promote an idea, event, or product. There are three million web users, and half of them—1.5 million people—view this one site every week.

Jakob Nielsen, a Ph.D. from Sun Microsystems, begins publishing articles (www.useit.com) calling for a rational approach to the development of the Web. Nielsen calls his approach "usability" and claims that it is based on scientific studies. The rift between designers and usability experts has begun.

Personal home pages are proliferating.

Yahoo! and other large sites begin running ad banners.

Netscape goes public.

1996

David Siegel creates "High Five" to honor and showcase the best-designed sites on the Web. (High Five is no longer active, but archives are available at highfivearchive.com/core/index.html.) He bestows the first High Five award on his own site. Some consider the gesture arrogant, but Siegel doesn't care; his book is selling like crack. And, to some extent because of his evangelism, the Web begins attracting greater numbers of design professionals and becoming better and better designed as a result. But this aesthetic boon comes at a cost. Because most of us are using hacks and workarounds to make our sites more attractive and readable, few of us are demanding the creation of robust standards that would provide better presentational capabilities without breaking the Web's structural underpinnings. And since we're not hollering for better standards, the W3C isn't rushing them out the door, and browser makers aren't hastening to support them. We will all pay for this later.

"Suck" (suck.com), a brilliantly written daily site created by Joey Anuff and Carl Steadman, offers sardonic commentary along with a radically flattened hierarchy. Instead of offering a splash page, followed by a contents page, followed by sectional header pages, and so on (the tedious architecture found in most early sites), Suck slaps its content on the front page where you can't miss it. Minds reel. The rift between web architects and graphic designers begins. (Architects think about streamlining and controlling the flow of the user's experience. Graphic designers think about reinventing the interface and blowing the user away on every page. Good web designers struggle to find a balance between these two approaches on a site-by-site basis.)

Anuff and Steadman will later sell their creation to their employers for more than lunch money, thus ushering in a period where "content is king," whether it's actually valuable or even read, and where everybody and her sister wants to be a millionaire. This is not Anuff or Steadman's fault.

Word.com begins offering intricately designed, well-written content. Like Suck, Word.com will be purchased later, with mixed results. One mass delusion ("content is dead") will briefly replace another ("we all get to be millionaires").

Netscape introduces JavaScript, a "simple" programming language that enables web pages to become far more interactive. Web designers begin stealing JavaScript from each other.

Netscape and Sun announce that Sun's new object-oriented Java language will "free" everyone from the "tyranny" of Microsoft's Windows operating system. Bill Gates smells the coffee. Microsoft creates Internet Explorer. The browser wars begin. Over the next four years, Netscape will invent one way of doing things while Microsoft invents another. Web designers will be forced to choose which technologies to support—or will support multiple technologies at considerable cost to their clients. Eventually, most everyone will realize that the medium can only advance with full support for common standards.

There are 12.8 million hosts and half a million websites.

1997

Amazon.com begins selling books over the Web. Marketers everywhere wake up to the promise of *e-commerce* and begin scrambling to launch e-commerce companies, add e-commerce capabilities to the offerings of their existing companies, or just put the letter "e" in front of whatever it is that they do. There are e-books, e-investments, e-architects, and e-communities. E-nough, already. A brief i-period will follow the e-period.

Internet Explorer 3.0 begins to support Cascading Style Sheets (CSS), an advanced yet simple-to-use design technology created by the W3C. Netscape Navigator 3.0 does not support CSS but does offer JavaScript (and JavaScript Style Sheets—a competing technology that nobody ever adopts). IE3 does not fully support JavaScript. The browser wars escalate, and the Web becomes still more fragmented.

There are now 19.5 million hosts, one million websites, and 71,618 newsgroups.

1998

There are over 300 million pages on the Web—and 1.5 million new ones appear online daily.

Internet traffic doubles every 100 days.

Investors become frenzied. Venture capitalists become stupidly wealthy. Anyone in a suit can raise $5 million by promising to sell anything to anybody. If we exaggerate, it's because this is a period of deep delusional dementia fueled by 80s style greed and 90s style buzzwords. Baby Jesus weeps.

The growth of e-commerce exceeds its one-year expectation by more than 10,000 percent. The projected growth of business-to-business services on the Web dwarfs even the growth of e-commerce.

With much money at stake, the browser war's fragmentation of the Web becomes intolerable. Developers spend at least 25 percent of their time working around incompatibilities between Netscape and Microsoft browsers.

A group of designers, developers, and writers, lead by Glenn Davis and George Olsen, forms The Web Standards Project (WaSP) at www.webstandards.org. The group hopes to persuade browser makers to support common standards so the Web can evolve rationally. The W3C, which creates most of the standards, lacks police power to enforce them; in W3C parlance, things such as CSS and HTML 4 are "recommendations." The WaSP sees these recommendations as an absolute necessity and will spend the next three years spreading that gospel by any means necessary.

Netscape goes open source, unveiling the secrets of its code in the hopes that thousands of programmers around the world will join together to create a newer, better version of the Netscape browser. The open source project for the Netscape Navigator source code is named *Mozilla*. The Department of Justice begins an antitrust lawsuit against Microsoft.

1999

America Online (AOL), though partially responsible for the growth and popularity of the Web, has long been despised by Internet connoisseurs. Many holding this view are die-hard Netscape users, who see AOL as a proprietary service for frightened "newbies" (neophyte Internet users). In a move that shocks the online world, AOL buys Netscape.

Netscape announces that its upcoming 5.0 browser, being built by the Mozilla open source project, will fully support the five key standards demanded by The Web Standards Project (www.webstandards.org/mission.html). The 5.0 browser never sees the light of day, but in late 2000 the project and Netscape will give birth to Netscape Navigator 6.

Microsoft announces that its upcoming 5.0 browser for the Mac will fully support two key web standards and offer "90 percent support" for others.

At least 100,000 web-related jobs cannot be filled because of lack of qualified personnel. Populi, the Web Talent Incubator, is launched to solve this problem. Your humble web author, who appears to enjoy typing the phrase "your humble web author," will later help Populi develop a curriculum in web communication design, which will still later become the basis for the book you are now reading, which will yet later be unearthed by archeologists of the thirty-first century, along with a Pepsi bottle.

2000

The year web standards broke, 1

Internet Explorer 5, Macintosh Edition is released in March, offering near perfect support for HTML 4, CSS-1, and JavaScript (www.alistapart.com/stories/ie5mac/).

The year web standards broke, 2

Netscape 6 is released in the wee hours of November 14. It supports XML, and the W3C DOM as well as the standards supported by IE5/Mac.

The year web standards broke, 3

Opera 5 (www.opera.com), released in December, supports HTML, CSS, XML, WML, ECMAScript, and the DOM (www.opera.com/opera5/specs.html).

The year the bubble burst

A number of ill-conceived web businesses fail, causing the usual dire predictions and market panics. A number of good web businesses are dragged down along with the unworthy ones. Overbuilt web agencies lay off staff; other agencies absorb them.

2001

You buy this book. And buy a second copy for a friend. And a third for your coffee table.

chapter 5

The Obligatory Glossary

SEVERAL YEARS BACK, Grey Advertising, Inc. felt it was perceived as a somewhat lackluster agency: large, dependable, and successful at delivering results, but not exactly cutting-edge in a world of Chiats and Weiden-Kennedys (the people who have made commercials for Apple and Nike).

Grey wanted to enhance its image, and as companies often do, it brought in an outside consultant. A depressing sum of money later, the consultant unveiled this recommendation: *make the logo orange.* A Grey company with an orange logo, get it? Unexpected. Cutting edge. Fresh. Or so the consultant argued, and the agency apparently agreed.

The story may be apocryphal, we hasten to add, because Grey has more lawyers than our publisher. We mention the whole thing because, as if Internet terminology itself weren't confusing enough, job nomenclature at web agencies can be dazzlingly baffling. This is thanks, in part, to consultants who think an orange Grey makes an Apple and "user experience transactional information architect" sounds better than "designer."

The Web is an insanely great medium. The young industry is exciting and challenging enough to fulfill you through a dozen lifetimes, but the business is so new that even people who work in it get confused over terminology.

Some companies have a dozen different titles for designers with slightly different jobs; other companies slap one title on everybody, and often enough the title makes little intuitive sense. Orange you Grey we've provided this little chapter to help you navigate the twin minefields of Internet buzzwords and ever-changing job titles? You bet you are. (Our apologies to Grey Advertising, consultants everywhere, and People for the Ethical Treatment of Animals, whom we haven't offended but just felt like mentioning because it's a good cause. Besides, if we don't mention it here, our cats will claw our eyes out—and they can do it.)

Web Lingo

Extranet

An *extranet* is a private network of computers that is created by connecting two or more intranets or by exposing an intranet to specific external users and no one else. Business-to-business collaboration often uses extranets.

In English: Extranets are websites that allow Company A to interact with Company B, and Special Customer C to interact with either or both—pretty kinky stuff. As a web designer, you may never be called upon to design an extranet. (If you are, it's the same thing as designing a website. We're sorry to bore you with these tedious distinctions, but that's our job in a section like this. We hear the American Movie Classics cable network is hosting an Alfred Hitchcock retrospective. Maybe you should go watch it until this chapter blows over.)

On the other hand, the Business-to-Business (B2B) category is one of the largest growth areas of the Web, so you may find yourself stuck, er, asked to design extranet sites anyway.

Websites are websites whether they're designed for the general public or for private businesses. However, because extranets are business-oriented, they tend to be more like software and less like magazines or television. In other words, the challenges are closer to industrial design and technical design and further from the consumer-oriented design many of us are used to. In still other words, this type of design work is not for everybody, though some designers adore and excel at it. (Excel is a trademark of Microsoft, and even though we didn't use it in that context in the preceding sentence, their lawyers read everything.)

HTML

Hypertext Markup Language (HTML) is an application of Standard Generalized Markup Language (SGML) and is used to construct hypertext documents (web pages).

In English: HTML is to web pages what PostScript is to print. But while PostScript is a complex programming language, best handled behind the scenes by software such as Illustrator and Quark XPress, HTML is a simple markup language best written by human beings. HTML breaks content down into structural components, much as an outline does.

The simplicity of HTML makes it easy to learn, but that simplicity also can be limiting. Soon, many sites will be built with more advanced tools, such as *Extensible Markup Language* (XML). You need not concern yourself with that now. Later on in this book we will show you what HTML is, how to use it correctly, and how to employ it creatively. See Chapter 8, "HTML: The Building Blocks of Life Itself."

Hypertext, hyperlinks, and links

For additional information, refer to the section titled, "Website" later in this chapter.

Internet

The *Internet* is a worldwide networking infrastructure that connects all variety of computers together. These connections are made via *Internet protocols* including (surprise, surprise) Internet Protocol (IP), Transport Control Protocol (TCP), and User Datagram Protocol (UDP). IP is used for addresses, TCP is used to manage sockets (and hence the Web), and UDP is used to manage Domain Name Servers (DNSs). See Chapter 4, "How This Web Thing Got Started," for further explanation.

In English: The Internet is to the Web as cable networks are to television or as phone cables and switching stations are to your Uncle Marvin, who always phones while you're away on vacation and then resents you for not returning his call the very next day. The Internet is a combination of hardware (computers linked together) and software (languages and protocols that make the whole thing work).

As a web designer, all you need to keep in mind is that you're not only communicating with readers and viewers ("users" if you must), you're also creating work that must fit into formats appropriate to Internet technology. In other words, it's not your job to manage networks (for instance) as long as you understand their implications for your work—such as bandwidth and cross-platform issues. See Chapter 2, "Designing for the Medium."

Intranet

An *intranet* is an internal or private networking infrastructure that uses Internet technologies and tools. Unlike what occurs on the Internet, only computers on the private physical network can access an intranet.

In English: As a web designer, in addition to creating sites for the public, you also might be called upon to create intranet sites, which are nothing more than websites for private companies. For instance, AT&T not only has websites for the public, it also has thousands of private intranet sites where its employees can communicate with each other, schedule appointments, keep track of company policies, and so on.

One other difference worth noting is that when you're designing an Internet site, it has to be usable by anyone in the world—Netscape, Opera, IE, and iCab users; 6.0 browser users as well as 2.0 browser users; the blind and the not-blind; WebTV users and AOL users alike. You get the picture. On an intranet site, by contrast, all visitors may be using the same web browser and computing platform, which can simplify some of your design choices.

Of course, even in such circumstances, it is best to design with open standards so that your client will not be locked into restrictive choices. For instance, if you had designed an intranet for a network of Netscape 4 users in 1998, you might have built the entire site using Netscape's proprietary LAYERS technology. But with Navigator 6, Netscape stopped supporting LAYERS in favor of W3C standards. Had you designed specifically for Netscape's previous browser, your site would not work when the client upgraded browsers. Clients dislike that sort of thing, even when they are the ones who insisted on using a specific technology. Proceed with caution.

Additionally, if all the site's users are connected via a local network, you can make bold use of bandwidth-intensive technologies such as streaming video. When designing for the Web, you need to worry about bandwidth. Full-screen video is out; smaller video images and heavily compressed audio might be okay. For more on this fascinating topic, see Dave Linabury's "The Ins and Outs of Intranets" at www.alistapart.com/stories/inout/.

JavaScript, ECMAScript, CSS, XML, XHTML, DOM

In English: Additional languages of the Web.

Briefly: *JavaScript* is a programming language that enables designers or developers to build dynamic interactivity into their sites, further separating the Web from print. *ECMAScript* is a standardized version of JavaScript. See Chapter 11, "The Joy of JavaScript," for more particulars on this topic.

Cascading Style Sheets (CSS) is a standard that enables designers to control online layout and typography. Like HTML, its basics are extremely easy to learn, though its subtleties elude many designers (as well as many browsers). See Chapter 10, "Style Sheets for Designers."

XML is a simplified version of SGML, designed for use on the Net. As of this writing, it is most often used to deliver database-independent query results between incompatible software applications. It is not yet universally supported in web browsers, though XML 1 is fully supported in Netscape 6, and much of it is supported in IE5 and Opera 5. As a web designer, at least for the next few years, you will hear about and see XML, but you will not be called upon to create it—unless you begin marking up your web pages in *Extensible Hypertext Markup Language* (XHTML).

XHTML is essentially an XML version of HTML that works in most browsers. It is currently the W3C-recommended markup language for creating sites, though most sites as of this writing are still created in HTML. The differences between HTML and XHTML, from the "writing the code" point of view, are rather small, like Japan, though the implications of XHTML are rather large, like China.

The *Document Object Model* (DOM) is a web standard that lets these other standards "talk to each other" to perform actions. (For more about this, see Chapter 11.)

With the increasing specialization of the Web, designers are no more expected to master all these technologies than Rabbis are expected to fry bacon. Web designers should learn CSS (which is easy), and most learn enough JavaScript to be dangerous. Developers rather than designers will likely do the XML and DOM programming as well as most of the heavy-duty JavaScript/ECMAScript. The longer you work in the field, the more knowledgeable you will become about these standards, but few employers will expect you to have more than rudimentary awareness of most of this stuff.

Web page

As explained in Chapter 1, "Splash Screen," a *web page* is a type of electronic document, just as a Microsoft Word file or a Photoshop document is, except that a web page does not require any particular brand of software for someone to open and/or use it. And that is the glory of it, brothers and sisters. Developers and designers build web pages in HTML but, as noted above, they also use stuff besides HTML, which we'll talk about in the relevant technical chapters.

Website

A *website* is a collection of related web pages published on the World Wide Web.

In English: Click here.

Additional terminology

Tech terms will come up like last night's chili burritos throughout your career. You can always look up the latest buzzwords (or refresh your memory about what you have learned) by turning to the Computer Currents High-Tech Dictionary at www.currents.net/resources/dictionary/.

Roles and Responsibilities in the Web World

As a web designer, you will be responsible for creating the look and feel of websites—or portions thereof. Web designers may create menu bar icons for sites designed by other designers on their team, or they may create animated ad banners for sites designed by others. Hey, you've read Chapters 2 and 3—you know the deal. (If you don't, read the next chapter, which describes the web designer at painful length.) Meanwhile, this seems as good a place as any to familiarize yourself with some of the other players on your team.

Web developer/programmer

The web developers on your team will be responsible for the technical implementation of the site. You might hear them talk about Perl, Java, ASP, PHP, SSI, XML, ColdFusion, and other technologies. Just smile and nod as if you get it.

Most sites seamlessly fuse design, content, and interactivity. For that to happen, teamwork is needed. You don't have to understand how developers work their magic any more than developers need to possess design or writing skills. But thoughtful collaboration and mutual respect for each other's disciplines are required to create functionally and aesthetically superb sites.

Many developers have their roots in UNIX. Some are old hippies; others look like preteen rejects from the cast of *The Matrix*. With the frantic need for qualified personnel, developers also might come from the ranks of traditional information technology (IT) services. Many of these people are wonderful, but some have a strong bias toward particular technologies and generally do not approach web development with a "Webby" mindset—by which we mean a preference for open standards and accessibility.

For instance, IT-trained developers with roots in Microsoft-only shops sometimes employ technologies that leave Mac, Linux, UNIX, and OS/2 users out in the cold. This is because they don't know any better; they are as trapped by their training as that sad little boy who shoots puppies. (We now make good on our earlier apology to People for the Ethical Treatment of Animals. You see, this book is really very skillfully woven together in spite of its strange, dreamlike quality.)

Before accepting a job, be sure to check the company's offerings using at least one of these non-Windows operating systems. If the sites fail, the developers may be biased in favor of proprietary technologies without realizing the harmful nature of that predisposition.

Designers who wish their work to reach the broadest possible audience might want to think twice before accepting a job at a place like that. We've even seen shops where Mac-using designers can't send email due to Windows-only gateway issues. This is not intended as a slam at Microsoft's many fine products, two of which were used in the creation of this book. It is simply cautionary advice for the job seeker. In our opinion, because closed systems lock out millions of potential users, serious web developers prefer open standards.

Project manager

These team members are like technologically savvy account executives. They help articulate the client's needs, develop schedules (timelines) and budgets, and are responsible for keeping the project on track. Just like the account executives you might have worked with in your traditional design career, project managers are usually good people with stressful jobs. As you used to do with account executives, you must employ tact and patience to negotiate with these folks.

Project managers will often produce things called Gantt Charts, which are frankly little more than fancy work schedules. Say "thank you" when you get these. It makes them feel good about themselves.

Do not actually look at the Gantt Charts, however. They will only frighten you and make you feel hopeless and uncreative. Don't worry about missing any deadlines. The project managers will be "casually dropping by" your cubicle every 15 minutes for the next 40 years, and you won't miss a single deadline. See, what did we tell you? They're exactly like account executives.

Systems administrator (sysadmin) and network administrator (netadmin)

Sysadmins and *netadmins* are also called network engineers, database administrators, directors of web development, webgods, UNIX guys, NT guys, Linux guys, and geeks (formerly often called "webmasters")—these are the people who run the server (computer) that houses the site you're developing. They also run the *staging server* where you might build the site before actually "publishing" it to the Web.

In some companies these folks are woefully underpaid juniors with extensive computing knowledge. In others, they're woefully overpaid juniors without any computing experience at all, which is why many old-school webmasters now call themselves systems administrators, network engineers, database administrators, and so forth, leaving the webmaster moniker to the temp who answers email about the site.

Most sysadmins are senior employees in charge of a staff. In small companies, they also might be the folks you go to when you need software installed on your computer or if you're having trouble with your email. In larger companies, an IT person typically handles those responsibilities. In some companies, sysadmins are also developers and in others, they are not.

Some companies call their sysadmins *developers*. Some call their juniors *seniors*—because titles are easier to come up with than salary. Some say love is like a flower. Don't let any of this drive you mad. Above all, respect the sysadmins. Without them, we'd have no Web.

Web technician

Web technicians, also called producers, web producers, HTML jockeys, webmonkeys, web practitioners, HTML practitioners, design technicians, HTML technicians, geeks, and many other things, are folks who do a job similar to that of the studio people in an ad agency. As studio people take an art director's comp and make technologically-oriented changes to it so that it can be handed off to a printer, web technicians take a web designer's Photoshop comp, cut it apart, and render it in HTML, JavaScript, and other languages as needed. They also will render the graphic elements in web-appropriate formats.

If you were wondering, the difference between web technicians and web developers is largely a matter of experience, knowledge, and salary. A web technician may cut your comp apart and write HTML; a web developer is more like a technology designer who envisions powerful transactions and writes advanced code in several different languages to bring those visions to life.

Web developers are as critical to the process as lead designers, whereas web technicians are more like junior designers. Junior designers might create buttons or develop alternate color schemes under the supervision of a senior designer; similarly, web technicians generally do lower-level programming tasks than web developers. Some don't program at all but simply use cut-and-paste JavaScripts (as do many web designers).

In smaller companies (or in large companies when there is a time crunch), there are no web technicians; web designers execute their own designs in HTML, JavaScript, and other languages as needed. This book will prepare you to do that part of the job, making you that much more employable and giving you that much more control over the process. (And as designers, we all like control.)

Even if you always work in large companies, your knowledge of these processes will enable you to work closely with web technicians, often in a supervisory capacity—as if they were junior designers helping you execute your campaign. It also will enable you to self-publish your creative work if you find, as many of us do, that the Web is the greatest thing since sliced bread, and you have an urge to do creative work even after hours.

We started this chapter by mentioning that titles are often confusing in this business. The same thing holds for job responsibilities. While there are plenty of junior and mid-level web technicians, there are also web developers who handle these tasks. Regardless of anyone's stature, it goes without saying that you should be respectful to all your teammates because that makes life better.

And speaking of you...

Your Role in the Web

Will be covered in the very next chapter. Go there.

chapter 6

What Is a Web Designer, Anyway?

WE'VE EXPLORED THE STRENGTHS AND LIMITATIONS of the Web as a unique medium; considered architecture and navigation as key components of the user experience; glanced at the medium's history; defined technical terms; and examined the roles played by your coworkers. Maybe it's time to look at *your* job on the Web. We'll start with a working definition.

Definition

Web designers are professionals who solve a client's communication problems and leverage the client's brand identity in a web-specific way.

Complementing this focus on the client's needs, web designers must think like the site's anticipated audience. They foresee what visitors will want to do on the site and create navigational interfaces that facilitate those needs.

Pretty dry stuff, we'll grant you, but like marital bliss, it's better than it sounds.

How does all this fancy talk break down in terms of daily tasks? Below is a summary of deeds you'll do during the web development project life cycle. In Chapter 7, "Riding the Project Life Cycle," we delve into details.

Through the project life cycle, the web designer will need to:

- **Understand and discuss** the underlying technology—its possibilities and limitations as well as related issues—with clients and team members.
- **Translate** *client* needs, content, and branding into structured website concepts.
- **Translate** projected *visitor* needs into structured website concepts.
- **Translate** website concepts into appropriate, technically executable color comps.
- **Design** navigation elements.
- **Establish** the look and feel of web pages, including typography, graphics, color, layout, and other factors.
- **Render** design elements from Photoshop, Illustrator, and other visual development environments into usable elements of a working website.
- **Lay out** web pages and sites using HTML and other web development languages.
- **Organize and present** content in a readable, well-designed way.
- **Effectively participate** on a web development team.
- **Modify** graphics and code as needed (for instance, when technological incompatibilities arise or when clients' business models change—as they often do in this business).
- **Program** HTML, JavaScript, and style sheets as needed. In larger agencies, this work is often performed by web developers and technicians (see Chapter 5, "The Obligatory Glossary"), but the accomplished web designer must be ready to do any or all of these tasks as needed.
- **Try not to curse** browser makers, clients, or team members, as obstacles are encountered throughout the process. (Well, go ahead and curse browser makers if you want to.)

- **Update and maintain** client sites as needed. Though this job, too, often falls to web technicians or producers, don't think you're off the hook. You're never off the hook.

What We Have Here Is an Opportunity to Communicate

The work of web design involves understanding what your clients wish to achieve, helping them refine their goals by focusing on things that can be done (and are worth doing), and ultimately translating those goals into working sites.

While interacting with clients, you're also interfacing with research and marketing folks to find out who is expected to visit the site and what they will demand of it. You'll be translating the anticipated needs of projected visitors into functional and attractive sites—and hoping that visitors want what your client wants them to want. (Try saying that with a mouthful of peanut butter.)

If visitors seek in-depth content, but your client envisioned the site mainly as a sales channel, either the client has fundamentally misunderstood his market (it happens), or your design is sending the wrong messages. To build sites that clearly convey what they are about and how they are to be used, you must first communicate unambiguously with clients, marketers, and researchers.

The site can't communicate unless the people who build it communicate. Ever try to design a logo for a client who could not articulate the target market, product benefits, or desired brand attributes? The same problems crop up in web design unless you are blessed with great clients or are willing to work with the ones you have. Listening may be the most important talent you possess. If your listening skills have grown rusty, you'll have plenty of meetings in which to polish them.

Good web designers are user advocates as well as client service providers. They are facilitators as well as artists and technicians. Above all, they are *communicators*, matching client offerings to user needs.

As designers, we often look down on clients for reacting according to their personal taste ("I don't like bold type") instead of viewing the work through the eyes of their intended market ("That's just what our customers are looking for"). But web designers commit the same offenses. Some of us become so enamored of our aesthetic and technical skills that we end up talking to ourselves or sending encoded visual messages to our fellow web designers.

As a design professional, you are presumably free of this affliction most of the time. (If not, you'd have found some other line of work by now). Retain that focus (Who am I talking to? What are they looking for?) as you pick up the tools of your new trade. If you emphasize communication above all other goals, you will find yourself enjoying a significant competitive advantage. You'll also design better sites.

Let's expand our definition of the web designer's role.

Definition (Revised)

A web designer is responsible for the look and feel of business-to-business and business-to-consumer websites. Web designers solve their clients' communication problems, leveraging brand identity in a web-specific manner (in other words, in a manner that respects the limitations and exploits the strengths of the Web). A web designer understands the underlying technology and works with team members and clients to create sites that are visually and emotionally engaging, easy to navigate, compatible with visitors' needs, and accessible to a wide variety of web browsers and other devices.

The Definition Defined

Let's break this definition into its components:

> A web designer is responsible for the look and feel of business-to-business and business-to-consumer websites.

Look and feel

Just as in print advertising, editorial work, and graphic design work, the look and feel reflects the client's brand, the intended audience, and the designer's taste. Is the site intended for preteenage comic book fans? Is it a music site for college students? An entertainment site? A corporate site? An informational or shopping site for a wide, general audience? Is it intended to reach an international visitorship? Or just people from Ohio? (Is visitorship a word?)

As with any design assignment, you first find out all you can about the client's brand and the audience the client intends to reach and then make appropriate decisions. The terrain will be familiar to you. It includes choosing typefaces, designing logos, selecting or creating illustrations or photographs, developing a color palette, and so on. As we discussed in Chapter 2, "Designing for the Medium," these familiar tasks change a bit when applied to the Web because the medium embraces certain things (flat color fields, text) while hiccuping on others (full-screen graphics, high-resolution images and typography).

More significantly, "look and feel" decisions extend beyond traditional graphic design and art direction to encompass site-wide navigational architecture (as discussed in Chapter 3, "Where Am I? Navigation & Interface"). Technological issues play their part as well. A site in which database queries generate results in HTML tables will have a different look and feel than a more traditional content site, or one created in Macromedia Flash. The technological choice does not *dictate* the look and feel: It can be any kind of HTML table-based layout, any kind of text layout, or any kind of Flash-based design. The choice of technology merely establishes parameters.

Business-to-business

Business-to-business means one company communicating with another or selling to another. Annoying dot-com types and techno-journalists refer to this as *B2B*.

The B2B category includes intranet sites (the private, company site of Ogilvy & Mather or Pepsi Cola) and extranets (a steel company's site linked to a broker's site linked to the sites of five customers). Flip back to Chapter 5 if these terms make you edgy. Though this part of the web business is hidden from most folks, it is vast and growing. There's no doubt that in your web career, you'll be asked to design some B2B sites. You'll also have to avoid slapping people who say "B2B."

In fact, we'd like to apologize right here for using acronyms such as B2B and B2C. They annoy us as much as they do you. But you might as well get used to them because you'll be hearing them constantly at your job. Besides, as annoying as these acronyms are, they're not nearly as nerve-wracking as ubiquitous venture capitalist phrases such as "burn rate," "built to flip," or "ad-sponsored community play."

We've never understood why these phrases arise, let alone how those who talk that way manage to avoid being beaten with large polo mallets on a daily basis. Our theory is that such phrases make the speakers feel important. As you can probably tell, we didn't have much to say about the business-to-business category because, basically, web design is web design regardless of the acronym attached to a particular category. Vanilla, chocolate, or strawberry—ice cream is ice cream, Jack. (But do look back at Chapters 2 and 5 for hints on coping with intranet-design-specific issues).

Business-to-consumer

When most folks think of the Web, they form a mental picture of business-to-consumer sites such as Amazon.com—a business that sells products to consumers like us. Not all B2C sites are overtly hawking products. Yahoo.com is a B2C site. Yahoo! (the business) provides web users with information. It isn't selling anything per se, but it's still B2C because it speaks to consumers and is open to all. It's not hidden on a private network and password-protected, as a B2B site would be. The B2C segment is the most visible part of the web. (We apologize for using the word "segment.")

Solve Communication Problems

Let's continue with the next part of the job description:

> Web designers solve their clients' communication problems, leveraging brand identity in a web-specific manner (in other words, in a manner that respects the limitations and exploits the strengths of the Web).

Using HTML to lay out web pages does not make you a web designer—nor does making pretty pictures in Photoshop. A web designer, like any other designer, is a communications professional who solves problems. Just as a CD cover says something about the music it contains, the band that created the music, and the likely customer, so the site must clearly communicate its structure, content, and purpose in a way appropriate to a specific audience.

Gosh, haven't we made this point before? Yes we have. And yet many web designers will read these words, nod their heads sagely (or maybe just nod off), and then continue to create sites whose appearance has nothing to do with the product, user, or brand.

Brand identity

As a designer or art director, you know what this means. But what does it mean on the Web? In simplistic terms, and on the most basic level, it means the same kind of work you've done all your professional life: *Make the logo bigger. Use the client's color palette.*

But on a deeper level, the web designer doesn't merely "use the client's colors" and slap the client's logo on a web page. The web designer *uses the site to express and extend the client's brand identity.*

In Chapter 3 we discussed the way IBM's brand positioning as a solutions company influenced not only the site's look and feel, but also the depth and nature of its architecture and the type of enabling technology employed in its construction (see Figure 6.1). Good web designers are always thinking beyond the surface, extending and translating the brand through function as well as form.

Web-specific

No surprises here. In the case of the IBM site, "leveraging brand identity in a web-specific manner" means designing a site that provides solutions, not problems. Clear navigation and a search engine that works help the site support this aspect of the brand. This is an example of using the Web's strength as a searchable database to convey brand attributes.

Figure 6.1

Did the designers of IBM's website (www.ibm.com) succeed in their quest to translate the IBM brand to the Web? Front-page graphics tell only part of the story. The site's functional performance tells the rest. Web design encompasses graphic design but extends beyond it.

Restrictions of the Medium

Every medium has limitations. This book, for instance, lacks hyperlinks and a soundtrack. You can't bookmark a motion picture (at least, not in the theater—the management might complain), and you can't save printed magazine images to your desktop (though you can often save newsprint to your fingertips).

The Web's restrictions, as well as its strengths, were discussed in Chapter 2. Respecting those limitations and playing to those strengths is a key difference between design and *web* design. A web page that ignores the medium's restrictions (for instance, by forcing the viewer to download 100K of bloated imagery) or that fails to play to the medium's strengths (for instance, by offering limited interactivity), may be visually beautiful—but it will still be poor web design.

Let's look at the last part of our definition:

> A web designer understands the underlying technology and works with team members and clients to create sites that are visually and emotionally engaging, easy to navigate, compatible with visitors' needs, and accessible to a wide variety of web browsers and other devices.

Technology

Web designers have a lot to say about the appropriate technological level for sites they design. Choosing appropriate technology is part of your job as brand steward and user advocate. Consider the following:

- You wouldn't design a general shopping site that depended on the visitor having the Flash plug-in, the latest version of Internet Explorer, or a particular operating system because you'd lose many customers that way. The owners of Boo.com, a technologically overwrought shopping site, learned this the hard way when their business imploded in 2000.
- On the other hand, when designing a gaming site for Playstation or an entertainment site for a high-tech sci-fi flick, using Flash (or designing for newer, more capable browsers) could be entirely appropriate.
- You or a developer on your team might have fun coming up with a nifty *Dynamic HTML* (DHTML) menu geared for Internet Explorer 5, Netscape 6, and Opera 5—three recent browsers that to greater or lesser degrees support the World Wide Web Consortium (W3C) standard Document Object Model (DOM). You would not create a menu like that, however, for a women's health care center because patients and their families are not going to download a new browser when seeking medical help or information.

Technology choices are essentially decisions about who the site is for. As a communications professional, you should cultivate an informed opinion on this matter. If you don't decide these issues for yourself, somebody else will decide for you, which can have potentially tragic results.

It's also worth repeating that even if you decide the site is primarily for bleeding-edge web enthusiasts, you will want to create alternative pages that are accessible to anyone.

Works with team members

Although sites are often driven by a lead designer and technologist (or a lead information designer), web design is nearly always a group effort. Think of your team members as friends. In fact, think of them as family. You'll probably see more of them than you do your friends and family anyway. Then again, as a designer, you may already be used to that.

Visually and emotionally engaging

Like we have to define this for you.

Like that ever stopped us.

Beyond functioning appropriately for its intended use and supporting the brand, if your site lacks visual appeal or a coherent and engaging message, all but the most dedicated users will pass it by in favor of a more fulfilling experience elsewhere.

"Form follows function" does not mean "form doesn't matter." Form matters a heck of a lot. Given two functionally equivalent sites, only one of which delights the eye, where would you choose to spend your time? Okay, you're a designer. But given the same two sites, where would your Aunt Martha choose to spend her time? Okay, well, yes, we forgot about Aunt Martha's problem. Anyway, you get the idea.

Visually appropriate does not mean visually unengaging. Most of the screenshots in Chapter 3 are of appropriately designed sites, very few of which are lackluster or emotionally unappealing. We adopt kittens but run from buzzards and rats because, well, to be honest, because buzzards and rats are filthy, disgusting animals—but also because kittens are cuter than buzzards and rats. We idolize babies and movie stars for much the same reason.

You did not go into design to make the world duller or uglier. Anyone who tells you a functional site has to be visually plain is suffering from an emotional problem. Don't make their problem yours. (But don't give them ammunition by designing a beautiful but hard-to-use site.)

Sites cannot be emotionally engaging if they don't have a clear purpose and a distinctive, brand-appropriate look and feel. It also helps a great deal if they're well written. Few commercial sites are. If you end up supervising budgets for some of your projects, be sure to leave money for good writers and editors. Great cinematography can only go so far when the script is bad.

Easy to navigate

Refer to Chapter 3.

Compatible with visitors' needs

Refer to this chapter's previous discussion of the three partners in any website (the designer, the client, and the end-user) and to Chapter 3, which covers scenario development as a means of getting inside the user's head.

We get inside the user's head (to the best of our abilities, anyway) to structure and design a site that meets that user's needs. Aside from your Uncle Marvin's personal home page, no site appeals to just one user. We construct multiple scenarios to forecast the needs of multiple users.

Accessible to a wide variety of web browsers and other devices

We've already pointed out that the Web is accessed by a wide range of browsers and that each of them has peculiarities, also referred to as incompatibilities. (Other words are also used, but we gave up swearing for Lent.)

Until all browsers support a core group of common standards, you will have to learn the ins and outs of each distressingly different browser and confirm what you think you know by testing your completed designs on as many browsers and platforms as possible. (We'll discuss testing in the next chapter.) In addition, your sites might need to work in nontraditional browsers and Internet devices such as Palm Pilots and web phones.

Can You Handle It?

By this point, the job of a web designer may appear too difficult. How is it possible to reconcile the needs of the user with the demands of the client and the heritage of the brand—not to mention coping with bandwidth limitations, browser incompatibilities, and the unknowable behavior of each individual visitor? Is it really possible to do this job well?

Obviously, we think so. Here are some not-so-obvious reasons why.

For one thing, web work is teamwork. Project managers, developers, web technicians, writers, producers, and other designers on your team will help you keep your eyes on the prize.

Moreover, as a design professional, you already possess most of the skills and talents needed to design great sites, including:

- The ability to research your client's products and end-users, creating work that promotes the former while speaking to the latter.
- A deep understanding of branding and identity.
- A comfortable familiarity with the processes of learning from and presenting to clients and colleagues. You know how to sell and when not to. You've learned how to listen.
- Maintaining schedules and deadlines. You deliver on time.
- A thorough knowledge of design principles.
- Expertise with digital design tools, such as Adobe Photoshop and Illustrator.

You can count on your teammates. You can count on yourself. And the process itself also will help you meet the goals you, your clients, and partners set for each project. Virtually every web agency employs methodologies and processes to guide you and your teammates from the initial meeting to the launch (and beyond). By a strange coincidence, you'll start learning about that very subject as soon as you turn the page.

chapter 7

Riding the Project Life Cycle

IN HOLLYWOOD, THE DIRECTOR IS KING. No matter how brilliant the work of the actors, producers, screenwriter, cinematographer, composer, editor, set designer, or other professionals, when the lights go down it is the director's vision that fills our eyes and forces us to respond.

On the Web, compelling sites begin and end with the vision of a lead designer or a small, high-level design team. Other professionals certainly play invaluable roles in defining and executing sites, however. Sites would not work at all without the efforts of information architects, programmers, producers, systems administrators, writers, and quality assurance teams—to say nothing of focus groups, testing groups, marketers, and the occasional consultant. And then there's the client, who not only foots the bill, but also contributes marketing and product information, existing artwork and promotional materials, and his own ideas.

But sites that transcend mere adequacy depend on the consistent vision of web designers. That means you.

Design at this level is broad and deep. It does not end with the creation of graphic design elements. In fact, it does not even begin there. It starts with the first meeting and continues straight through the launch. Under ideal conditions, it goes on to include training and maintenance. For web designers to stay actively involved in every step of the process, they must thoroughly understand how the process works—hence this chapter.

Make no mistake: If you skip any part of the process, you pay for it later—with a site that falls short of your vision.

This chapter sketches life in the trenches of web development. It emphasizes the value of a methodology, outlines the life phases of most web projects, and explains the kind of contributions you'll be expected to make in each phase of the process. Living this life is exciting, rewarding, and sometimes quite stressful. Reading about it is dull as dirt. If you feel like skipping this chapter, we'll understand. It will be here when you need it. For instance, just before you take your next job.

What Is the Life Cycle?

Every project, from an ad campaign to the development of a new car, has a life cycle. In most shops, web designers are expected to see a project through from the initial discussion phase to completion and updating. In some shops, this is not required; but in those places, you'll want to participate anyway.

If you're not actively involved in the project from conception to "baby's first steps," somebody else will be making critical decisions for you. That person may not understand or care about consumer psychology, web usability, or the importance of design. By understanding and involving yourself in the entire project life cycle, you'll be able to keep the focus on practicalities, aesthetics, the client's goals, and the needs of the site's potential audience.

In your design career, you've undoubtedly toiled on projects that were misdirected long before you were brought into the loop. Designers can solve many problems, but they cannot undo fatally misguided business decisions. As an advocate for the end user and a spokesperson for the needs of your team, you must be present from the beginning to the end.

Some web shops are designer-driven; others have roots in information technology (IT). All good shops recognize the importance of involving the design group early and often. Many web agencies formalize this role of the design group by incorporating it into their methodology.

Why Have a Method?

All websites, from e-commerce projects to abstract multimedia experiences, contain elements of two types of activities:

- Information systems, involving computers and software
- Communication design, including advertising and marketing communications

Because of the size and complexity of today's sites, web development often resembles information systems projects or enormous advertising and marketing campaigns. It's not as big a job as coordinating the cast and crew of *Gladiator*, but it can come surprisingly close.

Though estimates vary, it's agreed that the majority of information systems projects fail. In case you missed that, we'll say it again. Most information systems projects fail. Why do they fail? It's generally because there is too much stuff to manage and keep track of, including the following:

- Scope (the size of the project)
- Budget
- Resources
- Timelines
- Functionality (the stuff the site is supposed to do besides look pretty)

To help manage such complexity, companies have available to them a resource that reduces the amount of unpredictability and surprise in a project. It is called a methodology. Every good company has one; no two are the same.

A methodology outlines steps required for a successful project, making sure no steps are missed and none are undertaken at the wrong time. A methodology also organizes these steps into phases. Phases help team members group activities, recognize progress, and notice red flags. A sound methodology provides documented, consistent, proven, repeatable processes. Projects that follow such methodologies work because they avoid reinventing the wheel.

With a method in place, the team is freed from having to develop unique support tools and processes for each new project. Without a method, the team is driving off-road, blindfolded, without a map. They may reach their destination safely, but it will be six months too late. They may end up in Timbuktu, trying to convince the client they're in Kansas.

The following story is true: Once upon a time, a web agency with no methodology agreed to take on a large but fairly simple project. The client delivered the copy 3 months late (they all deliver the copy late). The copy, when delivered, was completely unusable. The agency had to pay a team of freelance writers rush charges out of its own pocket because the client had vetoed a writers budget. The client restructured the entire site as the last graphic elements were being produced, invalidating all development and graphic design work done up to that point and causing everyone to work through Christmas to make up the difference.

Two weeks before launch, the client changed his logo and corporate colors. A week later he changed his business model. The client faxed revised (atrocious) copy from his vacation home, and it had to be manually retyped, edited by those now-deliriously-happy freelancers, and then put into HTML by freelance web technicians.

Just before launch, the client's boss (the CEO) was brought in to bless the work. Apparently, nobody had apprised him of the project plans. The CEO hated everything. The client halted all work and, fearful of losing his job, refused to send final payment. Attorneys were brought in. Agency staff was laid off to pay the attorneys. Then the freelancers sued the agency for non-payment. More staff was laid off. War was declared in Bosnia; Pinkerton did not return—all because the agency failed to follow a methodology.

Successful web agencies often fall so in love with their methodology that they broadcast it on their corporate sites. Whether they call it "our method," "our process," or "Uncle Joe," the discussion of corporate methodology is duller than fungus. So why do so many web agencies fill their sites with such wearisome stuff? It's because clients have been burned when working with web agencies that seemingly had no methodology at all. The trumpeting of methodology carries an implicit promise of performance. ("We won't be late or over budget. Look! We have a methodology!")

Every married couple takes vows, but many later break them. Similarly, the existence of a written methodology is no guarantee that the company that wrote it will practice it. Nevertheless, good companies do have methods that work for them, and you will want to master the methodology of your web agency. If possible, you will want to improve it. Every project tests the validity of the company's methods, thus every project presents an opportunity to improve the company's methods.

We Never Forget a Phase

Like all human endeavors, web projects may be broken down into phases. Each phase involves particular, predictable activities and results. We're not speaking of the mysterious spark of creative inspiration here; we're talking about process and workflow. Breaking a web project into phases allows companies to predict and plan for activities, ensuring that no steps are skipped. Reusing processes from one project to another also increases efficiency while reducing heartache, phone rage, and legal expenses.

Phases are plans, and plans are never static. Over the life of any project, activities move from one phase to another; activities may span several phases; and lines of delineation between phases may blur. Still, it is possible to sketch a general outline of the web project life cycle, which is what we've done here.

The five phases of site development are as follows:

1. Analysis
2. Design
3. Development
4. Testing
5. Deployment

Analysis (or "Talking to the Client")

In this phase, you will meet with the client as often as necessary to fully understand what the client wishes to achieve with the project, to determine the best ways of meeting those needs, and to sell those solutions to the client. You'll also continually interface with fellow team members to make sure these solutions make sense and can be executed.

Even before sitting down to brainstorm with the team, you must help the client articulate and clearly define the site's goals. Is the site selling something? If so, what is being sold and to whom? Is the site intended to serve as a portal—if so, a portal to what and for whom? How will this portal differ from its competitors? If the idea stinks, don't be afraid to say so. (First, of course, do enough homework to be certain that the idea really stinks and be prepared to offer the client a better idea.)

These responsibilities are not the web designer's alone. Project managers, information architects, and marketing folks will be all over these meetings, but the web designer plays an essential part.

Indeed, the web designer is often the only person in the room who even thinks about the end user. The project manager is scheming ways to get the project done on time. The programmer is itching to try out some new technology or lazily conceiving ways to reuse code from the previous project. The technology director is fretting about server farms. The junior designer is nursing a hangover, and the client is lost in fantasies of market domination.

The web designer must help the client articulate objectives, both broad and narrow, to begin delineating the project's scope. If this work is not done up front, it will haunt the project (and the whole team) later on.

In these early meetings, the web designer should be prepared to discuss possible site structuring options, technological baselines, and related issues. Even if these ideas change later in the process—and they will—the web designer must be comfortable articulating possible solutions "on the fly." This begins establishing a client comfort level, which will be essential throughout the process. If the client does not trust the web designer in the beginning of the cycle, the project will begin to self-destruct further down the line.

To summarize what we've just said: It is essential that the web designer possess the ability to understand a client's marketing goals and to discuss potential issues and solutions with regard to design, site architecture, and technology.

To assuage your fears, the only part of this that is new (from your perspective as a professional designer) is that technological issues have been added to the equation—much as ink, paper stocks, and such are part of the traditional design equation. You will learn what you need to know in this book and on the job.

The early phase

Earlier, we urged you to get involved at the very beginning of the process. There is one phase in which you cannot participate. That is the client's own analysis phase. You will not meet with your clients until they've sat down first to figure out their needs. Ninety-nine times out of ninety-nine, those needs will change once you're involved in the process.

How does the analysis phase operate? Just as in traditional design projects, it typically begins at the highest levels of detail and works its way down. In initial meetings, the focus is on broad strokes (such as, "We're a community for young women."). As the project progresses, lower-level decisions emerge (such as, "Should we put buttons or text labels on tertiary search results pages?").

Though most of us are happiest alone in our cubicles, staring at our monitors and though many of us would rather undergo gum surgery than face another meeting, in many ways this phase is the most critical and creative part of the job. The movement, over successive meetings, from the general to the particular takes place on many levels and extends beyond issues of graphic design and technology.

Many times, even the most sophisticated clients have only a rudimentary and confused idea of what they wish to achieve. In their own realm, they are kings. On the Web, they are lost little children. If your background includes marketing experience and if you have made yourself knowledgeable about the Web, you can guide your clients away from vague or even nonsensical plans and toward worthwhile, achievable goals.

Take a simple project. Your client wants to sell videotapes online. He has lined up a supplier and a fulfillment house, and after a full two hours of online experience, he is convinced that his site will be "the Yahoo meets AOL of online videotape e-tailing," whatever that means. Because his daughter, an art major, showed him the Monocrafts site (www.yugop.com), a brilliant and beautiful work done entirely in Flash, he figures his site should have "something like that" as well—oh, and a chat room. He read about those in an airline magazine while flying between Seattle and New York last year. He then describes the in-flight movie.

We wish we were making this stuff up, but it happens all the time. Not that this client is necessarily an idiot—he may be brilliant in his accustomed sphere of business. He may even read French literature and know fine wines. It's just that the Web is a mystery to him, and he's not used to admitting ignorance on any subject, even to himself. With tact and kindness, you and your team will guide him toward a workable plan. Six months from now, if you do your job well, he may have a fine site that includes movie reviews by Roger Ebert, streaming video clips of selected films, and a thriving movie lovers' discussion area. But it can happen only if you work with him during the sometimes painful early analysis phase.

Defining requirements

Before all else, the web team must define two types of requirements:

- **Technical.** These include anticipated performance, bandwidth, security issues, and so on.
- **Business.** These include needs and constraints (having to accommodate first-time web users), as well as overall marketing objectives.

These requirements are summarized in documents with impressive-sounding names such as "Functional Spec," "Requirements Document," or the ever popular "Use Cases Document." And the fun doesn't stop there: parent documents beget baby documents—all of which will be used to guide initial development, and none of which are carved in stone. The more stuff you figure out, the more you realize you have yet to figure out. Digital projects kill more trees than the Daily News. You will be buried in paper. Read it, absorb it, and set it aside.

Happy families are all alike, but every web project is different. Generally, though, the purpose of early analysis is to define goals, determine constraints and requirements, and establish trust. Without goals, constraints, and requirements, it will be impossible to know if the project is on target. Without trust, you are looking at months of sheer Hell. With trust in place, you may still be looking at months of sheer Hell, but you have a better shot at enjoying the process and creating something useful.

If this sounds familiar, it should. The only difference between analysis in traditional design and analysis in web design is the medium itself. Instead of die-cuts or film transfers, you'll be discussing bandwidth and browsers.

How it Works: Analysis in Action

Dishes Plus is a regional chain of successful retail outlets, known for its reasonable prices, wide variety, and "break proof" guarantee. Dishes Plus has decided to sell its product online. Naturally, you learn about the company's existing business, its competitors, and its brand image before the meeting. You and your team help Dishes Plus define large goals (selling dishes), small goals (branching out into soup tureens), and in-between goals (establishing a bridal registry division).

You find out about the company's audience (mostly women/mostly men, young/old, urban/rural) and sketch the impact that may have on technological and design considerations. If Dishes Plus has a loyal audience of people over 50, tiny type is out, and plug-in based multimedia is probably out as well. If selling is key, technological considerations leap to the forefront and should be examined carefully.

How many clicks from expression of interest to final sale? If the inventory is vast, a search engine will be needed. If Dishes Plus shoppers tend to spend hours poring over the goods, artificial intelligence may be called into play on searches ("If you like the Dixie Deluxe Classic Set, you'll love the Colonel's Tea Service").

Does Dishes Plus anticipate an overseas market? You might need to consider building the site in several languages and using iconography to facilitate navigation by non-English speakers. Do details matter? You can't assume that the client's photography is up to snuff. You may need to budget for a good shooter, conversion from photography to digital images, and a database to store and serve the relevant images.

How does the database work? Your developers know. Meet with them separately and then bring one or more to the next client meeting.

The possibilities are endless—when you first enter the room. After several successful analysis meetings, the possibilities should have focused into a set of meaningful and achievable goals. If you're still talking in generalities after two or three meetings, you're not doing your job. If you're talking in generalities after four or five meetings, the client is not serious. Timelines with cash consequences can sober up most clients. Have an attractive, friendly project manager explain to the client the additional costs incurred as his indecisiveness causes deadlines to shift.

Design

The design phase is a simple word for a heck of a lot of activity. The process nearly always unfolds something like this:

- Brainstorm and problem solve with your team.
- Translate needs into solutions.
- Sell ideas to the client.
- Identify color comps to be developed.
- Create color comps and proof of concept.
- Present color comps and proof of concept.
- Revise and repeat as necessary.
- Receive design approval.

Brainstorm and problem solve

As soon as your team has a clear understanding of the client's business problems, goals, constraints, and requirements, you can begin brainstorming solutions on your own, in partnership with other web designers, and in meetings with developers, producers, and information architects.

A project manager will join the team if she has not already done so. Make her your best friend. While you conceive grand notions or are daydreaming in Adobe Illustrator, she will be keeping track of and documenting schedules, deadlines, goals, and progress. We wouldn't last a minute in her job. Nor would most "creative" folks. Respect her for doing what you would pay not to do.

Methods of brainstorming vary. Some groups like to shout out ideas, writing everything down on a whiteboard. Others like to go off in small groups and then reassemble to critique each other's ideas. Sometimes you sit in the corner and type out ideas. Sometimes you draw on a traditional sketchpad. Some agencies dictate how the process should work; others let you figure it out for yourself.

Translate needs into solutions

The web designer and other team members will collectively come up with a number of solutions, which will then be narrowed down by group consensus, creative director fiat, or both. These solutions may be articulated internally through any combination of rough design sketches, internal Photoshop comps, written documents, or *wireframes* (functional visual storyboards showing the proposed site elements in relation to each other, but not in any way indicating how they will eventually look and feel).

To present these ideas to the client, you can once again use any of the following:

- Rough design sketches
- User interface documents
- Creative briefs
- Pencil sketches
- Wireframes
- Color comps

Sell ideas to the client

Using any or all of the tools just listed, the team presents their projected solutions to the client, answering questions, justifying decisions and methods, and discussing alternatives. As part of this discussion and "selling" process, the designer should be able to:

- **Articulate technology limitations.** Explain why the team supports a particular solution and avoid committing to alternatives that won't work.
- **Articulate design considerations and decisions.** As in a traditional design project, explain the rationale behind various creative decisions.

Articulating the limitations of technology and the needs of users can be tricky. The web designer must be familiar with technological issues involved in web development to be able to explain why the team supports a particular solution and to prevent *impossible* agreements and commitments.

Impossible agreements occur when the client asks for something that cannot be done, cannot be done within the budget and time frame, or just plain *should* not be done—and an inexperienced web designer or project manager commits the company to fulfilling that unreasonable or impossible expectation. Don't laugh. Plenty of web design teams have met their doom by committing to solutions that are technologically or graphically inappropriate, more costly than they're worth, impossible to deliver within the given time frame, or simply deeply stupid.

We were once asked to design the interface for a sophisticated, multi-user business software program that ran in a web browser. Essentially, the product was an intranet site with advanced functions rivaling that of expensive proprietary software. Though a sales force had lined up dozens of large corporate buyers, the developers were unable to deliver the product because its scope kept shifting as the executive in charge came up with one "neat idea" after another that he insisted on incorporating into the product. The design team and sales force sat on their hands while the developers burned out trying to fulfill constantly shifting objectives.

The executive then decided that the seemingly undeliverable product would sell better if users could visually customize it to their liking. He asked that a series of "skins" be developed, and the project manager added this requirement to the mountain of unattained goals. The last we heard, the product was still in development.

This kind of foolishness most often takes place in-house, where egos run unchecked and projects can drag on forever without obvious financial consequences—because those who do the work are on the company payroll anyway. But it also can creep into traditional client-vendor relationships if project managers accept impossible agreements.

That's the worst-case scenario. The only-slightly-better scenario is that your company will somehow fulfill the impossible agreement only to watch the client fail because everyone shook hands over a really bad idea. The client may want his e-commerce site visitors to enter personal data and create a unique user account before even seeing what he has to offer. He may request this at the last minute, and the web agency may manage to fulfill the request on time and within the budget. But nobody will use the site, and the client could bad-mouth the agency rather than admit his own folly, thus harming your business for years to come.

Even if the client has only good things to say about you, you don't want your clients to fail, and you don't want the press to associate your agency with widescreen, Technicolor flops. It will take all your expertise at client negotiation to avoid the Titanic effect (also known as the Boo.com effect). But it's better to face conflict than to knowingly deliver bad work.

The best-case scenario, of course, is to come up with and sell workable solutions that offer real value to the audience your client wishes to reach.

How Not to Do It

"Because I know what I'm doing, and you're a pathetic marketing flack who wouldn't know a good idea if it bit him on the thigh."

How to Do It

"We considered that very solution, Burt, but these studies show it would take 50% more time than we have—and we found that companies who tried that technique actually did worse than companies who did it the way we're suggesting. Marcie, could you show Burt that Tragic Failure Report you were sharing with me before the meeting?"

A good web designer will sometimes lie in the service of a larger truth. Pretend we didn't say that, and we'll pretend you don't know exactly what we're talking about.

Selling your ideas is not limited to unselling bad ideas, of course. And it's also not limited to explaining technology. You'll have the same design and brand identity discussions you've been having for years. They still want the logo bigger. They still prefer the obvious to the original. They still know just enough to be dangerous to themselves and the project.

Identify color comps

You've finally determined the direction; in this phase, you figure out what the client needs to see next. Typically, you'll be creating comps of the website's front page and one or two internal pages. These comps are not functional web pages; they are simply realistic renderings. At the same time, you (or you and an information architect) will be developing storyboards or wireframes outlining the flow of the site, from front page to order form, from bulletin board to help page. You will not comp all these pages; you simply need to know how they work.

Create color comps/proof of concept

Having identified the color comps necessary to prove the site concept, you execute them in Photoshop or another design tool. Today's web pages almost always interact with the visitor—changing in response to mouse movements and other events. Representing those interactive changes in a comp may sound like a challenge, but it's really not.

For instance, on most sites, an icon or menu item will change appearance when the visitor's cursor rolls over that icon. This change in appearance, not surprisingly, is called a *rollover*. A comp can demonstrate the active rollover state by showing one icon that is different from the others ("rolled over"). To make the effect crystal clear, capture an image of a mouse cursor and lay it on top of the "active" icon in Photoshop (Figure 7.1).

DER SENDER FANS JAZZ CITY

Figure 7.1

Is this a screenshot of an active rollover on a web page? Or is it a Photoshop comp? Only its hairdresser knows for sure.

Present color comps and proof of concept

You have presented, articulated, and sold ideas to the client. Now you do it again. The only difference is that the work is farther along in the process. In addition to explaining the rationale behind design decisions and discussing the underlying technology, you also should be prepared to aurally "sketch" what you have not yet comped up.

The client is interested not only in what you are showing; she is equally interested in what you are not showing. "Are all the sub-pages like this one? Will there be photographs on the message board pages, as there are on the content pages? What happens if the search shows up empty? What will that page look like? Does my hair look okay?"

You need to satisfy the client by describing (or "verbally storyboarding") these non-rendered pages. Prepare in advance. After all, you need to know this stuff as badly as the client does. By having your answers ready, you'll shorten the approval process when it comes time to design the next stage. (Client: "Oh, right, that's the area we said would have the yellow menu bar. Now I remember.") You also will further instill client confidence in the design team.

After the presentation, you will almost certainly need to make modifications. Web clients are no different than other design clients. They all have needs they can't quite articulate until they've seen some work. As in your current job, you must know the difference between minor changes, which may actually enhance the site, and major changes that could throw the entire project off course. It is your responsibility to communicate the full impact of suggested changes.

The presentation and revision process can go several rounds, demanding your tact as well as your expertise. You must be able to respond positively to client requests and return with a solution that demonstrates your responsiveness, without jeopardizing the end product.

Receive design approval

The great day arrives! The client has signed off (well, except for one more teeny tiny change). Now you gear up to begin translating your concept into reality. This phase is known as development.

Development

In the development phase, web designers work with other team members to translate site concepts into functional web pages. While you design additional graphic elements, create Style Sheets, and possibly code web page templates in HTML and JavaScript, producers will be marking up dozens, hundreds, or thousands of pages, and developers will be working to make the entire site far more functional than HTML alone allows.

Up until now, you've felt pretty certain about the way the site would shape up. After all, the front page and selected sub-pages have been designed and approved. Now, you must take the elements of all those pages and apply them to every single page of the site. Sometimes you do all this work; sometimes assistants or colleagues pitch in; and sometimes the work is carried out by the equivalent of production artists, whose work you may supervise. What is important in this phase is to maintain consistency.

Is the navigational menu on the right-hand side in all existing comps? Then it should remain there as new pages are designed, unless there is an overwhelmingly important reason to move it. ("It doesn't fit on this page" is not a legitimate rationale; it merely means you must work harder and rethink that page. Sometimes it means you must rethink the entire site.) The consistent location of navigational elements provides a vital pathfinder for visitors. Imagine trying to find your way in a strange city where the street signs kept changing color or location. No city would be that cruel or foolish. Neither should any website. (Flip back to Chapter 3, "Where Am I? Navigation & Interface," for more on this subject.)

Client-branding elements also must be treated with consistency from page to page. There are technological reasons for this, as well as psychological ones.

Psychologically, if the logo is always 32 x 32 pixels and always at the top left, visitors expect to see it there on all pages. Such consistency reassures visitors that they are still in the same "place" on the Web. After all, the Web is a fluid and limitless medium, and the client's site is just a drop in that vast ocean. Consistent branding orients web users; inconsistent branding disorients them. Love your audience and provide the markers they need to know where they are (and your clients will think you're doing it for them).

Technologically, once a graphic element is *cached* in the visitor's browser, it need not be downloaded again. Because most visitors use slow dialup modems, the less downloading, the faster the site and the better the user experience. Thus, if the same 32 x 32 image appears on every page, there is no need for additional downloads, and each page of the site will appear that much faster. (Refer to the discussion in Chapter 2, "Designing for the Medium," regarding bandwidth and caching if you've forgotten how this works or why it matters.)

During the development phase, you'll do things such as:

- Create all color comps
- Communicate functionality
- Work with templates

We provide tips and pointers in the following sections.

Create all color comps

As you have seen, the design phase demanded the creation of selected color comps. During development, one or more web designers will create color comps for all pages. Depending on client expectations, the design team also may show these comps to the client for approval.

As the team creates each color comp, technicians or junior designers will cut it apart in Adobe ImageReady or Photoshop 6, Macromedia Fireworks, or another similar software program. This process converts the color comp into component elements, and these are finally assembled into a working web page built with HTML and other web languages or with a *What You See Is What You Get* (WYSIWYG) web layout program, such as Dreamweaver. This is not the only way to create web pages, nor (in our opinion) is it necessarily the best way. It is the primary technique used in most shops, however, and every web designer should master the process.

Communicate functionality

Refer to the previous discussion on rollovers or *image swapping*, as it can be called. In some web firms, the web designer will code those image swaps in JavaScript. In other firms, the web designer merely articulates a desired effect (complete with Photoshop comps), and a developer or web technician writes the necessary code.

Functionality can include CGI and Java (for forms, e-commerce, message boards, and chat functions), JavaScript (for special interactive visual effects as well as less glamorous browser detection, plug-in detection, forms validation, and so on), plug-in technologies (Flash, QuickTime, or RealVideo), and beyond.

The communication travels both ways. At times the technologist will explain intentions or limitations to the web designer; at other times the web designer calls the shots. Web designers are not expected to know Java programming or MySQL. Many web designers do not even work in Flash. What's expected is that you know enough about these formats and languages to work with those who specialize in them, articulating your vision or responding to the direction of others.

By the way, we despise the word "functionality" even more than we hate phrases such as B2B or B2C. Alas, it seems to be the best word for the job. Former English majors, check your emotions at the door. This business has more buzzwords than a venture capitalist convention.

Work with templates

In some cases, sites change very little over time. More commonly, the site you design functions as a placeholder or shell for ever-changing content. Sometimes this changing content is managed by the web agency. If the client updates infrequently, you can simply write new HTML and create new images to accommodate occasional changes like these. More often, your clients will update their own sites, with mixed results. (We'll be whining about that later in the book.)

Today, content is often changed dynamically, by means of various *backend* technologies. In such cases, you are not so much designing pages as you are templates—visual and markup placeholders in which content will be updated by means of a publishing system or in response to dynamic database technology. The work is essentially the same as "traditional" web design but involves special considerations that will be articulated by the technologists on the team. (See Chapter 12 for more.)

Design for easy maintenance

In the best of all possible worlds, the web design team retains control over the site as it evolves over the months and years. Control is usually accompanied by a retainer fee, which is negotiated at the very beginning of the process. In reality, more and more clients assume control over the site when it is delivered.

Designers and coders should always create highly structured and well-documented work, so that they can easily go back to it and update it without hunting for missing files, debugging errant file references, and so on (or so that their clients, upon assuming control of the site, can perform these tasks without damaging the site).

Upon finishing the site, you'll accompany it with a style guide and documentation. These will be much easier to create if the site's file structure and naming conventions make sense to begin with.

For you, this means titling the logo image "logo.gif" instead of "uglyswirl-withstupidbevel.gif," calling the November header graphic "nov_head.gif," and so on. For the web technician (or you, if you write your own HTML), this means naming the disclaimer page "disclaimer.html," storing images in a single directory labeled "Images," and so on.

If care is taken throughout the development process, then updating and maintaining the site will be easy and logical, whether updates are performed by you, a production person, or your client.

Testing

Though a web development team will test its product throughout the project life cycle, many web projects plan for a distinct testing phase. In this phase, the development team has the opportunity to test the deliverable against the design and functionality specifications.

In some cases, real users may test a site. In other cases, a specially trained testing team will do the job. Testing by real users usually tells you more about the site. We often get the most useful feedback by showing work to the guys who deliver sandwiches. Be elitist in choosing typefaces but democratic in designing interfaces. The Web is for people, not for experts.

Regardless of the testing technique involved, team members must work together to track down the source of problems and implement solutions.

We guarantee that there will be problems. For one thing, no two web browsers interpret code and markup exactly the same way (see Chapter 2). For another, what seems clear to you may be baffling to the people who use your site. Web designers tend to live two years ahead of the curve; web users, who actually *have lives,* tend to live behind the curve. You know that little rotating box takes visitors back to the home page; visitors may not. Testing will reveal problems in browser compatibility and user acceptance; then it's up to you and your team to solve those problems.

Deployment

You've completed the site. The client has signed off on it. The files have been transferred to the web server. Think you're finished? Not quite yet. Successful projects demand a smooth transition from the web team to the client.

The updating game

In the early days, clients viewed the web designer as a species of magician. They knew they had to have a web presence, whatever that meant, and they felt that you held their fate in your hands. Not only were they eager to approve what you created (because it was all magic to them), they also were more than willing to retain you as the perpetual updater and refresher of their online identity.

Then came FrontPage, GoLive, and Dreamweaver—tools that theoretically let "anybody make a website," whether they knew what they were doing or not. Now, the possession of FrontPage does not turn your client into a web designer any more than ownership of a Roland Drum Machine turns the neighbor's kid into Keith Moon. But the ability to generate HTML, the language with which web pages are created, has convinced too many clients that they can save a buck or two by purchasing one of these web-editing tools and updating their sites themselves. The results are often disastrous, for reasons that will be obvious to any creative professional, but incomprehensible to many clients, whose esthetic sensibilities have been shaped by cooking up pie charts in PowerPoint. Not that we're bitter.

There are several ways to manage the transition. In one of the better scenarios, you've designed a database-generated site for a large client with much money and created a custom publishing tool enabling them to add fresh content to the mix without befouling the site.

Alternatively, instead of providing clients with a custom publishing tool, you might hook them up with an existing product, such as Zope (www.zope.org) or Allaire Spectra (www.allaire.com). Some of these tools use standard web languages such as HTML and XML; many use custom markup and are part of larger proprietary product families. Some are simple enough for a client to use; others require considerable developer involvement, which is one way of keeping your finger in the pie—if that's your idea of fun. What you gain in billings you may lose in IT people, who quit from the frustration of continually guiding clients through complex processes requiring specialized knowledge. This, however, is your boss's worry, not yours (unless you own the web agency).

In still other cases, your client will assign an in-house person or team to take over the site. Sometimes these folks are in-house designers with solid web experience. Sometimes they're overworked marketers with a copy of FrontPage.

Regardless of how the site is updated and by whom, in this final phase of development, you get one more opportunity to preserve your work and serve your client by creating documentation, providing client training, and maintaining contact on a consulting basis.

Create and provide documentation and style guides

"Care and Feeding" instructions accompany everything from puppies to houseplants, and websites demand the same loving attention. It is important to provide the client with detailed notes on the location of files, the fonts and color palettes used, photographers or illustrators involved, and so on.

As more and more clients plunge into the business of updating their own sites, it is vital to provide them with every possible scrap of information. If you don't take pains with this postpartum part of the process, your client may paint a moustache on your Mona Lisa or send visitors running for their lives when a Style Sheet or JavaScript file is accidentally deleted.

Remember: A book design is a book design, a finished ad is a finished ad, but a website is never finished, and the client can always louse it up. Do everything in your power to save your clients from themselves.

By the way, such documentation should be created even if the web agency retains control of the project (including updating and maintenance). After all, six months from now, do you really want to scratch your head trying to remember which font you used, where your navigational menu graphics were stored, or which script was responsible for a given function? Of course not. This documentation will be easier to create, and the site will be easier to update if you've followed the advice given earlier in this chapter and *designed for easy maintenance* by establishing and following logical naming and structural conventions.

Provide client training

Sometimes it is enough to tell your clients which fonts and colors you used. Sometimes it is enough to tell your children not to play with matches. Usually, it is not enough. That's why, whenever possible, the designer and other team members should have after-meetings to discuss the site in detail and provide as much client training as possible.

Besides helping the client avoid ruining a beautiful site, in-house training also sends the message that your company cares. Clients who know you care will come back with additional projects and will tell their friends on the golf course about the integrity of your company.

If your clients are going to be writing HTML or (bless us) creating new images, it is worth sitting down with them, at their computer or yours, and pointing out the fine nuances of what you've done. You might even buy fonts for them (matching the fonts you used), install the fonts on the client's computer, and show them how to work with Extensis Suitcase or Adobe Type Manager Deluxe.

You may feel ludicrous doing this, especially if the client is not a graphic designer, but it's foolish to underestimate other people's creative potential. Besides, if they're going to do the work anyway, you owe them and yourself every possible assistance.

This whole thing is fairly unsavory, we're afraid. It's rather like a dentist training patients to extract their own teeth, but it is an aspect of the business, and coping is better than lamenting.

Learn about your client's methods

Training is often bi-directional. While explaining your methods to an in-house peer (or turning a client into a junior web designer of sorts), you also should learn as much as you can about the way your client will work with the site. If possible, you should learn about the software your client will be using. It's highly unlikely that your client will create HTML and other web markup by hand. Fortunately, the number of WYSIWYG web editors considered good enough to use is fairly limited, so you can learn the basics and pitfalls of your client's software of choice even if you never touch the stuff yourself.

We recently ran into a puzzling problem where the web typography we had established via Style Sheets kept disappearing from the client's site after he took it over. We had written a Global Style Sheet, placed it in a secure location, and instructed the client never to touch it. Yet every time he updated the front page, the Style Sheet reverted to an early, inferior vision, and the client was constantly contacting us to ask why the site was going to Hell.

Eventually we discovered that a site maintenance feature built into the client's software was the culprit behind the Case of the Changing Style Sheet. When the client updated his index page, his software program asked if he wanted to "upload related files." Because that sounded like a pretty good idea, the client always clicked Yes. The program then automatically uploaded dozens of files from his hard drive to the server. An old Style Sheet on his hard drive was automatically replacing the newer one we had created. We re-sent him the updated Style Sheet, instructed him to turn off the site maintenance feature, and from then on, all was well.

Work the Process

The process you've just read about varies by agency, but the general outlines and the lessons involved should hold true for most companies and projects. Some agencies keep themselves fairly aloof from their clients and manage to do wonderful work in spite (or because) of it. Others become deeply involved with their clients, establishing long-lasting, trust-based relationships.

Some hold their clients to ironclad contracts and schedules, while others are loose and almost playful in their approach. Some shops show the client exactly one comp—take it or leave it. Others cover the walls. Some agencies charge astronomical fees merely to write a proposal; others write proposals, design comps, and create storyboards on spec—a terribly ill-advised approach, but not as rare as it ought to be.

The main thing to remember is that every phase, every step of the process, is potentially empowering. If you use initial meetings to establish trust and help sharpen the client's vision, you will find yourself working on sites worth designing—for clients who respect you instead of mistrusting and fighting with you. If you use the design phase to fully explore possibilities, you will come up with richer designs and avoid structural problems in the implementation phase. If you cooperate with team members and your client during the production phase, you will encounter fewer problems during testing. If you train your clients respectfully, your best efforts will be preserved, you'll be able to look at your old sites without experiencing nausea, and the credibility of your work will win you new and better projects.

Part III

HOW: Talent Applied (Tools & Techniques)

chapter 8

HTML, the Building Blocks of Life Itself

AS WE'VE SAID THROUGHOUT THIS BOOK, HTML is a simple language for creating documents that adhere to structured outlines.

```
<h1>Headline</h1>
   <h2>Subhead</h2>
<p>Paragraph.</p>
<p>Second paragraph.</p>
<p>Third paragraph.</p>
   <h3>Subordinate subhead</h3>
<p>Paragraph.</p>
<p>Second paragraph.</p>
<p>Third paragraph.</p>
<address>Contact information, copyright, date of publication</address>
```

Rocket science it's not, nor was it intended to be. All great ideas should be this simple. Notice that the *tags* (that's what the lines are called—tags) suggest their functions: <p> for paragraph, <h1> for first-level headline, <address> for contact information. Notice also the fine symmetry in this simple example. You open a <p> and you close it </p> when you're done. You open a <h3> subhead and </h3> close it before moving on to another tag. In this way, the browser knows that one tag has closed before another begins. In HTML, the closing of some tags is mandatory, while with other tags it's optional. That inconsistency has led to sloppy markup, which in turn has caused browser problems, especially when other web standards (such as CSS) begin to interact with your HTML. So it's a good idea to close most HTML tags whether it's strictly required or not. (In XHTML, the successor to HTML, all tags must be closed.)

Code Wars

As five minutes of web browsing will show you, HTML has been twisted every which way to enable web designers to create documents that are not so logical in their construction nor so restricted in their presentation. Cascading Style Sheets (CSS) and JavaScript are additional technologies that enable designers and developers to create attractive, accessible, dynamic web documents.

In theory, web designers should let HTML be HTML, using it merely as a structured container for content, while relying on CSS to format pages. In practice, web designers had to design pages long before CSS was invented, so most of us developed methods for using HTML as a design tool. Even after CSS was invented (1996), the first reliably CSS-capable browser did not hit the market until 2000. As of this writing, support for CSS is still tragically far from complete in many popular browsers. More about that—including solutions—in Chapter 10, "Style Sheets for Designers."

Table Talk

As a result of the Thousand Year March toward CSS compliance and while waiting for better browsers, designers still use HTML for tasks it performs reliably, if grudgingly, such as creating visual layouts by manipulating HTML tables:

```
<!-- Begin menu bar. -->
<table border="0" cellpadding="0" cellspacing="0" align="center">
<tr>
<td>
<a href="reading.html"><img src="reading.gif" width="20" height="20" border="0"
alt="Reading"></a>
</td>
```

```
<td>
<a href="writing.html"><img  src="writing.gif" width="20" height="20" border="0"
alt="Writing"></a>
</td>
<td>
<a href="arithmetic.html"><img  src="arithmetic.gif" width="20" height="20" border="0"
alt="Arithmetic"></a>
</td>
</tr>
</table>
<!-- End menu bar. -->
```

The previous code, in conjunction with the appropriate <img> images (reading.gif, writing.gif, arithmetic.gif), will result in a clickable navigational menu in visual web browsers such as IE, Netscape Navigator, Opera, and iCab. The table is used not to present tabular data (such as the contents of a spreadsheet) but rather to hold images in place. Setting the border to "0" disguises the tabular structure to facilitate pure visual purposes. Typing the width and height for each image helps the browser more quickly calculate how the data is supposed to lay out on the page. The <ALT> attribute in each image tag makes the content accessible to users of audio browsers and nontraditional browsers such as Palm Pilots, as well as for those who surf with images turned off.

XHTML Marks the Spot

We keep emphasizing that HTML is logical and orderly. Let us return for a moment to the question of closing tags after they are opened. This practice may seem redundant, but there is a logic to it. Refer again to the preceding example. Say that your paragraph is followed by an image. If you don't close your paragraph </p> before starting the image <IMG> tag, the browser has to guess whether you intend the image to be part of the paragraph or to follow it. Depending on what the browser guesses, your image might be preceded by a carriage return, or it might not be. If you're using a style sheet that includes leading (*line-height* in CSS parlance), the browser might attempt to impose that leading on your image—or it may not. These are merely the visual complications that can arise from something as simple as an unclosed tag. The structural ramifications can be more serious.

HTML recommends that you close most tags, but it does not force you to do so, and it does not uniformly recommend tag closure. Images <IMG>, line breaks <br>, and list items <li>, for instance, are never closed in HTML. Most older browsers will accept and attempt to display all kinds of shoddy markup, including markup with unclosed tags that should be closed. And some browsers choke on optionally unclosed tags when, according to the rules of HTML, they should simply process the markup without qualms. For instance, Netscape's 4.0 browser refuses to display web pages with unclosed table rows, even though the rules of HTML 4 state that table rows need not be closed.

This inconsistency in HTML (and browsers) has resulted in sloppy markup on a surprising number of professional sites. Living in filth promotes diseases in human beings; slinging dirty markup can have equally dire effects on the health of the Web, particularly as the medium attempts to move forward.

For this reason, among others, in 2000 the W3C stopped evolving HTML and came up with a new standard called XHTML. Don't sweat it. For a web designer's purposes, XHTML is essentially HTML that forces you to close your tags—including those (such as <img>, <br>, and <li>) that never required such closure before.

We don't want to confuse you with yet another acronym, but the reason XHTML works this way is because XHTML only looks like HTML. It is actually the offspring of XML, which is the standard toward which the Web is evolving. (Technically, XML is a *meta-language*. That is, it is a set of rules for creating languages. HTML is a markup language based on the *SGML* meta-language. XHTML is a reformulation of HTML using *XML* as the meta-language. You don't really need to know this, but it's great at parties, particularly when you're trying to make someone stop talking to you.)

Minding Your <p>'s and q's

Instead of trying to grasp the mind-numbing sentences above, you can think of XML as a much smarter—and necessarily more complex—adaptation of the idea behind HTML; as Homo sapiens to HTML's Cro-Magnon, if you will; as a structured meta-language for containing data, if you must. In XML, you construct your own tags. Not only that, an XML tag "knows" what other tags on the page are doing. An HTML tag does not. Neither does an XHTML tag (at least, not yet). But XHTML follows the rules of XML, chief among them the demand that all code be "well-formed." Tags that close after they open are demonstrating *well-formedness* in XML parlance.

Exploring XML is beyond the scope of this book and is also beyond your immediate job requirements as a web designer. In all probability you will spend the next few years working with HTML or XHTML. In practical terms, working with XHTML is just like working with HTML, except that it enforces cleaner coding practices. HTML doesn't care if you clean up your room. XHTML does.

Looking Ahead

What you need to understand:

- Web designers must learn HTML, even if most of the HTML work at their jobs is performed by web technicians. Web designers who choose not to learn HTML will limit their creative thinking as well as their employability. Frankly, few good web firms would hire a designer who lacks at least basic knowledge of the technology that drives the medium, though many would hire a great designer whose initial HTML skills are merely adequate. Fortunately, HTML is very simple and thus very easy to learn.
- HTML was not created as a design tool, and within the next year or two, we will no longer be using it as one. However...
- ...the Web is in transition, from an anything-goes "tag soup" to a more usable and logical division of labor between technologies that structure content (HTML, XHTML, XML) and companion technologies that format its display (mainly CSS).

When you begin working at a web shop, you or your coworkers will likely be formatting your pages in HTML (or XHTML) to make them compatible with late 1990s browsers. You will use CSS as well, but initially only in limited ways (more about that in Chapter 10). Soon, CSS will do more and more of the design work, and HTML and its successors will be used as the Web's creators originally intended.

Directory Assistance

On the Web, files are referenced by Uniform Resource Locators (URLs) like this one:

http://www.populi.com/index.html

These URLs are to cyberspace what street addresses are to the real world—no two addresses are exactly the same.

UNIX was used to serve most sites at the dawning of the Web, and consequently, URLs follow the conventions of the UNIX Operating System (for instance, URLs are case-sensitive because UNIX is case-sensitive). UNIX is still used to serve heaps of sites due to its stability and its deep roots in the history of the Internet.

Other popular web-serving operating systems include Windows NT and, increasingly, Linux. Linux is a free, open-source version of UNIX. Macs also can serve websites, though most companies prefer to host on UNIX or NT because these platforms were designed for the job. That may change somewhat now that Apple has unveiled Mac OSX—its next-generation operating system with UNIX underpinnings.

In UNIX, slashes separate directory names from each other and from document names, and all web servers follow these conventions.

The names of web documents (including images, movies, and audio files) generally end in a three- or four- character abbreviation that clues the web server (and the browser) as to what they are (and thus, how they should be handled). HTML documents end in .html (or sometimes .htm); JPEG images end in .jpg (portrait.jpg); Flash files end in .swf (grandioseintro.swf); and so on.

All web-serving platforms follow these conventions in naming. Windows 3.1 is limited to three-letter abbreviations, so .htm is used on that platform. Few sites are served from Windows 3.1, however, and you are astronomically unlikely to encounter Windows 3.1 servers in your professional career—at least in the United States, Canada, and Europe.

Apache is a powerful web-serving platform with many conventions that designers follow even if they don't know why they're doing so. For instance, at the root level (www.populi.com), if you include a document titled index.html, that document will open automatically when the visitor types www.populi.com. This is why the ads can say "Visit www.spamulator.com" instead of "Visit www.spamulator.com/index.html." This is also why, in writing code, you can save bandwidth with URL references such as:

```
<a href="http://www.nostril.com/">
```

Instead of:

```
<a href="http://www.nostril.com/index.html">
```

It's also why you can reference internal files in this way:

```
Visit the <a href="contact/">CONTACT</a> page.
```

Instead of:

```
Visit the <a href="contact/index.html">CONTACT</a> page.
```

Or:

```
Visit the <a href="http://www.nostril.com/contact/index.html">CONTACT</a> page.
```

The systems administrator can override this default if she desires, allowing welcome.html (for instance) to serve as the default opening document. In fact, welcome.html was the default opening document on many systems before index.html gained ascendancy. The default page at www.zeldman.com is still welcome.html. (The old CERN server used Welcome.htm, complete with initial caps.)

These conventions vary by system. Internet Information Server (IIS), on Windows, uses default.html or default.asp. Again, the systems administrator is free to override any such default. (Pickledherring.html could be set up as the default document if desired.) If your server or systems administrator prefers a particular filename, you'll be told about it on the job.

Getting Started

There are plenty of books about HTML, and heaps of free online resources. After all, what better place than the Web itself to learn about the markup language with which the Web is created?

The beginner's tutorials at Project Cool's Gettingstarted.net (www.gettingstarted.net) and Jay Boersma's Web Work (www.ECNet.Net/users/gallery/webwork/www.html) can teach anyone, even your Uncle Phil, how to apply basic HTML tags to create simple web pages. A more detailed tutorial, Ian S. Graham's "Introduction to HTML," may be found at www.utoronto.ca/webdocs/HTMLdocs/NewHTML/htmlindex.html, and our own "Ask Doctor Web" (www.zeldman.com/askdrweb/), online since 1995, provides a readable overview on HTML and related technologies along with the psychology of web use and similar topics. After you're further along, you are sure to enjoy Lance Arthur's Design-o-Rama at www.glassdog.com/design-o-rama/, a wittily written treatise that includes a good introduction to frames and JavaScript.

These are but five of many such resources online. Most of these resources are noncommercial in nature. They exist only to share knowledge. We told you the Web was different, didn't we? (On the Web, this would be a hyperlink back to Chapter 2, "Designing for the Medium.")

Being noncommercial, such resources might not always be completely up-to-date. For instance, parts of Ask Dr Web show their age visually, and in places, the advice offered might not be up to current standards. Nevertheless, they are all excellent places for those who don't know their HTML from their elbow to begin absorbing vital knowledge. We urge you to visit them all before moving on to the following more advanced resources.

For a superb, hand-holding tutorial that walks you through the entire realm of HTML, you can't beat W3C member Dave Raggett's "Getting Started With HTML" (www.w3.org/MarkUp/Guide/). It's simple and complete; it touches on CSS, JavaScript, and Image maps as well as HTML; and it comes from a definitive source. (Raggett has been closely involved with the development of HTML since the Web's earliest days.)

The Web Design Group's "Web Authoring FAQ" (www.htmlhelp.com/faq/html/all.html) is yet another fine source of HTML knowledge. It even answers questions such as "How can I get my own domain name?" "Where can I announce my site?" and the ever-popular "How can I make a frame with a vertical scrollbar but without a horizontal scrollbar?"

After you've gotten a handle on these basics, you'll be able to learn from the fine tutorials and articles at Webmonkey (hotwired.lycos.com/webmonkey/), Builder.com (home.cnet.com/webbuilding/), and our own A List Apart (www.alistapart.com). Along with technical exercises and techniques, these three resources offer a bevy of useful tips, tricks, opinions, and (best of all) insights into the changing nature of web code, design, and content.

You'll be able also to visit the W3C's "HTML 4.01 Specification" (www.w3.org/TR/REC-html40/) without experiencing heart palpitations. This spec is the Mothership, though it can leave a neophyte feeling somewhat shaky. Also worth getting to know is "The Bare Bones Guide to HTML" (www.werbach.com/barebones/) and Ron Woodall's HTML Compendium (www.htmlcompendium.org). These three resources provide a head-to-toe anatomy of the HTML language. Forget an HTML tag? Not sure how one is supposed to work? Consult these guides.

But don't start with them. You'll just upset yourself. HTML is simple, but viewing dozens of pages of HTML tags and their scientific-sounding definitions can daunt the staunchest heart. Begin at the beginner's sites, which are written in civilian-friendly language. And learn to do one other essential thing:

View Source

Most of us learned HTML, not from each other's tutorials, but by studying the markup with which others' web pages were built. Imitation is the sincerest form of theft, and every one of us started out by copying and pasting other people's markup, changing it around, and seeing what happened. Before we discuss the ethics, here's how to get started:

When you find a web page you like, select **View, Source** from your browser's menu bar, and save the file to your hard drive. (In Netscape, choose **View, Page Source.**) Reopen it in a basic text editor (such as Simple Text or Write) or an HTML editor (such as Barebones Software's BBEdit, Optima Software's PageSpinner, or Allaire's HomeSite) and stare at the code until it stares back. Plug your own words in between the HTML tags, save your work, and open the file in your favorite web browser. Result: your first (offline) web page.

Unless the layout you've stolen is extremely basic, you should keep it offline. You don't want to upload what you steal. You just want to learn and move on. Here are the links for the editors mentioned previously:

- **Bare Bones Software BBEdit.** www.bbedit.com (for Mac OS)

- **Optima-System Page Spinner.** www.optima-system.com/pagespinner/ (for Mac OS)
- **Allaire HomeSite.** www.allaire.com/products/homesite/ (for Windows)

A Netscape Bonus

In addition to View Source, Netscape Navigator's browser includes a nifty **File** menu option called **View Page Info**. Choose it, and the entire page will be deconstructed for you in a new window, image by image. Beside each image's name you'll find its complete URL (you remember...its address on the Web), its file size, how many colors it contains, and whether or not it uses transparency. Click the link beside each image, and the image will load in the bottom of the window.

The way this works is not immediately intuitive; it was laid out by engineers, not by designers or usability experts. But once you get the hang of it, you'll find View Page Info a useful tool for understanding how other people have created web pages. IE does not offer this feature.

The Mother of All View Source Tricks

Viewing source is all well and good, but what's even better is viewing that source code in your text editor of choice. That way, you can continue to work in your chosen HTML editing environment instead of dragging and dropping (or cutting and pasting) between different software programs. You also will have less clutter on your screen. And if your editing program wraps text, you won't have to cope with the endless lines of markup that browsers often spit out by default in their built-in View Source windows.

Doin' it in Netscape

On the Mac: Pay a visit to your Netscape Options menu. Under **Options, Applications, View Source**, switch from the default program to your HTML editing program of choice (for instance, BBEdit or PageSpinner). Now when you view the source of any of your existing web pages, the resulting HTML document will automatically open in your preferred HTML program, ready for further editing. Pretty nifty. Similarly, when you View Source on someone else's site, the code will open in your HTML editor of choice, tempting you to steal other people's work and condemn your soul to Hell.

In Windows: First of all, you need to install the entire Communicator program, not just the Navigator component. From Composer (the extremely limited semi-WYSIWYG "page creation" tool bundled with Netscape's browser), choose Edit then Preferences. Click Composer and register your external editor for HTML Source. There. That really wasn't so bad.

Doin' it in Internet Explorer

First, open Explorer's Preferences. Go to File Helpers and click Add.

In a new, blank dialog box, type **Source Code** under Description, **.html** under Extension, and **source/html** under MIME type.

In the File Type area, click Browse. It sounds as if you're about to browse the Web, but you're not. You are actually navigating your hard drive to locate your web editor of choice. Select it, and the File type and File creator areas will be filled in automatically.

You're not done yet. Under Handling, choose Post-Process With Application. Hit the second Browse button, select your web editor one more time, and then hit OK. Then stand on your head and recite the Cub Scout pledge. Just kidding about the pledge thing.

Now when you View Source, the code will open in your favorite web editor. Not push-button easy, but it works—and you only have to do this once.

We figure these tips alone justify the cost of buying this book, and we expect you to dog-ear this page and fondle it quietly when you think no one is watching.

Absolutely Speaking, It's All Relative

HTML links can work several ways. The simplest link (and often the easiest to maintain) is the relative link.

Two files reside in the same directory:

```
index.html
thankyou.html
```

A relative link from index.html to thankyou.html looks like this:

```
There is a special message for you on our <a href="thankyou.html">Thank You</a> page.
```

By contrast, an absolute link might look like this:

```
There is a special message for you on our <a href="http://www.ourcompany.com/
thankyou.html">Thank You</a> page.
```

Or even this:

```
There is a special message for you on our <a href="http://www.ourcompany.com/
customerrelations/special/thankyou.html">Thank You</a> page.
```

These are called <ABSOLUTE> links because they refer to an absolute, concrete location in web space. (Well, as real or concrete as "web space" gets, anyway.)

When two pages reside in the same directory, there is no need to use absolute links. Using relative links lowers your character count (you can get rid of http://www.ourcompany.com/customerrelations/special/), and that, in turn, conserves bandwidth.

Relative links are easy to maintain on simple sites (though they become fiendishly complex as a site grows and uses more and more directories). For instance, if all images are kept in a directory called Images, the URL to an image file might read like so:

```
<IMG SCR="images/image.gif">
```

We have left out the image's height, width, and <ALT> attribute to simplify the presentation of this idea. However, as previously mentioned, it is always important to include an image's height and width to help some browsers display the layout more quickly. And, as also previously mentioned, it is essential to include <ALT> attributes so that those with visual disabilities or those who surf with images turned off will have some idea of the image's function.

The more complicated the site's directory structure, the likelier relative links are to require debugging. For instance, the reader is here:

```
somesite.com/julyissue/index.html
```

And you wish to direct her back to the index page at:

```
somesite.com/index.html
```

The URL would read as follows:

```
<a href="../index.html">Back</a> to the Index Page.
```

The two dots (..) preceding the slash mean "go up one directory level before locating this file."

With more directories, you have more and more complex links:

```
<a href="../../../../index.html">Back</a> to the Index Page.
```

This can quickly lead to madness. Are you stuck writing out full, absolute URLs? Heck, no.

Instead, you can use a shorthand form of absolute linking to retain the advantages of relative URLs (portability, low bandwidth) while maintaining the clarity of absolute URLs.

Absolute URLs also can be written like so:

```
/index.html
```

Where the slash represents "root directory."

By using this method, if you wished to move from the July Issue index page up one directory to the root level index page, your URL would look like this:

```
Return to the <a href="/index.html">front page</a>.
```

Or like this (which is even smaller and doesn't hardcode the default directory index filename):

```
Return to the <a href="/">front page</a>.
```

And reversing the direction, a link from /index.html to /julyissue/index.html would look like this:

```
Read the <a href="/julyissue/">July issue</a>.
```

Unfortunately, absolute URLs of this kind cannot be tested offline. You must load these pages to your web server to make certain the links work correctly.

By contrast, relative links work on or offline, which enables you to keep one or more fully functioning web sites on your hard drive.

That was relatively painless, wasn't it? Absolutely.

What Is Good Markup?

Technically, good HTML is code that validates—that is, code that fully complies with current W3C standards and contains no errors. To make sure your HTML validates, run it through the W3C validator at validator.w3.org, a free service from those wonderful people who brought you the Web. For more on this topic, see "HTML Standards Compliance: Why Bother?" in the Web Developer's Virtual Library (WDVL.com/Authoring/HTML/Standards/).

For the validator to work properly, you need to include a <DOCTYPE>. This is a simple declaration that specifies what kind of HTML (or other markup language) you are attempting to write. For instance:

```
<!DOCTYPE HTML PUBLIC "-//W3C//DTD HTML 4.01//EN"
"http://www.w3.org/TR/html4/strict.dtd">
```

This declares the document to be HTML 4.01 strict. HTML 4.01 strict emphasizes structure over presentation and balks at "deprecated elements" such as background colors in table cells, <FONT FACE>, <FRAMES>, and other stuff we're supposed to do with CSS instead of in HTML.

Newer browsers such as IE5/Mac, Netscape 6, and Mozilla render HTML 4.01 strict documents according to web standards and use a "quirks" mode for older or unspecified document types to emulate rendering bugs in older browsers. The engineers responsible for these browsers applied these techniques to offer full standards support for new sites without breaking old sites that were written to the quirks of the companies' older, nonstandards-oriented browsers. Those older browsers generally ignore the <DOCTYPE> declaration completely, but the validator requires it.

```
<!DOCTYPE HTML PUBLIC "-//W3C//DTD HTML 4.01 Transitional//EN"
"http://www.w3.org/TR/html4/loose.dtd">
```

This <DOCTYPE> declares that the web page is written in HTML 4.01 transitional markup, which tolerates deprecated presentational HTML attributes (<FONT FACE>, for example) so that such documents will render correctly in older, less standards-compliant browsers. IE5/Mac, Netscape 6, Mozilla and IE 6 will render these documents the same way older browsers would. This affords web designers the ability to support older and newer browsers while making the transition from a buggy Web to one that relies on standards. (See the section, "The 18-Month Pregnancy" in Chapter 2 to understand why a transitional or interim period is accommodated in this way.)

Other <DOCTYPE>s include HTML 3.2, HTML 4.01 Frameset, and XHTML Strict and Transitional.

What Is Sensible Markup?

Conceptually, good markup is code that gets out of its own way and helps communicate your message in the simplest, most intuitive way possible—just like good design.

Beginning writers use too many adjectives. Beginning designers use too many shapes, fonts, and colors. Beginning HTML authors often fall so in love with the medium that they forget to communicate. Instead, they cram every page with embedded MIDI (music) files, pointlessly scrolling JavaScript messages, huge full-color photographs, animated GIFs (flames and dripping blood are especially popular), and blinking and moving text, often in a dozen different font faces and sizes.

That is bad design, and (we think) bad markup, even if it validates—which is pretty unlikely because folks attracted to dripping blood animations tend not to spend much time learning about web standards.

Figure 8.1

This site for the Web Standards Project contains almost no graphics. The shapes and colors are created using nothing more than HTML and CSS. It is possible to fill the screen with color and content without wasting bandwidth on images. As a bonus, the code validates (www.webstandards.org).

HTML AS A DESIGN TOOL

Though this won't always be the case, one of the beautiful things about HTML (and eventually, CSS instead) is that it can be used as a powerful design tool—a design tool that loads instantly. No images are required; there are no fancy plug-ins and no worries about every user having the latest browser.

Consider the front page of The Web Standards Project (www.webstandards.org). Aside from one large Seymour-Chwast-like illustration, the rest of the front page is designed entirely with HTML and CSS. Now view the source.

An HTML color in the <BODY> tag defines the entire background. The content grid is made up of a table, and the grid areas and background colors are defined with table cell colors.

The content area is enclosed within a black outline created with one line of CSS. Originally, the same effect was created by wrapping one HTML table inside another.

CSS is used to create the typography and leading.

Creating a layout like this in Photoshop, cutting its elements into pieces, and assembling those pieces via HTML, would have resulted in a large web page composed of many small files that would take a long time to download. (And if the visitor had images turned off, the visual effect would be lost.)

Creating the layout in HTML and CSS means that the page loads almost instantly, no matter how slow the visitor's connection may be. And the layout is backward compatible with browsers dating back to Netscape 3 (a 1997 browser), although the CSS formatting will be lost in that browser. Actually, the site is viewable in any browser. Older browsers will lose the design branding effects, but the content will still be readily accessible.

Note that this is a transitional web design strategy. It respects bandwidth by using web technology (instead of image files) to create visual and branding effects—but at the cost of relying on deprecated presentational HTML attributes. Most of these effects can be generated in CSS alone, with HTML serving simply as the structural container of content. This is what the W3C recommends, and this is the way we will build all sites in the near future and forever after. (We're doing it at alistapart.com.)

However, as we mentioned in Chapter 2, old browsers that do a poor job at understanding CSS are still widely used in the market we serve. And as you'll see in Chapter 10, browsers that stumble over CSS don't simply render it incorrectly. They can actually crash and burn. For this reason, as you begin your career in web design, you will undoubtedly be using HTML tables and other deprecated presentational HTML attributes to control your web layouts and visual effects. Thus there is value in learning how to do this in ways that minimize wasted bandwidth and comply with the letter (though not the spirit) of W3C standards. The lessons you learn in building sites this way will apply equally well when you are free to control your site designs exclusively with CSS.

Other sites that use HTML or XHTML as a creative design tool (abetted by CSS):

- www.glish.com (designed by Eric Costello)
- www.harrumph.com (designed by Heather Champ)
- www.assembler.org (designed by Brent Gustaffson)
- www.kottke.org (designed by Jason Kottke)
- www.blogger.com (designed by Derek Powazek)
- a.jaundicedeye.com/weblog/ (designed by Steven Champeon)
- www.zeldman.com (designed by Zeldman)
- www.alistapart.com (designed by Zeldman)

Use View Source to see how these sites use HTML table cells and table cell colors, CSS fonts, leading, margins, and background images to create full-

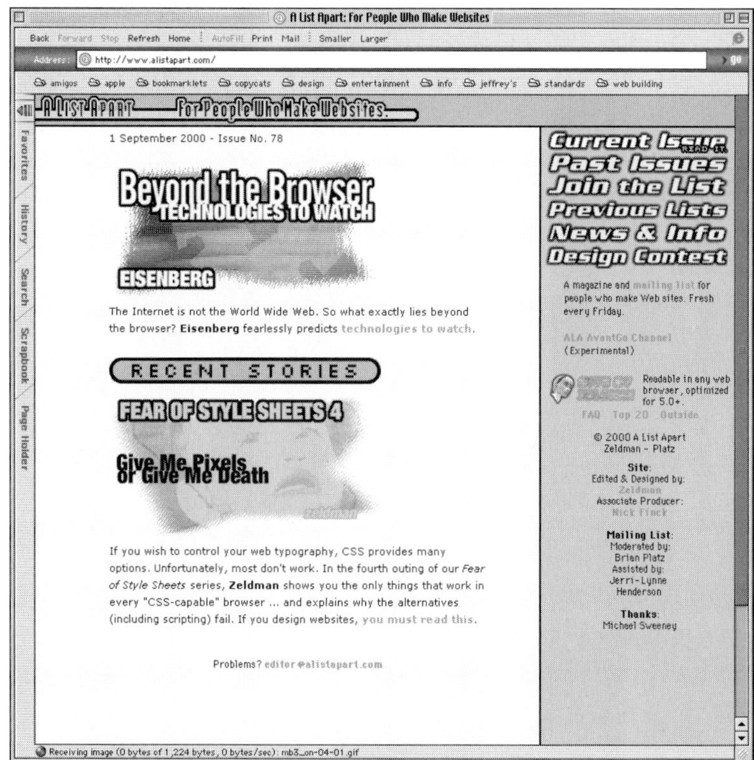

Figure 8.2

This site, though colorful, contains few graphics. Big color sections are created with CSS and HTML <DIV>s. The technique facilitates Liquid Design, reduces bandwidth, and makes the site more accessible (www.alistapart.com).

fledged visual experiences using nothing more than code (and a few low-bandwidth images).

Plug-ins and Tables and Frames, Oh My!

In the transitional Web, designers use HTML tables to lay out pages, as just described (with additional commentary and how-to-do-it type verbiage to come in the next chapter). We also use <FRAMES>, a Netscape "extension" to HTML which has temporarily made it into the HTML 4 Transitional standard but which will eventually go the way of the Dodo bird.

Frames are nothing more than pages within pages, for example:

```
<FRAMESET COLS="80,2,*" frameborder="no" border="0" framespacing="0">
<FRAME SRC="nav.html" NAME="nav" marginwidth="0" marginheight="0"
noresize scrolling="auto">
<FRAME SRC="black.html" NAME="black" marginwidth="0" marginheight="0" noresize
scrolling="no">
<FRAME SCROLLING=auto SRC="content.html" NAME="content" marginwidth="0"
marginheight="0">
</FRAMESET>
```

In this markup, <FRAMESET> tells the browser that the page contains frames. <COLS> (short for columns) specifies that the frameset contains three columns. The first is 80 pixels wide; the second is 2 pixels wide; and the last fills the remaining width of the browser window.

We also can tell the browser whether or not we want borders on our frames; whether or not each frame should permit the viewer to scroll content; whether or not each frame is user-resizable; and what size margin we'd like on each frame. Because we're designers, we turn margins off entirely (marginwidth="0" marginheight="0") and use CSS or tables to control the margins on each individual frame—each frame, of course, being nothing more than an HTML document (nav.html, black.html, content.html).

We also name each frame for targeting purposes. After all, when visitors click in a menu area, we want the content they've chosen to show up in the content frame—not in the menu frame. Assigning a target name to each frame enables us to write links like <a href="companypolicy.html" target ="content">. Naming also enables us to perform JavaScript stunts, which are mainly useful for avoiding the maddening usability hazards associated with frames, such as the following.

The Frames of Hazard

Through a search engine such as Google.com, Aunt Moira finds one of our client's content pages. Unfortunately, that's all she finds—the naked content page, immodestly lacking its associated navigational menu frame. Aunt Moira has no idea where she is, where she can go next, who created the site, or even how to find its home page.

We always had it in for Aunt Moira, who never failed to point out when we had gained weight or burst out in pimples, but our client would like her to be able to use the site. Because we have named our frames and because the good Lord (well, actually, Netscape) gave us JavaScript, we can instruct the browser to load named frames if they are not already visible on the page.

Thus when Aunt Moira (the old biddy) blunders her way into companypolicy.html, the browser is instructed to load the missing frames. Code like this would appear on each HTML document that made up the frame, though not on the frameset document itself:

```
<!-- This one makes sure the left nav is loaded. -->
<script LANGUAGE="JavaScript">
    <!--
    if (top == self) self.location.href = "frameset.html";
            // -->
</script>
```

Such a script tells the browser to make sure that frameset.html has loaded. If it has not loaded—if Aunt Moira's browser is about to show a confusing single frame no more illuminating than a single puzzle piece—the browser gathers and assembles the missing pieces before the dear old thing has a chance to notice that anything is amiss. We don't want to get ahead of ourselves by discussing JavaScript in the HTML chapter. Suffice to say, the need to rely on such scripts points out *some* of the hazards of HTML <FRAMES>, and helps explain why they are on their way out.

Everything we now do with frames (and more) we can do with CSS, which is standards-compliant and avoids the usability and accessibility hazards <FRAMES> engender. But to switch from <FRAMES> to CSS, we must wait for some browsers to improve their CSS support and all users to upgrade to these better browsers.

Please Frame Safely

Some old browsers do not understand frames. Neither do text and audio browsers. Nor do Palm Pilots and web-enabled telephones. To accommodate these devices and browsers, your frameset should include a <NOFRAMES> tag. Browsers that can't read frames can read the plain HTML that you insert between opening <NOFRAMES> and closing </NOFRAMES> tags. Copy the content that appears in your frames, paste it between the <NOFRAMES> tags, and you are on your way to creating a site everyone can access, regardless of their browser's capabilities.

Framing Your Art

Despite these hazards and hassles, frames can be quite useful to web designers. Frames allow you to present a menu bar that stays in place while content frames change. They also enable you to create layouts where, for instance, your content will always appear in the center of the screen, regardless of the visitor's monitor size. View Marc Klein's Creative Republic (www.creative-republic.com) to see this in action, and then view the source to see how Marc crafted his framesets.

One other maddening thing about frames is that though Netscape invented them, it never got them exactly right. When you tell the browser to make your menu bar 25 pixels tall, you may get 25 pixels in Netscape 4, but you're just as likely to get 32 or 16. If this suggests that you're better off avoiding frames whenever possible, we won't argue.

In addition to tables and frames, web designers use applets and multimedia files to create designs that are frankly unimaginable in print. We will discuss those in Chapter 12, "Beyond Text/Pictures." Don't skip ahead, we're watching.

Figure 8.3

Creatively used frames keep design elements fixed in the center of the screen, whether the visitor's monitor is large...

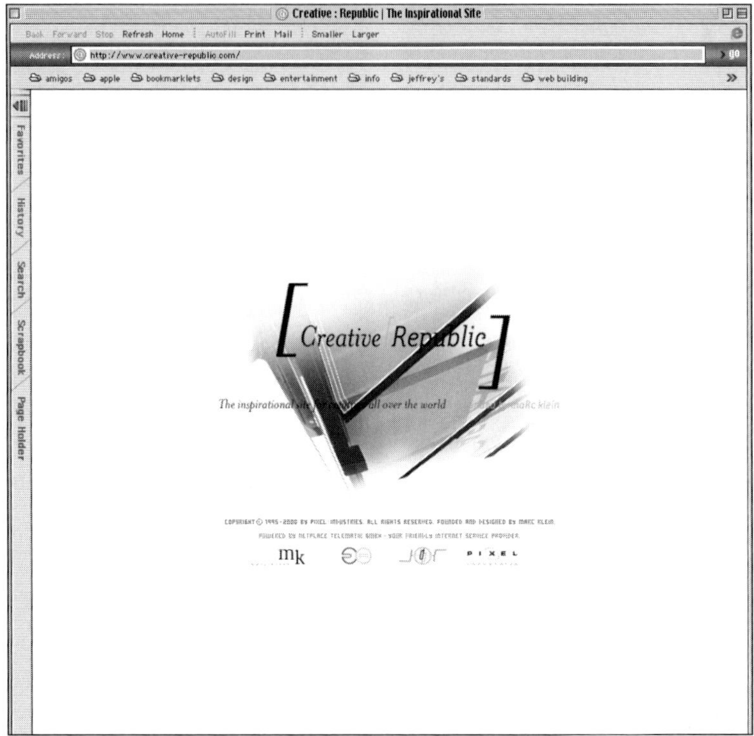

Figure 8.4

...or small. Designer: Marc Klein (www.creativerepublic.com).

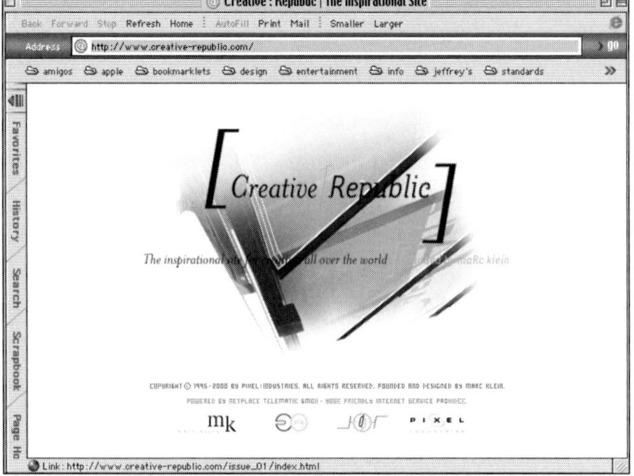

<META> <META> Hiney Ho!

Though <META> tags have many purposes, web designers and developers most often use them for one of two reasons:

- Accommodating search engines
- Reloading pages or forwarding visitors to an updated page

Regardless of the application, <META> tags are placed in the <HEAD> section of HTML markup. That is, all <META> elements show up between the <HEAD> and the </HEAD> tags. Now let's wrap our own <HEADS> around them to see how this all works:

Search Me

When Aunt Moira (the old battleaxe) enlists the help of a search engine to find a topic or subject, one way in which the search engine might sort data is through <META> tags. Some search engines compare search words with <META> descriptions, and they return the web pages that provide the best matches, as in the following:

```
<META NAME= "author" CONTENT= "your name">
<META NAME= "description" CONTENT= "page description">
<META NAME= "keywords" CONTENT= "keywords that apply to your page">
<META NAME= "generator" CONTENT= "the editor you used to create your page">
<META NAME= "copyright" CONTENT= "date of copyright">
<META NAME= "expires" CONTENT= "expiration date">
```

Most corporate and business-to-business sites will include only the <DESCRIPTION>, <KEYWORD>, and <COPYRIGHT> tags. After all, AT&T does not need its customers to know who designed the site, what tool they used to edit the HTML, or how old (and outdated) the page may be.

Aside from <HTTP-EQUIV> (the widely accepted predecessor to <DOCTYPE>), there is no reliable standard for <META>. Most search engines rarely use them (Google, for instance, ignores them). Those such as Altavista and Hotbot, which once relied on them extensively, pay them less and less heed as time goes by. Good <TITLE> tags and good, descriptive page copy are more effective at scoring with search engines and directories.

In spite of everything we've said, some search engines and directories do pay attention to these tags, and it sometimes falls to the designer to write them. So let's look at some good and bad ones. Here is a good one:

```
<META NAME= "description" CONTENT= "Widgets.com builds reliable widgets for the lubrication industry. As the American Midwest's largest developer and supplier of industrial-strength widgetry, we offer a product line of 2,000 parts as well as custom products built to your specifications. Standard products ship in 48 hours in the Continental U.S., and within three business days to lubricant concerns in Europe, Asia, and Africa.">

<META NAME= "keywords" CONTENT= "widgets, lubricants, lubrication, industry, U.S., midwest, developer, supplier, industrial strength, widgetry, 2,000, standard, parts, custom, product, development, shipping, 48 hours, Canda, Europe, Asia, Africa">

<META NAME= "copyright" CONTENT= "12 January 2001">
```

And here is a bad use of <META> tags:

```
<META NAME= "description" CONTENT= "Welcome to our home page on the World Wide Web! We are happy to serve you. Please do not hesitate to call on our reliable staff if we may serve you better in any way, shape, or form. This site is under construction. Some links may not work and some pages that we are going to make later have not shown up yet because we are still arguing about them in the boardroom. All our products are proudly made in the good old U.S. of A. We are a good company that has serious social concerns. Kids, stay in school. Hugs, not drugs. Have a nice day.">

<META NAME= "keywords" CONTENT= "welcome, to, our, home, page, which, is, under, construction, serving, you, proudly, since, 1955, but, not, the, website, which, as, we, mentioned, is, under, construction">

<META NAME= "author" CONTENT= "your name here">

<META NAME= "generator" CONTENT= "Hot Dog Pro">
```

The good <META> tags help search engines hone in on what the site actually has to offer. The bad <META> tags consign the site to the dung heap, where it will never be found by any living soul—unless they are searching for serve + kids + drugs.

Raw-elbowed marketing idiots, who are legion on the Internet, used to try to "upgrade" their search engine rankings by repeating certain keywords—a practice referred to as *keyword spamming.*

```
<META NAME= "keywords" CONTENT= "widgets, widgets, widgets, widgets, widgets, widgets, widgets, widgets, widgets, widgets, widgets, widgets, widgets, widgets, widgets, widgets, widgets, widgets, widgets, widgets, widgets, widgets, widgets, widgets, widgets,
```

widgets, widgets">

Needless to say, this no longer works, and if anything, you and the widgets you rode in on will be dropped to the very bottom of any halfway relevant search—or kicked out of the database altogether. Kids, don't try this at home (page).

As we say, most search engines ignore <META> tags, so if you want your site to be found, focus on developing relevant body text and <TITLE> tags. "Welcome to our home page on the World Wide Web" is not relevant text. "Widgets.com builds reliable widgets for the lubrication industry" is relevant, if unsavory, text. <TITLE> tags and body text are weighted more heavily than <META> tags, even by search engines that consider all three (<META> tags, <TITLE> tags, and body text). This is because it is easy for liars to lard their <META> tags with exciting buzzwords that have little to do with what the site actually offers. *Body text*—text seen by visitors—is therefore given precedence over the wishful thinking that goes on inside the <META> tag.

Everything we've just told you is probably outdated and irrelevant by now. Visit www.searchenginewatch.com to get the latest specifics on search engine ranking.

At a bad shop, <META> tags (and indeed, sometimes, body text) will be written at the last minute by a recent college graduate with no experience in marketing, communications, or the Web. When shopping for a job, don't simply judge the company by its graphic design. Peek under the hood for evidence of a caring, intelligent environment—or a sweatshop that bangs work out with little regard for its success or failure in the marketplace.

Wow, we've just saved you from taking a really bad job. This book is turning out to be worth every penny you paid for it, isn't it? You ought to buy copies for all your friends, and save them from taking bad jobs, too.

Another type of <META> tag (the <META HTTP-EQUIV>) does another type of job and is worth mentioning.

Take a (Re)Load Off

There are times where you want a page to hesitate and then reload. Though this may sound like a tricky process, <META HTTP-EQUIV> tags make it barnyard-simple:

```
<META HTTP-EQUIV= "REFRESH" CONTENT= "x; URL=http://www.widgets.com/">
```

In this code example, <x> represents the number of seconds before the refresh or reload occurs, and the URL refers to the page currently being viewed. (Obviously, you would replace <x> with <10>, <6>, or however many seconds you wish to have elapse before the page reloads itself. There is no limit, to our knowledge, on how many seconds that may be. The browser tells time via the operating system. Uncanny, is it not?) Given that the visitor is already at www.widgets.com, why spell out the full URL instead of a relative URL (such as index.html)? Trust us on this one. (If you don't trust us, using a relative URL will usually work, but can be problematic if the page you're refreshing gets moved or renamed, which web pages often do. Full URLs make for better, safer maintenance in this instance.)

You also can use this technique to forward the visitor from an old, outdated page to a shiny new one:

```
<META HTTP-EQUIV= "REFRESH" CONTENT= "x;
URL=http://www.widgets.com/newindex.html">
```

Many HTML experts, being spoilsports who live in Ivory Towers and probably never laugh even at really funny jokes like the one about the traveling salesman, the farmer, the hippie, and the bus driver, disapprove of this entire procedure. They recommend that you forward web users to new pages (if need be) by using JavaScript. However, this <META> tag technique does work, even with old, non-JavaScript-capable browsers.

A Comment About <COMMENTS>

In your career as a web designer, you will sometimes create entire sites by yourself from scratch. Most of the time, though, you will be working with a team. Occasionally, you will inherit an existing site that needs to be redesigned or updated. At other times, you will be creating a site for someone else to update. All these situations are best served if you *comment the code* as you write it. Referring once again to the code used earlier in this chapter:

```
<!-- Begin menu bar. -->
<table border="0" cellpadding="0" cellspacing="0" align="center">
<tr>
<td>
<a href="reading.html"><img  src="reading.gif" width="20" height="20" border="0"
alt="Reading"></a>
</td>
<td>
<a href="writing.html"><img  src="writing.gif" width="20" height="20" border="0"
alt="Writing"></a>
</td>
<td>
<a href="arithmetic.html"><img  src="arithmetic.gif" width="20" height="20" border="0"
alt="Arithmetic"></a>
</td>
</tr>
</table>
<!-- End menu bar. -->
```

<Begin menu bar> and <End menu bar> are the comments that help you (or a teammate or successor) figure out what was intended by all that wacky HTML. They are always enclosed within <!-- special brackets --> so that they will not be displayed on the web page. Even if you routinely work alone (say, as a freelancer), comments will help you find your way when you return to an HTML document you haven't looked at for six months. Professional web designers always comment their markup.

In Chapter 2 we mentioned that designers could save bandwidth by removing white space from their HTML documents. We also mentioned that most of us refrain from this practice because it interferes with the need to continually update existing web documents. Comments exist to facilitate that need. No further comment.

WYSIWYG, My Aunt Moira's Left Foot

We've all seen the ads: "Create web pages without learning a single HTML tag!" We've also seen ads that tell us how to lose weight while eating candy bars all day long. Strangely enough, we know no one who's lost weight that way.

Today's "What You See Is What You Get"(WYSIWYG) programs are far more powerful than the early, lame-o programs that gave WYSIWYG a bad name. But most professional web designers continue to use text-based web editors. Why? In a word, control. In four words, to avoid bad markup.

Code of Dishonor

Though we hope to see this change soon, nearly all WYSIWYG editors tend to write bloated (and often invalid) HTML markup. To make sure that every browser—even one that's five years old—will be able to display your page as the program thinks you want it to be seen, these programs will grind out all kinds of unnecessary workaround markup, adding unsightly flab to every web page.

Other programs, notably one famous one we won't mention for fear of lawsuits, tend to generate markup that works only in one browser. Coincidentally, this browser is made by the company that also makes the WYSIWYG program. Is this just bad design or an insidious marketing ploy? Ask their attorneys.

Beyond the twin plagues of page-swelling bloat and browser-specific "HTML," there is the problem of artificial limitations imposed upon you by the designers of any WYSIWYG program you may use. Unless you work the code yourself, you cannot expand its capabilities or explore new creative terrain.

Citizen Kane was not shot with an autofocus lens. Great web pages are not built by using defaults. Use the markup, or you'll be forced to depend on the kindness of strangers (otherwise known as software companies), to determine what you can and cannot do with your site.

With an autofocus camera, the man in the striped hat will be in perfect focus; too bad if you wanted to focus on the bird in the bush. Likewise, even with an advanced WYSIWYG editor, your options as a designer will always be limited. Comparing WYSIWYG editors to autofocus cameras is probably unfair—to the cameras.

Yes, these WYSIWYG programs are getting much better. Yes, a substantial number of pros do use them, particularly to rough out web pages quickly. But these pros always end up revising the end product by hand.

WYS Is Not Necessarily WYG

With a WYSIWYG tool, if you slap an image down 30 pixels to the right of another image, it stays 30 pixels away, even if you want it to move as the user's window widens. If you drop an image onto the exact center of the WYSIWYG editor page, you might think the image is "centered," but it's not—it is stuck in an exact location, which may bear no relation whatsoever to the relative center of your users' respective browser windows. (This is also the problem with using more advanced WYSIWYG editors to generate DHTML pages or CSS-based layouts. But we'll get to those issues in time.)

WYSIWYG editors give you a false sense of control and a false sense of the Web. As explained in Chapter 2, the Web is not fixed like a printed page. It is fluid and variable and should be designed for accordingly. The tightly-rendered page that looks great in your WYSIWYG editor may look terrible on Aunt Moira's monitor because your default fonts are larger than hers, or she doesn't have the same fonts installed that you do, or just because she's a silly thing who is going to leave her money to her cats, not you.

Suppose we intend to create a three-column layout with an image in the center column. Using HTML, this is no problem—we write a three-column table, set its borders to 0, and in a few moments, we are done. If we've used relative widths when constructing our table (<width="33%"> for example, instead of <width="200">) the design will reflow to accommodate any user's monitor, as discussed back in Chapter 2.

We can do the same thing with CSS, and before this book reaches its second edition, that's what we'll all be doing. With CSS such layouts are faster and easier to achieve, and the resulting web pages render more quickly.

Now let's build the same layout in a WYSIWYG editor. We drag three columns over a grid and place our image in the middle column. Unfortunately, we were two pixels off when we dropped our image, because the program lacks a "snap-to-grid" feature (or we forgot to turn the feature on). What does the program do? It calculates an 18-column cubist mess of code, using <ROWSPANS> and <COLSPANS> to make sure that our mistake gets perfectly rendered.

The program doesn't know that our inexact placement of the image was an accident. The program cannot think; it can only execute, using tortured workarounds to honor our errors as hidden intentions. The result is a slow-to-download, tortuously coded fiasco—one which, after all that absurd markup and lengthy downloading, looks like garbage because the layout is subtly "off."

And of course, it will never reflow to fit each user's monitor just so.

Knowing HTML doesn't make you a web designer any more than knowing your native language makes you a writer. But choosing not to know is senseless. Don't trust the ads. Learn the markup. If you wish to use the better WYSIWYG programs to rough out your layouts, go ahead, but be ready to get in there later and refine your code.

Browser Incompatibilities: Can't We All Just Get Along?

Not only is there no WSY in WYSIWYG web editors, there's no guarantee that any two browsers will display your page the same way or even that your page will work in every browser. Even if you write perfectly valid and standards-compliant code, old browsers are not standards-compliant, and the dream of "write once, publish everywhere" has not yet been attained.

Moreover, even on that great day when all browsers fully support W3C standards, extensive platform and hardware differences (as described extensively in Chapter 2) mean that the Web will remain evanescent and unfixed: a little different with each browser, in each monitor, and on each operating system. That kind of incompatibility is perfectly okay—there's nothing we can do about it anyway. Incompatibilities that result in page failures are not okay.

One thing you can do is author in accordance with commonly supported web standards instead of to "nifty new features" that work only in one browser. By definition, you will be including more people if you avoid proprietary, browser-specific markup. Given that support for these standards varies widely and browsers may legitimately differ in the way they interpret some standards, you and your company's Quality Assurance (QA) team will spend much time testing designs on a variety of browsers and platforms. (See Chapter 7, "Riding the Project Life Cycle," if you skipped it earlier.)

Another thing you can do is visit The Web Standards Project (www.webstandards.org), read our Mission Statement (www.webstandards.org/mission.html), and use the Project's Resources section to learn more about standards (as well as incompatibilities). (In Chapter 10 we'll talk about CSS incompatibilities and how to work around them.)

Publish That Sucker!

After you have created a website, how do you publish it? You publish it by sending your files and directories to the web server. This is done by means of an FTP program, so called because it uses the File Transfer Protocol (FTP) to do its work. Fetch is one common FTP program for the Mac; Interarchy (the FTP program formerly known as Anarchie) is another; and Panic Software's Transmit (www.panic.com/transmit/) is a third—and the most Mac-like. We still use Fetch, which has not been updated since the Pleistocene era, because the crusty old tool makes us feel that we are in UNIX, and that makes us feel all hardcore and stuff. WinFTP and CuteFTP are common Windows FTP programs.

To use an FTP program, you open it, type in the FTP address, user name, and password, and upload your files by dragging them from the open window on your desktop to the open FTP window. You can drag and drop hundreds or even thousands of files at once.

Note that unlike the Mac OS, an FTP server will not warn you if you are about to overwrite your files. Nor is there a comforting "Are you sure?" dialog box, such as in Windows. (Well, maybe the "Are you sure?" box is not comforting, exactly, but it does help prevent mistakes. FTP does not.) Existing files, if present, will simply be deleted and replaced by the new file. Many a life, or at least, a weekend, has been ruined when a web designer dragged one file on top of another. So use care when naming your files. Many web designers rename old files before they update them (personnel.html becomes, for instance, personnelbak.html, or ~personnel.html).

Equally important is that depending on the rules of the FTP server, text files might have to be uploaded as text, or they will not work. Image files, along with Flash movies, sound files, and so on, might have to be uploaded as binaries, or they will not work. Doddering old Fetch has a checkbox for "automatic" detection of text or binary. That checkbox is your friend. Check it and you will not be faced with the mysteries of the nonworking site.

Finally, as we've emphasized all along, it's important to make sure that your files end in appropriate extensions (.jpg for JPEG images, .html for HTML documents, and so on) and that you have paid attention to their capitalization—or lack thereof.

Offline, you can get away with mismatched cases. For example, <IMG SRC="mydog.gif"> might work just as well as <IMG SRC="MYDOG.GIF"> or <IMG SRC="mYdOg.gIf"> when you're testing the web page offline on your hard drive. But almost all web servers are case-sensitive. (Windows IIS does not seem to care one way or the other.) On most servers, if the file is named mydog.gif and your HTML refers to <MyDog.gif>, the image will not show up on the Web.

Many web designers avoid this problem by using only lowercase for their filenames: mydog.gif—never MyDog.gif or MYDOG.GIF.

Sticking to lowercase and coding all references in lowercase may save hours of tedious labor. You'll also protect your clients and your site's potential visitors. Because most folks who've spent time on the Web have noticed (consciously or unconsciously) that nearly all URLs are lowercase, when they hear your client's ad they'll type http://www.widgets.com. They will *not* type HTTP://WWW.WIDGETS.COM. Stick to lowercase so your client's visitors can actually view the site.

Besides, all-caps filenames are annoying. Who wants to view MYDOG.GIF on MYHOMEPAGE.HTML? Come to think of it, who wants to view mydog.gif on myhomepage.html? Never mind.

One of our clients performs his own site maintenance and updating. Well, actually, many of our clients do this, but we're not talking about those clients. We're talking about a particular client who wreaked havoc by renaming a certain directory <PRODUCTS> after linking to it throughout the site from its original name, <products>. One little word, eight little letters that simply meant he got fired.

HTMHELL

This chapter and the resources to which it points are not sexy because HTML is not sexy. It is a dull, baseline standard that behaves in predictable ways (give or take a few browser compatibility problems). As a web designer, you'll be hired because of your visual skills and your thinking, not because you can upload files correctly, write good <META> tags, or have committed the various <DOCTYPES> to memory. Nevertheless, without a thorough understanding of HTML and the ability to write it, detect and fix errors in it, and use it creatively as a design tool, you cannot be an effective web designer. So take the time to learn this simple, logical markup language before moving on to the more exciting stuff. (The exciting stuff begins in the very next chapter.)

chapter 9

Visual Tools

IN THIS CHAPTER, you'll learn how web designers use Adobe Photoshop and related software to design comps, prepare typography and images, and convert the whole shebang into working web pages. Along the way, you'll get the lowdown on image file types, learn design techniques that make a virtue of web images' limitations, and see how the issues of color, bandwidth, and navigation discussed earlier in this book apply to the creation of web layouts in image editors. We'll also chat about alternative web design methods that produce lighter, more accessible sites.

If you've read other web design books, some of the initial material in this chapter will be familiar to you, though we might take it places other books haven't.

In short—pour yourself a tall one, fluff up your seat cushions, and get ready to burrow in.

Photoshop Basics: An Overview

Coming from the world of print, most art directors and designers are familiar with Adobe Photoshop as an image editing tool. In web design, Photoshop is that and more. In fact, Photoshop, along with its included ImageReady module, is most web designers' primary imaging, layout, and production tool.

Some web designers use Macromedia Fireworks (www.macromedia.com/software/fireworks/) to supplement or even replace Photoshop. Fireworks is a fine tool created specifically to serve the needs of web design. But as a transitioning designer or as one adding web work to an existing repertoire of design services, you will want to use the tools you know. And that means Photoshop/ImageReady and Illustrator. You will encounter Fireworks in some web agencies—Photoshop and Illustrator in all of them.

We're assuming that you already know how to open an image in Photoshop, resize it as necessary, apply color correction, make selections, run filters, save the image in a particular format, and scream when the client tells you your multilayered masterpiece is "too busy." If not, now might be a good time to brush up on your basic Photoshop skills (www.adobe.com/products/tips/photoshop.html).

Following is an overview of key Photoshop functions in addition to the familiar tasks of resizing, color correction, blurring, and sharpening. Material that might be new to you will be covered in detail following the overview.

Comp Preparation

Unlike in the print world, where Quark XPress, Illustrator, and InDesign hold sway, most web designers create their page layouts entirely in Photoshop. You'll use it to conceive designs and show them to clients.

Dealing with Color Palettes

In print, color is practically unlimited. Not so on the Web. Photoshop 5.5 (or higher) and its bundled sister product, ImageReady, handle this issue with ease and grace.

Exporting to Web-Friendly Formats

Each computing platform sports a native, bitmapped image format—PICT for Mac users and BMP for Windows. But web browsers are configured to display special, cross-platform image formats that trade quality for bandwidth. In designing web pages, you'll use the compressed GIF and JPEG formats almost exclusively. The PNG format, an open standard with advantages including alpha channel transparency, is also beginning to enjoy support in newer browsers. Photoshop exports to all these formats, with advanced functions that make your job easier. It is also a fine tool for applying image compression during the exporting process.

Gamma Compensation

Photoshop easily handles the cross-platform gamma dilemma we discussed earlier in this book. (See "Gamma, Gamma, Hey!" in Chapter 2, "Designing for the Medium.")

Preparing Typography

Photoshop, together with Illustrator, enables you to prepare typographic images for the Web. Photoshop has become so adept at this task that many web designers now use it exclusively.

Slicing and Dicing

To turn a comp into a web page, most professionals find themselves slicing the comp into smaller component images and using HTML markup to put the pieces back together. Photoshop and ImageReady make this easy and painless, relieving you of the burden of hand-coding complexly nested HTML table cells and their associated image files.

Rollovers (Image Swapping)

The ever-popular *rollover* effect, in which one image is replaced by another when the visitor's cursor "rolls" over it, is not just a meaningless gimmick. By emulating familiar Graphical User Interface (GUI) behavior, in which user actions trigger software reactions, rollovers can provide important cues to the way the site functions. Or they can just be meaningless gimmicks. Rollover effects are powered by JavaScript (or ECMAScript, as it now prefers to be called).

We'll explore JavaScript in Chapter 11, "The Joy of JavaScript." While there is no substitute for learning JavaScript and employing it creatively, in this chapter you'll learn how ImageReady can automatically generate appropriate rollover scripts for you. These rollovers can be extremely sophisticated and might exceed many web designers' hand-programming abilities.

GIF Animation

On the Web, images need not be static. Animated GIFs create the illusion of motion without requiring visitors to download and install third-party add-ons such as Flash, Shockwave, or the Adobe SVG plug-in (not that there's anything wrong with Flash, Shockwave, or SVG, all of which are discussed in Chapter 12, "Beyond Text/Pictures").

GIFs can contain more than one image, and the format was originally prized for its utility as a kind of multiple image storehouse. In the mid-1990s, some smart soul figured out that these multiple images could be "played" in sequence, creating the illusion of motion. The animated GIF was born, and the Web has never fully recovered. Photoshop's ImageReady module enables you to easily create GIF animations. These can be free-standing, but might just as easily be incorporated into rollovers.

Create Seamless Background Patterns (Tiles)

These patterns or tiles formed a staple of web design in its early years. Many were downright ugly, and few appear in today's sophisticated sites, but the technique can still prove useful when creatively reimagined by web designers with taste.

From this brief overview, it should be clear that the Photoshop/ImageReady combo is a powerful tool for web designers. Basically, with Photoshop and your HTML editor of choice, you can perform almost any web task.

Now let's look at some problems peculiar to web design and see how you can solve them with Photoshop and ImageReady.

Color My Web: Romancing the Cube

Glance back at Chapter 2 for a refresher on the 216 color palette—or the Netscape Color Cube.

Designers work with computers that support millions of colors. But most web users are limited to thousands (or hundreds) of colors, and your design must work well in these environments.

Monitors limited to thousands of colors (16 bits) might seem to display realistic color, but it is never the actual color specified by the web designer. For mathematical reasons, colors shift slightly "off" in the 16-bit color space. This problem is insoluble and will haunt you like Jacob Marley's ghost until cheap 24-bit graphics cards find their way into most PCs and vendors ship them configured to use the higher resolution and bit depth. (One of the tragic stupidities of the computer industry is that computers that can display millions of colors come configured to show thousands; those that can show thousands come configured to show hundreds, and so on. It's tragic because ordinary citizens rarely realize that they can increase their PC's graphic power with a quick trip to the appropriate control panel.)

Eight-bit (256 color) systems face an additional problem in that up to 40 of these 256 colors are "used up" in advance by the operating system itself. For instance, Windows reserves 40 (count 'em) Windows system colors for its own display purposes. Knowing Windows, we should be glad it's *only* 40. Nevertheless, that leaves exactly 216 colors at your disposal. (And GIF, as an "indexed" file format, only supports 255 colors anyway, two of which—black and white—are always present.)

What happens to viewers with lower-end graphics capabilities when you design with millions of colors they can't see? The browser tries to simulate your color choices by combining adjacent pixels of color the visitor *can* see. This visual side effect is known as *dithering*, a verb that also means "babbling inconsequentially," which is kind of what we're doing here.

Dither Me This

You've chosen a subtle shade of off-white for your typography. The viewer's graphics processor cannot reproduce that exact color, so the web browser breaks up your type into a series of adjoining pink and white pixels. If the viewer squints, she will get an approximation of the color you intended to use (see Figure 9.1).

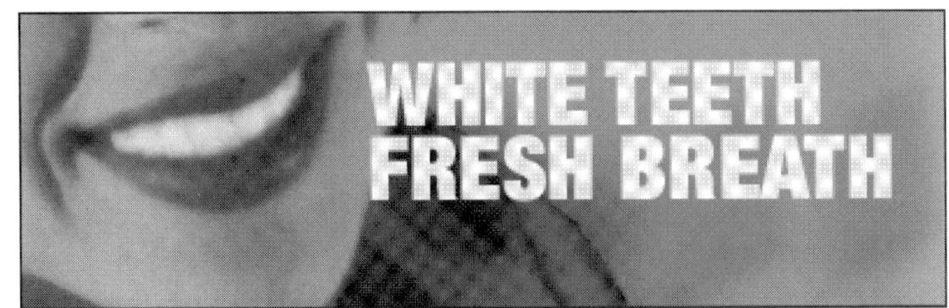

Figure 9.1

The toothpaste may get teeth their whitest, but it doesn't do much for this off-white typographic headline. On 8-bit systems, the type gets pixellated, and we suspect the web designer will, too. (Image enlarged 200%.)

In small, transitional areas, dithering is okay. But when it occurs across large areas of solid color—or when it is visible in the primary letterforms of typography—the result will be visually hideous, and legibility can be seriously impaired. (Usability experts and web artists alike can agree that hideous, illegible type is not a good thing.)

Because the discrepancy between computers' graphic capabilities is so enormous, it initially seems as though it would be impossible for a designer to create web pages that do not dither and degrade on most viewers' monitors. The Color Cube saves the day (see Figure 9.2).

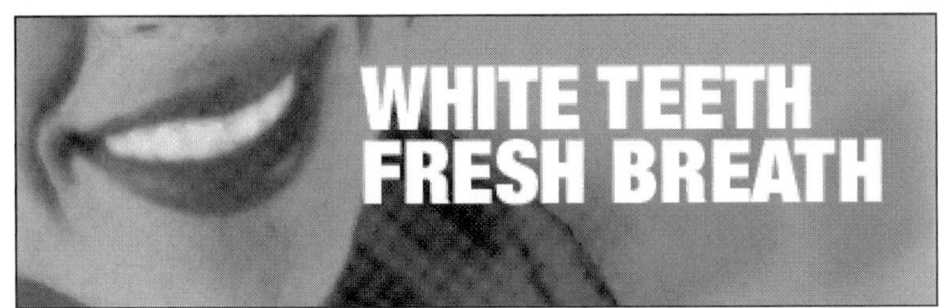

Figure 9.2

With the typography recast in web-safe white (#ffffff), the headline is no longer pixellated, increasing the chances that it will actually be read. The background image is still dithered, but users of 8-bit systems will accept that. (Image enlarged 200%.)

For typography, CSS or HTML background colors, or any other area of large, flat color, if you stick to the web-safe color palette, you will avoid causing dithering and its resulting illegibility and aesthetic problems on 8-bit systems. As explained in Chapter 2, the practice will not help those with 16-bit systems, but nothing can save those folks except a graphics card upgrade in their future.

Death of the Web-Safe Color Palette?

Creative people complain about everything. Web designers certainly complain about being limited to 216 web-safe colors, but to us this is like griping about the nip in the air while enjoying the scenic beauty of rustic New England. You want fall foliage, so put on an extra sweater.

Lulled by the music of these constant complaints, pundits perennially proclaim the death of the web-safe color palette, usually on the grounds that 16-bit systems enjoy a major market share. That 16-bit systems are widely used is undeniable: They are installed in 46% of PCs as of this writing. That the web-safe color palette is therefore dead is wishful thinking.

The web-safe color palette cannot die as long as it continues to solve problems for millions of web users. It does not solve every problem, but neither does penicillin, and nobody talks about the death of penicillin. We bring this up now because you will hear about it at the office and read about it in web design newsletters, mailing lists, and bulletin boards.

Who spreads these obituaries? Sometimes it's information architects and interface developers who conduct meaningful research but draw debatable conclusions from their data. The *Webmonkey* article, "Death of the Web Safe Color Palette?" (http://hotwired.lycos.com/webmonkey/00/37/index2a.html), proves beyond all doubt that 16-bit systems are hopelessly inadequate and invariably reveal the rabbits hiding in a web magician's hat. But the article nihilistically concludes that all color palettes and traditional methods are meaningless in the chaos of the Web; whereas we judge simply that 16-bit users are hosed until they upgrade. Not long ago, 16-bit color was considered luxurious; cheap graphics cards changed the market, and the next generation of cheap 24-bit cards will change it again.

Few discussions of the topic have been as carefully researched as *Webmonkey*'s. The death of the web-safe color palette is generally announced by the same people who tell us that bandwidth no longer matters because "everybody" will "soon" enjoy high-speed access. These folks often go on to proclaim that presently every site will be pumping out full-screen video productions to rival Hollywood blockbusters.

A moment's analysis will tell you that many people around the world are not online yet. That those who are online are mainly limited to slow connections over untrustworthy phone lines. That even in the major urban areas of industrialized nations, high-speed access is often hard to come by and frequently comes at a premium many cannot afford—or are not willing—to pay. That major Hollywood productions cost millions and can make a profit (when they *do* make a profit) only by charging admission. That websites generally do not charge admission, and web clients generally do not have millions of production dollars at their disposal. And finally, that most people do not seek big-budget entertainment from the Web. They seek information, services, and communities—all of which the Web can deliver with a minimum expenditure of bandwidth.

In other words, much of what you hear about how the Web works and where it is going is bunk—including, we think, the death of the web-safe color palette. Ask us again in a year or two when (hopefully) most PCs come standard with 24-bit color or higher.

A Hex on Both Your Houses

Reared on RGB and CMYK, many designers find the Web's hexadecimal color nomenclature strange, at first. But the predictability of recurring hexadecimal pairs (00, 33, 66, 99, cc, ff) makes it easy to tell if you are using web-safe colors or not. It also makes it easy to specify web-safe background colors and text colors in HTML and CSS.

You will find, after you work with these colors, that it is possible to create pleasing combinations with them, and you will develop your own techniques for doing so.

In this quest, you will be greatly aided by Photoshop's own tool set and by the VisiBone color palette included in Photoshop 5.5 and higher and available free online. The VisiBone palette is a superb tool for establishing visual relationships between web-safe colors. And, as you already know, visual relationships are the key to creating pleasing and effective color schemes.

Color relationships are essential to branding, can support navigational structures, and may greatly enhance a site's aesthetic appeal at a minimum expenditure of bandwidth. Fill an entire page with a CSS background color, devise complementary link and text colors, and you begin to have the rudiments of an attractive design using just a few kilobytes of bandwidth.

Was Blind, but Now I See

It should be noted that a small percentage of women and a larger percentage of men suffer from various forms of color blindness. Designs that rely exclusively on color to convey essential information and relationships could therefore be inaccessible to some viewers. So, while taking color extremely seriously, you must also test your designs for accessibility—ideally by running them past test subjects who manifest different forms of color blindness. If you can't do it that way, use the Color Blindness Simulator at www.vischeck.com. Viewing your web layouts in grayscale mode is a nice gesture but not a truly accurate means of testing how they will appear to, say, a person with red/green color deficit (deuteranopia).

From Theory to Practice

The following three exercises introduce you to the effects of dithering, describe how to set up the Photoshop Color Picker so that your color choices are always web-safe, and explain how to locate and install the VisiBone color palette. You will notice that we begin each exercise by cautioning you to set your monitor to 24- or 32-bit mode before launching Photoshop. If you accidentally launch Photoshop while in 16-bit mode, all your colors will shift, and the images you design for the Web will always be mismatched from their backgrounds.

Exercise 1: In a Dither

Be certain your monitor is set to 24- or 32-bit mode. Launch Photoshop 5.5 or higher.

Open a new, blank document (600 x 400 pixels) and paint in it randomly, using the Paintbrush and Airbrush tools.

Also be sure to use the Type tool to set some large type in a variety of colors.

Stop when you are satisfied.

In the Mac Finder or Windows desktop, switch your monitor to 256 colors.

Look at the image you've created. Those ugly dots are dithering, and that's what millions of viewers will see if you do not learn to incorporate the web-safe color palette into your work.

Close the image without saving it, quit Photoshop, and restore your monitor to its normal color settings (millions of colors).

Exercise 2: You Sure Can Pick 'em

Be certain your monitor is set to 24- or 32-bit mode. Launch Photoshop 5.5 or higher.

Open a new, blank document (600 x 400 pixels).

Open Photoshop's Color Picker (see Figure 9.3). Note the Only Web Colors checkbox and check it.

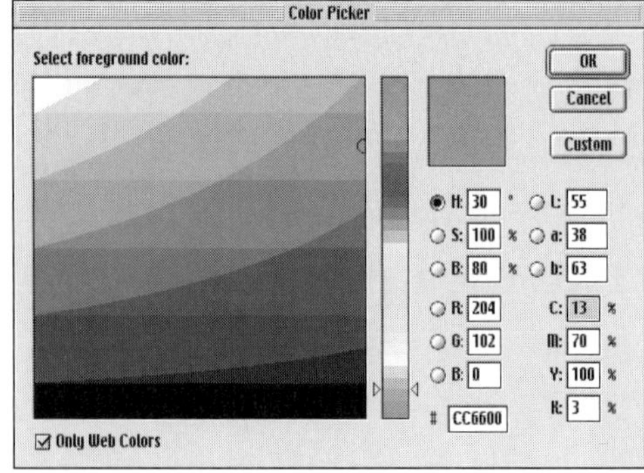

Figure 9.3

The Photoshop Color Picker provides RGB, HSB, Lab, CMYK, and hexadecimal readouts for any color you choose. The familiarity of RGB and CMYK will help acclimate you to hexadecimal nomenclature. Click the checkbox that reads Only Web Colors, and your choices will always be web-safe.

Watch your universe of color options shrink down to 216 choices. On the plus side, the various graphic dialogs help you see the relationships between web-safe colors.

Close the Color Picker dialog.

From now on, *Photoshop's Color Picker will always be web-safe*. You can also use Photoshop's Color Picker to *shift* a near-web-safe color so that it is fully web-safe.

Photoshop's web-safe Color Picker is a vast improvement over what the program used to offer in the way of support (namely, nothing).

Now that our Color Picker is web-safe, let's do the same for our color palette dialog. Jeepers, but we are moving along quickly here.

Exercise 3: Rolling the 'Bones

Be certain your monitor is set to 24- or 32-bit mode. Launch Photoshop 5.5 or higher.

Open a new, blank document (600 x 400 pixels).

Refer to the Colors dialog. Note that there is a web-safe palette included in Photoshop. Note that the color combinations are not especially intuitive and have no meaningful relationship with the color wheel or other color theory models.

Let's fix that.

In the Swatches dialog box, choose Replace Swatches. A dialog box opens, allowing you to navigate to a new palette located on your hard drive. Steer your way to the VisiBone color palette (VisiBone1.aco), which is most likely located in Adobe Photoshop 5.5, Goodies, Color Swatches.

Handsome, isn't it? (See Figure 9.4.)

Figure 9.4

The VisiBone color palette, located in the Color Swatches folder within the Goodies folder in Photoshop 5.5 and higher, makes it easy to choose harmonious or contrasting colors from within the web-safe palette. Don't leave home without it.

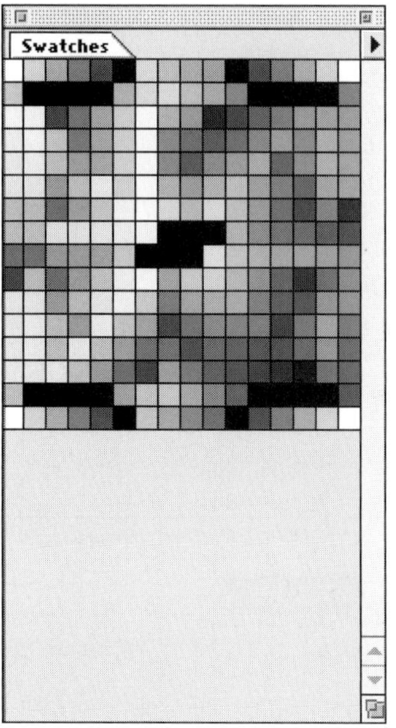

This is still the web-safe color palette. But unlike Photoshop's built-in, default version, the VisiBone palette offers a meaningful arrangement built around the color wheel model we all learned about in school (unless we spent our time in school doodling and learned almost nothing except how to draw guitars in the margins of our textbooks). Colors move in a circle across the spectrum, and related colors are geometrically aligned with respect to one another.

The VisiBone color palette not only helps you choose web-safe colors, it helps you choose web-safe colors *that relate to one another in a meaningful way, man.* Harmonious and contrasting color relationships are easy to see and thus easier to create.

In other words, the VisiBone palette helps you start doing beautiful work within the limitations of the Color Cube. For instance, it helps you quickly find a web-safe approximation of a client's logo color and begin experimenting with complementary and contrasting web-safe colors for your layouts. (It goes without saying that if original logo development is part of the project, you will design the logo using web-safe colors. It also goes without saying that your client might want you to design a logo that matches the color of their new Beetle or their favorite coffee mug, but that is where tact and client education come in.)

Save the VisiBone swatch so it is always available when you work in Photoshop.

Now pat yourself on the back. Many of your peers have no idea that this special swatch exists, that it comes bundled with Photoshop, and that it can greatly ease the creation of meaningful and attractive color schemes for the Web. You are ahead of the game.

If you're stuck using an older version of Photoshop or an alternative image editor, you can download the VisiBone palette free of charge at www.visibone.com. While there, help yourself to additional VisiBone palettes for other software programs you or your teammates use, including Adobe Illustrator and ImageReady, Macromedia Fireworks, Bare Bones BBEdit, Jasc Paint Shop Pro, Allaire HomeSite, MetaCreations Painter, or the GIMP (an image editor for Linux). You need it; they've got it.

For additional wisdom on the Color Cube, see Lynda Weinman's site at www.lynda.com and David Siegel's at www.killersites.com. You also might want to buy Weinman's *Designing Web Graphics* and *Coloring Web Graphics*, both of which are available from New Riders Press, and are pretty much the standard industry texts. They are full of practical examples and offer stimulating and innovative ideas from the earliest days of web design.

Another standard industry text, David Siegel's *Creating Killer Websites*, is also available from New Riders and also provides extensive information on the subjects we cover in this chapter. It's a beautifully written book full of great ideas, but it is also a book of its time (1996), and many of the practices it preaches would now be considered harmful to the development of a semantic Web based on W3C Recommendations. We own and cherish this book, which was greatly influential in our development, and we recommend it as long as you know which of its visual techniques to shun. (If you're unsure, wait for the book's third Edition...we hear it's coming soon.)

Format This: GIFs, JPEGs, and Such

Raster images come in at least as many formats as there are software programs and operating systems. On the Web, however, we tend to use two formats almost exclusively: GIF and JPEG. (As explained previously, animated GIFs are a special instance of the GIF format.)

PNG is yet another web format, one that has been little supported in the past. Some newer browsers have begun to support PNG, though it is still far from ubiquitous. We will discuss it after thoroughly examining the GIF and JPEG formats—how they work, which types of images they deliver best, and how you can evolve strong stylistic concepts by understanding their limitations.

GIF

The Graphics Interchange Format (GIF) is older than the Web. In fact it is older than some web designers. GIF was developed in the 1980s by CompuServe, and you'll often hear old-timers speak of "CompuServe GIFs." You'll also hear them talk about walking 12 miles to a one-room schoolhouse.

The Compuserve folks pronounced the word as if it were the name of the peanut butter ("Jiff") and because they were the inventors, that is the correct pronunciation. Millions of people pronounce GIF with a hard "G," however, so you might as well be a sniveling conformist and spend the rest of your career mispronouncing GIF while secretly suffering great guilt over it. GIFs are usually seen with a .GIF file extension, as in payme.GIF or payme.gif.

The GIF format renders in 8-bit color or lower, at your discretion. Two-color GIFs are not uncommon. GIF permits you to achieve crude transparency effects by marking one of your 216 (or fewer) colors as "transparent." However, you must take care to anti-alias the foreground image against the transparent color, lest mismatched halos surround your graphics. Fortunately, GIF renders specific colors exactly, so it is an easy matter to match web page backgrounds to image backgrounds. The only caveat there is the previously mentioned heartbreak of 16-bit systems.

Above all, GIF enables you to save bandwidth without sacrificing quality. It employs the *Unisys-patented Lempel Ziv Welch (LZW) algorithm* (www.dogma.net/markn/articles/lzw/lzw.htm) to efficiently compress solid color areas while preserving crisp detail. Though the format necessarily discards colors—for instance, when rendering a 24-bit image as a 16-color GIF—it does not blur or eliminate significant image details. For this reason, the GIF algorithm produces what is known as *lossless compression*.

Loves logos, typography, and long walks in the woods

This combination of crisp detail and efficient compression makes GIF the format of choice for line art including typography, logos, and illustrations. As mentioned earlier, the GIF format can also be used to create animated images. When combined with JavaScript rollovers, animated GIFs can lend life and dynamism to a website. They can also create nausea and ennui. With animation and rollovers, as with Tabasco, a little goes a long way.

Animated GIFs have been supported in all graphical web browsers since Netscape 2.0 (1995), and nonanimated GIFs have been supported in graphical web browsers since before time began. For now we will continue to discuss the merits and uses of static (nonanimated) GIFs.

In spite of the fact that GIFs are found on millions of sites, the GIF format is not a W3C-recommended web standard. That's because GIF gets its power from a patented algorithm. Unisys, the patent holder, is entitled to charge royalties on any software that employs the LZW algorithm—in other words, any software that can read or write GIFs. The revelation of Unisys' right to charge a "GIF tax" spread panic among early web designers when it became widely known only after the entire Web seemed to be built with GIF images. It also led to the development of PNG, a GIF-like format with more advanced features and a nonproprietary compression algorithm.

GIF "royalties" do not work in the way that, say, photo rights work. You do not pay a fee each time you create a GIF image. Instead, software companies such as Adobe, Macromedia, and Corel render these tributes to Caesar. You pay your share one time only, and it is hidden in the purchase price of Photoshop, Fireworks, or any other software program that exports to the GIF format.

GIFs are *not* the format of choice for photography, paintings, and other subtly modulated images because they lack sufficient colors to reproduce these types of images and because the nuances in those images do not lend themselves to LZW compression. Photographic images tend to render better in the JPEG format (or PNG), and we'll get to those formats soon enough.

GIFs in Photoshop

In Photoshop, you can choose whether to save your image as a standard or interlaced GIF. The standard format is like a reader, taking in one letter after another, one word after another, one sentence after another. Standard GIFs store and display the bytes comprising an image's pixels in their order of appearance: The first pixel in is the first pixel out. Thus, standard GIFs scroll onto the viewer's screen pixel by pixel and line by line.

The interlaced format is like a nervous reader who keeps skipping ahead—from paragraph one to paragraph five, then back to paragraph one. Interlaced GIFs load in a parallel rather than linear sequence, allowing the total image to be rendered more quickly and then with greater detail as additional pixels are downloaded. This allows viewers to get a sense of the image before it has finished downloading.

Under the right conditions, interlaced GIFs might thus appear to load faster—and so may your site. The appearance is deceptive given that interlaced GIFs are often a few bytes *larger* than standard GIFs and therefore take a fractionally longer time to fully download. Moreover, the slight benefits of interlaced GIFs often evaporate when other conditions are factored in.

For one thing, the effectiveness of progressive GIFs depends on the viewer's access speed. With a super-fast connection, images load so quickly that any progressive rendering benefits are lost. The format was something of a godsend not so long ago, when most web users were limited to 14.4 modems. Today, few are stuck with such abysmal speeds.

The effectiveness of progressive GIFs also depends on the browser. Some browsers do not show anything at all until all images are fully loaded; in those browsers, the progressive aspects of the image are entirely wasted. If anything, in such browsers, progressive GIFs delay the page by adding a few bytes to the overall download time.

Some browsers, such as Internet Explorer, give users a choice. Users may view each image as it downloads (best with slow connections), or they may choose to wait for the entire page to download and assemble itself in memory before appearing full-blown on the screen (best with fast connections). Users choose a viewing method in the Explorer Preferences dialog box. You have no way of knowing or controlling these user preferences.

Beginning web designers often ask if they can control the loading order of images on a web page. Given what has just been explained, the answer is obviously "no," because web users can choose (or their browsers may force them) to wait for the entire page to load. Beyond that, HTML has no means of controlling the loading order of images. And even if it did support such nuances, the unpredictability of HTTP calls (explained in Chapter 2) means that one image might halt in mid-download, not even appearing until another, called much later, has already popped into place. The more images per page, the greater the randomness of load order. View a busy thumbnail image gallery sometime to see this in action, assuming your browser allows you to watch images download one by one.

Avoid progressive GIFs when creating an image to be used as a background. Backgrounds do not appear until they have fully downloaded, so any "progressive" effects will be lost. Moreover, progressive GIF backgrounds can crash some older browsers.

Progressive GIFs also can be hazardous to animations because each succeeding frame of a progressive animated GIF will appear blurry, thus defeating the effort to create smooth motion effects.

They're not great for JavaScript rollovers, either. You can offset the harmful, blurred quality of progressive GIFs in rollovers by preloading the images, a technique explained in the Chapter 11, "The Joy of JavaScript." When preloaded via JavaScript, images download and are stored in the viewer's cache even though they do not appear on the web page until triggered by some action on the viewer's part (typically, moving the mouse over an image to which rollover effects have been applied). Any sane web designer who creates rollovers starts by preloading the alternate (replacement) images. But if the images are going to be preloaded anyway, there's no sense in having them render progressively because the user will never see them until they have fully downloaded and cached.

One last tip while we're in this area. Given that text loads instantly and images take time (see Chapter 2), designs that use HTML text above the fold will appear to load more quickly than those that bury their text further down on the screen. A web user waiting for images is a web user with nothing to do (except, perhaps, hit the Back button). A web user reading text has less anxiety about the fact that some images may not have finished downloading. With sufficiently engaging text, the user will feel that the site is responsive. Keep this in mind when designing sites that require a great many images.

JPEG, the Other White Meat

The Joint Photographic Experts Group (JPEG) format should be familiar to you from stock photo houses, digital cameras, and the Photoshop tutorial itself. Usually seen with a .jpg file extension (as in landscape.jpg), JPEG supports 24-bit color and preserves the subtle hue and brightness variations found in photographs and other continuous-tone images. JPEG is therefore usually the format of choice when creating photographic images for the Web. Like GIF, JPEG is widely supported in visual web browsers.

Just as MP3 music files toss away audio harmonics to achieve compact file sizes, JPEG's compression works by selectively discarding bits of image data. Because a loss of quality is involved, JPEG compression is referred to as *lossy compression.* "Lossy" is an annoying word that looks wrong, but we appear to be stuck with it. In theory, the material discarded by the JPEG optimization process is data that is nearly invisible to the human eye (just as audio data discarded by the MP3 format is supposed to go practically undetected by your ears, though we've never met a music fan who could not hear the difference). The greater the JPEG compression, however, the more visible the "missing data" becomes. At extremely high compression ratios, JPEG images can display funky artifacts (see Figures 9.5 and 9.6).

Although JPEG is generally preferred for photographic images, when sharp detail is important, GIF is the better choice. JPEG tends to soften images as it compresses them. Particularly when you are working with typography, the softness of JPEG images can ruin the effect of a web graphic. Naturally, there is a workaround, as explained in the "Combining Sharp and Blurry" section later in this chapter.

Unlike GIF, the JPEG format does not retain specific web-safe (or other) colors. It promises you a rose garden, but the rose might be umber. In a silhouetted portrait where the edges of the image must match the background of the web page, you would therefore use GIF, not JPEG.

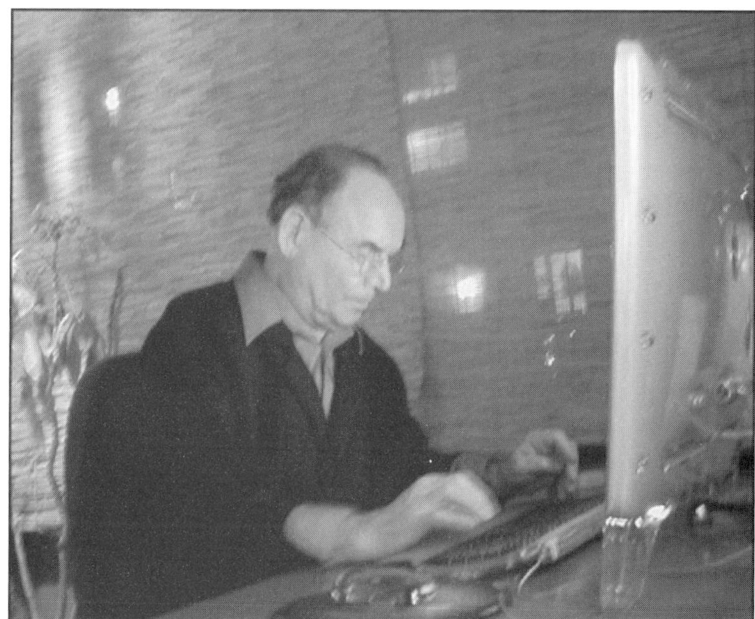

Figure 9.5

At moderate JPEG compression levels, image details are clear, but file size is high.

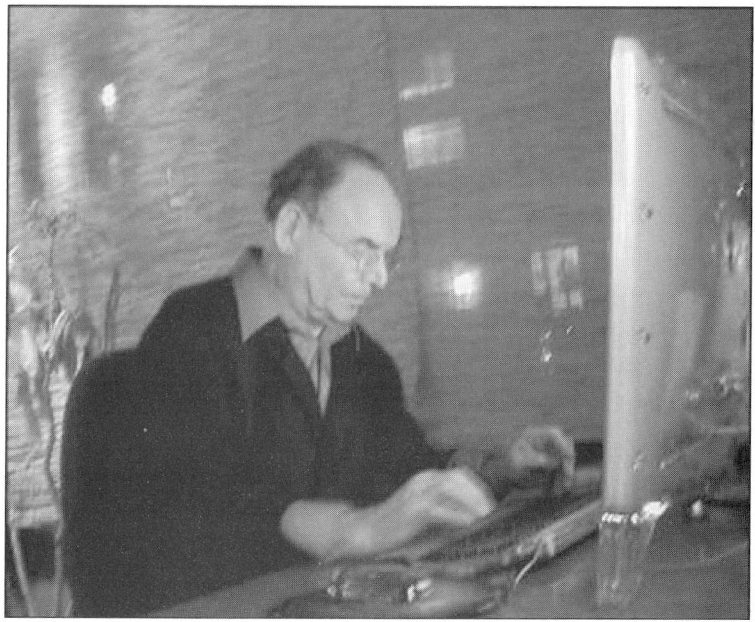

Figure 9.6

At high JPEG compression levels, file size is low (minimizing bandwidth) but so is the quality. Each JPEG optimization is an exercise in balancing file size versus quality of detail.

Photoshop's Save For Web function provides a small, Matte Color dialog box that purports to save an exact background color of your choice, even in the JPEG format. (Skip ahead to Figure 9.7, if you must. The Matte Color dialog appears at mid-right.)

Photoshop does all it can to fulfill this promise, but the JPEG format really is not built to handle specific colors like this. To viewers with 24-bit and higher systems, the background color will appear to match. For 16-bit and lower users, the mismatch may be clearly visible. So stick with GIF when you absolutely, positively, have to deliver a specific web-safe (or other) color.

In Photoshop, you can choose whether to save your JPEG as a baseline (standard) JPEG or as a *progressive* JPEG. Progressive JPEGs display a low-resolution version of the image almost immediately and then gradually come into crisper focus.

As with progressive GIFs, under the right circumstances, progressive JPEGs can create the illusion that the site is loading faster. As previously discussed, this varies depending on the viewer's access speed, browser functionality, browser preferences, and the caprices of HTTP. And as in the discussion of GIFs above, when intended as background images, progressive JPEGs are a no-no unless you want some of your visitors to crash-crash.

Optimizing GIFs and JPEGs

When we export images such as GIFs and JPEGs, we choose the format most appropriate to the type of image we're dealing with and then optimize it to create the best appearance possible, while using the least amount of bandwidth and computing resources.

In addition to *optimizing* (reducing file sizes), the exporting process allows us to further exert control over the color of our GIF images.

Photoshop 3, 4, and 5 offered early web designers very little in the way of optimization and color controls. As a result, a number of inexpensive, third-party, shareware plug-in products specifically tailored to the needs of web designers sprang up in the mid-1990s, most notably Boxtop

Software's PhotoGIF, ImageVice, and ProJPEG (all are available at www.boxtop-software.com). These products were dandy (still are), but they did not come as standard equipment (still don't). Arguably, they do a better job than Photoshop at handling some tasks.

Fortunately, Photoshop 5.5 and higher, together with ImageReady, offers a number of tools to help web designers create the best-looking image while using the least amount of bandwidth. Photoshop's Save For Web command (found in File, Save For Web) enables web designers to preview the effects of various compression settings on their images and then execute those settings and save the resulting web-ready images (see Figure 9.7).

The Save For Web dialog is powerfully compelling in the breadth and subtlety of its tools. You can preview GIF versions using as few as two colors, as many as 256, or anything in between. You can use Adaptive, Selective, Perceptual, or web-safe color, with or without dithering, transparency, or interlacing (the "progressive" setting). You can skew images closer to or further from the web-safe palette as you desire. You also can name and save custom settings for later application to similar images.

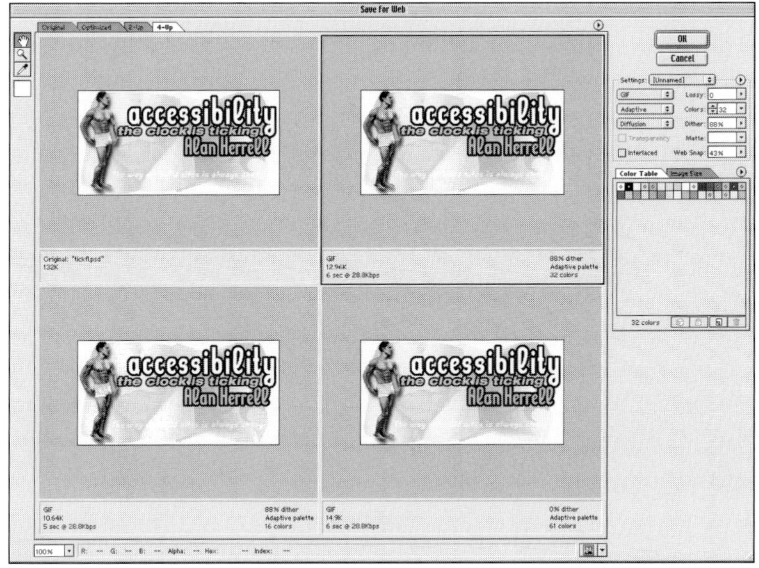

Figure 9.7

Photoshop's Save For Web dialog in action. In this "four-up" view, the original image appears at the upper left for easy comparison with various optimization schemes of your choosing.

Work on one optimization setting at a time or view three at once—and compare them with the original to check for image degradation and color shifting. Get an instant readout of the effect your decisions will have on file size and downloading speed. Enlarge images to check fine details. Lock selected colors before trying a new set. Shift one color at a time to its closest web-safe equivalent. We feel like press agents. We feel giddy. We love this dialog box. You will too.

Images in Save For Web mode also may be previewed at various JPEG settings, both baseline and progressive, and again the tools are remarkably powerful.

In general, the fewer the colors used in a GIF, the better it compresses. This is not because the color palettes themselves eat bandwidth; rather it is because of the way LZW compression works. More on that in a moment in the "Expanding on Compression" section that is coming up next.

Dithering images produces more photographic-like effects at the cost of slightly higher file sizes; images without dithering are smaller. We find that typographic GIFs are often cleaner and more legible when saved without dithering. Your mileage may vary. You can create either type of image (and preview the results) in Photoshop's Save For Web dialog box.

After you decide which optimization scheme works best for a given image, the image can be saved in that format. Your chosen settings may be retained indefinitely, and can even be applied (as a droplet) to an entire folder of images.

Photoshop lets you name and store as many of these settings as you like. If a series of images you've created for Acme Widgets happens to work well in 12 colors with no dithering at 60% web-safe, you can name that setting 12color_nodither (or acme_widgets or 60websafe or donaldduck if you prefer). You can then save it forever—or at least until your backup media deteriorates and what's left of your hair is white and listless. By then we'll all be living on Mars while our clones do the work, anyway.

Alternately, you can use the ImageReady module to satisfy your wanton image compression and formatting needs. But Photoshop's Save For Web is just as effective, and the true power of ImageReady comes later in the process (and this chapter).

Expanding on Compression

As explained previously, we compress images to minimize wasted bandwidth and speed the arrival of the web page. We've shown you how Photoshop optimizes images when preparing them for the Web, so you know all you need to know to handle the basics. The following are some extra tips.

Make your JPEGS smaller

You can make your JPEGs even smaller in file size (and reduce the appearance of JPEG artifacts) by blurring them slightly before compressing them. Not all areas of all images react well to blurring, but it's surprising what you can achieve by blurring, say, a distant sky and sunset while preserving the sharpness of a human subject in the foreground.

This kind of work requires selecting the parts of the image you want to blur, feathering the edge of the selection slightly, and masking out the parts of the image where sharper focus is important. As we said in the beginning, we assume you already know how to do these things in Photoshop.

If you prefer, you can apply subtle (or not-so-subtle) blurring effects to your entire image in the Save For Web dialog box, but we generally find this method too coarse. Blurring, say, an entire portrait makes the subject look drunk—or the viewer feel that way. Selectively and subtly blurring large areas of undifferentiated skin tones, while preserving the sharpness of eyes, brows, hair, and lips, will usually be much more effective. And that kind of work you do in the main Photoshop window before entering the Save For Web dialog.

Combining sharp and blurry

Subtle problems can arise when choosing the appropriate image format. Say you've designed a header graphic that includes both photography (a shot of the corporate board of directors) and typography (a superimposed headline in Meta or Helvetica Neu Condensed Black). The headline requires sharp focus and crisp handling—thus it begs to be a GIF. The photograph wants to be a JPEG. What's a mother to do?

Usually, what you do is give greater weight to the need for crisp typography and export the entire image as a GIF, accepting that the photographic imagery will not render as well as it would have in a JPEG (see Figures 9.8, 9.9, and 9.10).

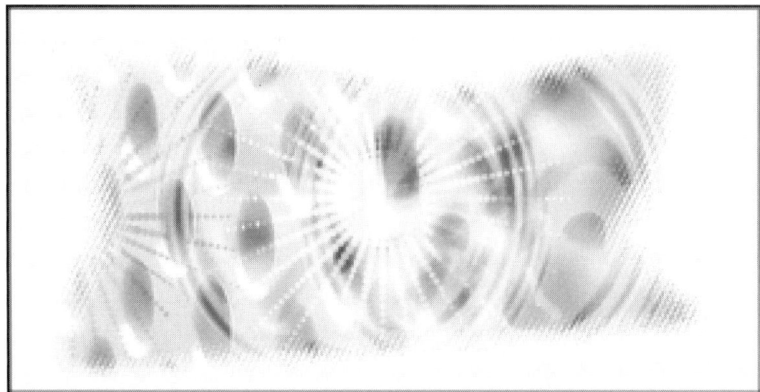

Figure 9.8

The background image, a layered photomontage, wants to be saved as a JPEG because JPEG would best reproduce its subtly modulating hue and brightness variations. But...

Figure 9.9

...the typography insists on being saved as a GIF because only the GIF format will reproduce the crisp, clear lines of type. A JPEG would soften the headline and render the small type as an illegible blur. So...

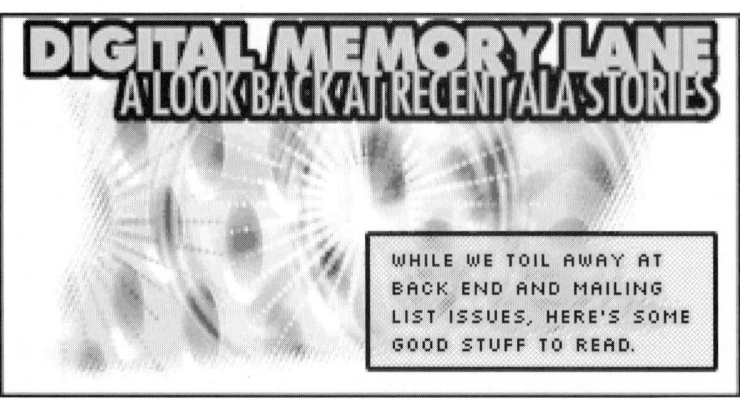

Figure 9.10

...the image is saved as a GIF because type takes precedence over photographic nuances. The image could also have been saved as a PNG. But the PNG would have been far larger and not enough browsers fully support the PNG format yet.

Alternately, you could export the human subjects as a JPEG, export the typography as a transparent GIF, and superimpose the GIF over the JPEG using any number of web sleights of hand. For instance, you could employ CSS absolute positioning to layer a crisp, transparent typographic GIF on top of a soft photographic JPEG. (This would not work in Netscape 3 or IE3 and might destabilize Netscape 4. Thankfully, these browsers are finally limping away from the playing field, although not as fast as we'd like.)

Depending on the layout, you alternatively could use the old, nonstandard <bgimage> attribute of the HTML table cell <td> tag to position a photographic image in the background of a table cell and then place a type GIF in the foreground. The type GIF would have to be the same size as the background image and would require GIF transparency to allow the background to peek through. The size of the GIF would be marked up in the table cell attributes to ensure that the cell was the correct size. Though this technique works well in almost every graphic browser since the svelte boyhood of Fred Flintstone, it is a lot of silly (and nonstandard) markup—and it's probably not worth the bandwidth.

Or you could do what Magdalena Donnea did on the front page of her award-winning personal site, "Water," at www.kia.net/water/. (Use View Source to see exactly what Magdalena did.)

As we said, most of the time, you'll use the GIF format to ensure that your text is legible. You also might consider rethinking the entire design idea in favor of one that is more in keeping with the limitations of the Web (see Figure 9.11).

Figure 9.11

The ever-popular "striped" effect that dominated the web in the late 1990s had its roots in a technique to minimize bandwidth by making the most of the GIF compression algorithm's preference for straight horizontal lines.

Compression Breeds Style: Thinking About the Medium

The GIF format not only compresses by removing millions of colors, it also employs the LZW algorithm to keep track of those colors and further reduce file sizes. A clever web designer can create large images that use little bandwidth by designing with LZW compression in mind. To understand how that is possible, we must take a closer look at how LZW compression actually works.

Onscreen images are like diners inside a burger joint. A mentally challenged waiter says, "The first gentleman at Table One would like a cheeseburger. The second gentleman at Table One would like a cheeseburger. The third gentleman at Table One would like a cheeseburger. The fourth gentleman at Table One would like a cheeseburger."

This is how a noncompressed image works. The computer looks up the color of a pixel and then displays it. It looks up the color of the adjoining pixel and displays that—and so on and so on for every pixel on the screen.

A smart waiter says, "Four cheeseburgers," which is how LZW compression works.

LZW compression looks at an image line by line and says, "Row #1 is all red pixels" (assuming that Row #1 actually *is* all red pixels). Obviously, the greater the number of pixel rows that are identical to each other, the better the compression engine works (for example, four tables of four cheeseburgers). Thus, horizontal and vertical elements compress better than diagonal elements because with horizontal or vertical elements, more rows of pixels can be exactly the same as each other.

Without getting too technical, horizontal lines tend to compress even better than vertical ones because LZW compression "reads" images left to right and line by line, the same way you're reading this book. If every pixel in a given line is the same color, that line compresses better, and therefore so does the GIF (there's more to it than that, of course). Ten lines containing all the same color compress better still. Basically, GIF compression likes large areas of flat color, whether they are confined to a single line or bleed down across several. The main point is that an image containing one or more lines of identically colored pixels will compress much better than the average image whose colors are arrayed at random.

In 1995, when 14.4 modems prevailed, some clever web designers began masking every other horizontal line in an image to maximize LZW compression and minimize bandwidth. This technique of masking images with evenly spaced horizontal lines is known as CRLI compression (www.infohiway.com/faster/crli.html).

What started out as a bandwidth-oriented tool had become a stylistic design fetish by the late 1990s, as newcomers to the field fell in love with the CRLI "look" without understanding its utilitarian purpose as a tool of bandwidth compression. To these designers, stripes were "webby," and "webby" was cool. As the Web exploded into public consciousness, consumers and ad agencies seemed to agree with this link between "Web" and "cool." The ever-popular striped effect was soon seen not only all over the Web, but also in print and television.

Among many ironies, some web designers exported these striped images in the JPEG format, where, far from saving bandwidth, the technique actually wasted it. They knew not what they were doing. CRLI compression is a GIF thing, baby.

The strengths and limitations of LZW compression are equally profound. For instance, because LZW prefers straight horizontal and vertical lines to all others, Roman type tends to reproduce better than oblique. Roman type is also better at hiding its anti-aliasing artifacts at screen resolutions—another reason it works better onscreen than oblique does.

Considering these limitations of the medium may lead you to set your headlines in Roman type more often than oblique. Of course, Roman type is far more frequently used than oblique to begin with, so this situation is hardly tragic. But you should be aware of it. Oblique type can certainly be used for headlines—we do it all the time—but it never reproduces as well as upright type.

You will run into the same difficulty with lines at almost every angle. The 45-degree angle is the exception: It works perfectly with LZW, like a diagonal in a game of tic-tac-toe. As you might expect, 45-degree angles came into vogue around 1999 because they reproduce well on the Web, and within six months they were popping up in print and TV as a meaningless design fetish after everyone had tired of the striped effect. And as you might also expect, many web designers employed 45-degree angles in JPEGs, then saved the JPEGs at the highest possible quality settings to preserve the crispness of their lines. The result: wasted bandwidth.

PNG

The PNG format was developed in hopes of establishing it as an open standard for graphics on the Web—which it now is (see www.w3.org/Graphics/PNG/). But while PNG was slowly being developed, working web designers had to create websites, and all browsers supported GIFs. In effect, then, GIF is a long-standing, unofficial *defacto* standard based on a proprietary compression algorithm, while PNG is a nonproprietary, officially sanctioned standard that is not as well supported as it ought to be.

There are two forms of PNG. PNG-8 is an 8-bit format (like GIF). PNG-24 offers 24-bit color (like JPEG), yet its sharpness and quality put JPEG to shame. To create PNG images for the Web, simply choose PNG-24 or PNG-8, 128 Dithered in Photoshop's Save For Web dialog box or in ImageReady.

PNG is still not natively supported in enough web browsers, and though support is growing, PNG is unlikely to supplant GIF or JPEG any time soon. For one thing, PNG, while high in quality, is often high in bandwidth as well. For another, while PNG stays crisp in milk (like GIFs do), the PNG format does not support animation. GIFs are therefore seen as more versatile by those who even bother to lift their heads out of their cubicles and think about these issues.

To see why PNG can be cool indeed, if your browser can handle it, visit the Audio site at www.panic.com/audion/faces.php, click any thumbnail, and a PNG image will pop up on the screen. Drag the image from place to place on the page at your pleasure. You can even drag it off screen (as shown in Figure 9.12).

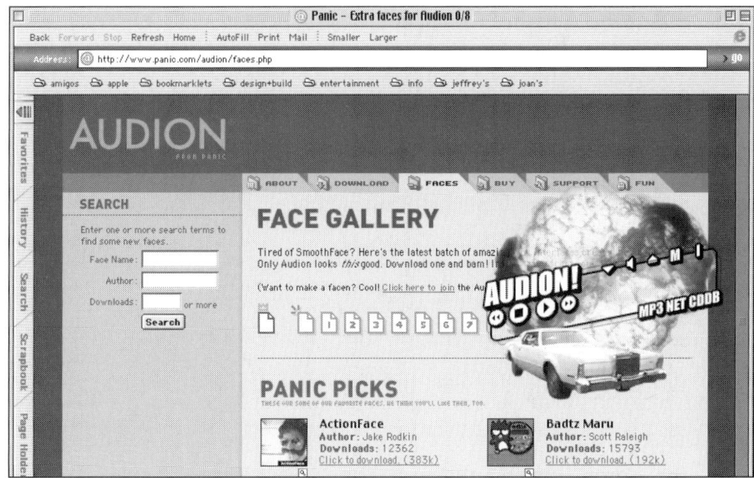

Figure 9.12

PNG a ding-ding. On the Audion site, you can bask in the glories of the PNG format—glories that include true alpha channel transparency, rich color, and crisp detail. (But only if you're packing the right browser.)

Notice that the PNG format offers true alpha channel transparency—it matches any background you drag it over. No more halo effects caused by mismatched anti-aliasing, no more ring around the collar. Notice too that PNG offers crisp imagery as well as rich color.

Notice that the page only works in IE5 for the Macintosh. Bummer. Eventually all browsers will support PNG natively.

Animated GIFs

Animated GIFs are nothing more than a series of frames (or individual GIFs) that have been joined together to create the illusion of motion. They can loop endlessly or play once and then stop. We could include a screenshot here, but what's the point? If you haven't seen animated GIFs, you've never used the Web. (Hint: look at the ad banners that clutter most commercial content sites—web animation in a nutshell.)

Although the GIF format supported the embedding of multiple images in the late 1980s, it was not until 1995 or so that Netscape figured out how to hack the format's multi-image capability to create flip-book-style animation. (Basically, Netscape did this by appropriating a Comments field and some unused but reserved bits in the GIF89A file format.)

Back in the day, web designers used free shareware tools to create animated GIFs, after first preparing each individual image, saving it as a GIF, and then running all resulting GIFs through DeBabelizer, a cumbersome color management tool that ensured that the colors would match between frames. (Nothing ruins the illusion of motion faster than an unexplained color shift between one frame and the next.)

Today all that work is merely a memory because Photoshop comes with ImageReady, and ImageReady makes it easy to create, optimize, and save GIF animations.

Animation for its own sake is charmless, abrasive, and amateurish. Good web designers use animation as they use everything else: with taste and skill in support of a concept and brand image. The creators of www.k10k.net employ animated GIFs well. The animations are revealed when rolling over the miniature content header graphics.

Care should be taken to avoid wasting bandwidth when creating animated GIFs. If one image uses *x* bytes, then ten images theoretically use *10x* bytes, and your web page might bloat as a result. Fortunately, web designers can trim excess fat from their animations by telling the software to animate only the parts that change, rather than redrawing each frame in its entirety. This process is explained in the next sections. Web designers also can optimize their animations by leaving out inessential in-between frames, by keeping their images small (50 x 50 is better than 100 x 100), and by creating graphics that can be rendered in as few colors as possible.

Creating Animations in ImageReady

Adobe ImageReady simplifies the process of creating animated GIFs by allowing web designers to use Photoshop's layers as a series of frames and enabling them to manually change the location of elements from one frame to the next.

For instance, if you wish to animate an arrow, you can draw the arrow on one layer in Photoshop then jump to ImageReady and open the animation palette. Create a new frame and drag the arrow manually to the left or right. Create a third frame and drag the arrow again. ImageReady "remembers" the location of each arrow and will render an animation as a result of these manual movements.

ImageReady can also generate *tweens* automatically. Start with an arrow on the left. Create a new frame. Drag the arrow to the right. Choose the Tween command and instruct ImageReady to tween between the first and second frames. ImageReady generates a smooth flow of images. You can then use the Optimize palette to ensure color consistency from the first frame to the last. Keep in mind that the more you tween, the smoother the motion but the larger the overall file size.

We could blab on about this, but the Photoshop owner's manual does a great job of explaining everything. The way we see it, if you own Photoshop, read the manual. If you don't own it, there's no sense in reading about it here and probably not much sense in planning a web design career. (Gosh, that sounds like a product endorsement.)

Typography

A designer's interest in typography usually borders on obsession. On the Web, you'll get plenty of opportunities to indulge your fetish. As part of establishing the look and feel of a site, the web designer is responsible for all of its typographic choices, including

- Body text typography (CSS)
- Logo (if not preexisting)
- "Type GIF" headlines, subheads, and so on
- Navigational typography (menu bar)

Body text typography is controlled with Cascading Style Sheets (CSS), a subject so important we devote an entire chapter to it (Chapter 10, "Style Sheets for Designers") and still scarcely do it justice. All we'll do here is remind you that 99% of the Web is text, most of it intended to be read, and that there is neither a reason nor an excuse to create hard-to-read text on your web pages.

The logo, if not preexisting, will be designed in Adobe Illustrator or Macromedia Freehand, just as it would be in print projects. All we need to say about that is to remember to start with web-safe colors, keep your design simple so it can reproduce at small sizes (32 x 32 web buttons, for instance), and pay attention to the following discussion about serif versus sans serif faces in the limited 72ppi screen environment.

Remember the VisiBone color palette we mentioned earlier in this chapter? Download the Illustrator version and use it to develop logos and other graphics intended for the Web.

Before copying Illustrator artwork to Photoshop, convert to RGB via Illustrator's **Filter, Colors** menu. The process is not perfect; web-safe colors may shift, and you might need to select large areas in Photoshop and refill them with web-safe colors.

The main thrust of our look at typography will not be body text (covered in Chapter 10) or logo design (covered previously in this chapter). Instead, we will discuss the basics of using Adobe Photoshop and ImageReady to create typographic GIFs for the Web. We'll also further examine how anti-aliasing can work for or against your web designs.

The ABCs of Web Type

As you know, Photoshop and ImageReady let you add horizontal and vertical type to any image. As of Photoshop 5.5, you can specify the typeface, leading, kerning, tracking, baseline style, size, and alignment of the type and edit its characters. Photoshop 6 improves on its predecessor's already remarkable power.

Previously, such details as leading, kerning, and tracking were the exclusive province of Illustrator, and most serious web designers would create their typography in Illustrator and then cut and paste it into Photoshop. Some still do that, and you might prefer to as well. Illustrator offers useful keyboard shortcuts for kerning and other typographic functions. Many of those keyboard shortcuts are missing from Photoshop, making the process a bit less streamlined.

But keyboard shortcuts aside, Photoshop has advanced tremendously in its handling of type and now offers essentially the same typographic functionality that Illustrator does. As a result, many designers use Photoshop for everything.

Photoshop 5.5 and higher also allows you to select an anti-aliasing option for type, apply simulated styles to type, and turn off fractional character widths to improve the appearance of small, bitmapped type displayed at low resolution.

Anti-Aliasing

As all designers know, *anti-aliasing* enables you create the appearance of smooth-edged type by partially filling in the edge pixels with intermediary colors. For those who don't know, we provide the following handy exercise.

Exercise 4: The Great Intermediary

Launch Photoshop and create a new blank document with a white background. Work at 72ppi. (We always work at 72ppi on the Web.)

Select the type tool. Click in the image to set an insertion point.

Enter some text in the Type Tool dialog box (Photoshop 5.5) or directly on the image (Photoshop 6). Format the text however you like. For the sake of argument, we'll type our names in black, 24pt. Helvetica. "Crisp" anti-aliasing is chosen by default. (If it is not, choose it now.)

Close the Type dialog.

Go to Photoshop's Navigator menu and blow up the image by 400%. Look at the edges of any letter. Those soft gray pixels are anti-aliasing. Now you know.

The purpose of anti-aliasing is to fool the eye into seeing type as smoothly rounded in spite of the low resolution of computer monitors.

Anti-aliasing is also used for images unless you're deliberately going for a bitmapped, pixellated look. And you're usually not. Whether for type or images, it can cause problems when working with GIF transparency.

Exercise 5: Match 'Em Up

Open Photoshop and create a new blank document with a white background.

Choose any two web-safe colors from the Photoshop Color Picker or the VisiBone web palette. For the sake of argument, we'll choose a dark purple and a light green.

Select a circular area and fill it with the foreground color (dark purple).

Save the image as circle.psd.

Hide the Background layer so that it becomes transparent.

Save for Web.

Choose GIF (choosy mothers choose GIF) and click the Transparency checkbox.

Select the background (light green) color as your transparency color.

Optimize at 16 colors with dithering on and the web-safe slider dragged to about 40% web-safe.

Save the image as circle.gif.

Open BBEdit or your HTML editor of choice.

Create a new basic HTML document with a background color to match the light green (transparent) background of your GIF image.

Save the file as circle.html.

Open it in any web browser.

The circle should look good and should have a soft edge thanks to anti-aliasing.

Return to the HTML document and change the <BODY> background color to a new, contrasting color. Say, black (#000000).

Save the file and reopen it in the web browser.

The circle should be surrounded by an ugly light green halo.

That is improper anti-aliasing. What have we learned? Always anti-alias against the color you expect to use in the finished web page.

How do you anti-alias a transparent type (or image) GIF when the site uses a gradient background image or a random texture?

You can't. So avoid using those types of backgrounds unless you never need to set transparent GIFs in the foreground.

You should avoid gradient background images anyway because they will dither horribly on 256-color monitors, don't render properly in the GIF format, and if exported as JPEGs cannot be web-safe.

And you should avoid busy random textured backgrounds as well because they are generally hideous, and they make text harder to read. Even beautiful pages developed with subtle background tiles are not much use if no one can read the text they contain.

The PNG format mentioned earlier offers real transparency, which means a PNG image could be used against any type of web background without ill effect. But the trouble with PNG is...well, we've covered that to death already.

Specifying Anti-Aliasing for Type

Anti-aliasing options in Photoshop and ImageReady allow you to choose from three levels of anti-aliasing to modify the appearance of type online. You can choose to make type appear crisper, smoother, or heavier.

Exercise 6: Shape Up—Sizes and Faces

Create a new type layer by typing in a new, blank Photoshop document.

In the Type Tool dialog box, select an anti-aliasing option from the pop-up menu. Choose:

- **None** to apply no anti-aliasing. Useful for bitmapped fonts such as Joe Gillespie's Mini 7 (www.wpdfd.com/mini7.htm), Jason Kottke's Silkscreen (www.kottke.org/plus/type/silkscreen/), or the Fountain Type Foundry's Sevenet (www.fountain.nu).
- **Crisp** to make type appear sharp. This is the default setting. It renders well and uses less bandwidth than Strong or Smooth.
- **Strong** to make type appear heavier. This is an impressive setting, but because it requires additional anti-aliasing to create its effect, it fights the LZW compression algorithm and results in larger file sizes. We are talking about very small differences here, but these differences do add up.
- **Smooth** to make type appear, well, smoother.

Experiment with different sizes and faces to get a feeling for which type of anti-aliasing is appropriate for each face, size, and weight. This also varies depending on the background being used, the visual interaction of other elements on the page, and so on. Most web designers choose Crisp most of the time.

General Tips

As just mentioned, the smoother or heavier the anti-aliasing, the greater the number of edge pixels in various shades, and the more bytes the resulting GIF image will require. When bandwidth is at a premium—and it is always at a premium—err in the direction of Crisp.

Not all type needs to be anti-aliased. Smaller type might be easier to read with no anti-aliasing at all. For instance, 10px Helvetica will be easier to read (and will use up less bandwidth) if you choose "None" in the Anti-Aliasing dialog box. But rather than create GIF type of that nature, a more responsible course would be to use HTML and CSS to create small bits of web type because such text may be easily copied, pasted, and indexed by search engines—whereas type GIFs are simply images.

General Hints on Type

Pardon the pun. (Get it? Type? Hints? Never mind.) Every aspect of web design involves trade-offs and potential problems for some web users. When setting typography for the Web, here are some points to keep in mind.

The Sans of Time

Let's just get it over with: Sans serif fonts are far easier to read onscreen than serif fonts. This is the exact opposite of what is true for books. But printing is high-resolution; the computer screen is low-resolution. There are simply not enough pixels to correctly render the tiny details required by serif typefaces. This is especially true with smaller type, such as body text and subheads. (It is also true for CSS text.)

It helps to think of your type GIFs as icons, which must be rendered pixel by pixel in a 72ppi environment—because that is essentially what they are. Anti-aliased fringe colors must use up an entire pixel (there are no half-pixels). Now add subtle ascenders and descenders to this mix, attempt to wedge such nuances into discreet pixels, and you can see why serifs work poorly onscreen.

You also can see why typographic colors should be web-safe. Add dithering to the unholy mix of anti-aliasing and serifs, and you have an illegible mess.

This inherent preference for sans serifs on the Web might be behind the present resurgence in Helvetica. We could be talking through our hats, but we haven't heard a better theory, and as we've shown earlier, web styles have been entering mainstream media as fast as designers could rip each other off.

From this discussion, it might seem that the Web is no place for fine typography. But that is not the case. Juxt Interactive is one agency that creates superb type treatments online, and their work repays careful study (www.juxtinteractive.com).

Space Patrol

In most cases, web type is more readable when it is widely spaced because such spacing makes allowances for the imprecise spreading of unruly edge pixels. So when setting type, try loosening your tracking in the Type dialog box. If you've done any TV design, it's pretty much the same thing. If you haven't, just trust us.

Lest We Fail to Repeat Ourselves

Always start with web-safe colors for your type and your background to avoid ugly dithering in low-end monitors.

Accessibility, Thy Name Is Text

The more text you create graphically, the less a search engine will understand about your client's web page and the more problems you create for readers with disabilities or those using alternative web browsers.

As mentioned elsewhere in this book, use <ALT> and <TITLE> attributes in your HTML <IMG> tags to explain what the search engine and the disabled visitor cannot see. If HTML and a text GIF look equally good, choose HTML because it increases the accessibility and usability of your page, makes it easier for search engines to locate the relevant information, and almost invariably uses less bandwidth than graphics.

In most cases, HTML text can be resized by the user. Type GIFs cannot. Keep in mind that small type that looks great to you might be difficult or impossible for folks with impaired vision to read.

If you were wondering why you see so much large bold sans serif typography on the web, now you know. It's not that web designers are copycats. Well, we are, but it's not *just* that. It's that we've learned by experience that small fonts, sans serif fonts, and tightly kerned text can all be problematic for the people who use our sites.

As support for CSS improves, it becomes a little easier to sell clients on CSS-style text instead of type GIFs. But resistance to this notion is widespread because clients seek branding, and designers like creating it. And, most of the time, type GIFs just work better for that purpose, regardless of their accessibility issues.

Navigation: Charting the Visitor's Course

We covered the guiding principles of navigation in Chapter 3, "Where Am I? Navigation & Interface." And in Chapter 7, "Riding the Project Life Cycle," we learned that developing a branded, intuitive navigational menu—or a series of hierarchical navigation menus—is only the beginning and that most web firms perform interface testing, asking volunteers to work with the developing site. And as problems are identified, the designer is asked to rethink and redesign.

Focus group testing in advertising often results in mediocre campaigns, but focus group testing of a web interface can result in a better site—if those who run the tests know what they are doing.

What this means in the context of Photoshop is that you will be creating a lot of comps until you truly crack the interface problem, and then you will be refining your comps based on feedback from user tests.

When the perfect interface has been designed in Photoshop, there is still more to do. Often, the design team will implement a menu bar that *changes state* via JavaScript as the visitor navigates the site. On the simplest level, changing state means that the menu bar subtly indicates where the user is within the site structure. For instance, when the visitor reaches the About section of PlanetRX (http://www.planetrx.com/information/about.html), the About portion of the menu bar is highlighted to remind the visitor "you are here." Refer back to Chapter 3's Figures 3.2 and 3.3 to see how this "you are here" state change is handled on the Gap site.

Changing state to reinforce the visitor's position within the site can be accomplished by simple HTML, via JavaScript, or with the help of publishing systems that swap visual elements on-the-fly. The choice of implementation varies by the scope of the site and the size of the budget. On a small site, the menu bar can be changed via HTML or JavaScript. On a very large site that is constantly updated, a publishing system will probably be used.

No matter how the technique is implemented, it is up to the designer to create the alternate state graphics on separate layers in the Photoshop document. (These will come in handy later in the process when the work is sliced and produced in ImageReady.)

Typical navigation menus also "light up" or otherwise change state when the user drags the mouse cursor over a given menu item selection. Again, this is accomplished via JavaScript, and again, though there is no substitute for home-cooked code (or working with good developers), ImageReady can help out, as we are about to see.

Slicing and Dicing

Photoshop is the primary tool used to design navigational menus and their associated text (unless these menus are created in CSS, per the preceding discussion). Photoshop and Illustrator are also used to create assorted navigational elements such as arrows and buttons. The larger and more commercial the site, the greater the pressure to create uniquely branded elements.

These elements can be created in separate image documents. For instance, you might create hundreds of arrows in Illustrator before choosing one for your design. Similarly, you might (and probably will) go through several rounds of logo development.

But after they are created and chosen, all of these elements are generally layered into a single Photoshop comp, which is used to sell the work to the client (see Figure 9.13). Of course, as we've just said (and as Chapter 7 explained), this "selling" is a multistage process, with continual refinement occurring based on research, user testing, and the client's strange whims.

Figure 9.13

Here is a Photoshop web layout that combines photography, logos, and interface elements. We used this layout to sell a final web design to JazzRadio.Net (www.jazzradio.net).

After it's sold, production begins, and at this point Photoshop's ImageReady module comes into its own. Knives were made to slice cake, and ImageReady was made to slice web comps. The process begins by dragging Photoshop guidelines across any area that will have to be sliced—for instance, dragging guidelines to separate one menu bar item from the next (see Figure 9.14).

Figure 9.14

The next phase is dragging Photoshop's guides to mark areas to be converted to slices in the ImageReady module. (Photoshop 6 can create the slices itself.) Though slicing such comps is the normal next step, for this project we opened a text editor and re-created the layout in HTML and CSS to minimize bandwidth and enable the layout to squash or stretch in true "liquid" fashion.

With Photoshop 6, you can create and name slices right in the Photoshop program itself. With Photoshop 5.5, having dragged guides, you "Jump to ImageReady" via the File menu and automatically convert your guides to slices at the touch of a button. ImageReady generates the relevant HTML, animations (if any), and JavaScript rollover functions (if any). We don't mean to imply that this happens instantly, of course. There is a great deal of typing, dragging, and layer selection involved.

Rollovers are created by selecting new layers for each rollover state and typing the relevant URL and text (if any) in the Slices dialog box. Now you can see why rollover states are visually designed during the comping phase. Not only does this satisfy the client, it also enables you to focus on production tasks without worrying about previously unconsidered design issues.

Performing all these production tasks is a fairly straightforward process, and the Photoshop manual spells it out so completely that we won't bother doing so here. One thing Photoshop's manual does not emphasize (but we will) is that you can often replace selected slices with bandwidth-friendly HTML and CSS equivalents. For example, instead of generating a large brown GIF image, you can generate an empty table cell filled with the appropriate background color, merely by choosing No Image from the Type drop-down menu.

This by no means converts a browser-centric, brand-heavy site into a light, accessible one. It does, however, help reduce overall file size, and it does make life a bit easier for those using nontraditional browsers, given that this will be one less pointless image to trouble them with its incomprehensibility.

After the process is completed, sophisticated web designers take the HTML and JavaScript generated by ImageReady, open it in an HTML text editor such as BBEdit, PageSpinner, or HomeSite, and edit as needed. For example, you might substitute a simpler JavaScript function for one generated by ImageReady.

ImageReady's JavaScript is verily a two-edged sword. Novices and experienced web designers in a hurry can rightly consider ImageReady's automated scripting a godsend. But it is equally easy to generate massively confusing or even completely dysfunctional scripts until you familiarize yourself with the process. The first time we used ImageReady to automatically generate image rollovers, we ended up with a folder full of bizarrely named duplicate slices and a script that changed every image on the page at the slightest movement of the mouse.

Then we read the manual.

Most professionals will use ImageReady to generate slices and raw HTML, then tighten up its markup for better standards compliance and lower bandwidth, and replace its often complex scripts with simpler ones. In large web agencies, web technicians will perform these tasks.

Thinking Semantically

Photoshop and ImageReady perform vital tasks splendidly, but what they cannot do is generate semantic websites predicated on the separation of style from content. Being visual tools, they necessarily create visual sites—and of course this is what most clients want and what most designers are comfortable with. But this is not the only way and not necessarily the best way to create websites.

Visual sites are a comforting link to the past, to our history of print and package design—of concrete objects made beautiful and intelligible through precise design. Semantic sites are something else again.

Because they are rooted in images, and images are necessarily of fixed and specific sizes, Photoshop and ImageReady generate image-laden sites laid out in HTML tables with specific heights and widths. They do not generate the Liquid Design we discussed in Chapter 2 because it is not in the nature of a pixel-based program to develop abstractions of form. And certainly they cannot separate style from content because style *is* their content.

So separating style from content becomes your job, if you choose to accept it. As an interim step, what we've done in our shop over the past two years is confine ImageReady's slicing skills to key elements that must be precisely sized—for instance, to branded navigational menu bars. But whenever possible, instead of slicing entire comps to create precise graphic web layouts, we use our comps as guidelines to create HTML (or, even better) CSS equivalents that are loose, flexible, and fairly minimalist.

This process enables us to create templates that function as "content containers." Such sites are still branded and still function as all sites function, but they are less tied down by fixed elements than traditional sites. This makes them easier to revise and update (just change a style sheet) and harder for clients to screw up when they take over the maintenance chores. It also makes them easier for nontraditional browsers to process and positions them for the next phase of web development.

We have now broached the vital next step in the web's history: the separation of style from content. Meanwhile, in our discussion of web typography, we have so far avoided the specifics of coping with actual web texts as opposed to decorative elements. So maybe it's time to look at a technology that handles *both* the separation of style from content *and* the need for precise typographic control of web text.

The people of earth call it CSS, and the next chapter will explain how it works—and what to do when it stops working.

chapter 10

Style Sheets for Designers

IN THE BEGINNING WAS THE WORD: without style and unadorned on a plain gray background.

The scientists who envisioned the Web saw it as a place for reasoned discourse conducted through documents whose structure was as logical as the arguments they propounded. HTML would present content and structure, and the browser (or *User Agent*) would interpret it visually, according to its own built-in rules of display. <h1>Headlines</h1> would look like whatever the browser decided they should look like (typically, 24pt. Times). <p>Paragraphs</p> would look like whatever the browser decided they should look like (typically, 12pt. Times).

In early browsers such as Mosaic and Netscape 1.0, web page backgrounds were generally gray. Why did browser developers choose this dingy color? The answers are lost in the mists of time. In other words, we have no idea. But we do have a theory. Namely, images seemed to want to appear against a black background for maximum contrast and impact. Text, of course, wanted to appear on white. We're guessing that the makers of the first browsers compromised by giving us a washed-out gray that would provide rudimentary contrast for either type of foreground element. Regardless of their reasons, the resulting web pages were not much to look at.

Tag Soup and Crackers

Designers and their clients, however, were not about to sit still for such limited presentational capabilities, so browser companies (mainly Netscape at first) began "extending" HTML willy-nilly to offer web designers more control over the visual appearance of their sites. Netscape extended the <BODY> tag, allowing us to choose background colors as well as text and link colors. Microsoft gave us proprietary <BODY> tag extensions that allowed us to create margins of a limited sort.

Netscape gave us the <FONT> tag. We could control the size of our text, regardless of its structural context. (We could, for instance, make paragraphs really big <FONT SIZE="7"> and headlines really small <FONT SIZE="1"> even if such approaches contradicted the underlying document structure.) Microsoft gave us the <FACE> attribute for the <FONT> tag. We could control typography in a limited, Flintstonian fashion. <FONT FACE="ARIAL, HELVETICA"> would make text on the page appear in Arial if the visitor's operating system offered that font. If not, the text would appear as Helvetica. If neither font were available, visitors would see their default typeface (probably Times).

While browser companies corrupted HTML in a well-meaning but wrong-headed effort to serve designers and their clients, designers began setting their text in Photoshop and saving the images in web-friendly GIF format. 14pt. Meta or Futura, with precise kerning and leading, looked a lot better than <FONT FACE="ARIAL, HELVETICA">. Instead of using HTML to present text, designers used it to embed visual representations of text.

What we gained in presentational spiffiness, we lost in usability. GIF images of text could not be searched, indexed, copied, or pasted. They could not even be seen by some people or in some browsers.

At the same time, designers began using HTML tables to control their layouts, a practice most of us still follow, though it runs counter to the structural nature of HTML. The practice has another downside as well: It yokes our presentation to our content, making it harder or even impossible for those with disabilities or those using nontraditional browsers to access the information on our sites.

Many of us went beyond using tables and text images. We harnessed invisible powers to our task. As you know, in Photoshop any layer may be fully or partially transparent. Images in the GIF format are limited to 256 (or fewer) colors, any one of which may be designated as transparent. Using Photoshop, web designers created small (1 pixel by 1 pixel) GIFs filled with a single, transparent color. We then used these transparent GIF images to control the positioning of elements on the page, as if we were designing for a fixed medium like print.

We used these transparent GIF images again to simulate leading, inserting "spacer GIFs" between lines of HTML text.

```
<IMG WIDTH="100" HEIGHT="100" ALT=" " SRC="transparent.gif">
```

Notice the height and width. Netscape's browser likes it when you indicate the size of images used. This helps the browser leave space for the images, even before they have finished downloading. A tangential aspect of the whole affair is that browsers will display your images at any size you tell them to. Thus a 1 pixel by 1 pixel transparent.gif could be 100 pixels wide by 100 pixels tall if you marked it up that way in your HTML. These crude feats provided rudimentary layout control, while HTML itself did not.

That was the key. HTML, practically the only tool at our disposal, provided no typographic or layout control. So most of us deliberately deformed the simple markup language in hopes of forcing it do our bidding. We made a "tag soup" of the Web, using <TT> ("typewriter text") to force the browser to display a monospaced font (usually Courier). To create vertical space, we deployed transparent GIFS or typed structurally meaningless carriage returns such as:

```
<br><br><br>
```

or went so far as to create "invisible headlines" which were never intended to be read. To create invisible headlines we used the nonstandard <FONT COLOR> attribute to set a headline to the same color as the web page's background. For example, on a page whose background color was white, we might use the following:

```
<H1><FONT COLOR="#FFFFFF">Don't read this headline</FONT></H1>
```

By means of these stunts, the Web began to look better on the surface, but the markup that was supposed to hold it together was becoming less and less meaningful, more and more fragmented. Documents made less and less structural sense and were more and more tied to the quirks of specific browsers. "Use Netscape so you can see this page!" we screamed at our viewers in the mid-1990s.

CSS to the Rescue...Sort of

In 1996, Microsoft, Netscape, and other members of the World Wide Web Consortium (W3C) came up with a brilliant new standard technology—one intended to give designers far more power over the display of web pages, without further corrupting the structural meaning of their HTML documents. The name of that technology was Cascading Style Sheets (CSS).

CSS is the best friend a visually oriented web designer ever had, but support for this crucial standard has been a long time coming. In the following section, we'll gently introduce you to CSS, showing how and why it works. Afterward, we'll talk about what can go wrong with CSS and present a detailed No Fault CSS Plan that enables you to harness the power of style sheets without running afoul of buggy browsers. The good news about all of this is that most current web browsers now offer good-to-excellent CSS support. The bad news is that older, inferior browsers are still in use, though they are fading away over time (see the section, "The 18-Month Pregnancy" in Chapter 2, "Designing for the Medium," for comments on this topic).

As a last prefatory note, you might find yourself working at a large web agency—one where web designers spend most of their time in Photoshop and Illustrator, while HTML production chores are handled by a separate group of professionals. Even at job like that, you will still need to know CSS. Why? It's because even when HTML chores are assigned to web technicians, it is almost always the web designer's job to create the style sheet.

That may seem puzzling. If web technicians and developers handle all other markup and coding, why wouldn't those professionals also be called upon to write the site's style sheet? The answer is simple—style sheets control typography and layout, and that makes them the designer's responsibility. (You don't really want a programmer deciding how your web typography should look, do you?)

Designing with Style: Cascading Style Sheets (CSS)

CSS is a developing web standard whose purpose is to control the display of web pages. Cascading Style Sheets Level 1, the initial version of CSS recommended by the W3C in 1996, is well (or fairly well) supported in current browsers including Opera 5 or higher, Internet Explorer 5 or higher, and Netscape 6 or higher. CSS empowers web designers to control such elements as:

- Font families, font sizes, and leading ("line-height" in CSS-speak)
- Margins and page divisions
- Colors, backgrounds, whether or not backgrounds tile, whether or not they scroll, and so on
- Positioning of elements in relation to each other, and to the edges of the browser window
- Borders, HTML elements (such as <FORM> elements), and more

As this list suggests, CSS is a very powerful standard that can replace the use of HTML tables to control layout; end the use of <FONT> tags to control web typography; and do much more than tables and <FONT> tags ever could (see Figure 10.1).

Figure 10.1

The New Year's 2001 Greeting at zeldman.com. The background image, text, and "core" button are exactly positioned via CSS, which also creates the black outline and background colors. Notice that the image hugs the upper left corner of the browser window, a feat that is easily achieved by using CSS to set margins and padding at "0." JavaScript was used to route Netscape 6 users, IE5 users, and Opera 5 users to subtly different pages (www.zeldman.com/2001.html).

Separation of Style from Content

Beyond providing designers with a powerful tool set, CSS serves an additional purpose—that of formally separating a website's *style* (or design elements) from its *content* (otherwise known as writing and such).

Disadvantages of Traditional Web Design Methods

The way web designers have historically designed pages, style and content are hopelessly intermingled. Text appears inside table cells. <FONT> tags are wrapped around every paragraph.

While this old system works, and while it is used in literally millions of sites, it has two powerful disadvantages:

1. **Problems in the present: wasted bandwidth and HTML abuse.** HTML tables were never intended to be used as design tools; when used for that purpose, they slow the rendering of web pages in the browser and can cause problems for users of text-based browsers—such as people with disabilities. While they do work in most browsers, these tags and tricks slow down web pages and contribute to bandwidth problems by forcing the user to download unnecessary text (namely, the tags themselves). They also clutter the markup.
2. **Problems for the future: retarding progress.** By mingling content with style, the present system makes it much more difficult for web designers and programmers to create sites that can be used by non-graphical browsers and devices, such as web phones, Personal Digital Assistants (PDAs), and audio browsers for the blind. Such devices represent a growing and vital market. On the other hand, if content and style are formally separated, then nongraphical browsers can simply display text and links, while computer users with graphical browsers still enjoy a rich visual experience created by web designers. In addition to the harmful effects on web-enabled devices, the mingling of content and style also makes it more difficult to design and build robust interactive sites, including the e-commerce sites you will inevitably find yourself designing.

CSS Advantages: Short Term

Under the present system, designers who wish to control the appearance of text on the Web must type <FONT> tags for every paragraph of client content. This adds up to hundreds of kilobytes of wasted bandwidth on every site and hundreds of hours of tedious labor for the web designer and/or the HTML technician.

After all those hours of labor, if the client requests a design change, many more hours of labor must be put in, as the designer or web technician manually searches for and replaces all those annoying <FONT> tags.

It's a dumb way to work. With style sheets, the web designer can change just one document—a global style sheet—and the layout and typography of the entire site will be instantly changed. Hundreds of hours of the dullest sort of labor can be saved in this way. If style sheets are used to control layout as well as typography, the savings in labor (and client costs) can be even more profound.

What can you do with the client dollars saved? You can spend them on design, programming, writing, photography, illustration, research, testing, marketing, and maintenance. With less of it wasted on monkey work, the same budget now enables you to create a richer, more powerful site.

Another bonus is that after putting every ounce of our experience and talent into the design of web pages, we typically turn the sites over to our clients, who then update the sites as needed. Websites are not carved in stone; a site that's not minty-fresh is a dead site. How many clients have a background in design and extensive knowledge of web technology? We've been lucky enough to find precisely one such client in nearly six years of doing this work.

As explained in Chapter 7, "Riding the Project Life Cycle," often during the hand-off and maintenance phase, a junior or mid-level person with no design experience and little web knowledge is made responsible for the site's maintenance and updating. Frequently, "refreshing the site" is merely one of that employee's daily duties. The more our pages are filled with <FONT> tags, complex tables and framesets, the sooner that overworked web coordinator can turn the site into an eyesore as well as a usability nightmare. By separating design elements from content, we make it much harder for our clients to destroy the sites we've worked so hard to create for them. CSS is our friend.

CSS Advantages: Long Term

As indicated, CSS provides a way for web designers to create richly visualized, robustly interactive sites that also might function well outside the traditional web browser environment. As more and more people begin to interact with the Web through new, nontraditional Internet devices—and as more and more powerful web standards are brought to fruition in the browser as well as at the W3C bargaining table—the need to separate content from style becomes even more important. So it's pretty darned crucial that web designers come to grips with this concept of style/content separation and learn to use style sheets effectively in designing for the Web.

Compatibility Problems: An Overview

The CSS-1 standard was created in 1996 but was not completely supported by any web browser before the year 2000. As of this book's publication, it is still imperfectly supported by browsers most often used to access the Web. This has slowed the adoption of CSS in the field given that no client wishes to pay for a site that might not work correctly for many users.

Poor, partial, or incompatible CSS implementations in browsers also have persuaded most web designers who do use style sheets to employ them only in very limited ways. For example, many designers now use CSS to control the fonts on a site. But these same designers continue to use HTML tables to control the layout of text and graphical elements on each page (see Figure 10.2) because poor or incompatible CSS implementations in the browser might otherwise render their layouts illegible. They can even cause one browser to crash (more on that shortly).

Figure 10.2

The Daily Report at zeldman.com uses CSS to control typography but traditional HTML tables to lay out the page. CSS-capable browsers are on the market, but so are Netscape 4 and IE3—two old browsers whose support for CSS is problematic. Because Netscape 4 users can crash from CSS layouts and IE3 users can barely see them, an interim approach was taken. When these old browsers have faded into disuse, the same page will be designed entirely in CSS (www.zeldman.com/coming.html).

We refer to this two-pronged, "safe" approach as *No-Fault CSS*, a technique we began recommending in 1998 in the *A List Apart* "Fear of Style Sheets" series:

- www.alistapart.com/stories/fear/
- www.alistapart.com/stories/fear2/
- www.alistapart.com/stories/fear3/
- www.alistapart.com/stories/fear4/

The series was designed to evangelize CSS use in spite of browser compliance problems by showing which CSS techniques to avoid and which could be safely used.

Browser companies such as Netscape and Microsoft have sometimes been slow to realize that what is good for designers and web users is also good for browser makers themselves because fewer problems mean fewer complaints and better word of mouth. Nevertheless, by fits and starts, the browser companies have increasingly supported CSS in earnest. Eventually, web designers will be able to dispense with HTML tables and other forms of HTML abuse altogether and use CSS to design robust sites that conserve bandwidth while offering true separation of style from content.

In turn, this separation of style from content will enable designers, programmers, and web technicians to more capably use additional web standards, such as JavaScript and the Document Object Model (DOM), to build truly dynamic, interactive sites.

Working with Style Sheets

Style sheets are composed of "rules." Rules have two parts: a selector that is followed by a declaration. Consider the style sheet below:

```
BODY {background: white; font-family: helvetica, arial, sans-serif;}
H1 {font-weight: bold; font-size: 24px; }
P, LI {font-size: 12px; line-height: 150%;}
```

BODY is the first selector, while the text within brackets is the declaration. Each declaration consists of one or more properties, followed by its associated values. For example, in the first line, background is a property, and white is declared as its value. font-family is a property, and the fonts listed are possible values for that property. This terminology is confusing at first, but working with style sheets is actually very easy. Let's look more closely at the following example:

```
BODY {margin-top: 0; background: white; font-family: helvetica, arial, sans-serif;}
H1 {font-weight: bold; font-size: 24px; }
P, LI {font-size: 12px; line-height: 150%;}
```

The first line indicates that the BODY of the HTML document will use a white background and that typography throughout the entire page (unless otherwise noted via an additional selector) will be in the Helvetica family. If the user does not have Helvetica on his or her system, the type will be displayed in Arial. If Arial is not available, a generic sans serif will be used. Finally, margin-top: 0 tells the browser to start the web page at the top of the browser window, rather than "helpfully" offsetting it with an unpredictable or inconsistent vertical margin.

Font families are displayed in the order with which they are written. If the user has both Arial and Helvetica on her system, Helvetica will be displayed because it is listed first. In this way it is possible for designers to specify "best-case" scenarios while providing backup options. Remember: The first font listed will be displayed if it is available. The old <FONT> tag worked the same way.

It is crucial to provide typographic alternatives to compensate for cross-platform differences and to end every font declaration with a generic alternative, such as "serif" or "sans serif." Additional generic alternatives include "monospace" for monospaced fonts such as Courier and "fantasy" for ugly and cancerous fonts such as Microsoft Comic Sans.

Recognize the awesome power of style sheets. *In a single line, the typeface has been provided for an entire site.* Imagine typing all those <FONT FACE="HELVETICA, ARIAL, SANS-SERIF"> tags instead. Yuck.

```
BODY {margin-top: 0; background: white; font-family: helvetica, arial, sans-serif;}
```

Note also that the background color has been written out as "white." Any color may be used, though as has been discussed before, it is always best to use web-safe colors.

Colors need not and usually should not be specified by name because names do not necessarily trigger web-safe colors. Instead of white, the designer could have specified the hexadecimal code for that color: #ffffff. It is even possible to use "shorthand" and specify only the first letter of each hexadecimal pair (#fff). This will be clearer with a color such as #ff9900, which can be written as #f90 in the style sheet, saving the designer three strokes of the keyboard and saving the user an infinitesimal amount of bandwidth.

Note that the H1 (headline), P (paragraph), and LI (list item) have had their sizes specified in pixels:

```
H1 {font-weight: bold; font-size: 24px; }
P, LI {font-size: 12px; line-height: 150%;}
```

It is possible (though not always useful) to specify a size of 1px or 200px (or even larger type). Besides pixels, style sheets can use points, inches, centimeters, .ems, percentages ("font-size: 75%;") and even absolute font size keywords. We will discuss the advantages and disadvantages of each further on in the chapter. Oh, brother, will we discuss them.

Note also that it is possible to specify bold (or light, or italic, or italic bold) and that for the first time in web design history, it is also possible to create Quark-like leading in HTML text. Okay, you're new to web design, so you're not impressed. We've had leading in desktop publishing tools since Nixon wore short pants—but not on the Web, sister. On the Web, this is some cool new stuff.

```
line-height: 150%
```

This declaration means that the text will have leading of 150%. Any number may be chosen. Line-height can be 110%, 200%, or 75% (for special effects involving overlapping text). Assume 100% as a default, which need not be written. (Actually, the built-in leading seems to be closer to 110%, but again, unless you are specifying leading for a reason, leave it out to avoid creating problems.)

Line-height, like font-size, can be specified in points, pixels, .ems, percentages, centimeters, or inches.

```
line-height: 18px;
```

Because 150% of 12px equals 18px (12 + 6 = 18), a line-height of 18px would look exactly the same as a line-height of 150% on 12px type. If the font-size were 24px, then 150% would yield a line-height of (24 + 12) 36 pixels.

It is also possible and often desirable to indicate font-size and line-height in the same declaration, using CSS shorthand:

```
P, LI {font: 12px/18px;}
```

The first number (12px) is the font-size; the second (18px) is the line-height. All CSS-capable browsers understand this shorthand.

Leading on the Web serves exactly the same purpose as leading in print: it adds air to the "page" and enhances readability. On the screen-based Web, with its low typographic resolution, anything we can do to encourage readability is all right by us. By contrast, reading may be discouraged when we fail to apply leading and other CSS niceties to our text (see Figure 10.3).

Figure 10.3

The Adobe web column, written by your humble author, but laid out by Adobe's online design team. CSS is used to control typography, but the small text is tough on the eyes. CSS leading and a larger font-size would make the reading experience more pleasurable. This typographic approach works well for image captions, a staple of the Adobe site, but it is less well-suited to longish articles (www.adobe.com).

Now that we've taken a brief look at the rudiments of CSS, let's see how web designers can make this work on a site.

Types of Style Sheets

There are three main ways to use style sheets on a website:

1. By linking to an external style sheet from the HTML document
2. By embedding a style sheet within each HTML document
3. By adding styles inline in an HTML document

Additionally, it is possible to import one style sheet into another. Unfortunately, this technique is not supported by Netscape Navigator 4, so we will confine our discussion to the first three items. If Netscape 4 has gone to its reward by the time you buy this book, you can read up on "CSS import" at www.w3.org/Style/CSS/.

External style sheets

Linking to an external style sheet enables you control multiple web pages (or even an entire site) using a single CSS document. The more pages controlled by the same CSS document, the easier it becomes to make design changes to that site. It is literally possible to change the appearance of a 5,000-page website in under a minute, simply by editing one external Style sheet. Trust us, this is one maintenance chore you will genuinely enjoy.

Five steps to paradise: creating an external style sheet

1. Essentially, in BBEdit, PageSpinner, HomeSite, or any other HTML editor, the designer creates a style sheet. For simplicity's sake, here is a basic one:

```
BODY {background: white; font-family: helvetica, arial, sans-serif;}
H1 {font-weight: bold; font-size: 24px; }
P, LI {font-size: 12px; line-height: 150%;}
```

2. The designer saves this document with a filename ending in .css. For instance, the name could be style.css, or clientname.css.

3. This CSS file is then uploaded to the server via FTP, just like an HTML file.

4. Next, in the website's HTML files, the designer inserts one additional line of code within the <HEAD> tag:

```
<html>
<head>
<title>Welcome to Widgets.com</title>
<link rel="stylesheet" HREF="style.css" TYPE="text/css">
</head>
<body>
```

...and so on.

5. The <link> tag calls up the separate syle sheet file (style.css) and uses its contents as instructions for displaying the page.

Note that it is possible to link to a CSS file using a relative path ("../styles/style.css"), a rooted URL ("/path/from/server/root/style.css"), or a full URL (http://www.widgets.com/styles/style.css). This style sheet will now control any web page that links to it via the additional line of code within the <HEAD> tag. An entire site can be controlled in this way.

Embedding a style sheet

Web designers who wish to affect only one page may do so by embedding a style sheet within the <HEAD> tag of that web page.

```
<html>
<head>
<title>Style Sheets Rule!</title>
<style type="text/css">
<!--
BODY {background: #ffc; font-family: palatino, georgia, times new roman, serif;}
P {font-size: small; line-height: 125%;}
.sub {font: large bold arial, helvetica, sans-serif; margin-top: .25in;}
-->
</head>
```

Note the use of commenting to prevent older, non-CSS-capable browsers from being confused by the code and to prevent search engines from pointlessly indexing your style sheet:

```
<!--
```

(Anything within comments will be ignored by browsers that do not understand the code, and ignored as well by search engines. Have a nice day.)

```
-->
```

What else is new in this example? The CSS is preceded by a tag that tells the browser how to interpret it:

```
<style type="text/css">
```

A more complete heading tells the browser not only that what follows is an embedded CSS, but also tells what type of media the CSS is intended to support:

```
<link REL="StyleSheet" HREF="style.css" TYPE="text/css" MEDIA="screen">
```

The idea is that a document can link to several style sheets. For instance, one controls screen presentation (MEDIA="screen"), another printing, and a third audio browsers. Not all browsers support this as of now, though it's a good idea to begin fully spec'ing your CSS anyway.

In a Class by Itself

All of the preceding is straightforward, but what does .sub mean in this line?

```
.sub {font: large bold arial, helvetica, sans-serif; margin-top: .25in;}
```

The selector labeled .sub is a unique class, created by the web designer for his or her own particular design needs on this page.

That's correct. CSS not only gives web designers the power to style traditional HTML markup, it also enables them to create and style unique items to suit their needs.

For instance, here, the web designer wished to create a special subhead class with a quarter-inch margin at the top. She decided to call it sub because the name was easy to remember and indicated the purpose (subhead) for which the class was created. The designer could have called this class unclecharlie if she wished.

To make use of this special class, the web designer will refer to it in the HTML document in this way:

```
<div class="sub">Here is my subhead, with a quarter-inch margin at the top.</div>
```

In the web page, the line, Here is my subhead, with a quarter-inch margin at the top would be large, bold, Arial or Helvetica (or generic sans serif) with (surprise!) a quarter-inch margin at the top.

Style sheets rock.

Adding styles inline

The inline method is used when the web designer wishes to change the appearance of a single tag or group of tags on one page, and not for changing the entire page or site. Adding styles inline does not offer web designers the true power of CSS because it forces them to restyle text one item at a time. Still, it can be very useful at times.

For instance, an entire page or site may be set in medium-size Verdana (Helvetica, Arial, sans serif). But one line of text needs to stand out from the rest. Perhaps this line of text represents a letter from a customer—or a message from the U.S. Internal Revenue Service. The web designer decides that this particular line of text should be set in 12px Monaco.

She could create an entire class just for that line of text and include that class in the site's global style sheet, but why create an entire class for one line of text on a single web page? Inline styling does the job better:

```
<p style="font: 12px monaco, monospace;">
Greetings from the I.R.S.</p>
```

Inline styling seems like an oddity, but it is actually a wonderful supplemental tool—much like a tube of touch-up paint that is used to correct a small detail.

Inline styling is also quite effective for improving the appearance of <FORM> elements:

```
<div align="center">
<form>
<input
type="button" style="font-size: 12px; font-family: geneva, arial; background-color:
#ff6600; color: #ffffff;"
value="Previous Reports"
onClick="window.location='com0400d.html';"
onMouseOver="window.status='More of same.'; return true;"
onMouseOut="window.status='';return true;">
</form>
</div>
```

Form elements also may be styled via DIV classes in a global style sheet. If every <FORM> button on your site is supposed to be orange (#ff6600) and use 12px Geneva or Arial type, by all means create an orangebutton class for the site, declare it on the global style sheet, and then refer to it in individual HTML pages, like so:

```
<div align="center">
<form>
<input
type="button"
class="orangebutton"
```

```
value="Previous Reports"
onClick="window.location='com0400d.html';"
onMouseOver="window.status='More of same.'; return true;"
onMouseOut="window.status='';return true;">
</form>
</div>
```

Trouble in Paradise: CSS Compatibility Issues

The first web browser to attempt to support CSS was Microsoft Internet Explorer 3.0 (1997). It supported about 30% of the standard. A year later, Netscape 4 came out with support that was marginally better than that of IE3. During three years of hell, while Netscape sought to rebuild its browser from the ground up, Navigator 4 sat rotting on the market—its once-proud CSS support looking more and more shoddy. IE4 got more of it right and was soon replaced by IE5, which got still more of it right. No browser got it absolutely right, and baffled web users were often reluctant to upgrade to incremental (4.52 anybody?) versions of these browsers.

Thus support for CSS lagged, and problems abounded. In 1998, The Web Standards Project (www.webstandards.org) was formed to advocate and shore up support for CSS and other web standards, and *A List Apart* (www.alistapart.com) began running the "Fear of Style Sheets" series.

Fear of Style Sheets: CSS and Layout

One of the great strengths of CSS is its ability to position elements on a web page. Elements may be positioned by exact pixel coordinates (400 pixels from the top, 32 pixels from the left, for example). They may be positioned relative to each other. They may be positioned via percentages, permitting web designers to easily set up liquid layouts, as previously discussed.

Unfortunately, CSS positioning is not supported in IE3 and is poorly supported in Netscape Navigator 4. In fact, it can cause the browser to crash, as detailed in *A List Apart*'s article, "The Day The Browser Died" (www.alistapart.com/stories/died/).

So until IE3 and Netscape 4 leave the market, many of us will probably keep using HTML tables to create our web layouts. Web pages laid out with HTML tables will work in Netscape 1, 2, 3, 4, and 6; in IE 2, 3, 4, 5 and beyond; and in all other graphical browsers, including Opera and iCab.

If you've been following along, you'll realize this means that web designers still cannot safely separate style from content on commercial projects and will continue to face difficulties in creating sites that work well outside the traditional desktop computer-based browser. But in the trenches, where work gets done, it also means that we can create sites that work for our clients and our clients' audiences.

By late 2001 or soon after, we should be free to truly harness the power of CSS. Meanwhile, on personal, noncommercial projects, we can explore the full potential of CSS and other web standards without fear of hurting our clients' customers (see Figure 10.4). It is hoped that these noncommercial usages of CSS and other web standards help widen interest in emerging technologies and encourage quicker adoption of newer, more standards-compliant browsers.

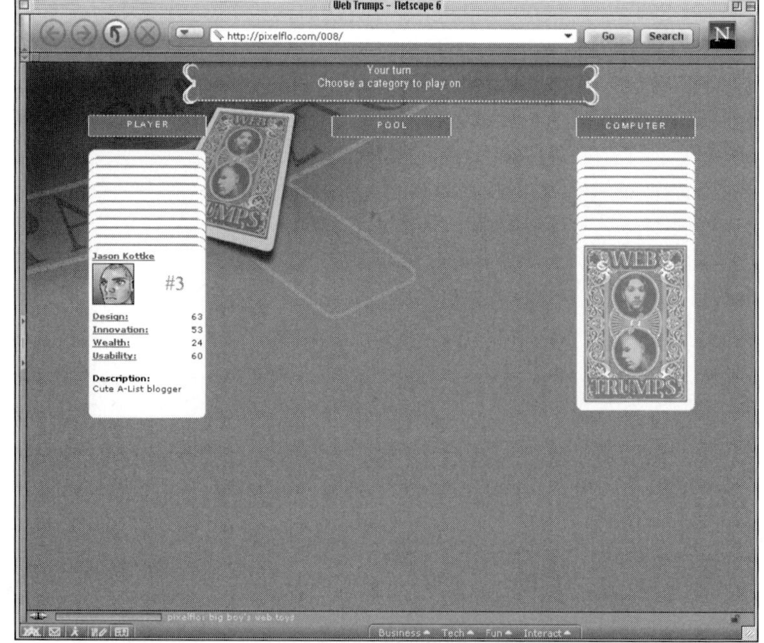

Figure 10.4

Web Trumps, a card game featuring well-known web personalities, uses CSS to control the positioning and layering of every image on the page and JavaScript to reveal new layers during game play. Web Trumps is a mini-masterpiece of graphic design and web programming—but one requiring the use of a modern browser. Experiments like this help hasten the day web designers can apply the same level of sophistication to commercial designs without worrying about browser incompatibilities (http://pixelflo.com/008/).

Fear of Style Sheets: Leading and Image Overlap

As mentioned earlier in this chapter, CSS leading provides a standard means of improving the legibility and aesthetics of textual presentations on the Web—something every site designer should care about. And it does this while avoiding all the problems associated with transparent GIF hacks and other nonstandard visual workarounds.

The CSS line-height property solves all the old problems, but it can lead to new ones, particularly in older browsers whose support for CSS is largely theoretical. For instance, in the following example, if CSS line-height is specified for the <p> tag, the image will float on top of the text in both IE3 and early versions of Navigator 4:

```
<p><img src="dog.gif" width="100" height="100" alt="My dog, Pookie." title="Pookie is a
friendly mutt." align="left">My dog Pookie liked this text so much, he decided to sit on it
in IE3 and Navigator 4.</p>
```

This problem is more prevalent in Mac OS than in Windows, largely because big browser companies spend more time and resources developing browsers for Windows than for other operating systems. (All the more miraculous then, that in the year 2000 the best browser on the market was IE5/Mac. Arguably it is still the best.) The solution to image overlap is to keep images outside of paragraphs and <div> tags. Unfortunately, doing so brings up yet another problem in Netscape Navigator 4:

```
<img src="dog.gif" width="100" height="100" alt="My dog, Pookie." Title="Pookie is a
friendly mutt." align="left">
<p>My dog Pookie liked this text so much, he decided to shove it to the right in its own
little column in Navigator 4.</p>
```

With a left-aligned image placed outside the <p></p>, some versions of Netscape Navigator 4 will stick all the paragraph text in an imaginary column to the right of the image, as if the web designer had desired to create such a column. New paragraphs, in turn, will appear also in that unwanted column. Many a simple layout has been ruined in this way.

There is no solution to this problem. No matter which approach is used, some Netscape 4 users are going to get an ugly layout. Because an unwanted and mindlessly stupid column is preferable to text that is hidden behind an image, it is best to hope and pray that most Netscape 4.x users are equipped with a more recent version of the browser. Alternately, the designer can create pages that use no images whatsoever—scarcely an attractive option. Finally, the designer can wrap images inside table cells, given that doing so seems to solve most of these problems—at the terrible cost of adding needless, bandwidth-wasting and time-consuming code to every single web page.

The good news of course is that Netscape 6 avoids all these problems, and Netscape 4, like other old browsers, will gradually wither away. The bad news is it hasn't withered away yet. So proceed with caution.

Fear of Style Sheets: CSS and Typography

Guerrilla warfare pays little heed to niceties and neither can designers in the trenches. Too much of CSS still does not work in millions of web users' browsers. To prepare you for battle, we will now pay little heed to the way things should work. Instead, we will show you what does work in any CSS-capable browser, no matter how old, inadequate, or semi-standards-compatible it is. In other words, the following is an interim strategy for use until nearly all web users are packing a CSS-compliant browser. If you wish to control your web typography with CSS (and why wouldn't you wish to do that?), there are only two things that always work:

1. Use pixels (not points, not .ems, not percentages, not keywords) to specify your font sizes.
2. Or use nothing. Do not specify font sizes at all, and let the browser's stylistic defaults and the visitor's preferences take care of the relative size relationships. This approach is detailed in the "Dao of Web Design" article at *A List Apart* (www.alistapart.com/stories/dao/)

Promise and performance

By now you understand that CSS is an important standard. It allows web designers to specify the font family, size, margins, and leading of type on the web; permits web designers to create advanced web layouts without abusing HTML; and enables web designers, web practitioners, and programmers to separate design elements (presentation) from content.

This ability to separate presentation from content theoretically empowers us to create attractive sites without excluding visitors who cannot use graphical browsers—a highly desirable goal. It also paves the way for the expansion of the Web beyond the desktop computer and onto a variety of hand-held and other Internet-enabled devices.

Yet many times our best CSS efforts fail in one browser or another.

Even though the CSS Level 1 standard was finalized in 1996, the first browser to meaningfully support it did not appear until the year 2000 (Internet Explorer 5, Macintosh Edition). Fortunately, Netscape 6 (multiple platforms), Opera 5 (multiple platforms), and Konqueror (Linux/UNIX) soon followed, with commendable CSS support of their own. But each of these fine browsers enjoys only a relatively small market share as of this writing.

At present, the market is dominated by IE for Windows—a browser that comes teasingly close but misses the mark in a few critical areas. The Windows version of Microsoft's browser did not fully support CSS-1 before the release of IE6—if then. And Netscape Navigator 4, still used by tens of millions, does such a poor job of handling style sheets that it has been known to crash upon encountering them, as detailed in *A List Apart*'s "The Day the Browser Died."

Faced with these inconsistencies, many web designers have avoided using CSS altogether. A few brave souls have leaped ahead to fully exploit the power of CSS in spite of the dangers posed to old browsers. Other web designers and developers have followed the "No-Fault CSS" plan outlined in *A List Apart*'s "Fear of Style Sheets" series, whether they picked it up at *ALA* or figured it out on their own.

Still others—tricky devils—have created platform and browser detection scripts to serve a variety of "appropriate" style sheets to specific user agents—for instance, serving one style sheet to an IE4/Mac user and another to a Navigator 4 user on Windows NT. This approach was always unpleasantly complicated, but at least it used to work. As we'll show you in a moment, it no longer works.

What works? Pixels or no sizing at all works. How can we make this audacious claim? We'll let an expert make it for us. Take a sad look at Web Review's Master List and see the inconsistencies for yourself:

The Master List

www.webreview.com/style/css1/charts/mastergrid.shtml

"The mother of all CSS (Cascading Style Sheet) charts," which lists every aspect of the CSS spec and identifies how well it is supported by various Mac and Windows web browsers.

If the Master List did not convince you (or if you could not quite grasp its meaning), we'll look at the alternatives one by one:

Font Size Challenges

Among many other capabilities, CSS allows web designers to specify the size of typography on web pages. As shown below, font sizes can be indicated using any of the following: points, pixels, absolute keywords, relative keywords, length units, and percentage units.

```
H1 {font-size: 14pt}
H1 {font-size: 14px}
H1 {font-size: x-large}
H1 {font-size: larger}
H1 {font-size: 1.5 em}
H1 {font-size: 125%}
```

Too bad most of the stuff doesn't work everywhere...yet.

Points of contention

Points are the units of measure with which designers are most familiar—from their years of creating print layouts in Quark XPress or similar programs. Unfortunately, points are meaningless on the Web. Points function as units of print, not as units of screen space. (Pixels are the only meaningful unit of screen space.) Due to platform and resolution differences, 14pt. can mean many things. What it does not mean is a specific unit of screen size.

Points are included in the CSS spec so that designers can set up a second style sheet for printouts, as mentioned earlier in this chapter—one CSS document to control the way the display looks on the screen and a second for printing.

In your print-oriented style sheet (if the browser supports this), it makes perfect sense to use points because printers understand points and can be thrown for a loop by pixels. In some older browsers, 12px type gets printed as 12 pixels, and those pixels are computed against the printer's resolution. Got a 1200ppi printer? Your 12px type could be .01 inches tall. To avoid that kind of lunacy, points should be used in style sheets devoted to the printer—and nowhere else. (Better browsers recalculate style sheets according to the needs of the printer, but your visitors may not be using these browsers.)

In the world of print, there are approximately 72 points per inch. To match this, Mac OS offers a default resolution of 72 pixels per inch, mapping pixels to points (give or take a fraction). Of course, as soon as the Mac user changes her screen resolution, all bets are off. In Windows and other PC operating systems, there are 96 pixels per inch—until the PC user changes her screen resolution, and then all bets are off.

What this means is that point sizes are incompatible between Mac OS and Windows right from the get-go. For instance, when a Windows client sends a Microsoft Word document to a Mac-based graphic designer, the type is often too small for the designer to read. The same problem traditionally plagued web pages.

Leaving aside the fact that most users change their screen resolution (and therefore all bets are off), savvy developers have used JavaScript to serve appropriate point-size-based style sheets to Mac users versus PC users. It's more complicated than using pixels, but at least it *used* to work.

Point of no return: browsers of the year 2000

In IE5/Mac and Netscape 6, this has changed. (See *ALA*'s "Why IE5/Mac Matters" for a complete discussion of this issue.)

IE5/Mac sets as its default typographic preference 16px type at 96ppi. In other words, it brings the default Windows typographic resolution to the desktop of Mac users. Netscape 6 does exactly the same thing.

This is not evil hegemony; it is simply common sense in that the more closely browsers adhere to commonalities, the less likely web users are to get hurt. Windows' default resolution is no better or worse than Mac resolution. But it is the most commonly used resolution, so more sites are designed to accommodate it. Treating it as a de facto "standard" prevents Mac users from being hurt by the poor authoring practices of some web developers.

"Aha!" cries the Scripting Brigade. "So all we have to do is add a few more lines of code to our browser detection scripts, and we can serve Windows-size type to Mac users if they are surfing with IE5 or Netscape 6 and Mac-size type if they are using older browsers?"

Not so fast, buckos. IE5/Mac starts at this default resolution but enables users to change it. They can change it back to standard Mac resolution (and how will you know if they've done that?). Adept users can change it to a size based specifically on their screen resolution, and Netscape 6 users can change their font size to any arbitrary value that strikes their fancy. You have no way of knowing if they've done this or not. Therefore, using JavaScript to detect the user's browser and platform tells you exactly nothing about their default font size and its relationship to standard point sizes. There is only one thing of which we can be certain: If you use points to control sizes, you are kidding yourself.

What works? Pixels.

Pixels for fun and profit

Though screen resolutions vary, a pixel is always equal to a pixel. Pixels are the only reliable means of sizing typography if the web designer absolutely must control the size of type on the web page. Unfortunately, this practice might cause problems for some readers. For instance, if the designer has specified 10-pixel type:

1. The visually impaired might have difficulty reading the type. This is not a problem in IE5/Mac, which allows users to resize type at their discretion by using the included "text zoom" function. Netscape 6 offers similar functionality, and Opera 5 zooms the entire page at the touch of a button. So in those browsers, you can use pixels without causing accessibility problems for anyone. (But these, as we've already explained, are not the most popular browsers.)

2. Older browsers do not allow visitors to resize most CSS type—particularly type set in pixels, and IE5.5/Windows still does not offer text zooming at all. Thus, there will always be a potential accessibility hazard involved when you specify text in pixels—at least until IE for Windows offers text zooming or an equivalent solution. As explained in Chapter 2, we might have to wait 18 months or more for Netscape users to upgrade to the 6.0 browser and for Microsoft to implement text zoom in its Explorer browser for Windows.
3. If your style sheet calls up a scalable True Type font and if the user's operating system includes that font (and supports True Type), your pixel-based style sheet will work just fine. But if the user's system does not include a scalable version of that font or a suitable substitute or does not natively include True Type fonts (Linux for example), type set in pixels can display jaggedly and may be illegible.

Accessibility problems are deadly serious. This is not idle, theoretical chitchat. When people can't read (or even access) your site, it hurts them, it hurts you, and it hurts your clients.

Accessibility problems aside, some designers quibble that pixels are bad because they vary according to screen resolution. A 400 x 400 pixel square fills most of the screen at 640 x 480, and very little of it at 1600 x 1200.

To which we reply, so what? A 100 pixel-tall CSS headline will be the same height as a 100 pixel-tall GIF image. A 200 pixel-wide CSS div will be equivalent to a 200 pixel-wide JPEG image.

If you intend to create print-like layouts on the web—or even liquid layouts that depend on the relative sizing of elements—you have exactly one choice: pixels. If you can get away with a looser type of design (as you can, for instance, in a personal diary or an academic paper), so much the better. Most of us have to size the elements in our layouts, and most of us designers like it that way.

Besides, our other options simply do not work. For instance:

Absolute size keywords

There are seven absolute size keywords in CSS Level 1:

xx-small	medium	large
x-small		x-large
small		xx-large

If implemented correctly and uniformly, these seven keywords would allow designers to specify approximate sizes without running into the accessibility problems associated with pixels. For that reason, the W3C recommends their use. The W3C is wise, and the recommendation is sound—except that it fails in too many browsers.

One size fits nobody

Unfortunately, absolute size keywords are unusable in many browsers. Netscape 4 largely ignores them. Netscape 4.5 and higher and IE3 render them at illegible sizes. (For instance, Netscape 4.5 and IE3 render xx-small at 6 pixels, which is 3 pixels below the threshold of legibility.) In Netscape's case, the engineers were following an early recommendation of the W3C, which was that each size should be 1.5 times larger than the size below it. If small was 10 pixels, medium (one size larger) would be 15 pixels.

The W3C later changed its recommendation, but not before Netscape had followed it. We can't fault Netscape for trying to support standards that changed, but we can point out the absurdity of using absolute size keywords if even one of your visitors is using Netscape 4 or IE3. And millions of folks use those browsers.

Small means medium, war means peace

Does IE5.x/Windows get it right? Not in our estimation. In IE5.x/Windows, there is a logical disconnection between the keyword and the way it is rendered. "Small" is displayed as medium; "medium" is larger than normal; and so on. (IE/Windows gets keywords right.)

The engineers who developed IE for Windows are not hacks and are not evil. They were trying to do the right thing. Remember the seven <FONT SIZE> settings supported by Netscape? Sure you do—<FONT SIZE=1>, <FONT SIZE=4>, and so on. Rather deftly and cleverly, the IE developers mapped the seven CSS keywords directly to the seven Netscape font sizes. In many ways, it was a logical and even brilliant thing to do. (The IE/Windows developers were also the first group to attempt to support absolute font size keywords. We should credit them for that before carping about the results.)

The problem, of course, is that, logically, the sizes do not map to the keywords. In old-style browsers, <FONT SIZE=3> is the default or normal size that the user has specified in her preferences. In Netscape's extended HTML markup, <FONT SIZE=3> is assumed unless you specify another size. Logically, a default size should map to the "medium" CSS keyword. Unfortunately, in the IE/Windows scheme, <FONT SIZE=3> maps to "small" instead of "medium" because small is the third size up from the bottom of the list.

Who goofed—the W3C or the IE/Windows team? It doesn't really matter. What matters is that the keywords don't map to expected sizes, and an incompatibility exists not only between different manufacturers' browsers but between the Mac and Windows versions of the same browser.

If you think of the seven sizes the way the IE/Windows team did, your sizes will be off on Mac users' desktops. (You also will go nuts. It's like trying to drive a car where Park means Neutral.) If you think of them the way the keywords actually read (small, medium, large) your display will be off in Windows. You can trick the Mac browser into emulating Windows behavior by specifying a <DOCTYPE> of HTML 4 Transitional and leaving off the W3C URL. (For details, see http://www.alistapart.com/stories/ie5mac. But this is forcing the browser to emulate nonstandard behavior, and that's not good. Besides, it won't work in Netscape 4, Opera, or Konqueror.

So what can you do? Sadly, until your entire audeince uses browsers that render absolute keywords, all you can do is ignore the W3C recommendations and use pixels in your style sheet. Or do not use sizes at all.

Relative keywords

Relative keywords are limited to two: smaller and larger. These in turn refer to the size of the parent element. For example, consider the following example, in which the <BODY> is 12px, and <BOLD> is "larger."

```
<HTML>
<STYLE TYPE="text/css">
<!--
BODY {font: 12px verdana, arial, geneva;}
B {font-weight: bold; font-size: larger;}
-->
</STYLE>
```

Bold type would theoretically be 14px tall in this example because 14px is one "notch" up from 12px. Like absolute size keywords, relative keywords are ignored or bungled in some popular browsers (Explorer 3 ignores them, as does Navigator 4 for the Mac). And even if they worked correctly, they would be insufficient for the needs of most web designers and their clients. Normal, larger, and smaller is not exactly a robust vocabulary for the needs of professional designers.

So what can you do? You can use pixels in your style sheet; that's what you can do.

Length units

Length units sound smutty (those W3C folks should get out more...or maybe it's just us) and include the following:

- **em**—Is a unit of distance equal to the point size of a font. In 14pt. type, an em is 14pts. wide—named for the size of the capital "M." But you knew that.)
- **ex**—Refers to the height of lowercase letters.

When used with the font-size property, em and ex units refer to the font size of the parent element.

```
<HTML>
<STYLE TYPE="text/css">
<!--
BODY {font: 12px verdana, arial, geneva, sans-serif;}
STRONG {font-weight: bold; font-size: 2em;}
-->
</STYLE>
```

In this example, <STRONG> would be 24px tall, or 2em (two times the font size of the parent element, which is the <BODY> tag). In theory, a web designer could create a layout using em or ex units, where all elements were sized relative to each other. This would avoid the accessibility problems associated with pixels.

Unfortunately, the browsers make this impossible for the time being. Netscape 4 ignores em and ex units. IE3 treats em units as pixels. Thus, 2em is mistranslated as 2 pixels tall. It takes a village to raise a child, and it takes at least 9 pixels to render a font. Length units are therefore not recommended. What is recommended? Pixels or nothing.

Percentage units

Percentage units, like length units and relative keywords, refer to the size of the parent element.

```
<HTML>
<STYLE TYPE="text/css">
<!--
BODY {font: 12px verdana, arial, geneva, sans-serif;}
STRONG {font-weight: bold; font-size: 200%;}
-->
</STYLE>
```

In this example, <STRONG> would be 24px tall, or 200% of the font size of the parent element, which is the <BODY> tag. In theory (notice how we keep saying "in theory"?), a web designer could create a layout using percentages and avoid the accessibility problems associated with pixels.

Nothing is sadder than the murder of a beautiful theory by a gang of ugly facts. Netscape 4 for Mac renders percentage units when they are used for line-height (leading) but ignores them entirely when they are used to specify type sizes. And some versions of Netscape 4 for Windows treat percentages as pixels. (Thus, 200% is dementedly translated as 200 pixels. Mmm, nice layout.)

Lest we forget, good old IE3 drops the ball by sizing percentages relative to the user's default font size rather than to the parent element. In English: If the web user has set her browser's default to 10px, IE3 will display <STRONG> at 20px and not the 24px you intended. If her browser defaults to 16px, <STRONG> will be 32px. Too bad for you. Too bad for your visitor.

In spite of their accessibility benefits, percentages still fail in too many browsers. What works? Pixels—pixels or nothing. In case we've failed to communicate, we will summarize our findings as follows:

Looking Forward

Web designers will continue to be limited to using pixels in their style sheets—despite the accessibility hazards associated with that practice—until fully standards-compliant browsers exist and are widely used. The approach might have its drawbacks, but failure to work correctly is not one of them. As web designers, our job is to control the visitor's visual experience to communicate. For the time being, the approach outlined here will allow us to do exactly that. And soon enough, Lord (and browser companies) willing, the full power of CSS will be ours.

Can you take CSS further today? Quite possibly. It depends on the makeup of your audience and your salesmanship with clients. As explained in Chapter 13, A List Apart converted to an all-CSS layout in February 2001, and many sites have since followed suit. For details and encouragement, see http://www.alistapart.com/stories/99.

chapter 11

The Joy of JavaScript

WE'VE SAID ALL ALONG that the Web is not print. If you've harbored lingering doubts on that score, this chapter should clear them up pronto. If this chapter does not clear them up, try club soda and a semiabrasive cloth.

A primary reason the Web is not print is that websites don't just sit there; they do things—responding to clicks of the mouse, hovering motions, and other user activities. JavaScript is behind much of that interactivity. In JavaScript parlance, user actions such as mouse clicks are called *events*, and you handle them via *event handlers* ("onClick," for example). Similarly, in JavaScript, the components of a web page, such as GIF images and form buttons, are considered *objects*. Web pages are known as *documents*, and the whole shebang is held together by a Document Object Model (DOM).

See, it's not that hard, and you are learning already.

In this chapter you'll find out what JavaScript is, where it came from, how it brings websites to life, where to learn all about it, and how to begin using it even *before* you learn all about it.

You'll also learn how to communicate desired JavaScript functions to the developers on your team, who will handle the heavy scripting when it is needed. If you freelance or work in a graphic design shop instead of a web agency, you'll learn how to communicate with freelance programmers. But before you can begin doing any of that, a few basics are in order.

What Is This Thing Called JavaScript?

JavaScript is a programming language designed specifically to work in web browsers. Its purpose is to bring interactivity to sites. Though JavaScript is powerful and complex, it is relatively easy to learn—at least it is easier to learn than many other programming languages.

Even before JavaScript, sites could be somewhat interactive. After all, clicking a hyperlink loads a new page. The nonlinear nature of hypertext allows the reader to decide where to go next—to structure her own voyage through the site (and, indeed, through the Web).

That is an interactive process and a rather profound one. But it is not a terribly *sophisticated* form of interactivity. JavaScript puts the top hat and tails on web interactivity.

The Web Before JavaScript

Before JavaScript, programming languages such as Perl were used to facilitate interactive processes, for example typing text into a form and clicking a button, thereby sending requested information to the site's owners. Perl is still often used for this purpose on a great many sites.

But Perl is a *server-side* scripting language. That is, when a visitor clicks the Send button, the web server itself must process the script. If the server goes down or malfunctions, nothing will happen. Likewise, a web page not connected to a web server—say, a web page on your hard drive—would not be able to process such a script except in special circumstances (permanent Net connection, full URL specified in the <FORM ACTION>, burning of incense, wearing of magic ring).

While the script is being processed, the web server is momentarily tied up—just as your Mac or PC gets tied up when you apply motion blur to an image in Photoshop. Imagine constantly applying motion blur while receiving and sending email, and you begin to see what web servers were up against. (This is, of course a crude picture, and if you like it, we have other crude pictures available at a nominal price.)

As the Web's population grew, more and more users were clicking more and more Send buttons. More and more web servers were thus spending more and more time processing scripts in between serving web pages. Meanwhile, the user's browser sat there, doing nothing. A tool was needed to transfer the process from the server to the *client* (the user's computer). Enter JavaScript.

JavaScript, Yesterday and Today

In 1995, the company formerly known as Netscape Communications Corporation introduced a *client-side* programming language designed to transfer the burden of interactive processing from the web server to the end-user's browser. Unlike other programming languages (such as Java or C), this new language was built into the browser. It even understood HTML.

Netscape called its new client-side scripting language LiveScript, but soon changed the name to JavaScript to capitalize on the growing excitement about Sun's Java language. To this day, as a result of their similar names, many beginning web designers (and users) confuse Java with JavaScript. The relationship between the two is mainly one of marketing.

Netscape quickly promised to release JavaScript as a web standard so that other browsers could use it too. But for competitive reasons, the company initially held back on its pledge. Old browsers like Mosaic could not use JavaScript at all. Neither could Microsoft's newly unveiled Internet Explorer.

To offset Netscape's advantage, Microsoft's browser engineers developed a JavaScript-like language called JScript. Web design quickly became a circle of Hell, as serious developers were forced to work with these similar but incompatible technologies. Freelancers and small firms, lacking deep resources, often chose to support only one technology. That one was nearly always JavaScript, especially in the beginning when Internet Explorer enjoyed only a tiny share of the market. Thus JavaScript functioned as a sort of standard before it really was one.

Around the Millennium, JavaScript finally became an official web standard, available to all. As reported in Chapter 2, "Designing for the Medium," the European Computer Manufacturers Association (ECMA) supervised the standardization of JavaScript, renaming it in the process. The universal web scripting language is now officially known as ECMAScript or ECMA-262, though no one we know calls it anything but JavaScript. (Our Scandanavian friends pronounce it "Ya-va-script," which we find incredibly endearing. That has nothing to do with any of this, but it does lend this chapter a certain international flair.)

The point is that JavaScript/ECMAScript is a standard that works in all current browsers, though there are still some subtle incompatibilities being worked out between the latest versions of Netscape, Internet Explorer, Opera, and other browsers. Meanwhile, the DOM has been standardized by W3C. Prior to that, JavaScript had its own ever-changing DOM in Netscape, and Microsoft had its own DOM as well.

As all browsers finalize complete support for these standards, web designers and developers are being empowered to create sophisticated interactivity that works for everyone. Conversely, as browsers lag in their DOM and ECMAScript support, web designers and developers are stuck programming alternate versions of every site function, often going so far as to develop alternate versions of the sites themselves.

Now that we've concluded our mini-history lesson and you've finished your nap, let's move on to the good stuff.

JavaScript, Unhh! What Is It Good For?

Absolutely lots of things. Through this web-friendly programming language, designers and developers can:

- Replace cryptic status bar URLs ("http://www.doglovers.com/poodles.html") with text messages ("Learn about poodles"), a somewhat controversial practice, for reasons we'll discuss in a moment.
- Create the ever-popular image rollover effect discussed in Chapter 9, "Visual Tools."

- Compensate for browser incompatibilities.
- Open new, precisely sized "pop-up" windows, with or without various bits of browser chrome.
- Test for the presence or absence of Flash, QuickTime, or other plug-ins (more about plug-ins in Chapter 12, "Beyond Text/Pictures").
- Rotate content and images depending on the time of day, the number of times the user has viewed a certain page, or simply at random.
- Enable the client to inject 50 links on a page without cluttering that page at all.
- Provide alternative means of navigating the site.
- "Remember" that a user has visited the site before, sparing her the pain of reentering personal data or passwords. This is accomplished by means of *cookies* (Netscape terminology for little bits of text that reside on the end-user's hard drive and can be recognized by JavaScript on subsequent visits to the site).
- Cause images or text boxes to scroll horizontally or vertically, another controversial and often annoying practice.
- Verify the credibility of email addresses entered on "customer feedback" forms. JavaScript won't tell you if a person is using her email address or someone else's, but it will tell you if the address is well formed or not. (If malformed, it is probably a nonworking address.)
- Control complex frames—of less importance than it used to be, as frames are gradually being phased out. Similarly, JavaScript can protect sites from a third party's poorly crafted frames.
- Create *nested* navigational menus that reveal secondary and tertiary levels in response to cursor movements—a wonderful idea because it enables visitors to navigate directly to the information they seek, but problematic because not all browsers fully support a standard means of doing this.
- ...and much more.

Add the W3C DOM to what JavaScript does already and you can change that phrase to "much, much, *much* more."

We know what you're saying. "Sounds great, but I'm, like, an artist. Do I really have to learn this stuff?"

Sounds Great, but I'm an Artist. Do I Really Have to Learn This Stuff?

The politically correct answer is, yes you do, because adding interactivity to your clients' sites is part of what makes you a web designer. The gentle answer is, learning JavaScript is an iterative process: You can begin by cutting and pasting and gradually come to understand what you're working with. The Richard Nixon Memorial answer is, not at first, and maybe never.

Not at first and maybe never is an answer because many working web designers get by for years doing nothing more than cutting and pasting other people's scripts. By the way, we're not talking about *stealing* code. Many developers freely offer their scripts in return for an acknowledgement in the source code, and some don't even ask for *that* (http://javascripts.earthweb.com/).

Likewise, many other web designers get along by using WYSIWYG editors such as Macromedia Dreamweaver and Adobe Golive and image editors such as Macromedia Fireworks—programs that can create many standard JavaScript functions for you. Some respected web designers have never programmed a line of JavaScript code; they let Dreamweaver do it.

But *most* web designers do learn at least the basics of JavaScript because, sooner or later, they run into problems they cannot solve without it. A problem like this can occur: A certain page does not display properly in Netscape 4. The solution would be to create an alternate page that *does* work in Netscape 4 and use JavaScript to send Netscape 4 users to that alternate page. For nearly every design problem like this, there is a simple JavaScript solution.

The other problem with cutting and pasting (or relying on a WYSIWYG editor) is that browsers change, web standards evolve, and cut-and-paste scripts as well as WYSIWYG editors tend to lag behind.

Hopefully, Microsoft, Netscape, and Opera will soon patch the holes in their ECMAScript and DOM support, and Macromedia and Adobe will vastly improve their support for these standards in Dreamweaver and Golive, respectively. If both things happen, you might be able to spend the rest of your life banging out advanced JavaScript functions with no clue as to what you are doing or why it works.

If you intend to work primarily as a graphic designer and merely wish to create simple sites for your existing clients, you can probably get by with cutting and pasting or relying on Dreamweaver or Golive—at least for the time being.

But if you intend to plunge into full-time web design or if you simply want to master the craft, you will want to learn JavaScript. So let us tell you how you can do that, and then we'll move on to examine how JavaScript helps web designers solve typical problems that arise in the development of any professional site.

Educating Rita About JavaScript

We've called JavaScript a relatively "easy-to-learn" programming language, but it *is* a programming language, and teaching it is beyond the scope of this book. In some ways, teaching it is beyond the scope of fat books dedicated entirely to that pursuit. However, we can recommend two books on the subject:

- Nick Heinle's *Designing With JavaScript: Creating Dynamic Web Pages* (O'Reilly: 1997) is a wonderful, readable, detailed introduction that any designer can understand and is chock-full of examples and explanations of the basic terminology and theory behind JavaScript. The book is somewhat out of date (at least as of this writing), but it will raise your comfort level tremendously while teaching you the basics.

- *JavaScript for the World Wide Web: Visual Quickstart Guide, Third Edition*, by Tom Negrino and Dori Smith (Peachpit Press: 1999) provides a series of quick exercises, complete with screenshots, that demystify JavaScript while explaining how to perform useful functions and avoid common mistakes. From plug-in testing to creating dynamic menus or from controlling frames to baking your first "cookie," pretty much everything you need to know can be found here. The scripts also are freely available at the authors' www.javascriptworld.com site.

Speaking of free online resources, you also can learn much about JavaScript by studying Thau's JavaScript tutorial at Webmonkey (http://hotwired.lycos.com/webmonkey/javascript/tutorials/tutorial1.html). Give yourself at least two days to go through all the exercises in this five-part tutorial. The *JavaScript School* at www.w3schools.com/js/ is another great place to learn. Classic and recent JavaScript/DOM articles may be found at http://www.javascript.about.com/.

We highly recommend that you buy these books and study these free online tutorials. We also recommend that you take it slow, breathe deeply, and avoid freaking yourself out over this stuff.

Don't Panic!

As a web designer, you will not normally be expected to do advanced JavaScript and DOM programming. Instead, your knowledge of what JavaScript is and what it can be used for will enable you to work more closely with team members to create engaging websites.

But don't think you're getting off scot-free, either.

JavaScript Basics for Web Designers

As a professional web designer, you really should be able to use JavaScript to do simple things such as replacing meaningless URLs with text messages as a means of extending the site's branding. (And ducking when some visitors complain about it.)

You should be able to create *rollovers* (image swaps) that help your visitors experience the site as a responsive, interactive entity. (Yes, by hand.)

You should know how to open new browser windows (when doing so serves a purpose), use browser detection to solve compatibility problems, and enhance your site's navigation through JavaScript's ability to manipulate simple HTML <FORM> elements.

The techniques involved are as simple to learn as they are to demonstrate. Don't mistake simplicity for stupidity: Some of the simple things we're about to show you are among the most effective ways of adding interactivity to your sites.

Indeed, though we recommend learning all you can (and putting that knowledge to use with taste and restraint), too much knowledge can sometimes lead to too much inappropriate JavaScript: scrolling text that moves so quickly no one can read it, full-screen pop-up windows containing rigidly designed 800 x 600 sites that look ludicrous on large monitors, or complex, dynamic menus on general audience sites or on sites whose lack of in-depth content is made pitifully obvious when these complex menus end up pointing to single-paragraph pages.

While other jazz musicians blew fast and frantic, Miles Davis played very few notes. The way he played them, *when* he played them, and the many times he did not play at all, all combined to create a timeless creative legacy. This is our highfalutin' way of reminding you that less is more, a little goes a long way, and slow bakin' makes good eatin'.

So let's look at some of these simple tasks and simple scripts. And let's see how ordinary web designers with no programming experience use basic JavaScript techniques to solve everyday design and communication problems.

The Dreaded Text Rollover

Problem: Your client is insane about branding. In his restaurants, he brands everything from the napkins to the silverware. He expects the same level of branding on his site.

Solution: The JavaScript text rollover lets you brand even HTML links (see Figure 11.1).

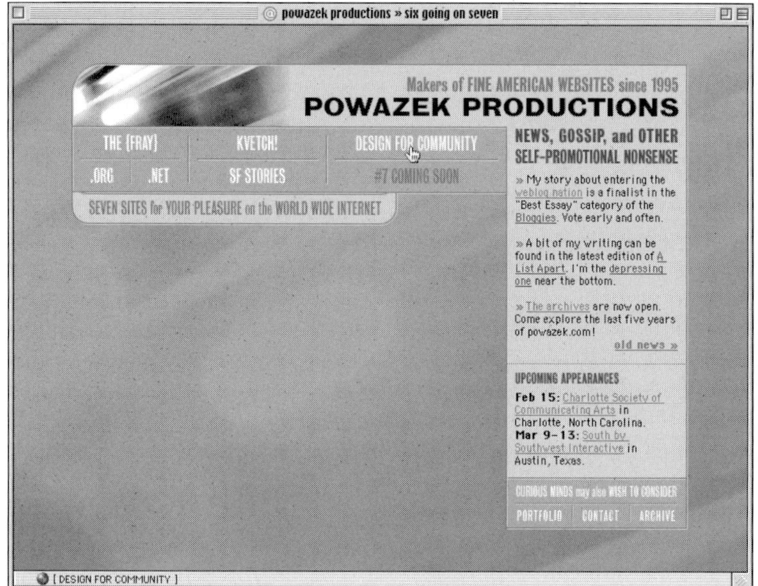

Figure 11.1

The status bar text rollover in action at the personal site of Derek Powazek. Placing the mouse over DESIGN FOR COMMUNITY in the menu bar causes the phrase [DESIGN FOR COMMUNITY] to appear in the status bar at the bottom left of the browser. By mastering the basic text rollover, even beginners can emulate at least one Powazek design trick (www.powazek.com).

Visit a typical site, and hold your mouse cursor over a link. You usually see something like this:

http://www.fashionmaven.com/fashions/men/index.html

Not terribly interesting, not very informative for the average citizen, and it certainly won't help your brand-happy client. How much better would it be if the visitor saw a message like this?

FASHION MAVEN fashions for men.

Many visitors might find this message far more useful than a bare-naked URL. And your client would certainly dig it. Fortunately, it is easy to accommodate these visitors and your client with JavaScript. Text rollovers are one of the easiest effects you can possibly create.

First, let's look at a typical HTML link:

```
Explore FASHION MAVEN <a href="/fashions/men/">fashions for men</a>.
```

Notice that we've used an absolute link, as explained in Chapter 8, "HTML, The Building Blocks of Life Itself." There is no need to waste bandwidth by including http:// or the company's domain name in the link; both the http:// and the domain name are understood. There is also no need to waste bandwidth on "index.html" because the systems administrator will have configured the server to display index.html when no other document is specified. (Some systems administrators specify welcome.html or index.htm or default.htm instead, but the same rules apply. If default.htm is the default document on your server, you can link to it without typing it. But we digress.)

A visitor dragging her mouse over such a link will see the page's URL and nothing more:

```
http://www.fashionmaven.com/fashions/men/index.html
```

Let's give the visitor something more informative than the page's URL.

The Event Handler Horizon

Built into JavaScript are two powerful event handlers: onMouseOver and onMouseOut. Event handlers enable you to create functions that take place during an event. In this case, the event is that the visitor is dragging her mouse cursor over a link—pretty simple stuff.

Many event handlers are built into JavaScript, but these are the two that will help us right now. Let's take the link just listed and make it more illuminating using JavaScript's onMouseOver event handler:

```
Explore FASHION MAVEN <a href="/fashions/men/" onMouseOver ="window.status=
➥'FASHION MAVEN fashions for men.'; return true;">fashions for men</a>.
```

What is going on here?

We've used the onMouseOver event handler to tell the browser that something is supposed to happen when the visitor's mouse hovers over this link. The event handler is followed by the equal sign in the same way that links and other standard bits of HTML use the equal sign.

As you may have guessed, window.status is JavaScript's charming way of referring to the status bar at the bottom of the web page. (The status bar is the part of the browser that usually displays the bare-naked URL, generally at the lower left.) Without getting too hairy, JavaScript gives each object in its document model an address based on the object's position within the document's hierarchy, moving from the top level of the hierarchy down to the details: window is a top-level object; status is the object being modified via JavaScript. (Like we said, buy the JavaScript books if you want a better explanation, and you probably do.)

Notice that the status bar message text 'FASHION MAVEN fashions for men.' is enclosed within single quotation marks. This is because the JavaScript itself is enclosed within double quotation marks. If the text also used double quotation marks, the browser would not know how to distinguish the quoted JavaScript from the quoted text.

Observe also that both the description and the phrase return true end in a semicolon. This is basic JavaScript syntax, so get used to it. There are more semicolons in JavaScript than in all Charles Dickens's novels combined. Technically, the semicolon is not required when a JavaScript statement ends the line. So,

```
window.status = "some thing"
```

is perfectly valid JavaScript in the context of a function, a la:

```
<script type="text/javascript">
function rollover() {
  window.status = "some thing" // no semicolon
}
</script>
```

But if you are placing two or more statements on a single line, as you would inside an event handler attribute, you must separate the statements by semicolons.

Finally, note that return true is used at the end to handle the event. It tells the browser to follow the HTML link. Return false would tell the browser *not* to follow the link, which can be useful when you don't want to load a new page.

Status Quo

So far, so good—now let's make our little example even more exciting. (Well, as exciting as this kind of stuff gets.) Let's craft a message that shows up in the status bar when the visitor *stops* hovering over the link:

```
Explore FASHION MAVEN <a href="/fashions/men/" onMouseOver ="window.status=
➥'FASHION MAVEN fashions for men.'; return true;" onMouseOut="window
➥status='Welcome to FASHION MAVEN.'; return true;">fashions for men</a>.
```

What have we done? (Besides further prostituting ourselves to FASHION MAVEN, that is.)

We've used exactly the same syntax to replace the onMouseOver message with a default status bar message. When the user places the mouse pointer over the link, he'll read "FASHION MAVEN fashions for men." When he releases the mouse, our insistent client will replace that link-specific brand message with a general one: "Welcome to FASHION MAVEN." This general message will remain in the visitor's status bar until he moves the mouse over a new link. If we had not done this, "FASHION MAVEN fashions for men" would have been "stuck" in the status bar window even after the visitor removed his mouse from that link.

None of what we've just shown you requires any custom scripting or preparation in the <HEAD> of the HTML document. The onMouseOver and onMouseOut event handlers are as old as the hills, and any JavaScript-capable browser will handle this code natively. (As we'll see later, other JavaScript techniques require a script before the function itself.)

Well, this is fine for a single link, but coding identical onMouseOut messages for a dozen links seems like a lot of work, doesn't it? There ought to be a shortcut! And fortunately, there is. (Programmers are always creating shortcuts.)

In the <BODY> tag of our HTML document, we can add this line of code:

```
<body onLoad="window.defaultStatus='Welcome to FASHION MAVEN.'">
```

For the sake of simplicity, we've left out the rest of the markup you might normally include in the <BODY> tag, such as the default background color, text color, and so on. Of course, if you're following W3C recommendations and using CSS to handle your site's stylistic elements, then your <BODY> tag *can* be as simple as <BODY> with no extra junk inside it.

As you have probably deduced, onLoad is another event handler. In this case, the event is the loading of the web page itself. When the page loads (the event), a function must be performed. In this case, you've instructed the browser that the required function is a change in the status bar message. Thanks to your cleverness, even before the visitor hovers over a link, the status bar at the bottom of the browser will proudly proclaim, "Welcome to FASHION MAVEN." Can you feel your client's love? We can. You have now carried your client's brand down to the level of the status bar. Had you not done this, the status bar would read "Internet Zone" or something equally meaningless (as far as your client is concerned).

But wait, there's more! Because the onLoad event handler in our <BODY> tag is telling the browser to proclaim "Welcome to FASHION MAVEN." by default, we can simplify our JavaScript link as follows:

```
Explore FASHION MAVEN <a href="/fashions/men/" onMouseOver ="window.status=
➥'FASHION MAVEN fashions for men.'; return true;" onMouseOut="window status='';
➥return true;">fashions for men</a>.
```

What changed? Look closely. We've removed the redundant text "Welcome to FASHION MAVEN" and replaced it with Folger's Crystals. Just kidding. Actually, we've replaced it with an empty pair of single quotations, which tell the browser to revert to the default text specified by the onLoad event handler ("Welcome to FASHION MAVEN"), We no longer have to type "Welcome to FASHION MAVEN." in the JavaScript text link itself.

That may not seem like much of an achievement. That's because it's not much of an achievement. But if there are a dozen links on this page, all requiring JavaScript text messages, we've saved ourselves the trouble of typing the same onMouseOut text 12 times. We've also saved the viewer the trouble of downloading those few kilobytes of redundant text.

Notice that it is possible to create dynamic web effects in web pages that live on your desktop—without requiring a web server. Hooray for JavaScript!

A Cautionary Note

Like everything you can do on the Web, modifying the default status bar message involves trade-offs and thus requires thought. Browsers use `defaultStatus` to communicate with users, letting them know if they've connected or not, informing them when an object is being downloaded, and letting the geeks in the house keep track of the actual URLs to which your links point. Modifying `defaultStatus` can enhance site branding and please your client, but it might upset some users, so don't use JavaScript in this way unless the benefits outweigh the drawbacks.

Kids, Try This at Home

Before we go any further, try reproducing the JavaScript effects we just described in a simple HTML page you've written. Needless to say, you will not win any innovation awards, but it might help you conquer any lingering fear of programming. If you can do this simple thing, you can do other, somewhat more complex things.

When it works on a page you've created, you'll begin to feel like a web designer. If it *doesn't* work, you'll *really* begin to feel like a web designer.

Then you'll go back and fix your syntax. Speaking of which...

The fine print

Because single quotation marks are used to denote the beginning and ending of text messages, what do you do if your text includes an apostrophe? After all, in HTML, an apostrophe is exactly the same as a single quotation mark.

What you do is "escape" the single quotation mark by inserting a backslash character in front of it.

```
Lip smackin' good! Get <a href="/recipes/stupidcomeon.html " onMouseOver
➥="window.status='Our chef\'s favorites.'; return true;" onMouseOut="window status='';
➥return true;">the recipes</a>.
```

Notice that we don't refer to our chef's favorites; we refer to our *chef\'s* favorites. The backslash character tells the browser to treat the quotation mark as a quotation mark, not a string terminator (meaning, not the end of a JavaScript statement). Forgotten backslashes have caused many a web designer her share of sleepless nights.

Return of the son of fine print

Yep, one more tip. Forget the semicolon, and you will create JavaScript errors in many browsers, which unfortunately will not show up in many others. That's unfortunate because if you can't see the error, you might not realize it's in there—so you may not know to fix it.

For some reason, Macs seem especially forgiving of the missing semicolon error. Many a Mac-based web designer has uploaded a web page (or an entire site) and gone off to smoke reefer, little realizing that he has left a trail of JavaScript syntax errors behind him. The moral, of course, is to check your JavaScript syntax carefully, test on multiple platforms, and avoid smoking reefer—especially that overpriced brown stuff they're selling uptown.

The Not-So-Fine Print

It's worth pointing out again that some web users, including hardcore geeks, detest this flippant toying with the sanctity of the status bar. These users want to know which URL your link will take them to. They deeply resent your hiding this information from them with stupid text about FASHION MAVEN. Some might even avoid clicking the link out of paranoid fear. ("Dude, if I can't see the link, I don't know where you're taking me.") Thus they will never learn about FASHION MAVEN's extensive selection of plaids and corduroys for tall men, short men, fat men, and cadets, all at prices 10% below what department stores usually charge.

You think we are making this up, but you haven't read our email and haven't spent years watching flame wars erupt on web design mailing lists. You think people will click links without worrying about or even noticing these changes in the expected status bar message. Many people, of course, won't notice; many others will notice and not care; some will notice and be pleased. But others will be displeased, and a few may even write letters of complaint.

These people are out there, and some of them might be among your clients' favorite customers. Thus, your infinitesimal gain in branding could be offset by a commensurate loss of audience. Even this small a decision is worth considering carefully.

It's also worth mentioning that, with the rise of HTML's <TITLE> attribute:

```
<a href="somelink.html" title="Information about this link.">
```

...there is now an easier way to enhance the information conveyed by a link.

In IE4 (and higher), Netscape 6 (and higher), Opera 5, iCab, and Mozilla, the <TITLE> attribute will cause a Windows-like Tool Tip or Mac OS Help balloon to pop up when the user hovers over the link. (In Opera, the message appears in the browser's status bar, just like a JavaScript mouse-over text.) This Tool Tip or Help balloon will contain the text you've written inside the quotation marks following the word title and the equal sign. To avoid overwhelming users with flying tool tips, there is usually a slight delay before the Tool Tip appears. There is also no need to worry about escaped characters when writing <TITLE> attribute text:

```
<a href="somelink.html" title="It's exciting not to worry about apostrophes, isn't it? Gosh,
➥it's really swell."
```

Of course, if your <TITLE> text includes a double quote, the browser could get confused:

```
<a href="/" title="We say "no!" to drugs.">
```

Instead, use single quotations:

```
<a href="/" title="We say 'no!' to drugs.">
```

Not only is this <TITLE> attribute method marginally easier to use than JavaScript, it is also, in some ways, more logical. When a user has her eye on a link (or a linked image), her eye does not wish to jump down to the browser status bar. Her eye wants to say where it is. In IE4+ and Netscape 6, the <TITLE> attribute accommodates this natural behavior of the human eye and mind because the Tool Tip or Help balloon pops up adjacent to the link itself.

Still, we do not wish to discourage you from using status bar messages.

They make a handy informational and branding tool, and they work in older browsers (like Netscape 4) that don't support the <TITLE> attribute.

The Ever-Popular Image Rollover

Problem: The site is pretty but feels lifeless. Visitors are encouraged to admire but not to click and explore. The site needs a shot of GUI-like, visual interactivity.

Solution: The JavaScript image rollover (see Figures 11.2 and 11.3).

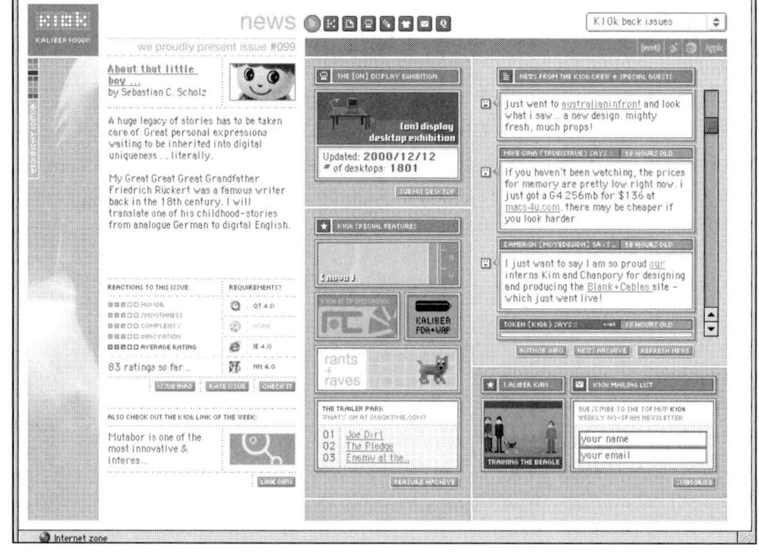

Figure 11.2

Kaliber 10000, "The Designer's Lunchbox," is a jewel of graphic and navigational design with numerous JavaScript tricks up its virtual sleeve. Note the "K10k back issues" pull-down menu at the upper right, the code for which is described later in this chapter. One of K10k's simpler (but very effective) techniques is using the ever-popular image rollover to replace static icons with animated ones. For instance...

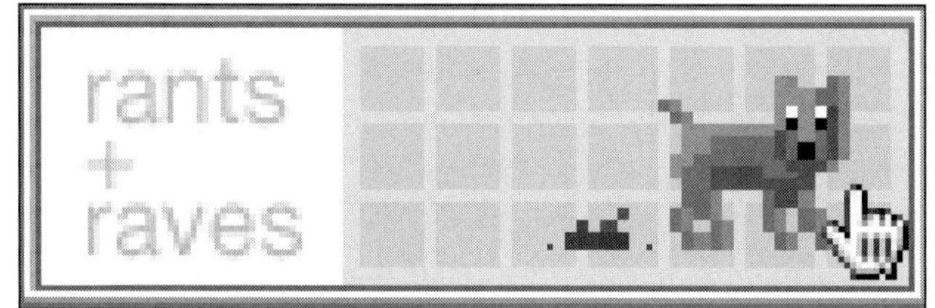

Figure 11.3

...dragging your mouse cursor over the Rants and Raves button replaces the static dog with a GIF animation of a pooping dog. Hey, we said they were brilliant web designers; we didn't say they were mature (www.k10k.net).

Let's assume that after reading Chapter 9, "Visual Tools," you opened Photoshop and ImageReady, designed a web page comp, sliced it, and used ImageReady to generate the JavaScript rollover. Now take those same sliced images, open your HTML text editor of choice (Allaire Homesite, Barebones BBEdit, or Optima-Systems PageSpinner), and, using the techniques you learned in the books or online tutorials mentioned earlier in this chapter, write yourself an image rollover by hand.

You can do it! It's okay to prop the books open in front of you or to refer back to Thau's web pages. You'll create links much like the text links we showed in the previous example. You'll also hand-code a *preload*, usually in the <HEAD> of your document. A preload ensures that swapped images will be downloaded to the user's cache before the page displays. In that way, those preloaded images are ready to leap into action the moment the user drags her mouse over them.

Why are rollover effects so popular? We think it is because users are accustomed to operating systems whose GUIs respond to their actions. Rollovers emulate this behavior, and they indicate that an image is more than an image—it is a dynamic trigger to an action the user can perform. Users dig that stuff.

A Rollover Script from Project Cool

On the assumption that you haven't bought those other books yet, haven't read any of the online tutorials, and still feel uncomfortable with JavaScript, we'll go ahead and show you another simple way to create JavaScript image rollovers.

The following was adapted from a basic script at Project Cool. And that's okay. Project Cool wrote their script back in the late 1990s so web designers would use it and learn from it. The future of Project Cool is doubtful because the site's creators left in late 1999, but this script and others like it were still available online as of this writing (www.projectcool.com).

```
<script type="text/javascript">
<!-- Adapted from Projectcool.com
if (document.images){
```

```
mainover = new Image; mainout = new Image;
   mainover.src = "/images/menubar_over_1.gif";
   mainout.src = "/images/menubar_out_1.gif";
   storiesover = new Image; storiesout = new Image;
   storiesover.src = "/images/menubar_over_2.gif";
   storiesout.src = "/images/menubar_out_2.gif";
}
functiover swapem(iname, gname) {
   if(document.images){
      iname.src = gname.src;
   }
}
//-->
</script>
```

This script goes inside the <head></head> of an HTML document. It might look complex if you're unfamiliar with JavaScript, but it is really elegantly simple.

The script begins by announcing the fact that it is a script and that its type is text/javascript. Older browsers expected to see a <LANGUAGE> attribute with the name and, optionally, a version of the scripting language being used ("Javascript1.2," for instance), but this attribute has been deprecated in favor of a more generic <MIME> type descriptor. Don't worry if you don't understand what we just said; simply relax and type:

```
<script type="text/javascript">
```

Similarly, the end of the script is announced by a </script> tag. As with HTML and CSS, <comment> tags tell search engine spiders (and non-JavaScript-capable browsers) to ignore everything written between <!-- and -->. You want search engines to help web users find your content, not your JavaScript.

Next, the Project Cool script sets a condition for running. Early versions of JavaScript did not support image rollovers. The script wants to make sure it is working with a browser that understands rollovers, so it tests the browser's receptivity to the *images array object* of *the document model:*

```
if (document.images)
```

The script could have accomplished the same thing by detecting for browsers and platforms (a technique known as *browser sniffing*). For instance, it could have checked for the presence of Netscape 2 and Internet Explorer 3, two browsers that did not support the images array of the document model (and hence would not be able to process this script). But the code to check for these browsers is somewhat long compared to a simple line such as

```
if (document.images)
```

Besides, some versions of IE3 *did* understand image rollovers. Rather than get tangled in browser versions, it is easier, more elegant, and more reliable to test for an understanding of the document images object. If the browser does not understand (document.images), the script will be skipped. If the required conditions are met, the script runs.

The script next declares two image conditions (Over or Out) and preloads the required images (mb3_on-01-01.gif, mb3_off-01-01.gif, mb3_on-02-01.gif, and mb3_off-02-01.gif):

```
if (document.images){
mainover = new Image; mainout = new Image;
   mainover.src = "/images/menubar_over_1.gif";
   mainout.src = "/images/menubar_out_1.gif";
    storiesover = new Image; storiesout = new Image;
    storiesover.src = "/images/menubar_over_2.gif";
    storiesout.src = "/images/menubar_out_2.gif";
```

Over corresponds to the onMouseOver state, and off corresponds to the default and onMouseOut state. The two images correspond to two named JavaScript objects (main and stories).

Finally, the script declares a swapem function, which works by swapping one image state for another:

```
function swapem(iname, gname) {
      if(document.images){
            iname.src = gname.src;
```

As we said, all of this takes place in the <HEAD> of the HTML document, though it could just as easily live in an external JavaScript document. Like an external style sheet as described in Chapter 10, "Style Sheets for Designers" external JavaScript documents can live anywhere on the web server and are referenced via links in the <HEAD> of each HTML page:

```
<script language="JavaScript" type="text/javascript" src="/daily.js"></script>
```

For more on external JavaScripts, see "Going Global with JavaScript," later in this chapter.

All that remains is to call up these functions in the <BODY> of the HTML document itself.

And here is code that does just that:

```
<a href ="/main.html" onMouseOver="swapem(main, mainover); return true;"
➥onMouseOut="swapem(main, mainout);return true;"><img name="main"
➥src"/images/menubar_out_1.gif " width="200" height="25" border="0" alt="Visit the
➥main page." title="Visit the main page."></a>
```

This code should look somewhat familiar to you because it is fairly similar to the dreaded text rollover.

Once again, here is a standard HTML link followed by two event handlers: one for onMouseOver, the other for onMouseOut. But now, instead of invoking a status bar message, our MouseOver and MouseOut states call upon the swapem function declared earlier in the document. The onMouseOver event handler declares two variables for the swapem function: a named object (in this case, main) and an appropriate image state (mainover)—over, because this is the "MouseOver" state for the image object. The onMouseOut event handler also declares two variables for the swapem function: a named object (main) and an appropriate image state (mainout)—out, because this is the "MouseOut" state for the image object. Semicolons follow the naming of the variables and the required return true declaration.

The image <IMG> tag that follows gives the source image a name (main), allowing the swapem function to recognize the image as the object that is supposed to be swapped. The remaining <SRC>, <WIDTH>, <HEIGHT>, and <BORDER> attributes should be familiar to you from the HTML chapter. The <ALT> and <TITLE> attributes are included so that the menu item will remain accessible to those who surf with images turned off or who are using nongraphical browsers such as Lynx. The link to /main.html will work even if JavaScript has been turned off in the user preferences (or the browser does not support JavaScript).

The code and the effect on the web page are much simpler than the descriptive text you've just waded through.

You might ask, can JavaScript text rollovers be added to an image rollover like the one just described? The answer is yes, and it can be done very easily:

```
<a href ="/main.html" onMouseOver="swapem(main, mainover); window.status='Visit the
➥main page.'; return true;" onMouseOut="swapem(main, mainout); window.status='';
➥return true;"><img name="main" src="/images/menubar_out_1.gif" width="200"
➥height="25" border="0" alt="Visit the main page." title="Visit the main page."></a>
```

Windows on the World

Problem: The site offers streaming video files. You, the client, or the information architect want these files to play back inside the browser via the QuickTime plug-in (see Chapter 12). It is easy to use the HTML <EMBED> or <OBJECT> tags to embed a QuickTime movie in a thoughtfully designed HTML page. But if you do this on the current page, the movie will begin streaming even if visitors do not have the bandwidth or patience to see it.

Solution: The JavaScript pop-up window.

Opening new windows via JavaScript is a simple task, though it's somewhat controversial. Some web users feel that everything should happen in their existing browser window. These folks hate pop-up windows, remote controls, and everything else that can happen outside the safe, familiar world of their existing browser window.

Are these users right? They are right for themselves.

What does this mean? It means that pop-up windows, remotes, and other such stunts should never be created lightly or purposelessly. (Why offend visitors if you can avoid it?)

Sometimes, however, you need pop-up windows. Sometimes, nothing else will do—as in the present example, when you wish to embed a streaming video file in a web page but don't want to force that streaming movie on users who don't care to (or can't) view it. Pop-up windows can also be used to provide additional information as needed (see Figure 11.4). In case of emergency, break glass and use JavaScript to easily create new windows.

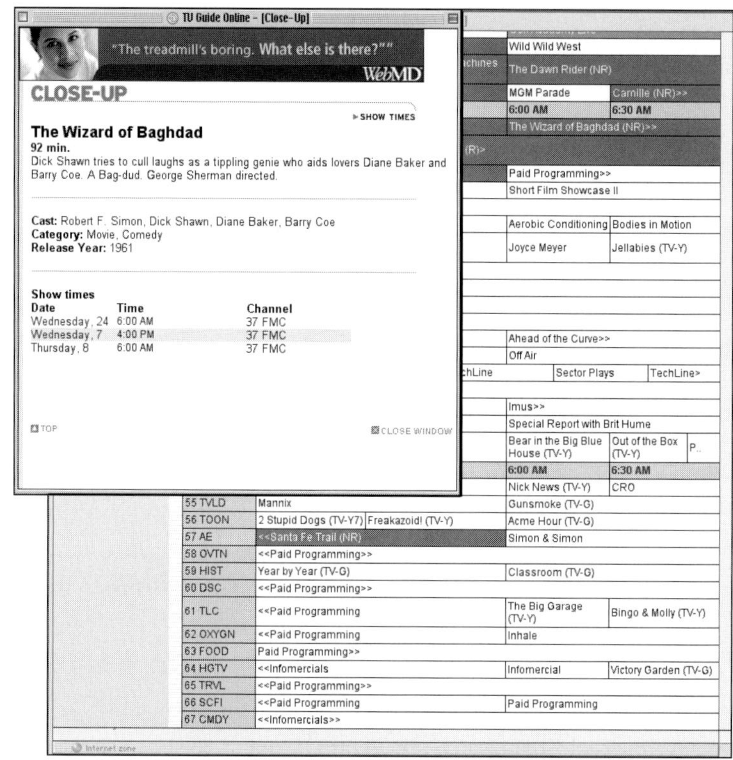

Figure 11.4

JavaScript pop-up windows annoy some web users but can be extremely functional. At *TV Guide's* site, the main page offers a compressed listing of all available cable channels. Clicking any program triggers a pop-up window that offers detailed information about the selected show. Here, for instance, we can read about Dick Shawn groping for laughs as a drunken genie in *The Wizard of Baghdad.* The point is that JavaScript allows the user to select exactly the level of detail needed (www.tvguide.com).

Get Your <HEAD> Together

Before you can create a new window, you must define it in the HTML <HEAD> of your HTML document.

Here is a typical way to do just that:

```
<html>
<head>
<title>Welcome to Porkchops.com!</title>
```

```
<script type="text/javascript">
<!--
function awindow(url) {
  return window.open(url, "thewindow", "toolbar=no,width=350,height=400,status=
➥no,scrollbars=yes,resize=no,menubar=no");
}
// -->
</script>
</head>
```

What are we doing? We have defined a function, given it a name (aWindow), and defined its properties: It will not have a toolbar (toolbar=no), it will be 350 pixels wide (width=350), it will stay the exact size we've specified (resize=no), and so on.

We have also, without even realizing it, declared a JavaScript variable—that is, an element that can be replaced, as in the swapem example. Our variable is the URL of any HTML document we would like to use in the pop-up window.

In the HTML page, we would trigger the function like so:

```
<a href="sucky_old_browser.html" onClick="aWindow('porkpops.html'); return false;">
```

When the event is triggered by the user's action (clicking the link), the named window.open function will be performed, and the appropriate HTML page will appear in a 350 x 400 pop-up window with no status bar or menu bar. The return false will prevent the browser from following the URL specified in the <HREF>, for backward compatibility.

As a courtesy, it's nice to include a <CLOSE WINDOW> function in the pop-up window itself, for the beginners in our viewing public. Porkpops.html should include a link like this:

```
<a href="#" onclick="window.close(); return false;">Close me!</a>
```

Onclick is another of those essential built-in JavaScript event handlers you'll come to know and love, and window.close is a built-in JavaScript function that, as you might have guessed, closes windows. In other words, we are telling the browser to close the window—pretty basic stuff.

Can we use graphics instead of HTML text to perform these functions? Oh, yeah! In the original HTML document, we can use a fancy-pants GIF image we'll call openwindow.gif:

```
<a href="sucky_old_browser.html" onClick="aWindow('porkpops.html'); return
➥false;"><img alt="Open new window." src="openwindow.gif" height="100"
➥width="100"></a>
```

And in the pop-up window we can use the dapper and elegant closeme.gif:

```
<a href="#" onclick="window.close(); return false">)"><img alt="Close this window."
➥src="closeme.gif" height="25" width="50">
```

And that's all there is to it.

Avoiding the Heartbreak of Linkitis

Problem: The client insists on a menu with dozens of choices. You know such a menu will be ugly and confusing and will cause visitors to scroll indefinitely (or more likely, leave). Your client "knows better." What's a mother to do?

Solution: The JavaScript pull-down menu.

Slip this in your <HEAD> and smoke it:

```
<script type="text/javascript">
<!--
function load_page(which_form)
{
self.location.href=which_form.modules.options[which_form.modules.selectedIndex].value;}
//-->
</script>
```

This sets up a load_page function with a replaceable variable (which_form) and uses the location object to swap links in and out.

Now, in the <BODY> of your HTML document, create a standard HTML pull-down form element and use the onChange event handler to trigger new pages in response to user actions:

```
<form name="hc">
        <select name="modules" onChange="load_page(this.form)" size="1">
           <option value="">Pick a Project!
           <option value="a.html">A List
```

```
        <option value="b.html">B List
        <option value="c.html">C List
        <option value="d.html">D List
        <option value="e.html">E List
        <option value="f.html">F List
        <option value="g.html">G List
        <option value="h.html">H List
        <option value="i.html">I List
        <option value="j.html">J List
        <option value="k.html">K List
        <option value="l.html">L List
        <option value="m.html">M List
        <option value="n.html">N List
        <option value="o.html">O List
        <option value="p.html">P List
        <option value="q.html">Q List
        <option value="r.html">R List
        <option value="s.html">S List
        <option value="t.html">T List
    </select>
</form>
```

This script will automatically change pages as soon as the user highlights any item in the list. If you prefer, you can use a button or other mechanism to actually initiate the action. You can also easily add inline CSS to add some style to the whole sorry affair:

```
<select name="modules" onChange="load_page(this.form)" size="1" style="font-size:
➥10px; font-family: verdana, geneva, arial; background-color: #336; color: #ccc">
```

The resulting mega-menu will look nice and take up very little space on the page (see Figure 11.5). Compared with an endless list of standard HTML links, the advantages of JavaScript-based navigation become obvious. To compensate for non-JavaScript-capable browsers, you should include a standard HTML menu somewhere on the page, but it need not be a mess if you consolidate these HTML links using subpages:

```
<a href="subpage_a-g.html">A-G</a>
<a href="subpage_h-n.html">L-N</a>
etc.
```

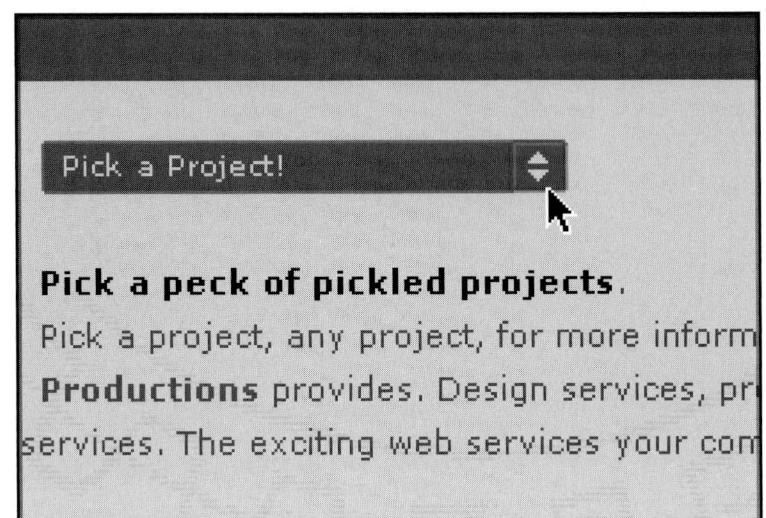

Figure 11.5

Add JavaScript to a standard HTML <FORM> element, throw in a dash of CSS for style, and you have a tasty alternative to the traditional navigation menu. Instead of the mess of links the client may have demanded, you have a clean, intuitive interface requiring very little space on the page (www.happycog.com).

Browser Compensation

Problem: You want to use particular technology—say, CSS—without causing old browsers to fail.

Solution: Browser detection and redirection.

As we've probably boasted 100 times already throughout this book, we publish a weekly online magazine for web designers that the gods call *A List Apart* (http://www.alistapart.com/). For our 19 January 2001 edition, we decided to create a special issue dedicated to employment problems being experienced in the web design field at that time, due to the collapse of many pre-IPO dot-com businesses in the last quarter of 2000.

In addition to running two articles on the subject, we were also introducing a new site feature: namely, message boards. We figured that the chance to commiserate over business troubles would be a natural inducement to use this new community forum.

Ordinarily, ALA's navigational architecture employs a flattened hierarchy: You hit the front page and are immediately presented with that week's content. But to highlight the special issue—to really alert our readers to the fact that this issue was different—we decided to break with our own convention and launch the issue with a splash page (see Figure 11.6).

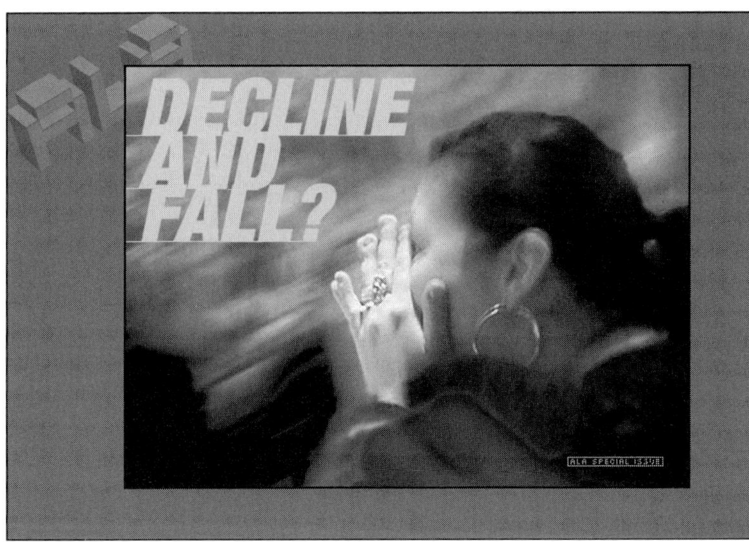

Figure 11.6

This is a splash page for a special issue of *A List Apart.* Using CSS rather than traditional HTML tables and image slices simplified the design and production, reduced the bandwidth required, and ensured that the photo's color would remain consistent. But this page did not work in old, buggy browsers. JavaScript browser detection saved the day (http://www.alistapart.com/stories/decline/).

We also decided to use CSS to lay out the page, instead of relying on the techniques described in Chapter 10. We did this for several reasons. For one thing, it's leaner. Instead of an HTML table filled with dozens of image slices, it's three simple images, one tiny rollover image, and a few lines of standards-friendly code:

```
<style type="text/css">
<!--
BODY {margin: 0; background-color: #930; background-image: url(/stories/decline/
➥alatop.gif); background-repeat: no-repeat; background-attachment: scroll; background
➥-position: top left;}
A:link, A:visited, A:active { text-decoration: none; font-weight: bold; color: #f90; }
A:hover { color: #cf0; text-decoration: underline; }
#grief {position: absolute; left: 115px; top: 50px; background-image: url(/stories/decline/
➥decline.jpg); background-repeat: no-repeat; background-attachment: scroll; background-
➥position: top left; border: 2px solid black; height: 400px; width: 550px;}
.special {position: relative; left: 425px; top: 365px;}
-->
</style>
```

For another thing, if we had followed the time-honored method of cutting the comp apart in ImageReady, the colors in the photograph might not have matched from one slice to another. And the bandwidth requirements would have been substantially higher.

CSS enabled us to create a page that looked and worked better than traditional methods allow—but there was one problem. As you'll remember from Chapter 10, Netscape Communicator 4 has fairly shoddy CSS support. It does not display CSS properly and can even crash when encountering CSS layouts.

Our referrer logs told us that 10% of our audience was using Netscape 4. How could we offer our splash page to 90% of the audience without offering ugliness (and possible browser instability) to the other 10%?

JavaScript to the Rescue!

We solved our problem by writing a simple browser detection script and embedding it in the <HEAD> of our HTML page:

```
<!-- This is for bugs in Netscape 4 -->
<script type="text/javascript">
<!--
bName=navigator.appName;
bVer=parseInt(navigator.appVersion);
if (bName == "Netscape" && bVer >= 5) br = "n5";
else if (bName == "Netscape" && bVer >= 4) br = "n4";
else if (bName == "Netscape" && bVer==3) br = "n3";
else if (bName == "Netscape" && bVer==2) br = "n2";
else if (bName == "Microsoft Internet Explorer" && bVer >= 5) br = "e5";
else if (bName == "Microsoft Internet Explorer" && bVer >= 4) br = "e4";
else if (bName == "Microsoft Internet Explorer") br = "e3";
else br = "n2";
//-->
</script>
```

This script defined Netscape 4 to keep an eye out for it. (We didn't worry about the earlier browsers because no one uses them to visit ALA.) When a Netscape 4 user hit the splash page, he was redirected to an alternate page via a second simple script:

```
<script type="text/javascript">
<!--
if (br == "n4") {
window.location="/stories/decline/main.html"
}
//-->
</script>
```

As you can see, this script checked for a condition (browser = Netscape 4). If that condition was met, JavaScript's built-in window.location object directed Netscape 4 users to main.html, the issue's table of contents page. The rest of the audience got to main.html by clicking the link on the splash page. Netscape 4 users missed the splash page but they didn't miss a drop of content, and they didn't realize they were missing *anything*. In this way their needs were accommodated without disturbing them or any other visitor to the site.

On a commercial project, we might have gone ahead and built a table-cell version of this page for Netscape 4 users and used browser detection and window.location to send them to that page instead.

Location, location, location

There is a drawback to using window.location. Because the redirected users don't realize they've been redirected, they bookmark the page to which they've been redirected instead of the actual index page. That's fine for them, but when they send their friends the URL or link to the site from a site of their own, they will be sending other users to an inner page instead of the cover.

There is a way around that—it involves frames—but it's a tired, messy hack, and we don't recommend it. If you insist on seeing how it works, visit Happy Cog (http://www.happycog.com/), where we combine browser detection and redirects with frames. Hopefully, by the time you read this, we will have redesigned Happy Cog, and you won't be able to see what we're talking about anyway. Never mind.

Browser detection is not always as simple as what we've just shown. Given that browsers can function differently on different platforms—and because incremental upgrades can also function differently (the 4.5 version might choke on code the 4.6 version handles with ease)—browser detection can get very specific and painfully complex. By a strange coincidence, we have more to say about that very thing.

WATCHING THE DETECTION

Problem: Your site absolutely requires that the user have a plug-in installed on her system (see Chapter 12 for more about plug-ins). Simply enough, use JavaScript plug-in detection (http://www.javascriptworld.com/scripts/script02.08.html). But some browsers do not understand JavaScript plug-in detection, even though they perform many other JavaScript functions perfectly. What on earth can you do about that?

Solution: Load o' code—JavaScript browser and platform detection code, that is.

Did someone say "complex browser and platform detection?" Oh, joy. An example of that very thing follows. Specifically, it is one of Juxt Interactive's (see Figure 11.7) browser detection scripts of late 2000, written, in part, to compensate for the fact that Juxt uses the Flash plug-in extensively, and IE4.5/Mac (and earlier) did not recognize JavaScript's plug-in detection method—though the browser was otherwise JavaScript-capable.

Figure 11.7

The gifted designers and programmers at Juxt Interactive rely heavily on the Macromedia Flash plug-in. Juxt must be certain its visitors have the plug-in installed before throwing heaps of Flash content their way. JavaScript plug-in detection is the answer, but plug-in detection fails in some browsers. Juxt's developers tackled this problem by writing the mother of all plug-in, browser, and platform detection scripts (www.juxtinteractive.com).

If this entire chapter so far has you seriously contemplating a career as an oil painter, we suggest you skip the next few pages, at least for now. However, we should point out that what you are about to see is not so much *complex* as *complete*.

At first glance, the river of code you're about to drown in looks like one advanced function after another. In truth it is just a few functions, repeated over and over again so that every browser version, on every possible platform, can be recognized and accounted for.

The first code torrent that follows lives in a global JavaScript file called sniffer.js. We'll discuss global JavaScript files in a later section, "Going Global with JavaScript," (just as soon as we get through *this* section).

The second river of 'Script lives in an HTML page called testSniffer.htm. Let's examine them both, shall we?

Please don't freak. Here's sniffer.js in all its glory:

```
//////////////////////////////////////////////////
// source: juxtinteractive.com
// description: Flash 3, 4 AND 5 Detection
// Author: anthony@juxtinteractive.com
// credits: netscape communications (client sniff)
// Permission granted to reuse and distribute
// Last Modified: 10-03-00
//////////////////////////////////////////////////

//////////////////////////////////////
// Convert userAgent string to Lowercase
//////////////////////////////////////

var agt=navigator.userAgent.toLowerCase();

//////////////////
// Browser Version
//////////////////
```

```
var is_major = parseInt(navigator.appVersion);
var is_minor = parseFloat(navigator.appVersion);
var is_ns  = ((agt.indexOf('mozilla')!=-1) && (agt.indexOf('spoofer')==-1) &&
➥(agt.indexOf('compatible') == -1) && (agt.indexOf('opera')==-1) &&
➥(agt.indexOf('webtv')==-1));
var is_ie   = (agt.indexOf("msie") != -1);
////////////
// Platform
////////////

var is_win   = ( (agt.indexOf("win")!=-1) || (agt.indexOf("16bit")!=-1) );
var is_win95 = ((agt.indexOf("win95")!=-1) || (agt.indexOf("windows 95")!=-1));
var is_win16 = ((agt.indexOf("win16")!=-1) || (agt.indexOf("16bit")!=-1) ||
➥(agt.indexOf("windows 3.1")!=-1) || (agt.indexOf("windows 16-bit")!=-1) );
var is_win31 = ((agt.indexOf("windows 3.1")!=-1) || (agt.indexOf("win16")!=-1) ||
➥(agt.indexOf("windows 16-bit")!=-1));
var is_win98 = ((agt.indexOf("win98")!=-1) || (agt.indexOf("windows 98")!=-1));
var is_winnt = ((agt.indexOf("winnt")!=-1) || (agt.indexOf("windows nt")!=-1));
var is_win32 = (is_win95 || is_winnt || is_win98 || ((is_major >= 4) && (navigator.plat-
form ➥== "Win32")) || (agt.indexOf("win32")!=-1) || (agt.indexOf("32bit")!=-1));
var is_mac= (agt.indexOf("mac")!=-1);

////////////////////////////////////
// Detect IE 4.5 on the mac
// Mucho Problemos with this browser
////////////////////////////////////

var is_ie45mac  = (is_mac && is_ie && (agt.indexOf("msie 5.0")==-1) &&
➥(agt.indexOf("msie 5.5")==-1) && (agt.indexOf("msie 4.5")!=-1));

////////////////////////////////////////
// Flash 3, 4 AND 5 Detection
// Last Modified: 10-03-00
// NOT checking for enabledPlugin (buggy)
////////////////////////////////////////

var is_flash5 = 0;
var is_flash4 = 0;
var is_flash3 = 0;
if (navigator.plugins["Shockwave Flash"]) {
   var plugin_version = 0;
   var plugin_description = navigator.plugins["Shockwave Flash"].description.split(" ");
   for (var i = 0; i < plugin_description.length; ++i) {     if (isNaN(parseInt(plugin_
   ➥description[i])))
   continue;
   plugin_version = plugin_description[i];
      }
```

```
    }
    if (plugin_version >= 5) {
    is_flash5 = 1;
    }
    if (plugin_version >= 4) {
    is_flash4 = 1;
    }
    if (plugin_version >= 3) {
    is_flash3 = 1;
    }

if (is_ie && is_win32) { // Check IE on windows for flash 3, 4 AND 5 using VB Script
    document.write('<SCRIPT LANGUAGE="VBScript"\>\n');
    document.write('on error resume next\n');
    document.write('is_flash5 = (IsObject(CreateObject("ShockwaveFlash.ShockwaveFlash
➥.5")))\n');
    document.write('on error resume next\n');
    document.write('is_flash4 = (IsObject(CreateObject("ShockwaveFlash.ShockwaveFlash.
➥4")))\n');
    document.write('on error resume next\n');
    document.write('is_flash3 = (IsObject(CreateObject("ShockwaveFlash.ShockwaveFlash.3"
➥)))\n');
    document.write('<'+'/SCRIPT> \n');
}
```

And now the browser and plug-in detector, as used in the HTML document: testSniffer.htm:

```
<html>
<head>
<title>testSniffer - juxtinteractive.com</title>
<meta HTTP-EQUIV="Content-Type" CONTENT="text/html; charset=iso-8859-1">
<SCRIPT TYPE="text/javascript" SRC="sniffer.js"></SCRIPT>
</head>
<BODY BGCOLOR="#000000" TOPMARGIN="0" LEFTMARGIN="10" MARGINWIDTH="10"
➥MARGINHEIGHT="0" LINK="#CCCC33" VLINK="#CCCC33" ALINK="#FFFFFF"
➥TEXT="#999900">
<br>
<font FACE="Verdana" size="2">
///////////////////////////////////////////////////<br>
// source: juxtinteractive.com<br>
// description: Flash 3, 4 AND 5 Detection<br>
// Author: anthony@juxtinteractive.com<br>
// credits: netscape communications (client sniff)<br>
// Permission granted to reuse and distribute<br>
// Last Modified: 10-03-00<br>
///////////////////////////////////////////////////<br>
```

```
<br>
<br>
<b>Function examples</b>
<br>
(the page uses the external JS file "sniffer.js")
<br>
<br>
<br>
<script>
<!--

if (is_ie45mac) {
   document.write('It seems you are using IE 4.5 on the mac – a extremly buggy browser,
   ➥you should consider upgrading to IE5 ASAP!\n');
}

// Check Flash
if (is_flash5)
{    document.write('This browser can play FLASH 5 movies<br>\n');
} if (is_flash4) {    document.write('This browser can play FLASH 4 movies<br>\n');} if
➥(is_flash3) {    document.write('This browser can play FLASH 3 movies<br>\n');} else {
   document.write('This browser CANNOT play FLASH movies<br>\n');}
//-->
</script>
<br>
<br>
</font>
</body>
</html>
```

Scared you, didn't it? Scares us, too.

Don't be alarmed. This is the province of web developers, not web designers. You would not be called upon to create JavaScript this detailed yourself. (Besides, if you ever are, you can use Juxt's script. Note the comment: "Permission granted to reuse and distribute," an act of grace and kindness that is typical of the way web designers share information with their peers.)

There are things we dislike about these torrents of code besides the fact that they are torrents of code. Mainly we're unhappy with the nonstandard, old-style "extended" HTML markup. This page would not validate. As HTML, it is not the best role model. As JavaScript, it will do 'til the next browser upgrade comes along.

Recognize that developers bash their brains out writing code like this because browsers behave so inconsistently from version to version and platform to platform. Be glad you're going into web design and not web development. Be kind to your programmers.

On the off-chance that you find this stuff enthralling or decide to switch from design to development, you'll find an abundance of good browser detection information at http://webreference.com/tools/browser/javascript.html and http://developer.netscape.com/viewsource/krock_v5.html. Unfortunately, there is always the chance that by the time you read this book, these pages will have moved or disappeared. If so, check the Resources Department at http://www.webstandards.org/ for the latest on browser detection.

Going Global with JavaScript

Just as with style sheets (Chapter 10), it is possible and often desirable to save time, hassles, and bandwidth by creating one or more global JavaScript documents, which can then be used to control whole sections of your site—or even the entire site.

For instance, the "My Glamorous Life" section at zeldman.com (http://www.zeldman.com/glamorous/) is controlled by a single JavaScript document (http://www.zeldman.com/glamorous/glam.js).

The document, in its entirety, reads as follows:

```
// Menubar preload. Pretty standard stuff.
function newImage(arg) {
   if (document.images) {
      rslt = new Image();
      rslt.src = arg;
      return rslt;
   }
}
function changeImages() {
   if (document.images && (preloadFlag == true)) {
      for (var i=0; i<changeImages.arguments.length; i+=2) {
         document[changeImages.arguments[i]].src = changeImages.arguments[i+1];
      }
```

```
    }
}
var preloadFlag = false;
function preloadImages() {
    if (document.images) {
        tocover = newImage("../omen2/coreover.gif");
        funover = newImage("../omen2/funover.gif");
        alaover = newImage("../omen2/alaover.gif");
        15over = newImage("../omen2/15over.gif");
        stealover = newImage("../omen2/stealover.gif");
        webover = newImage("../omen2/webover.gif");
        miscover = newImage("../omen2/miscover.gif");
        comingover = newImage("../glareon.gif");
        preloadFlag = true;
    }
}
// Get out of some idiot's frame.
   if (top != self) { top.location = self.location; }
// Popup window, 640 x 480
function open_window6(url) {
mywin = window.open(url,"win",'toolbar=0,location=0,directories=0,status=0,menubar=0,
➥scrollbars=0,resizable=0,width=640,height=480');
}
// Popup window, 500 x 500
function open_window(url) {
mywin = window.open(url,"win",'toolbar=0,location=0,directories=0,status=0,menubar=0,
➥scrollbars=0,resizable=0,width=500,height=500');
}
```

Pretty "light" after all that stuff from Juxt Interactive, eh? By now it should be obvious what this stuff means, but we'll spell it out anyway because we really, truly love you.

The double slashes // precede comments. The comments help the author remember what each function is for. The double slashes tell the browser to ignore these comments and proceed to the next function.

The menu bar preload and subsequent changeImages function are just another way of preloading images and creating image rollovers. The images in this case are referenced via relative URLs (../glareon.gif), as explained in Chapter 8. It would have been smarter to use absolute URLs, but we never claimed to be all that bright.

Get out of some idiot's frame is a simple *framebuster* script, consisting of just one line.

```
if (top != self) { top.location = self.location; }
```

A third-party site might link to yours. Sometimes that third-party site uses frames. Sometimes those frames are poorly constructed. Your site might load inside their frames instead of in its own window. This line of JavaScript prevents that from happening. In English, what it is saying is, "The HTML document referenced by this script should fill the browser window. If it does, swell. If it doesn't, get rid of any extraneous frames and fill the browser window with our page, not some other jerk's." Of course JavaScript syntax is a bit more formal than that.

The subsequent two functions are pop-up windows of varying dimensions. They are identical except for their dimensions and their names. (The 640 x 480 window is named window6; the other is simply named window.) The parenthetical URL (url) is a variable. If a pop-up window is needed on any HTML page that refers to this global JavaScript document, the address of the pop-up window will be inserted between the parentheses (popupwindow.html).

How do the HTML pages make use of this global JavaScript document? Just as with global style sheets, they do it by referring to the .js file with a link:

```
<script ""type="text/javascript" src="glam.js"></script>
```

The link appears inside the <HEAD> of each HTML document that requires these scripts.

```
<!DOCTYPE HTML PUBLIC "-//W3C//DTD HTML 4.01 Transitional//EN"
"http://www.w3.org/TR/1999/REC-html401-19991224/loose.dtd">
<html>
<head>
<link rel="StyleSheet" href="glam.css" type="text/css" media="screen">
<script ""type="text/javascript" src="glam.js"></script>
<title>Jeffrey Zeldman Presents: My Glamorous Life</title>
</head>
<body onLoad="preloadImages(); window.defaultStatus='Jeffrey Zeldman Presents.
➥Entertainment, free graphics, and web design tips since 1995.'">
```

Notice that the <BODY> tag includes these two onLoad functions: preloadImages and window.defaultStatus. The first preloads the images as referenced in glam.js. The second is our old friend, the default status bar message—the first snippet of JavaScript we learned in this chapter. The two are combined in one onLoad declaration and separated by a semicolon. Simple.

Learning More

There is so much that JavaScript can do. This chapter barely hints at the possibilities, and some methods used in this chapter could be out of date by the time you read this book.

With the arrival of full support for ECMAScript and the DOM, the dynamic possibilities for websites will expand exponentially. If you find, as some do, that you take naturally to JavaScript and want to learn more about the standardized version of JavaScript (ECMAScript) and the DOM:

- The W3C offers the DOM at http://www.w3.org/DOM/ in all its baffling glory.
- WebReference's "Doc JavaScript" (http://www.webreference.com/js/) offers many fine articles covering ECMAScript, JavaScript, and the DOM.
- Peter-Paul Koch maintains a DOM mailing list (http://www.xs4all.nl/~ppk/js/list.html).
- The Web Standards Project maintains links to the latest ECMAScript and DOM resources, beginning at http://www.webstandards.org/resources.html.

And *A List Apart* (http://www.alistapart.com/) offers the Eisenberg DOM series, an ongoing tutorial that includes:

- Meet the DOM: http://www.alistapart.com/stories/dom/
- DOM Design Tricks: http://www.alistapart.com/stories/dom2/
- DOM Design Tricks 2: http://www.alistapart.com/stories/domtricks2/
- DOM Design Tricks 3: http://www.alistapart.com/stories/domtricks3/

Whether you tackle this advanced stuff now or crawl off to recover from reading this chapter, be proud of yourself. You have faced your fears and at least *looked* at the part of web design that most designers find confusing and unintuitive. This is mainly because, compared to Photoshop and <p> paragraph tags, JavaScript *is* confusing and unintuitive.

But with practice and experience, it will get easier. And when browsers do a better job of complying with ECMAScript and the W3C DOM, it will get easier still. The *programming* will not be easy, but you or your development team will take comfort in the fact that you only have to code your site one way to work in all browsers.

There is just a little more to learn before you can consider yourself a full-fledged (or at least a fledgling) web designer. And by a strange coincidence, what you still don't know is covered in the very next chapter. Let's go for it, shall we?

chapter 12

Beyond Text/Pictures

On first discovering that the Web is not print, many designers see only the drawbacks: poor typographic resolution; a limited pool of installed user fonts; bandwidth bugaboos; the need to compensate for browser, platform, and hardware differences; and the awkwardness of trying to read a computer screen in the bathroom.

As we start to become genuine web designers, though, most of us see more advantages than disadvantages in the Web's distinctive differences from print. For example, instant worldwide distribution looks pretty darned good after wrestling with print shops and mail houses.

The longer we work at it, the more we marvel at the Web's ability to provide universal access across seemingly unbridgeable gaps of technology, nationality, economic and political systems, and physical ability or disability.

As these barriers are crossed, the human spirit becomes less isolated, suspicion and intolerance begin to fade, and we learn to appreciate each other's differences instead of fearing them. These benefits will greatly increase if the whole world gets to come along for the ride. They will greatly diminish if too many humans get left behind.

This, the substance of the vision of the founders of the Web, should be enough. But there is more. In particular, there are the two profound differences between the Web and print that we'll discuss in this chapter:

1. The ability to develop not simply static pages, but full-fledged, dynamic experiences
2. The visual, sonic, and interactive possibilities inherent in rich media, whether it is delivered through emerging web standards or popular plug-in technologies

These two unique strengths of the Web have tremendous implications for business and for art. Each has played a huge part in popularizing the medium. Each brims with powerful potential that designers and developers have barely begun to tap. Each also has the potential to be abused.

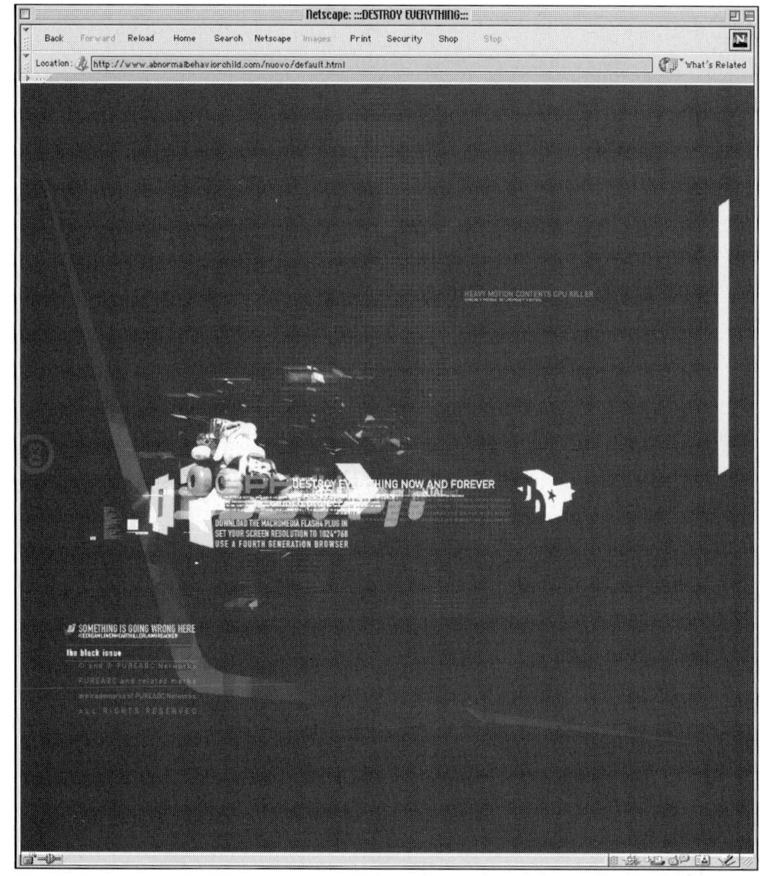

Figure 12.1

Nicola Stumpo's "Destroy Everything" is a noncommercial, nonnarrative Flash site that eats your screen alive. Stumpo's emotions are probably inexpressible in any medium outside Macromedia Flash (http://www.abnormalbehaviorchild.com/).

Prelude to the Afternoon of Dynamic Websites

In Chapter 11, "The Joy of JavaScript," we saw how JavaScript and its big brother, the Document Object Model (DOM), facilitate interactivity that printed media can only dream about. In the pages that follow, we'll look at additional and powerful ways of making the Web more interactive.

Dynamic sites enable web users to locate information, store phone numbers in a shared contact database, buy holiday gifts without braving crowded shopping centers, or view "adult" material without shame until the baby-sitter barges in.

In this chapter, we will see how web agencies use server-side applications to build sites that let users *do* things. We'll look at where the web designer fits in and how server-side applications help us manage immense content sites or change text and appearance in response to user actions. We'll also discuss how small shops and freelancers can get in on the action even if they don't have casts of thousands and budgets of millions at their disposal.

We'll also see how technologies like Java can compensate for "missing pieces" in our visitors' browser setups or unleash full-fledged software programs that run right in the browser. And we'll explore Java's potential beyond the desktop.

Figure 12.2

Here is a tranquil moment outside the Eiffel Tower, captured in all its panoramic, Sensurround glory courtesy of Apple's QuickTime VR—part of the QuickTime plug-in. Print cannot do this (http://www.apple.com/).

You Can Never Be Too Rich Media

After all that, we'll examine emerging "multimedia" web standards that are almost ready for prime time and take a peek and a poke at plug-in technologies that can radically enhance your sites—if used with respect for the realities of average web users.

These technologies are not for every site, but, when appropriate, they can enhance the web user's experience tremendously. Used poorly, of course, they lead to less satisfying experiences. We will explore all these technologies and consider what causes both kinds of experiences.

Knowing you as we do, we'll start with the drier, more technical stuff because if we saved it for later, you'd never read it.

The Form of Function: Dynamic Technologies

Think back to our earlier discussion of Perl versus JavaScript in Chapter 2, "Designing for the Medium." As far as the Web is concerned, Perl is most often used in *server-side* transactions, such as the processing of a visitor-submitted mail form. You might remember that a server-side technology is one in which the computing process takes place on the web *server* (hence the name) rather than the end-user's PC. With Perl, number-crunching tasks fall to the web server, while the visitor's computer sits idly, waiting.

We contrasted Perl with JavaScript, whose actions take place in the browser. With JavaScript, the end-user's computer (the "client," in geek parlance) does the heavy lifting. JavaScript is a *client-side* technology. Naturally, the dynamic technologies we're about to consider do some work on the client side and some on the server side. After all, the two sides are continually interacting. If the two sides, client and server, were *not* continually interacting, you would not have web transactions; you would just have machines sitting around doing nothing, like Teamsters.

But though they necessarily move from one realm to the other, most of the dynamic technologies we're about to discuss do the bulk of their work either on the server or on the user's desktop. Sometimes *where* they work is so important it becomes part of their name. For instance, as you might guess, Server Side Includes (SSI) is a server-side technology. Mostly, though, the names of web technologies give very little away. For instance, would you guess, from its name alone, that PHP (originally called Personal Home Page tools) is a server-side technology? Probably not.

Some versatile technologies work both sides of the street. Java, for instance, is frequently used on the client side, as a downloadable applet. But it also performs many server-side jobs. You'll hear developers and systems administrators talk about Java *servlets*, which are miniature Java applications that run the Apache server's mod_jserv component. Or you might host a site on Jigsaw, a W3C server that's written entirely in the Java language.

You don't really have to know any of this, as long as you get the general idea. Now let's move on to some specifics.

Server-Side Stuff

The days of slicing Photoshop comps and hand-coding every last HTML page are not dead—they just smell bad.

One day soon, web designers will be fully liberated from these crude production methods. It will happen when a core group of web standards is completely supported in browsers, enabling us to separate style from content, presentation from structure, and design from data. It hasn't happened yet, as any working web designer can tell you. It's coming soon, we tell you now. We'll talk more about it in Chapter 13, "Never Can Say Goodbye," so save your questions until then.

Meanwhile, we have interim solutions that let us create web pages without, well, creating web pages. Under the principles of dynamic site construction, we can establish the *conditions* for web pages instead of building each page individually.

The process is simple: To begin with, web designers create visual templates, while writers, editors, and marketers create content. (Hopefully the two teams are talking to each other so that design and content work together.) The content is stored and indexed in vast, humming "back-end" databases, and the site is launched. When visitors request data, server-side *middle-ware applications* fetch the appropriate content and pour it into the designer's template. The result: virtual pages that can be read, used, and bookmarked but that do not exist as conventional, self-contained HTML documents. Oh, oh, oh, it's magic. Let's descend to earth and see how it works.

Where were you in '82?

Ever used a search engine such as Google (www.google.com)? You type in the name of your former high school sweetheart and hit the Google Search button. Moments later, you're presented with page after page of links.

From these pages you learn that your old flame is the two-term governor of a large Midwestern state, honorary dean of a prestigious university, has had two charities, a hospital wing, and a Ben & Jerry's flavor named after her, and relaxes by participating in amateur kick-boxing tournaments.

The question, of course, is why did you ever break up with her? But for our purposes, the question is, where do these Google results pages come from?

The Google results pages are created on the fly by software that sucks query-related entries from a huge database, determines which links are probably most relevant, and pours the results into a preexisting HTML template.

Who made the software? Programmers. How does data get into the data-base? More software: specifically, a search engine *spider*, so named because it crawls around the Web indexing the content and location of individual web pages. Where does the designer fit in? The designer creates the template that the software uses to display the results. How does the designer do that? Let's see.

Indiana Jones and the template of doom

As a web designer, you might be called upon to design the front end of an application like Google, or you might work on vast content sites that rely on similarly dynamic processing. Or you could design a site that sells things, revealing new products in response to the visitor's desires.

Paradoxically, *your* job will not change that much from what we've described earlier in this book. You are still creating the part of the site that the visitor sees. You design it as you would any other web project. In a way, it's like designing a magazine's table of contents page. You create the master design; someone else designs the individual issues. It's also like designing corporate letterhead in that your responsibility ends when you deliver the approved letterhead design. You don't have to sit and type individual business letters. Creating website templates is as normal as those more familiar design processes. It's after the image pieces and HTML templates leave your desk that the voodoo kicks in.

Precisely what happens next is up to your team's developers—those who write the scripts that make these dynamic transactions possible. The developers take *their* lead from information architects, whose job is to figure out "user flow" through the transactional portions of the site. (Who will come here? What will they want to do? How can we best fulfill their needs? What can go wrong?) The very things we advised you to do when planning an entire site, information architects do as they envision and structure the site's transactions.

The data can be stored in an open source MySQL database, or in similar programs from Microsoft, Oracle, and other companies. As each visitor hits the site and begins to take actions, the middleware that lies between the visitor and the back-end database begins to do its thing.

It is the job of the middleware to process each request, fetch the appropriate document (or document fragment), and pour it into your template. Common middleware applications include open source PHP, Allaire Cold Fusion, and Microsoft Active Server Pages (ASP). MySQL is often found on UNIX Apache servers, Microsoft SQL and ASP on Microsoft Windows NT servers, and PHP can run on UNIX Apache or Windows/IIS.

Deciding on the appropriate database and middleware is not your concern. Technology officers and network administrators solve that problem. You aren't expected to write code that complies with these middleware programs' requirements either; developers do that, and we love them for it. You *can* learn to write code for PHP, ASP, or Cold Fusion if you wish, and we'll have something to say about that in the "Doing More," section that follows.

Ordinarily, the developers and project managers will provide you with guidelines in a document that might be called the *functional spec*. They will also discuss requirements with you in one or more personal meetings—probably more. "We can't have frames," they might tell you or, "we must have frames," could be their direction. Don't skip these meetings and don't rush to argue. Talk, listen, and learn.

The work process is but a variation on what you already do. You might take the comp no further than Photoshop; the developers will try to emulate it in, say, Cold Fusion, and show you the result. You might ask them to revise their code to bring the design up to your spec; they might ask you to revisit the design to accommodate limitations in the software or particular site requirements.

You will also write the Cascading Style Sheet (CSS) that determines colors, type sizes, margins, leading, and so on—same as always. You might find that some of these middleware technologies are unfortunately ill-suited to CSS, and you might need to do some HTML table work or have it done by your friendly neighborhood web technician.

It is sad but not surprising that some of these dynamic tools (Cold Fusion and the like) are more suited to old-style methods of web construction (<FONT> tags, table-based layouts, and so on) than to the newer, standards-based methods (structural markup, design via CSS). After all, these server-side tools arose in a market driven by browser quirks and proprietary technologies, not by universally supported web standards. As browsers improve their support for web standards and as web designers and developers begin using these standards instead of whining about them or pleading ignorance, the dynamic tools will likely improve in this regard.

Serving the project

As you might expect, database-driven sites, built with templates, are usually not the place to show off your deep Photoshop layering skills, your ability to bring complex layouts to life via frames, or your newly acquired mastery of *DHTML*. Low bandwidth, large areas of flat, web-safe color, reasonably sized web fonts: This is the terrain you must plow; these are the fields you must harvest.

Some web designers understand this as part of the discipline of the craft and strive to bring beauty, elegance, and utility to their simple designs. Others rebel and might be temperamentally unsuited to this type of work. The Web needs both kinds of designers, and there is plenty of work for both.

The need for simplicity is another reason that it's best to do as much of the design work as possible in CSS (as long as the middleware doesn't choke on it). There is little sense in asking the server to generate deeply nested table cells when you can achieve the same result with light, clean, structural markup and a single declaration in a global style sheet. By doing the work in CSS, you save processor cycles and bandwidth; and when it comes time to update the design, you can do it yourself in the style sheet instead of pestering the programmers to change their scripts.

Naturally, you will have to test to make sure that the middleware your company has chosen can handle the CSS you've written. You'll also have to test the site in multiple browsers, as described in Chapter 7, "Riding the Project Life Cycle." During testing, you also will want to turn off CSS in your browsers to make sure that the resulting pages work in non-CSS browsers (or in CSS browsers whose users have turned off CSS in their preferences).

What do we mean by "make sure the pages work with CSS turned off?" We mean that the pages work. We don't mean that the pages look the same with CSS and without it. Bad clients and stupid companies expect sites to look exactly the same in AOL 1.0 and Netscape 6. That's impossible without quadrupling the budget, and it's also pointless. Those who turn off CSS or use older browsers aren't hoping for a rich visual experience. If you stick with basic structural markup and the simple CSS techniques described in Chapter 10, "Style Sheets for Designers," you should be fine.

Doing More

Coding in PHP or ASP rarely falls within the web designer's job description, but after working in the field for a while, many web designers are pleased to discover that they have a knack for these simple programming environments. If you are one of them, this knack will not go unappreciated or make you any less marketable.

Mini-Case Study: Waferbaby.com

Waferbaby (http://www.waferbaby.com/), Daniel Bogan's delightful, personal site, makes smart use of PHP to facilitate dynamic content such as the site's "Brainstorm" section and to enable playfully user-centric design, as seen in the site's "Preferences" department (see Figure 12.3).

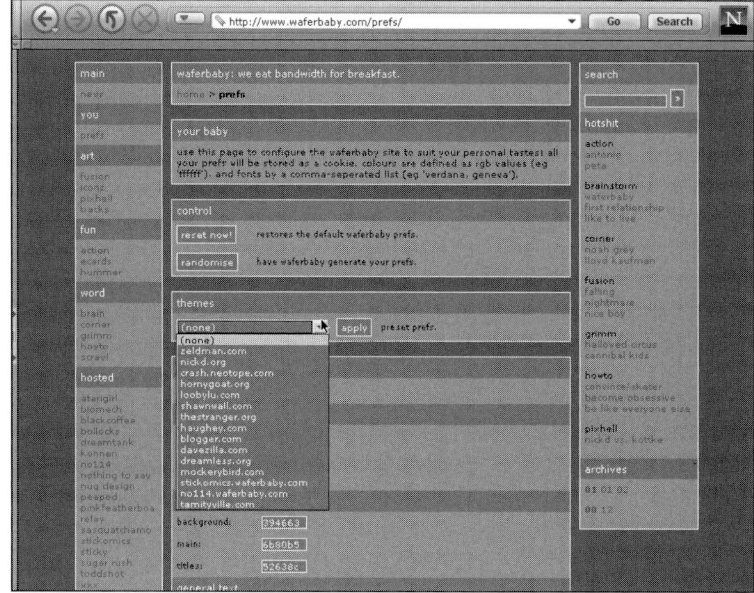

Figure 12.3

User-selectable "Preferences" at Daniel Bogan's Waferbaby. Choose a look, and the site changes. Though this might appear to be the brainchild of a programmer, Bogan is actually an animator-illustrator. If he can do it, you can do it (http://www.waferbaby.com/).

In "Brainstorm," readers respond to a provocative question on the site by typing their answers in a form. Instantly, these answers appear on the page, in reverse chronological order. Readers vie to outdo the wit and originality of previous answers. The audience creates the content; personal involvement and natural curiosity promote repeat visits.

In "Preferences," visitors can modify Waferbaby's appearance by choosing alternate color schemes and typographic choices modeled after well-known personal sites or create their own look and feel by editing a CSS document right in the browser. When the reader is happy with the color scheme and typography, it is stored as a JavaScript cookie on her hard drive. The site will use her chosen color scheme and fonts until she decides to change it.

Both "Brainstorm" and "Preferences" are made possible by a few lines of code in PHP, a JavaScript cookie, and a MySQL database to store and fetch the results.

Mini-Case Study: Metafilter.com

In 1999, Matt Haughey used Allaire Cold Fusion to create Metafilter (http://www.metafilter.com/), a community site for web authors who like to write about other people's web content. This site will be discussed again in Chapter 13. For the time being, it is worth noting how Metafilter accommodates two levels of dynamic change: instantaneous change based on user actions and evolutionary change based on user patterns observed over time (see Figure 12.4).

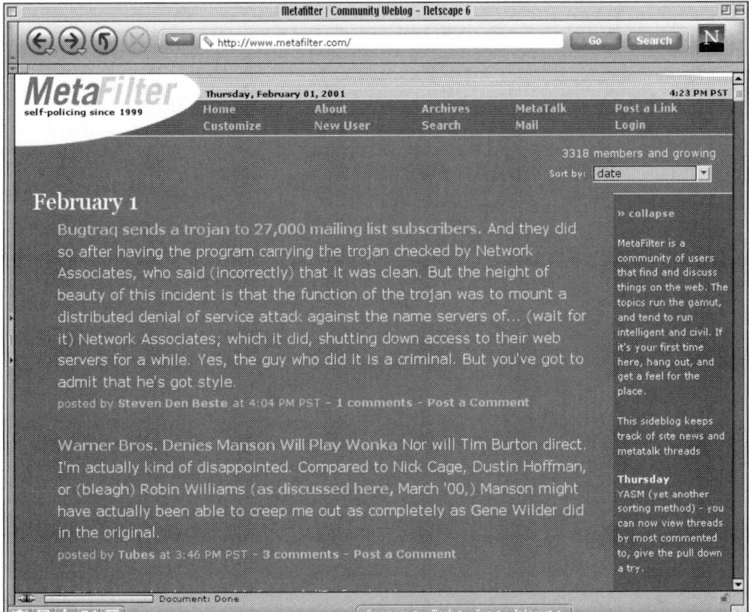

Figure 12.4

Matt Haughey's Metafilter community site, a web-based application that responds to its members' needs. The dark blue panel at right, introduced in January 2001, keeps members posted on changes in the way the site functions (http://www.metafilter.com/).

As in Waferbaby's "Brainstorm," at Metafilter, user participation fashions the content, generating loyalty and repeat usage. As usage patterns emerge, Haughey responds to them by adjusting the way the site works. A new feature is added, an old one removed. This in turn changes the way the site is perceived and used. New usage patterns emerge, and over time, new site-wide changes are instituted.

Every site owner studies usage patterns and changes the site accordingly: rotating content more frequently in the most visited sections; clarifying a text label if one section of the site continually goes ignored; changing the design to emphasize the least-visited section (or the most-visited); or removing front page links to sections the public simply seems not to care about (but keeping those sections alive to avoid link rot). The possibilities are many.

Add dynamic, user-generated content to the mix, and the potential grows even more interesting. On top of everything else, a psychological dynamic begins to emerge. Is the community shaping the site, or is the site shaping the community?

We don't wish to imply that this whole thing goes on like a scientific experiment or that the community in question serves as some kind of Petri dish slide. As in any good community site, the owner/moderator is as involved as any other member—but with the added ability to institute changes or solicit suggested changes from the members. What is interesting is the way that human dynamic behavior shapes *and is shaped* by basic web dynamism. This is the power of a site that changes when you type on it.

This is interactivity print cannot match.

Any Size Kid Can Play

We've confined our case studies to two relatively small-scale (but influential) projects to show that dynamic interactivity is within the reach of even the modest web shop or the lone freelancer. Large-scale projects require teams of information architects, project managers, web designers, developers, writers, web technicians, producers, network administrators, server consultants, marketers, advertising teams, editors, and content specialists. If you go into full-time web design, you will likely be part of such enterprises. But even sites created by tiny teams can use the techniques just discussed to add web dynamism to the mix.

For instance, a dyed-in-the-wool print designer wishes to service a few of his clients who've requested smallish websites: 10 to 20 pages of mostly static content. One of these clients urgently desires the ability to post customer feedback onsite in real time. Initially that seems beyond the reach of the print designer-cum-web designer, but a few hours with a book on PHP will change all that. The client gets his interactivity; the designer gets a higher fee. Hopefully the consumer is also better served.

You might think all this is "too technical" for you. If you don't believe you will ever be able to wrap your head around server-side stuff, let us now introduce you to Server Side Includes (SSI), the technology we mentioned earlier in this chapter.

Take a Walk on the Server Side

As a working web designer, you might find yourself cutting and pasting the same menu bar into page after HTML page. For instance, you might have cut and pasted something like this into all 500 pages of your site:

```
<!--Begin menu -->
<table border="0" cellpadding="0" cellspacing="0">
   <tr valign="top">
      <td width="20%" valign="top" align="left" bgcolor="#cccc00" height="25">
         <a href="/main.html"
           onmouseover="window.status='Current issue. You\'re soaking in it.'; return true;"
           onmouseout="window.status=''; return true;">
<img name="main" src="/menu3/main_o.gif" valign="top" align="left" height="25"
border="0" alt="Current issue."></a></td>
   </tr>
   <tr>
      <td valign="top" align="left" bgcolor="#cccc00" height="25">
         <a href="/stories/"
           onmouseover="window.status='Past issues.'; changeImages('stories',
            '/menu3/stories_o.gif'); return true;"
           onmouseout="window.status=''; changeImages('stories', '/menu3/stories.gif');
            return true;">
<img name="stories" src="/menu3/stories.gif" valign="top" align="left" height="25"
border="0" alt="Past issues."></a></td>
   </tr>
   <tr>
      <td valign="top" align="left" bgcolor="#cccc00" height="25">
         <a href="/news.html"
           onmouseover="window.status='Site news.'; changeImages('news',
            '/menu3/news_o.gif'); return true;"
           onmouseout="window.status=''; changeImages('news', '/menu3/news.gif');
           return true;">
```

```
<img name="news" src="/menu3/news.gif" valign="top" align="left" height="25"
border="0" alt="Site news."></a></td>
   </tr>
   <tr>
      <td valign="top" align="left" bgcolor="#cccc00" height="25">
         <a href="/join.html"
            onmouseover="window.status='Our mailing list.'; changeImages('list',
            '/menu3/list_o.gif'); return true;"
            onmouseout="window.status=''; changeImages('list', '/menu3/list.gif'); return
            true;">
<img name="list" src="/menu3/list.gif" valign="top" align="left" height="25" border="0"
alt="Our mailing list."></a></td>
   </tr>
   </table>
<!-- End menu -->
```

Ugly, isn't it? What if you could replace that entire chunk of repugnance with one comely line of code? Namely:

```
<!-- #include virtual="/includes/menu.inc" -->
```

You can do it!

To do it, let's assume that the menu mess was part of a page called index.html.

First, cut the menu mess out of index.html, paste it into a blank document, and save that document as menu.inc. The .inc stands for "include," though technically speaking, includes can have any file extension—even .html. Your systems administrator will tell you if includes require a particular or unusual file extension.

Now in index.html, where the menu mess used to be, type that one line:

```
<!-- #include virtual="/includes/menu.inc" -->
```

What do these tags mean? <!-- is a null tag containing a comment; <!-- #include --> is an include; virtual means that what follows in quotes is a URL pointing to the file you wish to include; and --> closes the comment and the include.

Next, you'll save menu.inc in an "includes" directory on your web server. You don't *have* to save it in such a directory, but it makes sense, just as it makes sense to save GIFs in a "gifs" directory, QuickTime movies in a "quicktime" or "movies" directory, and so on. As described in Chapter 7, this makes it easier to find pieces and write appropriate file references during the site's creation and subsequent maintenance. If for some reason you prefer to save your SSI files in a directory called "rosebud," the reference would read:

```
<!-- #include virtual="/rosebud/menu.inc" -->
```

Now simply use that line of code in every HTML document where you formerly had to cut and paste a heap of menu bar markup. Then upload your HTML pages to the web server.

Some folks use a different file extension, such as .shtml or .shtm, if their HTML file contains an include, and some servers require this. But if you can stick to the .html file extension, you'll avoid confusion and heartache down the road.

Why confusion and heartache? We knew you were going to ask. For one thing, imagine that your static .html pages have been bookmarked by visitors and search engines. You then start changing your file extensions. All of a sudden, your internal and external links are broken, your visitors are confused, and the search engines that ranked you so highly are pointing to nonexistent pages.

Are You Being Served?

You've replaced redundant markup with neat, clean includes. What's the next step? There probably isn't one. Most web servers natively support SSIs. If it doesn't work right away, you might need to contact the company hosting your site (or the network administrator if your company hosts its own sites) and ask that the configuration file be changed to permit SSIs. Unless the hosting company hires trained monkeys as tech support, complying with your request will take two minutes.

Of course, if you are sane, you will have made this phone call *before* changing all your HTML pages. Or you will have created a test HTML page, uploaded it, and confirmed with your own eyes and mouse cursor that it works.

More than one SSI can be put to use on each page. You can replace the "header," the "footer," or just about any piece of the puzzle. Using SSI, you can replace all or nearly all of the dull, repetitive junk that holds web pages together.

In turn, you can begin viewing HTML pages *as content containers* rather than tortuous masterpieces of visually oriented markup—because *content containers* are exactly what they are and were always intended to be. This might not be the true separation of style from content, but it will do until the real thing comes along.

SSI can do many things besides what we've outlined here. It can insert appropriate text, HTML, or CSS based on the user's browser. It can indicate when the page was last updated (`<!--#echo var="LAST_MODIFIED" -->`), give the current date and time, and do other funky tricks.

And, as we've said, SSI is the low end. Imagine the possibilities if you begin to work with more advanced server-side technologies.

Advantages of SSI

If a site changes—or perhaps we should say *when* a site changes (for instance, when a new section must be added to the menu bar)—the power of SSI is revealed. What was true for CSS is just as true for SSI: It is easier to edit a single document (menu.inc) than it is to change hundreds or thousands.

Hopefully, your client is not about to wantonly add new sections to the menu or demand changes to the appearance of the menu after the site is nearly built. In a perfect world, you have followed the suggestions in Chapter 7, and the client has signed off (and paid part of your fee) at each stage of completion. Therefore, the client has a vested interest in following through with the plan he committed to and paid for and has *no* vested interest in pulling last-minute changes to prove that he is the dominant monkey in this rainforest.

But clients are clients, and change happens. SSI is a simple way of protecting yourself from hours of tedious replacement tasks.

Disadvantages of SSI

Being a server-side technology, SSI eats up processing power from the server. Every time a visitor hits a page containing a replaced SSI element, the markup describing that element must be fetched from the server—like a stick in the jaws of a panting mastiff.

If you're building a professionally hosted site with plenty of server power in reserve, such demands on the server are no problem. If you're hosting the site on your home computer and connected to your home cable modem, there could be a problem. Given sufficient traffic, the toll on your PC might be noticeable, and the site might "slow down" for your visitors during times of peak traffic. On the other hand, if you're hosting an extremely popular site on your home computer, maybe it's time to upgrade your server.

If you are interested in server-side technologies, Jeff Veen's *The Art & Science of Web Design* (New Riders: 2001) discusses the subject in more detail—and using better words and stuff. If you are uninterested in server-side technologies to the point of anxiety, you'll be happy to know that we've finished discussing them.

Now let's look at a technology you will frequently encounter in your career but will never even contemplate programming yourself. Let's talk about Java. First of all, what the heck is it?

Cookin' with Java

Java is an object-oriented programming language developed by Sun Microsystems (http://www.sun.com/) primarily for the Web. And just what, you ask, is an object-oriented programming language? An object-oriented language is one that reuses software objects the same way you might re-use custom shapes you'd created in Adobe Illustrator or a sales executive might reuse chunks of boilerplate text about "tremendous synergies, should our two companies work together."

In Illustrator, you can recombine basic button shapes, spirals, or complex outlines to create new artwork from predesigned fragments. Similarly, a Java programmer can combine entire libraries worth of coded objects to build new programs from existing parts. Reusing graphic elements makes *you* faster and more productive; reusing code objects does the same thing for Java programmers.

Reusable parts: that's the idea. Sun's programmers called these parts *objects*. Sun didn't invent this idea. Windows, Mac OS, and UNIX also reuse code objects (Windows DLLs, anyone?). But in operating systems like Windows, Mac OS, and UNIX, these reusable parts are immediately compiled down to machine code. In Java, they are compiled to an intermediary format called "bytecode," which is then interpreted by a Java Virtual Machine, about which we'll have more to say in just a moment.

As mentioned earlier in this chapter, Java can be used to create full-scale programs (applications), miniature programs that download quickly when needed (applets), or server-side *servlets*. Servlets are full-fledged but small application fragments that run in the context of the server—as Photoshop plug-ins run in the context of Photoshop.

Ghost in the Virtual Machine

But there's a catch. Just as Windows programs require a Windows environment and Mac programs are designed for Macs, Java programs must run in a Java environment.

Does this mean that you have to go out and buy a Java computer? No, it simply means that Java programs are designed to run in Java-capable web browsers (Netscape Navigator, Microsoft Internet Explorer), Java-capable web-enabled devices, or special Java devices (such as Java-powered digital television-top boxes and remotes). They do this by means of Java Virtual Machines, which we promise, really truly promise, we will describe in just a moment.

Netscape was the first browser to support Java, and the point of the Sun/Netscape partnership, as explained in Chapter 2, was to smash Windows hegemony while getting Java onto as many platforms as possible, by way of the browser. They succeeded at getting Java onto as many platforms as possible. One out of two ain't bad.

Today most browsers and computer operating systems support Java. It gets a bit more complicated when the browser or OS maker offers an "improved" Java environment that Sun does not consider truly Java-compatible, but we'll get to that later. Java-capable browsers might run on any computing platform (Windows, Mac OS, Linux, UNIX, or BeOS) as long as the browser manufacturer supports that platform.

What makes all of this work? The Java Virtual Machine does. You might think of the Virtual Machine as a streamlined computer operating system (OS) running inside another computer OS—a Java computer running inside Windows, for example. Or you might think of it as an interpreter, turning spoken words into sign language for the hearing-impaired.

This Virtual Machine is sometimes included with the browser. Early versions of Netscape included a Virtual Machine customized for each OS. This added significantly to the download time but ensured that users would have the then-new Java technology at their disposal.

In other cases, the Virtual Machine is built into the operating system. For instance, Apple Macintosh OS9 includes "Mac OS Runtime for Java," a Java Virtual Machine whose sole purpose is to run Java programs on the Mac.

If you install IE5 Macintosh Edition on a pre-OS 9 Mac, you might get Java errors because IE5/Mac expects a more recent Virtual Machine than the one on your system. You can correct this problem by upgrading to OS9 or by downloading a more recent version of Mac OS Runtime for Java from http://developer.apple.com/java/classic.html. The program is free.

As you can see, the tantalizing potential of Java lies in its ability to work in any operating system equipped with a Java Virtual machine—in other words, theoretically at least, to run on any operating system. Practically speaking, developers could build a word processor or a full-blown office suite that runs in any Java-capable web browser and on any operating system with a Virtual Machine. Of course, companies that make word processors and full-blown office suites might not like that idea. They might dislike it so much that they would end up building their own web browser and taking over the market...not that we're mentioning any names. There is, in fact, a Java word processor (indeed, there is an entire Java office suite), and we hear it works quite well.

Where the web designer fits in

As a web designer, you might be called upon to embed a Java applet in an HTML page. (Again: An applet is a self-contained piece of code that runs within a Java-capable browser, as Photoshop plug-ins run within Photoshop.) This is simply a matter of using the HTML <OBJECT> or <APPLET> tag or another very basic HTML tag—no problem at all. At other times, you might use Java to compensate for a missing plug-in on a visitor's system.

For instance, the IpixViewer plug-in, like Apple's QuickTime VR (see the section, "Turn on, Tune in, Plug-in" later in this chapter), enables visitors to explore 360° panoramic views of any location that can be photographed. It's an extraordinary plug-in that does a remarkable job. But not many people know about this plug-in, so not many have downloaded it. Therefore you might feel that IpixViewer content cannot be used on your site. Not to worry! The missing plug-in can be replaced by a Java applet and compiled down to native, platform-specific code via the Java Virtual Machine:

```
<applet name="IpixViewer" code="IpixViewer.class" archive="IpixViewer.jar" height="210"
➥width="280">
<param name="URL" value="zabptcaj.ipx">
<param name="Spin" value="on">
</applet>
```

If the HTML just listed looks odd to you, don't sweat it. Your Java developer will tell you what needs to be included on the page. Your job will be to insert it, test it, and verify things such as height and width. (Is the resulting image in fact 210 pixels high? Does it look right? If not, change the numbers and try again.) By the way, this same technique works for other multimedia content, such as Flash. If the visitor lacks the Flash plug-in, a Java applet can display the Flash content. Your developers will create the applet and the complex code that determines whether or not the applet is needed on each visitor's system. Your job is simply to plug in some HTML and test.

The other reason you need to know about Java is that in spite of its utopian aims and utilitarian benefits, Java can sometimes be problematic. And as a *user-oriented* web designer, you need to be aware of that.

Java Woes

We can do this two ways: the short, brutal version or the long, boring, politically correct version.

Here's the short, brutal version: From a user experience perspective, Java often sucks. It can be as unstable as Norman Bates, drain resources like Australians drain beer steins, and crash more frequently than a drunk driver's Pinto.

For those who expect us to be fair, a long, carefully guarded, politically correct version follows. Feel free to skip it unless you are an attorney for Sun Microsystems. In which case, we meant to say that Java is the best thing since the Magna Carta.

Java Woes: The Politically Correct Version

At times, companies have created their own Java Virtual Machines that differ subtly from Sun's. Sun does not like that, and you can understand why. Java is not open source; it is a protected product. Differing Virtual Machines can sometimes prevent Java from fulfilling its promise. This has led some developers to avoid using Java. As a web designer, you will want to stay aware of these issues if there's a possibility of their affecting your site and your users.

Java can also sometimes drain the computer's memory resources because the user is essentially running a second operating system (Java) within his existing OS. Not to mention the fact that the user is likely running a Java-based application on an unstable web browser with all its memory-hogging plug-ins, on top of any other software programs he might have running in the background, and on top of a possibly unstable base operating system such as an older version of Mac OS, which can be wonderful but not entirely stable.

The older the computer and the less memory at its disposal, the greater the possibility of woe. Attention, Sun attorneys: We do not wish to overstate these issues. All that is usually required is for the user to increase the amount of memory allotted to the browser. Unfortunately, most web users don't realize this, so they don't do it. Result: instability.

The memory problem is not a Java problem per se; plug-ins like Flash and Shockwave also work better if the user increases his browser's memory partition. Fortunately, during the installation process, Shockwave and Flash alert users to the issue and offer to increase the browser's memory automatically if the user clicks the OK button. Java does not do this because Java is typically preinstalled on the user's machine when it arrives from the factory.

Given that browser makers know most users are going to encounter Java and are going to install and run plug-ins, why don't they increase the default memory partition of their browsers? In a word: competition. The browser makers want to prove that their product uses *less* memory than the competitor's, so the browser installs itself with the lowest memory allotment possible. It will operate under those conditions just fine as long as users rarely venture beyond all-text websites. Most users do venture far beyond, whether knowingly or not. So most users are practically guaranteed to encounter browser instability on sites that use Java or plug-ins or even large, memory-draining background images.

Though Java tends to work well in Windows and UNIX, it's a mixed bag in Mac OS. Even on top-of-the-line G4 Macs with 1.5GB of installed RAM, T3 connections, and system buses capable of transferring over 1GB of data per second, Java can sour.

These same Macs can rotate a 40MB Photoshop image faster than Google can track down your ex-girlfriend. At speeds exceeding 5.5 gigaflops, they can outperform Pentiums with twice the rated clock speed. But a stupid "rippling water" Java applet on a personal site at Geocities can take down these mighty Macs. Java is cross-platform but not always reliably so. Attention, lawyers: We do not wish to overstate these issues.

Then of course, Java does not work at all in text-based browsers such as Lynx, nor will it function in older browsers such as Internet Explorer 2. And users of even the newest browsers might "turn off" Java in their preferences, thus defeating the development team's efforts to use Java on the site.

This is not a Java problem per se. Users can also turn off JavaScript and style sheets. They can refuse to install plug-ins, tell the browser to use "their" background colors instead of yours, and in every other way imaginable assert their right to see the Web as they wish to see it, thus turning your beautiful site into a sea of sewage that strangely pleases them.

The workaround, as always, is to provide alternatives. Simple HTML menus and alternative content go a long way toward keeping sites accessible, no matter what technologies are intended for their use under optimal conditions. We do not wish to *understate* this issue. We wish to strongly emphasize it. Make accessibility part of the plan at all times.

Java Joys

Despite hiccups, Java is cross-platform, and it does many things very well, such as "stepping in" to replace missing plug-ins. For instance, as just described, Flash files can be run as Java applications in Netscape Navigator if the user does not have the Flash plug-in. That is fairly remarkable. It is handled by Flash itself. When saving the file, Flash generates code that will call upon a built-in Java action if the plug-in is not detected in the user's browser.

Beyond all that, Java applets and Java *servlets* (smaller, more stable mini-applications of Java that run on the server) can be used to help create dynamic, database-driven websites. Java is ideally suited for sophisticated tasks that take place under the hood. Because Java works cross-platform and cross-browser (despite problems just mentioned), it might be preferable to use Java for complex tasks, rather than relying on proprietary, platform- and browser-specific technologies such as VBScript and ActiveX.

Java seems less valuable to us when it is used to create dynamic menus or to trigger the rotation of ad banners. In both cases, JavaScript/ECMAScript is a lighter, more stable choice that is also a web standard, tends to use fewer computing resources, and works better across platforms.

Seeing as we've mentioned Java and JavaScript in the same paragraph, we might as well restate that the two technologies should not be confused, in spite of their similar names. JavaScript is a complex but interpreted programming language that works in web browsers. Java is a full-fledged, object-oriented programming environment that can drive entire devices or can be used to build complete applications. Nearly all web designers work with JavaScript, whether on the programming level or simply via cut-and-paste. No sane web designer attempts to program in Java. Even insane web designers avoid it.

The true power of Java is now being manifested beyond the browser. Instead of web surfing, consumers are channel surfing via Java-powered TV devices (www-us.semiconductors.com/news/content/file_501.html). Java and Linux are now creating Internet appliances that require no understanding of Java or Linux (http://www.linuxdevices.com/news/NS5323294840.html). Java is finding its way into Personal Digital Assistants (PDAs), cell phones, and even server-side technologies (http://www.alistapart.com/stories/beyond/2.html). Keep your eye on Java as your career unfolds, and use it judiciously as your sites evolve.

Rich Media: Exploding the "Page"

We say web "pages" because our minds cannot let go of the publishing model we grew up with. But rich web media give the lie to the "page" metaphor. These pages are *not* pages. This is not a pipe. This is not my beautiful wife.

Let's see how standard technologies and popular plug-ins push the Web way beyond the cosmologies of print design. We'll start with some web standards you might or might not know about.

Virtual Reality Modeling Language (VRML)

VRML, though nearly dead from disuse, is the standard language for the animation and 3D modeling of geometric shapes. It allows 3D scenes to be viewed and interactively manipulated on the Web. Using a special *VRML browser*, the web user can connect to an online VRML site, choose a 3D environment to explore, and cruise around the spooky "3D world." It is also possible to zoom in and out and to interact with the 3D environment in various ways. The Netscape Live3D VRML browser (built into Netscape 3) was the first to support the VRML 1.0 standard.

Think video game. Think cheesy, super-low-grade video game. Laura Croft it's not. It's more like Pacman 3D. Think wireframe and black backgrounds.

Besides being fairly crude, VRML is not a technology that lends itself to accessible alternatives. A GIF image might be described via <ALT> and <TITLE> text for the benefit of web users with visual disabilities. But you are either navigating a 3D environment, or you're not. <ALT> text just won't cut it: "If you could see and if you could physically manipulate a mouse cursor, you might enter a crude simulation of a living room and 'pick up' an illustration representing a pencil." Thanks for sharing.

VRML is fascinating but has few immediately apparent commercial benefits. Nor is it particularly dazzling in today's world of Flash 5, DOM-based interactivity, and improved monitor and color resolutions. Perhaps for these reasons, the technology has never caught on the way that JavaScript, for example, caught on. Web users have a tough enough time finding what they want on most websites without adding primitive 3D effects to the mix.

Of course, VRML was never about "web users finding what they want," and you might feel we've just slapped a straw man. But have we?

Web-using veterans might recall a similar 3D experiment called *Hot Sauce* that was created by Apple Computer in the mid-1990s. Hot Sauce turned text-based directories into virtual 3D environments containing (you guessed it) text—text that floated in fake 3D space. To move from one block of text to the next, you eased your mouse up and down your desk.

Instead of navigating Yahoo.com the conventional way and finding what you wanted in under 30 seconds, with Hot Sauce you could spend hours painfully navigating a 3D version of the Yahoo directory. This was not most people's idea of fun, and the technology soon petered out. Scientists do what they can; marketers do what sells. Hot Sauce did not sell, and neither did VRML because after you muttered, "Cool," there was little else to be said. Angry VRML and Hot Sauce fans, please send your protests to null@newriders.com.

Now that you know what VRML is, you probably don't need to know much more about it. If you're curious, more information is available at The Web Developer's Virtual Library:

http://wdvl.internet.com/Authoring/VRML/

SVG and SMIL

In the absence of finalized multimedia standards for the Web, plug-ins were developed that enabled websites to offer streaming video, animated vector graphics, music tracks, and the like. We are about to look at those very plug-ins. But first, let us pause to consider a recent development.

Over the past couple of years, W3C recommendations have emerged to suggest standardized ways of doing what proprietary plug-ins already do so well. One of these is SMIL, the W3C recommendation for multimedia; the other is SVG, intended to deliver vector graphics such as those already used in Flash (but with some essential differences from Flash).

What's up with these two new standards, and why do they matter?

SMIL (through your fear and sorrow)

SMIL (http://www.w3.org/AudioVideo/) stands for Synchronized Multimedia Integration Language and is pronounced, "smile." Isn't that cute? Oh, shut up.

SMIL is an easy-to-learn, HTML-like language for creating "TV-like multimedia presentations such as training courses on the Web," according to the W3C. The current SMIL recommendation is 1.0, and you can read all about it at the W3C address just cited and at another one we'll mention later. This is our way of avoiding adding another 50 pages to this book.

Aside from the fact that three Internet heavies (Real, Apple, and Adobe) are throwing their weight behind SMIL, why should you care about any of this? Let's see.

Harnessing media, helping users

SMIL packs accessibility features (http://www.w3.org/TR/SMIL-access/), including alternative text content that can be made available to Braille readers. Such content will also enable search engines to index multimedia web content authored in SMIL.

In English: slap a QuickTime video on your site and search engines such as Google or Altavista could care less. But add a carefully authored SMIL presentation to your site, and speeches made by the characters in your video could show up in Google and Altavista's search results.

The educational implications are enormous. A student researching Hamlet's soliloquy could find a SMIL-authored video of Sir Laurence Olivier performing it. The Web's potential as the world's library could suddenly become much richer.

The commercial implications ain't bad, either. A buyer searching for widgets could find your client's digitized promotional video on the subject. Existing multimedia formats obviously do not offer these advantages.

Lest you think SMIL is a completely wacky new technology, it is, in fact, simply a markup language that works with existing technologies like QuickTime and Real digital video and audio. What SMIL does is bring the traditional benefits of the Web (searching, finding, bookmarking) to non-text content. That is profound.

More reasons to SMIL

Other cool things you can do with SMIL:

1. With a single link, you can deliver audio to dialup users and video to broadband users. None of that "click here for audio, click here for video" junk.
2. Deliver different language versions of clips depending on a user's system-language setting.
3. Use back-end technologies to deliver multimedia content on the fly. No need for expensive, proprietary programs with steep learning curves. (SVG delivers similar benefits.)

...All with a few simple tags.

Author! Author!

Among the currently available Web tools and plug-ins that support SMIL are Apple QuickTime 4.1 (http://www.apple.com/quicktime/) and the unfortunately named RealSlideshow authoring tool by the makers of the RealPlayer (http://proforma.real.com/rn/tools/slideshow/index.html?). Adobe is presently developing a SMIL extension for its GoLive WYSIWYG tool, which should simplify the creation of SMIL content and might help accelerate the standard's adoption.

RealSystem's support for SMIL has been solid since 1998. Given the number of RealPlayers out there, SMIL can already reach almost as many web users as Flash does. Not that SMIL and Flash are enemies. SMIL is often used to integrate Flash content into the QuickTime and RealPlayers, and Flash 5 exports SMIL for use in RealSystem.

SMILsoftware's Flution 1.5 (http://www.smilsoftware.com/) for Windows can streamline the SMIL creation process. Tom Wlodkowksy's free Media Access Generator (MAGpie) for Windows (http://main.wgbh.org/wgbh/pages/ncam/webaccess/magpie/) adds accessibility features such as closed-captioning to SMIL. For a more detailed description of the goals of the SMIL language, see the W3C Activity Statement (http://www.w3.org/AudioVideo/Activity.html) on Synchronized Multimedia. For practical advice on putting SMIL to work, see Jim Heid's old-but-good tutorial at Macworld, SMIL: Markup for Multimedia (http://macworld.zdnet.com/2000/02/create/markupmultimedia.html).

SVG for You and Me

SVG (Scalable Vector Graphics) is a W3C standard in progress. As of this writing, the W3C describes its initial SVG activities as "currently nearing completion" (http://www.w3.org/Graphics/SVG/Overview.htm8). Though SVG produces vector graphics, it is a markup language. In fact, it is an application of XML, the super-meta-markup language we've mentioned throughout this book.

Like Flash vector graphics, SVG vector graphics can fill an entire screen with artwork while using very little bandwidth. Also like Flash, SVG can be animated via scripting. You'll find examples of this at Adobe's SVG site, which we'll discuss in a moment (see Figures 12.5 and 12.6).

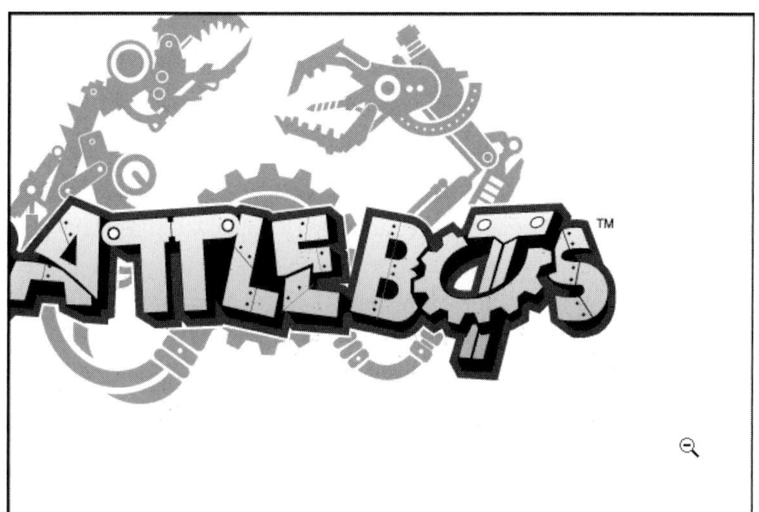

Figure 12.5

The Battlebots logo in SVG. At the user's discretion, the image can be enlarged again and again.

Figure 12.6

Vector artwork maintains quality at the highest magnifications while keeping bandwidth expenditure at a minimum (http://www.adobe.com/).

No matter its graphic appearance, SVG remains text. To understand the implications of that fact, let's contrast SVG with our present production techniques. We'll use an example that's close to every designer's heart: the client's logo.

Romancing the logo

For the purposes of this little exercise, we'll assume that the client's logo involves letterforms rather than nonverbal swooshes or swirls. We'll further assume that you're developing the logo in Adobe Illustrator and that you have not yet converted your text to outlines. After it becomes outlines, it ceases to be text, thus losing the SVG benefit we're about to explore.

First, the traditional methods:

If you export your client's logo from Illustrator to Photoshop and embed it on a web page as a GIF image, search engines will not index it because it is not text. You can work around that limitation by adding <ALT> text to your image tag, but not all search engines index all <ALT> text.

If you create that same logo in Flash, it can spin and whirl and glow, but search engines will not index it because it is not text. Flash 5 has added some accessibility features, allowing you, for instance, to include <ALT> text for a Flash file, but this is global text, not image-specific text, and we already talked about the limitations of <ALT> tags as a guarantor of search engine placement.

Now, the SVG method:

Take that same Illustrator logo and export it as SVG, using Illustrator's built-in support for that web standard. The resulting logo looks great, smells fresh, *and it remains text.* That means search engines can index it.

Your client's logo no longer blushes like a maiden when the search engine comes courting. From every page of the site, the text-based logo calls out to the search engine, and the search engine rewards it with the Web's greatest mark of love: a high ranking.

To the eye, the logo is a logo; to the search engine, it is a word. If the word "Widgets" appears at the top of every page of the site, that site will rank high when users search for widgets. When the client cries, "Make the logo bigger," you can answer: "We've made it number one." By contrast, under the old methods, when a *GIF image* of the word "Widgets" appears at the top of every page of the site, it is unlikely to seduce the search engines.

Because the SVG-formatted Widgets logo is a *word that looks like a logo*, users can also copy and paste it into a text document. It will lose its SVG formatting when users do this, but your client's name will remain intact. Your client will like that. And who knows? A year from now, it might not lose its formatting when pasted into a popular word processor, print layout program, or email message.

In fact that is one of the promises of SVG for graphic designers: that we will be able to use the same SVG image file in our print work and our web work—from Illustrator to Quark to the website, as easy as drag and drop. (Yes, you can also create SVG illustrations by hand-coding them—after all, SVG is really XML—but we doubt many designers will want to do that. We sure don't.)

Will SVG replace Flash? Not likely and certainly not any time soon. Will SVG evolve into a useful tool for creating scriptable vector graphics? We think it will.

Sounds dandy, but will it work?

SVG support is coming online slowly. A plug-in from Adobe (http://www.adobe.com/svg/main.html) supports SVG in all web browsers, though not equally well. The first version of the Adobe plug-in relied on Netscape-proprietary plug-in detection that was not supported in Internet Explorer for Macintosh. Users of IE5/Mac could not see SVG graphics at all with that plug-in version.

As of this writing, a newer Adobe SVG plug-in has greatly improved its support for non-Netscape browsers, though Internet Explorer support for Macs is limited to nonscripted SVG only. In other words, IE/Mac users can see SVG graphics on the Web but cannot see dynamic (animated) SVG graphics.

Still, things are looking up for SVG. You might find it odd that it takes a proprietary plug-in to support an open standard, but such is the state of the Web. After the SVG standard is finalized, we suspect that browser makers will begin investigating ways to support it.

Promises, Promises

While SMIL is well-supported via plug-ins, SVG is still a work in progress—a promising work in progress, an exciting work in progress, but a work in progress. It will be widely adopted when it is further along in development and can be natively supported in browsers.

Do these tools, SMIL and SVG, pose an immediate threat to Macromedia Flash? They certainly do not. In fact, we don't see them as anti-Flash technologies at all (though some might view them that way).

While SMIL is expanding and SVG is still taking shape, now would be a good time to download Adobe's SVG plug-in and explore SMIL presentations and tutorials. Over the coming months, you will want to remain open-minded about these emerging standards and keep your eye on their evolution. Before we know it, they will likely be part of every web designer's tool kit.

But in the meantime, you have a job to do. So let us turn our gaze to the Web's *de facto* multimedia "standards" (which are not, technically speaking, web standards at all). Let's consider the proprietary, often-maligned, sometimes-adored, widely used plug-ins that already bring rich multimedia experiences to hundreds of thousands of sites and hundreds of millions of web users.

Turn on, Tune in, Plug-in

Plug-ins are the chief means by which web designers currently add sound and motion to the Web, and web users employ them to extend the capability of their browsers, allowing them to see and hear these sound and motion effects. Browser can't play music? Pop in a plug-in. Browser can't show vector graphics? Pop in a plug-in. Browser can't show 360-degree panoramic views of the client's flagship $599 running shoe? Pop in a plug-in.

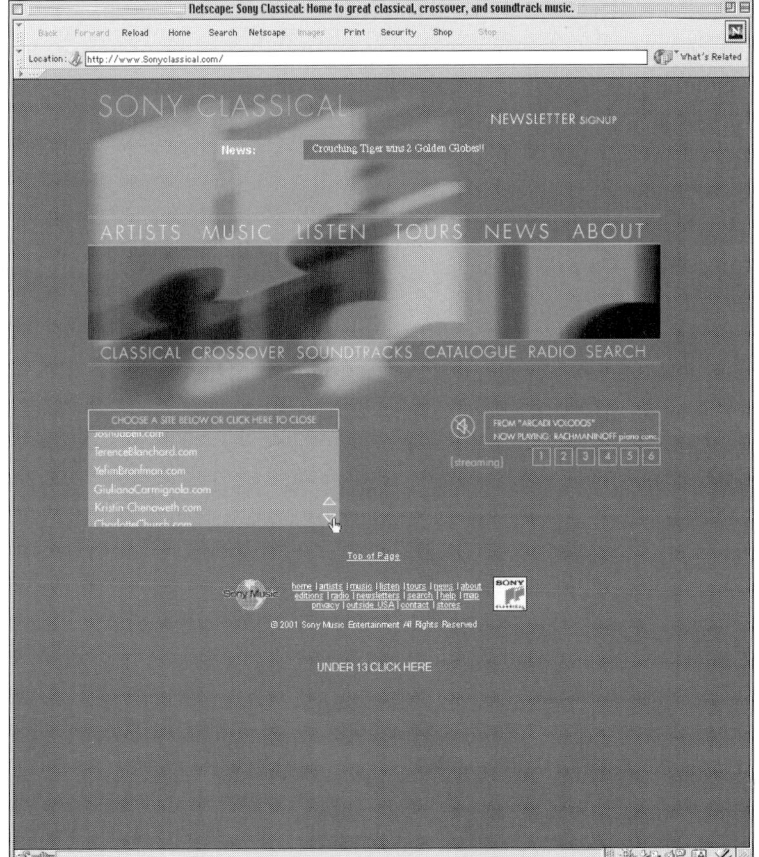

Figure 12.7

Sony Classical, a site that Flash built. What it loses in accessibility, it gains in form and function. Classical music greets the visitor as the site loads; as one piece of music replaces another, the company's musical offerings shift in the main window as though one were poring through record bins (http://www.sonyclassical.com/). You can do some of this in HTML and JavaScript but not as smoothly or reliably.

For graphic designers, plug-ins are nothing new. If you want to create strange blurs in Photoshop, you can buy and install Kai Krause's KPT Filters plug-ins. If you wish to work with preset masks in Photoshop, you'd purchase Extensis Photoframe. Photoshop and Quark have sparked entire industries devoted to creating such plug-ins. Plug-ins for web browsers function exactly like plug-ins for Photoshop and Quark, except that browser plug-ins are free. (Why are they free? How can they be free? We'll get to that.)

The other difference between designer plug-ins and browser plug-ins is that browser plug-ins are as essential to the end-user as they are to the creator. Your client does not need KPT Filters to see the way you've blurred his logo in Photoshop, but web users need the Flash plug-in to view your Flash work, the Real plug-in to see and hear your Real-encoded video, and so on.

A Hideous Breach of Reality

Some plug-ins are *true* plug-ins, invisibly doing their work inside the browser. Others are more like free-standing players, though their manufacturers still refer to them as plug-ins, and most web designers call them that as well. Of course they should be called "helper applications" if they aren't actually plug-ins, as they have been for years by persnickety people who also pronounce "GIF" correctly.

Still other multimedia add-ons can work either way. Depending on how you mark up your web page, Apple's QuickTime plug-in can lurk in the shadows, invisibly playing embedded video and audio files right in the browser window (like a plug-in). It also can spawn an overly ornate steel-burnished console player that lies atop the browser window like a misbegotten Cadillac ornament (*not* like a plug-in).

To keep it simple and to annoy the overly precise among you, we will follow the manufacturers' lead (as well as convention) and refer to all of these add-ons as "plug-ins," whether they behave like true plug-ins or not.

The ubiquity of plug-ins

Plug-ins have been a fact of web life and web design since the mid-1990s. Why plug-ins? How did it happen?

In the beginning, God created the Heavens and the Earth. A little later, the Web consisted of hyperlinked text. In the fullness of time, it became possible to include badly rendered images on web pages. This began to make the medium more attractive to creative and commercial enterprises, and there was soon a demand for sound, video, and other multimedia enhancements on the Web. There was also a demand for really good Chinese food in the American Midwest.

How to answer the clamor for sound and video and other fancy stuff? The engineers at Netscape were inventing what a web browser was supposed to be as they went along. Eventually they hit upon the notion of plug-ins. If it worked for Quark and Photoshop, it ought to work for them too.

At the time, the Web was hotter than Jennifer Lopez's Academy Awards dress, and Netscape's browser was the thing that was making it hot. Here was a marketing opportunity! Dozens of plug-ins soon flung themselves into the market. When new browsers began muscling in on Netscape's turf, they followed Netscape's lead and supported "Netscape plug-ins" simply to compete.

And here we are, more than half a decade on and still plugging away. (There is still no good Chinese food in the American Midwest, however.)

The Impossible Lightness of Plug-ins

Any web designer has much to say about plug-ins, not all of it printable, and we are no exception. Truth is, we could write a whole book about plug-ins. Come to think of it, we could write a book about just *one* plug-in. In fact, many people have. Hillman Curtis, for instance, wrote *Flash Web Design: The Art of Motion Graphics*, New Riders: 2000 (http://www.newriders.com/books/title.cfm?isbn=0735708967).

Want in-depth help with Flash, and penetrating insights into its nature? Try Hillman's book or Joshua Davis's upcoming *Flash to the Core* (New Riders: 2001). We have our hands full as it is. Meantime, let's assess a few well-known plug-ins.

Plug-ins Most Likely to Succeed

There are as many plug-ins as there are stars in the heavens. Plug-ins for specialty uses, plug-ins for novelty uses, plug-ins that support the needs of mathematical and scientific markup, plug-ins that let you print official U.S. postage from your web browser. No, we're not kidding. Pour yourself a strong beverage and hit http://home.netscape.com/plugins/ to take in the range of available plug-ins. Do you have to learn about all these plug-ins? No.

When designing content that requires plug-ins, the first question to ask is, which plug-ins? Which are most widely available? Which are likely to be sitting in your visitor's browser plug-in folder, just waiting for you to give them something to play?

Unfortunately, this question is easier to ask than answer. An assessment of which plug-ins come preloaded in which browsers does little to clarify the state of plug-in-hood. As mentioned in Chapter 2, both Microsoft Internet Explorer and Netscape Communicator include the Apple QuickTime plug-in in their distributions. That much is known.

Netscape also includes the RealPlayer and Shockwave/Flash. IE for Windows, the most popular browser/platform combination, includes the Windows Media Player but not RealPlayer. Most Windows distributions of Explorer include Flash (but not Shockwave); Mac Explorer distributions include neither. By the time you read this, all of this might have changed. That's marketing, kids.

Seeing that you're no better off than you were before, we've gone ahead and created a short list of plug-ins we think you'll run into during your long and splendid web design career. Herewith, please review our never-impartial assessment of the major multimedia plug-ins.

RealPlayer (www.real.com)

This popular plug-in/player delivers streaming video and audio, along with support for Flash and the SMIL standard. RealPlayer is the most popular streaming video format because it uses the least bandwidth and works on all computing platforms (though it's sometimes flaky on Macs).

As explained in Chapter 2, *streaming video* is video that plays while downloading. Early plug-in technologies did not stream. The viewer had to wait for an entire movie or sound file to download before she could see or hear the file in her browser. Real was the first to offer streaming playback.

Dull technical note

Even when a player supports streaming, a small amount of data must be downloaded and cached before streaming begins to ensure smooth playback. If the file were to begin playing immediately, playback could be interrupted later on—for instance, when other network traffic momentarily interfered with the stream. By preloading (downloading and caching) initial data, the player attempts to offer smooth, uninterrupted playback. Apple QuickTime and Windows Media Player, discussed in the following section, are also streaming formats.

Tool tips

The free Real Producer software available at Real's site is of sufficient quality for converting existing digital video to the Real format. An inexpensive "Pro" version provides more options, enables you to create MP3 files, and will help you create HTML files and stub files. *Stub files* are miniature text files that trigger the streaming of Real files over conventional http networks. You also can easily create stub files yourself:

If lopez_dress.rm is a Real-encoded file featuring Jennifer Lopez in her famous Academy Awards dress, and if that file resides at http://www.example.com/real/lopez_dress.rm, to force the file to stream over a conventional web server, you need to create a stub file. Open a blank text document (Write, SimpleText, BBEdit, Tex-Edit, any basic text editor will do). In this blank document, type the address of the Real file:

```
http://www.example.com/real/lopez_dress.rm
```

Close the document and save it as lopez_dress.ram. That's your stub file, Bubba. Upload it to your web server—for the sake of simplicity, we'll assume you've uploaded it to the same directory as the HTML file that references it—and then conjure it up with a link like this:

```
<a href="lopez_dress.ram">La Lopez!</a>
```

Can you refer to it with an image instead? Of course. It's just a link.

```
<a href="lopez_dress.ram"><img src="images/lopez_50x50.gif" height="50" width="50"
alt="Actress Jennifer Lopez" title="Watch Jennifer Lopez at the Academy Awards.
RealPlayer required." Border="0"></a>
```

You can also <EMBED> the file, thereby triggering the Real plug-in instead of the Real console:

```
<embed src=" lopez_dress.ram " autostart="true" volume="100" width="2" height="2"
controls="hidden" pluginspage="http://www.real.com">
```

What does all that extra code mean? We'll explain later.

The point is to link to the stub file, not the actual Real-encoded file. The stub file, being text, downloads almost instantly. If the user's browser is configured correctly, the stub file will launch the RealPlayer, which will then begin preloading the actual video clip. Your visitors will soon see Jennifer Lopez...and so will Ms. Lopez's attorneys. Be certain you have permission to publish the clip.

You can skip the need for stub files if your client or host purchases dedicated Real servers—recommended if you plan to serve much video to many visitors. For instance, on a site that constantly serves TV news feeds, cable comedy clips, or streaming video trailers, investing in Real servers would be a Real good idea.

Special indications

With the highest compression ratio (and consequently, the lowest quality), Real is the fastest streaming format, making it the plug-in of choice for news sites and others where quality is less important than a hardy constitution and the ability to deliver like James Brown. With Real, you are assured of supporting the largest number of users with the widest range of connection speeds.

If video files are meant to viewed and then forgotten (like a TV experience), Real is likely what you want. Conversely, if video files are meant to be stored and treasured on the end-user's hard drive, you would probably choose QuickTime instead. This is, of course, merely our opinion.

QuickTime (www.apple.com/quicktime/)

A high-quality streaming video format, QuickTime also supports a wide variety of streaming audio formats including the ever-popular MP3. It also delivers QuickTime VR panoramas and animated sprites. QuickTime supports hyperlinks in video, and offers some support for Flash and SMIL. An innovative multistreaming process serves appropriately sized material according to the end-user's connection speed, as described in Chapter 2.

Last time we checked, QuickTime was the second most popular streaming format. It uses more bandwidth than RealPlayer but delivers smoother video and audio. The QuickTime format is native to Apple Macintosh computers but thoroughly supports Windows PCs.

Tool tips

Delivering video over the Web should be impossible. The technology works by means of drastic compression methods. Even the best of these methods include visible artifacts. To minimize these artifacts and assure a better quality image, choose subject matter that compresses well.

"Talking heads" compress well. Swish pans and mad action sequences do not. This is because the compression works by seeking pixels that barely change from frame to frame, choosing one of these pixels as a "master" pixel, and repeating it from frame to frame in hopes of fooling your eye. The more jerky camera movement in your *mise-en-scene*, the more obvious the software sleight-of-hand is. This is true not only for QuickTime but for all digital video.

QuickTime VR panoramas can be breathtaking, and various software products are available to help you stitch together individual photographs into a full 3D panorama, including Apple QuickTime VR Authoring Studio (http://www.apple.com/quicktime/qtvr/authoringstudio/). You can insert sound effects in these panoramas and confine the effects to certain portions of the panorama. See Figures 12.8, 12.9, and 12.10 for nonprofit and noncommercial QuickTime VR panoramas at Heidsite and PBS.org.

Figure 12.8

Writer Jim Heid's personal QuickTime VR panoramas convey the rustic beauty of his community (http://www.heidsite.com).

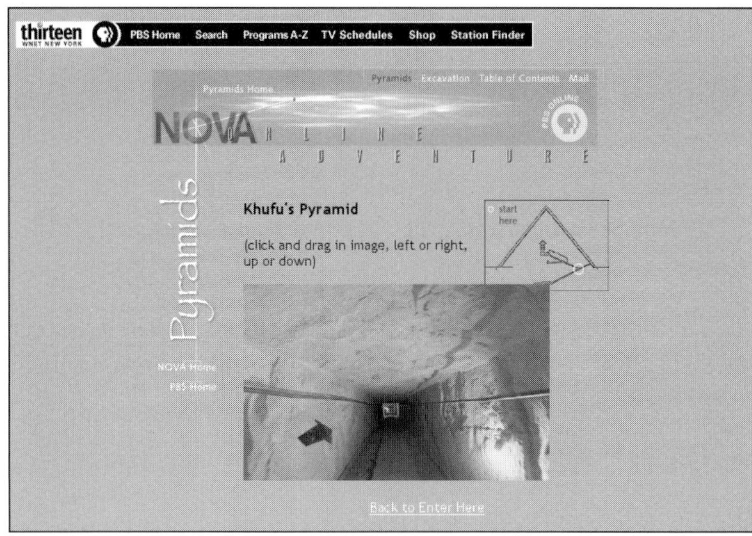

Figure 12.9

A virtual reality tour of Khufu's Pyramid lends needed "gee-whiz" appeal to an essentially educational enterprise (http://www.pbs.org/).

Figure 12.10

A hauntingly frozen moment in time (http://www.heidsite.com/). Print absolutely cannot do this, nor do these screenshots begin to convey the effect.

For instance, a 360-degree panorama of the downtown skyline might be filled with canned traffic effects until the viewer rotates the image to your company's office tower. Suddenly the sound of laughter is heard. As the viewer rotates away from your office tower, the laughter is drowned by the traffic noise.

Or a tranquil beach panorama could reveal the *Jaws* theme as the camera reaches the sea.

Or a 360-degree panorama of the client's company softball team could reveal the hidden thoughts of each individual as the camera's gaze passes over him or her.

You get the idea. QuickTime VR can be very cool.

Special indications

If you want high quality, you probably want QuickTime. If you want VR Panoramas, you need QuickTime. Other panoramic plug-in formats are available (some of them quite good—see iPix, mentioned previously), but none are nearly as widely distributed as QuickTime. Later we'll talk about how some plug-ins managed to crawl to the top of the heap while other good ones languished. It isn't really all that fascinating a story, but gossip is as good a reading motivation as any, and her attorneys have informed us that we can't keep referring to Jennifer Lopez's dress.

Windows Media Player (WMP) (http://www.microsoft.com/windows/windowsmedia/)

WMP delivers streaming video and audio in the Windows Media File (WMF) format and is included in all distributions of the various Windows operating systems, making it a popular plug-in indeed. Though WMP is viewed as a plug-in that primarily supports Windows users, a version is available for Macintosh folk, and it actually works well. The player supports real-time capture and broadcast of audio and video files (making it competitive with RealPlayer) and also handles MP3 audio as smoothly as its competitors.

According to Microsoft, Windows Media Player supports "near-DVD-quality" video and "near-CD-quality" sound. A free Windows Media Encoder makes it as easy to prepare video materials for distribution as streaming WMF files. As of this writing, the free encoder runs only in Windows 98 or higher.

The WMP URL we've listed was accurate as this book went to press, but contents might have settled during shipment. (Microsoft constantly changes URLs at its site.)

Special indications

For some reason, WMF has apparently become the format of choice for the streaming distribution of "adult" content, or so our informants tell us. We just thought it was kind of interesting, that's all. You try writing a chapter about plug-ins, and see if your mind doesn't start wandering where it shouldn't. We blame Jennifer Lopez's dress.

Beatnik (http://www.beatnik.com/)

Musician Thomas Dolby's Beatnik, though less widespread than the biggest hitters, is an intriguing plug-in that comes bundled with most Netscape distributions. Beatnik enhances MIDI (Musical Instrument Digital Interface) playback, easily surpassing the quality of most PC add-on sound cards and the Mac's built-in MIDI voices. It also offers strangely wonderful features, such as the ability to mix jam sessions on sites authored according to Beatnik's specifications.

Such stuff is unlikely to be part of a site for your local church, synagogue, or small business but might well add luster to the site for a recording artist. Beatnik was used to enhance the PBS "Jazz" site (http://www.pbs.org/jazz/) that accompanied Ken Burns's historic jazz documentary series of 2001.

Beatnik works in Netscape (all platforms) and IE (Windows only). It unfortunately does not work in IE5/Mac because its JavaScript functionality relies on proprietary Netscape Application Programming Interfaces (APIs). Beatnik is a cool plug-in, and IE5/Mac is an extremely polished, standards-compliant web browser. It seems a pity that the two cannot work together, but this raises the whole trouble with plug-ins, which we cover later in this chapter (see "The Trouble with Plug-ins").

Shockwave/Flash (www.macromedia.com, www.macromedia.com/software/flash/)

Two plug-ins now bundled as one, Shockwave and Flash, are the biggest, most-accepted, and possibly the most dynamic plug-ins on the market. They are certainly the most controversial. Entire sites have been created in these formats. Entire sermons have been written denouncing them. For many, Flash is a religion; for many others, it is the first sign of the anti-Christ. Flash artist Peter Balogh sums up the controversy in his witty essay, "Sympathy for the Plug-in" at http://www.alistapart.com/stories/sympathy/.

Figure 12.11

The "virtual piano" in the Jazz Lounge at PBS.org, created in Macromedia Director, rendered unto the Web in streaming Shockwave format. Print cannot do this (http://www.pbs.org/jazz/).

Though they share a similar blow-you-away quality and though the manufacturer now serves them like two peas in a pod, Shockwave and Flash are quite different.

Shockwave

Shockwave is a sophisticated, proprietary format that can do anything a CD-ROM can do. Full-fledged gaming environments; animated, hot-linked city maps; endless labyrinths deep within simulated subterranean worlds: If you can dream it up, it can be rendered in Shockwave. Essentially, Shockwave files are like self-contained software programs that launch in the user's browser.

As might be obvious, the more complex and multileveled the Shockwave file, the larger it must be to do its job. Thus there is a trade-off between sophisticated presentation and amount of bandwidth required.

There is also the risk that Shockwave programs will exceed the user's computing capacity. Linux users, who take justifiable pride in cranking tremendous computing juice out of old, cheap PCs, frequently hit a wall when Shockwave comes to town. Even Mac and PC users sometimes find Shockwave too rich for their blood. None of this is the fault of the operating systems in question. We're back to the problem we discussed with Java. When it works, it's magnificent; when it doesn't, it ain't.

Shockwave files are created in Macromedia Director, a multimedia production and programming package requiring tremendous expertise. No web designer is expected to know how to program in Director, though some specialize in it.

"Hip" web agencies generally have a Shockwave master or two in their design departments—so do many "unhip" agencies. (We're not sure what "hip" and "unhip" actually mean in the context of web design and development, but some web agencies seem to care a lot about it. In this, they take their cue from ad agencies.)

Shockwave development is an art unto itself. It coincides with web design but is not the same as web design. Shockwave has nothing to do with the structured, semantic Web of meaning and information—but then neither does a GIF image file.

Shockwave has largely escaped the fire and brimstone preached against its younger cousin, Flash, because Shockwave files are fiendishly difficult to create; therefore, gigantic Shockwave "intros" are not epidemic throughout the Web. Hence the usability experts rarely scream about Shockwave. But, oh brother, do they roar about Flash.

Flash

Flash is Shockwave's lighter, less-bandwidth-intensive, easier-to-program (but somewhat less powerful) cousin. Flash delivers animated graphics and sound, and it is completely interactive. At this point in the history of the Web, it is easier to create rich interactive presentations in Flash than by trying to use the open standards of the Web (HTML/XHTML, CSS, JavaScript, and the DOM). It's more reliable, too, sadly enough.

Flash files stream and can be highly compressed because Flash is built on vector graphics. (As you know, vector graphics, like PostScript, are mathematical in nature rather than pixel-based.) Thus it is somewhat ironic that Flash has become known as a bloated format. This has to do with poor Flash authoring, not with Flash. Flash presentations, even incredibly sophisticated ones, can be very low in bandwidth—and generally ought to be.

Flash files are created in the Macromedia Flash authoring program. They also can be authored with Adobe's LiveMotion software, which premiered in early 2000.

Sixty second software review: LiveMotion is easier for beginners to learn, particularly if they are familiar with the Adobe interface found in Photoshop, Illlustrator, and so on. It does one or two things Flash can't do. Flash, with a more baffling interface and a steeper learning curve, is initially harder to learn. But its programming depth, through Action Script and standard JavaScript, far exceeds that of LiveMotion (at least as of this writing).

Cult take: Flash designers take as much pride in mastering the tool's absurdly poor interface as they do in exploring its programming depth and complexity. Just as web designers who code by hand take pains to chuckle mockingly at Dreamweaver and GoLive users—and hold FrontPage users utterly beneath contempt—so the hardcore Flash jockeys shake their heads in bewilderment at the very notion that anyone would even think of using LiveMotion.

Remember, this is not necessarily our opinion; it is mere observation of a cultural milieu. If it sounds like Flash is a cult, it is. If it sounds like hardcore web design is also a cult, it is. If it sounds like you should reconsider getting involved in web design, you've read too far and know too much to escape unscathed.

Our opinion: Flash and LiveMotion are both fine tools, each of which caters to a different niche in the market. (There goes our cult status.)

Whichever authoring tool you use, you can do all the design work in the program itself or create your vector graphics in Adobe Illustrator or Macromedia Freehand and then export them to Flash (or LiveMotion). You also might find yourself working with audio and video editing programs and 3D design programs. If you think we're going to cram this book with quick 'n easy tutorials on those sophisticated software programs, you are very high and should lie down or consult a physician.

Tips on authoring Flash

Buy the program. Read the manual. What do you want from us?

Look at great Flash sites. Look at poor Flash sites. Emulate the good; learn from the bad.

Good Flash sites are dynamic, attractive, navigable, intuitive, communicative, and respectful of the visitor's bandwidth and time—just like all good websites.

Bad Flash sites are unresponsive, static, hard to navigate and understand, communicate poorly (if at all), and waste the visitor's bandwidth and time—just like bad websites.

As with all such proclamations, there are always exceptions that succeed in spite of being cryptic, initially confusing, or bandwidth-intensive. If you are a genius with a deserved cult following, feel free to ignore the previous two paragraphs. If you're not, respect your audience.

Choose vector graphics over raster graphics to conserve bandwidth. When you must use raster graphics, use images that have been optimized to death, rather than lovely images that suck bandwidth. A static four-color GIF might not cut it on a traditional, static web page, but once that low-grade image is set in motion, viewers will respond to the motion without scrutinizing the quality of the image.

Juxt Interactive (http://www.juxtinteractive.com/) has built an entire practice by bringing brilliant design to Flash without the high bandwidth baggage. Its prototype, the SHORN project (http://www.shorn.com/), makes extensive use of four-color GIFs, and no one has ever noticed or complained.

What Flash is great for

Flash excels as an environment for the creation of rich works of art such as Monocrafts (see Figures 12.12, 12.13, and 12.14), Volume One (www.volumeone.com/), Once Upon A Forest (www.once-upon-a-forest.com), and many others you'll meet in Chapter 13.

Figure 12.12

Those still perplexed by the popularity of Macromedia Flash need look no further than Monocrafts, Yugo Nakamura's multitiered masterpiece.

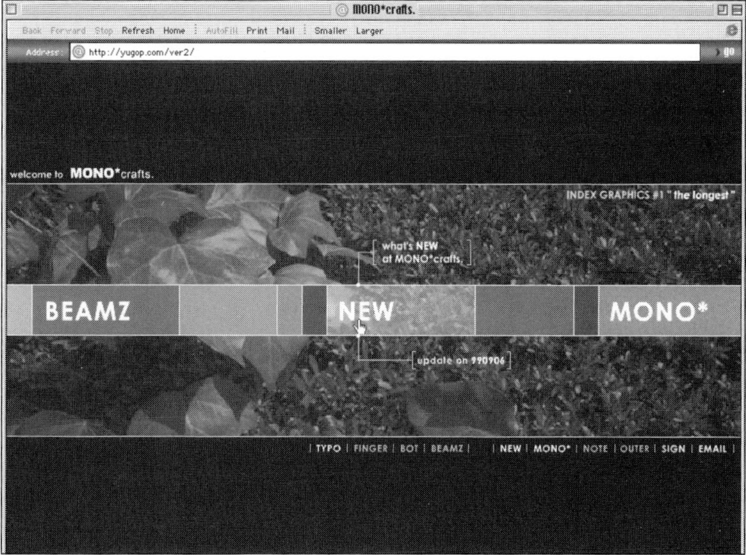

Figure 12.13

Nakamura studied civil engineering, architecture, and landscape design before focusing his crisply uncanny intelligence on issues of web art and interface. These screenshots are from a previous version of the site, which still stands as a remarkable achievement by anyone's measure but Jakob Nielsen's.

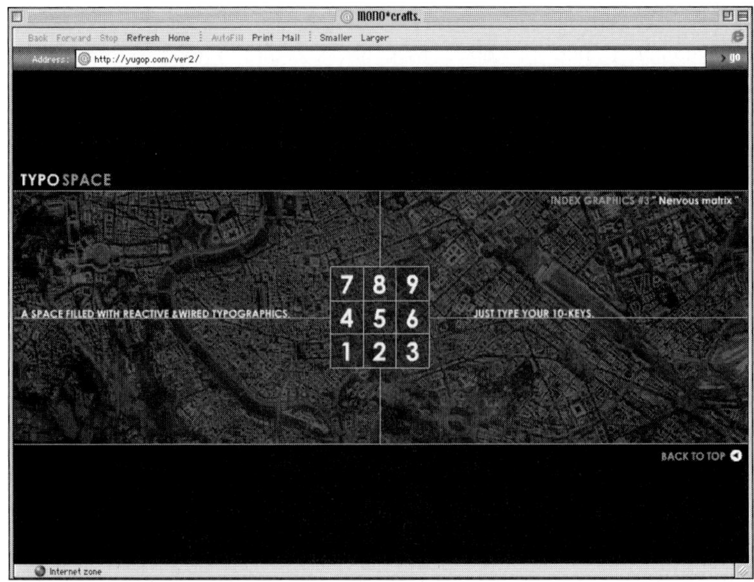

Figure 12.14

Reducing Monocrafts to a series of printed screenshots is like trying to explain a symphony by playing a single note (http://www.yugop.com/ver2/).

What Flash is not so great for

Flash is not so great for structured data, semantic markup, accessibility, searchability, indexability, and bookmarking. In short, nearly everything we associate with the Web.

Why Flash gets a bad rap

Refer to the previous answer.

Why else Flash gets a bad rap

Refer to the previous answer.

Still more reasons why Flash gets a bad rap

There are several things, really. For one, too many copycat designers use Flash in unimaginative, "me-too" ways. Thus, every other corporate site seems to launch with a giant spinning logo rendered in Flash.

These miserable things are called "intros" (as in introduction) to the site. They are the spiritual descendants of David Siegel's (www.dsiegel.com/) "entrance tunnels," meaning that while some of them can be beautiful establishers of mood, tone, and identity, too many feel simply gratuitous.

Here is a true horror story. The author of this book was supposed to speak at a web conference. He visited the conference site in hopes that it would tell him where the event was being held. He knew it was in a hotel, but which hotel, and where? Instead of providing that information, the conference site linked to the third-party site of the hotel itself (strike one). Not the most usable idea, but all right.

The hapless author clicked the hotel site link and discovered that he was trapped inside the conference site's frameset, an HTML error so basic he'd forgotten such things could even happen. Strike two.

Inside that tiny frameset, the hotel site presented, not its name or address, but a Flash intro (strike three), nor was this an optimized, bandwidth-friendly intro built largely with vector graphics. No, what it actually was, was something more akin to a QuickTime movie: a motion picture showing the beauty of the hotel. Strike four. In spite of his fast connection, the author had to wait several times while the overweight Flash file choked on its own girth before streaming resumed. Strike five. There was no way to skip this intro; it simply had to be endured. Strike six.

When the low-resolution but high-bandwidth graphic nightmare finally ended and the expiring Flash file triggered a standard HTML page, that page did not list the hotel's address. Strike seven. The author had to navigate three layers deep into the site before he could find that simple, essential bit of information. In baseball you get three strikes. On the Web, you might not even get one. We needed to locate that hotel's address because we had no choice but to show up there. Travelers planning a trip have many hotels to choose from. Word up.

And that's another reason that Flash gets a bad rap—because people who don't know what they're doing often use it poorly. There are bad painters, but no one criticizes paint. On the other hand, bad paintings aren't shoved in your face when you're trying to find information online.

A "Flash usability" site at www.flazoom.com can help you avoid designing useless or less-than-usable Flash movies; beyond that, the issues we discuss throughout this book are equally applicable to the world of Flash. Base your work on the needs of your audience; create intuitive structures that invite your specific audience to enter, explore, and linger; craft a memorable identity without wasting bandwidth...you know the drill by now.

Clients might salivate over the prospect of giant animated logos, but designers and web users are tired of this unimaginative use of Flash, and the plug-in is best reserved for truly creative and artistic purposes. You'll find sites exemplifying that kind of creativity in Chapter 13.

Another reason Flash gets a bad rap

Failure to provide alternatives, thus leaving some users in the dust, is a widespread problem. Macromedia has begun an initiative to make Flash sites more accessible, and this is commendable. But streaming audio and visual media, accessed by mouse movements, will always remain inaccessible for some (refer to the preceding discussion of VRML).

Unless Flash is able to overcome tremendous barriers to accessibility (http://www.alistapart.com/stories/unclear/) inherent in its very nature, it is vital to provide some kind of basic HTML alternative for those who might be unable to see or hear or move their limbs.

Embedding Flash files in web pages

Flash generates all the HTML necessary to embed a Flash movie in a web page. Isn't that nice? You might, of course, want to go in and further massage the markup.

Are we finished with Flash?

We will never be finished with Flash, but we've pretty much finished discussing it in this chapter.

Who Makes the Salad? Web Designers and Plug-ins

As a web designer, you will rarely be asked to develop content for plug-ins (with the possible exception of Flash). QuickTime and Real video files, for example, are usually created by web producers or design technicians—not by web designers. Sometimes the people who actually shoot and edit the film will generate digitized versions as part of the post-production process.

If you do find yourself pressed into service in these areas, the work is not hard. In agencies, you'll typically find a workstation with a video machine at one end and a Mac or PC at the other. Software like Adobe Premiere or Apple iMovie is used to digitize the film. Third-party compression software such as Terran Cleaner 5 (http://www.terran.com/) optimizes video for streaming web delivery. None of this is difficult, but rarely will a web designer be asked to do it. Your time is too valuable elsewhere.

Many web designers include Flash design in their skills repertoire; many others do not. Developing *exceptional* Flash content is a specialization all its own. Most web agencies keep a few designers on staff who excel at Flash development, allowing the bulk of the design crew to focus on interface and other design issues.

So if web designers generally do not create plug-in content, what do web designers have to do with plug-ins? They make them work on web pages—that's what.

Making It Work: Providing Options

Web designers use HTML to embed a plug-in file (or *object*) on a web page. Following is markup from an IPIX panorama page at the Travel Channel (http://travel.discovery.com/tools/gallerypages/ipix/noam/wmiss/zabptcaj.html):

```
<p>
<!-- java applets -->
<applet name="IpixViewer" code="IpixViewer.class" archive="IpixViewer.jar" height="210"
width="280">
<param name="URL" value="zabptcaj.ipx">
<param name="Spin" value="on">
</applet>

<!-- For MSIE 2 -->
<noembed>
<b>To view IPIX images you need to Upgrade your Browser. We recommend Version 3
or above of either Netscape or MSIE.</b><br>
</noembed>
<!-- end java applets -->
</p>
```

Notice the use of <!-- comment tags --> to help the web designer keep track of what she is doing and why.

Notice that room has been made for the space used by the plug-in image file (280 x 210 pixels). If the layout for this web page had been initially created in Photoshop, the web designer would have left a 280 x 210 space in the layout itself and then replaced it with HTML during the web-building phase. In all probability, this page was never individually designed in Photoshop but is simply one of many that share the same template.

Notice that a Java applet has been used to embed the file, as described in this chapter's section on Java. Visitors lacking the iPIX plug-in will be treated to a Java simulation, rather than simply encounter an error message about missing plug-ins.

But what happens to the visitor whose browser does not support either plug-ins or Java? That is taken care of by the <noembed> tags. Let's look just at that section of the markup:

```
<!--For MSIE 2 -->
<noembed>
To view IPIX images you need to Upgrade your Browser. We recommend Version 3 or
above of either Netscape or MSIE.<br>
</noembed>
<!-- end java applets -->
        </p>
```

The <noembed> tag basically says, "Listen up, old, dumb browser. What follows is for you." In such a browser, the text beginning To view IPIXimages... will be revealed. In other browsers (those that support Java or contain the iPIX plug-in), the text message will be hidden.

The designers also could have put this text and markup inside the <applet> element, like so:

```
<applet name="IpixViewer" code="IpixViewer.class" archive="IpixViewer.jar" height="210"
width="280">
<param name="URL" value="zabptcaj.ipx">
<param name="Spin" value="on">
<p>If you can read this, your browser does not support Java. Have a nice day.</p>
</applet>
```

As to whether anyone ever upgraded their browser in direct response to a website's message, well, that is something else again.

The "Automagic Redirect"

Whether bundled with the browser or not, all plug-ins are readily available online. In some cases, when a web user hits a page that requires a plug-in not found on her system, Java is substituted for the missing plug-in (as in the preceding example).

In most cases, though, Java is not pressed into service. After all, plug-in manufacturers want their plug-ins to be downloaded, not synthesized by a substitute technology. Typically, when a web user lacks a plug-in, she is "automagically" directed to the appropriate plug-in page so she can download it. In most cases, the magic is merely a matter of adding a <pluginspage> attribute to the HTML <OBJECT> or <EMBED> tag:

```
<embed src="http://build.kubrick.org/sounds/the.shinning/midnight.the.stars.and.you.mp3"
autostart="true" volume="100" width="2" height="2" controls="hidden"
pluginspage="http://www.quicktime.apple.com">
```

In this snippet lifted from our unfinished experiment at www.kubrick.org, the <pluginspage> attribute to the <EMBED> tag serves two functions:

1. The material in question is an MP3 audio file (midnight.the.stars.and.you.mp3), capable of being played by a number of additional plug-ins and players, including RealPlayer, Flash, and a variety of free and commercial applications. Specifying QuickTime in the <pluginspage> attribute tells the browser which plug-in to select: namely, Apple's QuickTime plug-in. More about why that's important a little later in this section.
2. It also provides a web address where the latest version of the QuickTime plug-in can be downloaded. If the visitor did not have QuickTime installed on her system, the browser would display a dialog box indicating that the plug-in was required and asking if she wished to download it. Clicking Yes or Okay would load the appropriate Apple plug-in page. The way the <EMBED> tag works, the browser does most of the work of supporting the web user (and the web designer).

Embed 'n Breakfast

```
<embed
src="http://build.kubrick.org/sounds/the.shinning/midnight.the.stars.and.you.mp3"
autostart="true" volume="100" width="2" height="2" controls="hidden"
pluginspage="http://www.quicktime.apple.com">
```

Heck, while we've got this markup in front of us, let's just go ahead and explain what the rest of it means:

- <EMBED>. This tells the (2.0 or higher) browser to anticipate content that must be handled by a plug-in.
- <AUTOSTART>. This tells the browser to begin playing the file instantly. (The default value is on.)
- <VOLUME>. This sets the loudness. (The default value is 100, or full volume.)
- <CONTROLS>. This specifies the presence or absence of on-screen controllers, similar to those on a video or audio cassette console. If controls are visible, they can be seen and used by the visitor. If hidden, they do not appear, and consequently they take up no space on the screen. (The default value is visible.) When would you use hidden? You'd use it, as we have here, when you simply want the file to play without prompting the visitor to do anything. Naturally, in such a case, you'll turn Autostart on. Otherwise, you're forcing the user to download a file they have no means of playing.
- <WIDTH>, <HEIGHT>. These attributes specify the size of an in-page controller, if any. Interesting paradox: If controls are hidden, why specify sizes at all? It's because Netscape 2, 3, and 4 might crash if some size attribute were not included. It also could crash if the size were smaller than 2. As to the number itself, "2" means "2 pixels." Though width and height are specified, they do not appear because the "hidden" value of the <CONTROLS> attribute makes them invisible. If you're working with hidden player controls, the default width and height attributes should be 2 to avoid crashing old versions of Netscape Navigator.

Before we close this fascinating portion of our narrative, we must add one more reason to specify the player via the <pluginspage> attribute: If you don't, the browser will choose one for you, often with hideous results. Read on.

The iron-plated sound console from Hell

Right up through its 4.0 browser, Netscape used to respond to WAV, AIFF, AU, and other traditional sound file formats by sprouting an ugly little console. But the console did not simply leap up and start playing. Oh, no. Nor was the console actually part of Netscape's browser, even though it was the default player. For reasons we can only guess at, Netscape chose Java as the foundation for the console.

When you encountered a site that contained a sound, the page would stop loading, and the browser would seem to freeze. In the status bar, the dreaded words "Starting Java..." would appear. After a Vietnam-like eternity, the ugly console would at last pop up and blast the stupid sound.

Now, suppose you did not feel like waiting for this mockery of a sham to run its course. Suppose you attempted to close the browser window or navigate to a previously visited site via the Back button. What would happen then? The browser would crash, of course.

If most people did not detest embedded sound files to begin with, this tragicomic exercise in non-user-centric design certainly encouraged them to think of embedded sounds as one of Satan's more diabolical efforts.

The Trouble with Plug-ins

While providing the visitor with linkage to the appropriate plug-ins page is certainly a friendlier gesture than simply abandoning her to chance, most professionals try to go one step further. They try to hide all the technological complexity from their users. Even something as simple as navigating to a plug-ins page can confuse and frustrate some users.

To work around this, most developers step in at this point and write a plug-in detection script. The theory is simple: If the user has the plug-in, the embedded content plays. If the user lacks the plug-in, some alternative is provided (perhaps something as simple as text). The user is never made to feel inadequate, never made aware that she might be missing something.

It's a beautiful plan, but as we mentioned in the JavaScript chapter, it has often broken down because plug-in detection is not universally supported.

Netscape, having created JavaScript, has always used it in the browser to detect the presence or absence of plug-ins. Let's take the Flash plug-in for argument's sake. If the plug-in is not detected, the visitor might be taken to a page that explains that the site uses Flash and offers her the opportunity to download the plug-in from Macromedia.com, as previously described in "The 'Automagic Redirect.'"

Because JavaScript was not originally a standard technology, Microsoft's Internet Explorer had to rely on another technique. Prior to IE5, Microsoft used IE-only ActiveX technology to handle plug-in detection.

Before writing plug-in detection scripts, developers had to write browser detection scripts. If the browser was Netscape's, the JavaScript plug-in detection script ran. If the browser was IE, ActiveX plug-in detection was triggered (and if the plug-in was missing, ActiveX would supply it).

None of this worked on the Macintosh version of Explorer, whose users generally ended up in a hellish loop of nonfunctioning technology and self-contradictory error messages. This cruel stupidity should not be blamed on the Macintosh Operating System, nor on developers who toiled long and hard to work around browser deficiencies.

IE now supports JavaScript on both the Windows and Macintosh platforms. As users upgrade to new versions of these browsers, these incompatibility problems should become a distant memory.

Yet software developers still sometimes confuse Netscape's proprietary JavaScript APIs with standard JavaScript. That's why two plug-ins mentioned earlier in this chapter (Adobe's SVG plug-in and Thomas Dolby's Beatnik plug-in) don't work properly with IE5/Mac.

And web designers who don't keep track of the ever-changing browser compatibility scene still make silly mistakes, particularly where IE5/Mac is concerned. For instance, even though IE5/Mac handles plug-in detection flawlessly, many Flash sites, when they detect the presence of IE on a Mac, refuse to let the user proceed until she has switched to Netscape's browser. This makes no sense, but it happens all the time.

We fear we are beginning to lose some of you in the back row. Snap out of it. We're almost done, honest.

If Plug-ins Run Free

Earlier we promised to answer a simple question: Why don't companies that make plug-ins charge web users to download them? After all, Extensis makes a bundle from its fine Quark and Photoshop plug-ins. Are the makers of the most popular plug-ins (Macromedia, Apple, Real, and Microsoft) simply beautiful altruists who want to teach the world to sing and don't desire a penny for their efforts?

That was, of course, a rhetorical question.

Companies distribute their plug-ins at no cost because the value of these products is commensurate with their distribution. Put simply, a plug-in that is on 100 million desktops is vastly more valuable than one that is on a million. How do you encourage a person to try something? Let them have it for free.

Indeed, as we'll see in a moment, companies not only gave stuff away free, they paid other companies to promote their free stuff. Never have so many spent so much to earn so little. (Excluding the browser wars themselves, of course. Those cost even more and made even less.)

Okay, so as a result of giving all this good stuff away for free, Macromedia, Apple, Real, and Microsoft have achieved what they sought: nearly everybody uses their plug-ins. So how do these companies recoup their investment and hopefully even squeeze out a profit?

They do it by creating and selling authoring tools. Web designers buy Macromedia Flash. Web producers buy Real Producer and professional QuickTime authoring suites.

Though Apple sells professional QuickTime suites, it also gives away some extremely capable video authoring tools with every new Mac. What is the sense in that? The sense in that is that these "free" products come with a Macintosh. If you want the free product, you buy the Macintosh computer. Similarly, Microsoft gives away WMF authoring tools to encourage you to buy Windows products. Some web businesses might have trouble coming up with revenue models, but software and computer companies generally don't.

While striving to reach ubiquity, plug-in makers have frequently partnered with content producers. For instance, at different times, downloadable trailers at a well-known movie company's empire of websites have been available exclusively in Apple's QuickTime format, and at others, exclusively in Windows Media Player format. The plug-in maker compensated the movie studio for favoring its product over competitive plug-ins.

Today the cash flows in the opposite direction. A movie studio might pay the purveyor of a popular plug-in to feature its studio instead of a competitive film conglomerate on the plug-in vendor's "Hot Downloads" page. Ubiquity makes for destinations, and destinations, if popular enough, can generate income. To up the income, the plug-in page sprouts ad banners—from free plug-ins to cold cash in twelve easy lessons.

As we feared, none of that was as interesting as Jennifer Lopez's dress.

Parting Sermon

In Chapter 2, we discussed the way most popular plug-ins stream their presentations to compensate for slow user dialup modem speeds. We also reminded you just how slow those dialup speeds really are. Please reread Chapter 2 before authoring high-bandwidth multimedia content or blithely adding it to a site for which it might be inappropriate.

We web designers, most of us, anyway, live in a spoiled world of hyper-fast Internet access, powerful desktop processors, and wide-screen monitors. Most of the world does not enjoy such niceties, or anything half so nice.

In fact, as the Web grows in popularity, the median average access speed declines drastically because there are more and more home users for every luxuriously appointed web professional. Though the field is expanding tenfold, the web-using population is growing at many times that pace. Even if the profession were to stop growing, the number of web users would continue to rise.

The day of universal high-speed access and fat bandwidth is not at hand. It's not even close.

While the prophets of high bandwidth high-five each other, millions in China and Africa and Alabama begin using the Web via a 14.4 modem that is shared by two or three families or 50 kids in a schoolroom. In libraries in America and around the world, those who cannot afford Internet access line up for hours to use public systems. Some of those systems are fast. Some are not. Few can afford to be tied up for hours just so some logo can spin.

Even those on the fortunate side of the digital divide rarely enjoy the fastest speeds or the most reliable connections. When the *Daily Show's* Jon Stewart jokes about the AOL busy signal, the entire audience laughs. They've been there. Most of them still are there. They are not only Jon Stewart's audience, they are every web designer's audience. And *they're* the ones in the good seats.

So treat rich media like you'd treat Jim Beam: responsibly.

We end this chapter on a somber note, but the book on a happy one. Kindly proceed to Chapter 13.

chapter 13

Never Can Say Goodbye

YOUR DIALOG WITH THE WEB has now begun. And though this book, like young love, must end, our conversation will continue. You will find us, and we will find you on the pages of the World Wide Web.

No book (indeed, no five-year program, if one existed) could teach you everything you need to know to design smart, attractive, user-focused websites. You will learn as you work—from teammates, partners, and even your clients.

You also will learn a great deal from the people who visit your sites. You'll be surprised at how many write—and not merely to complain when your single-spaced, 10px type sends them scurrying to the optometrist.

But some of the best places to learn are on the Web itself, hence this chapter. In it we share our favorite online resources and explain the importance of continuing your education as the Web and your career experience growth and change.

SEPARATION ANXIETY

Throughout this book, we've shown methods used to design today's Web and shared theories about how people interact with the medium. You need to know these things to begin working now.

But as we've also pointed out, the Web is changing; indeed, like the sea, or like some other Zen metaphor we can't quite put together here, the Web's very nature is one of constant change. Currently the Web is changing in an intriguing way—one that will move it closer to its founders' original vision of an open medium, accessible by all people and available to all sorts of Internet-enabled devices.

What will empower that happy change? It will come with the separation of style from content. What does that mean? It means you'll stop welding your texts and functions and images together through overextended HTML. Instead, you'll keep your visual design in one place (a Cascading Style Sheet) and your content in another (a series of HTML or XHTML documents; a database of XML-formatted text). The twain will meet on the web page, but their behind-the-scenes separation will considerably enhance your working conditions and your audience's experience.

Instead of painstakingly slicing apart images in Photoshop as described in this book or spending hours hand-tweaking hundreds of individual HTML documents, you'll have time to spend on more interesting pursuits such as design itself—which is, after all, what you do.

This change in the nature of web design as a practice will come when all web users employ browsers that fully support the standards that empower us to separate style from content: HTML/XHTML, CSS, XML, JavaScript/ ECMAScript, and the DOM.

Not only do browsers have to change (and they are changing), web designers must also change—a proposition that requires the willingness to continue learning and to risk discarding methods we've spent years perfecting.

In February 2001, *A List Apart* reinvented itself with a standards-compliant design that separates style from content (http://www.alistapart.com/stories/99/). As you might expect, the site (www.alistapart.com) is a good resource for information on that subject.

The reinvention of ALA coincided with The Web Standards Project's Browser Upgrade campaign (http://www.webstandards.org/upgrade/), which urges web designers to learn about and use the W3C recommendations we've discussed in this book, even if the resulting sites look less than delicious in older, nonstandards-compliant browsers. The Browser Upgrade campaign also asks web designers and content creators to seek ways to encourage user upgrades so that the Web can improve without leaving anyone behind.

The Browser Upgrade campaign and the ALA redesign were logical next steps in the evolution of the Web. We launched them while writing this book, which brings up the problem with books. Namely, while books have the virtue of permanence, they cannot update themselves as websites can. We encourage you to continue learning by visiting educational and inspiring websites and reading and participating in web design mailing lists and forums.

The remainder of this chapter will provide you with plenty to choose from. Use these resources to amplify parts of this book and to learn more about the emerging, standards-based Web. At the end of the annotated list below, we'll return to offer a final thought about the Web and you.

From Tag Soup to Talk Soup: Mailing Lists and Online Forums

Learning by trial and error is part of any process and is certainly part of web design. Learning from other members of your team is a deeply bonding experience, but learning (and sharing your own knowledge) on a mailing list is a pleasure no web designer should miss.

There are many, many mailing lists and online communities for web designers and developers. Some focus on specific technologies; others are vast, crowded, and general. Some function as job referral services while others mainly promote the people who created the list. Some are chaotic, others restrictive. With a little effort, you will find the ones that make you feel most comfortable.

Following, in alphabetical order, are some of our favorites.

A List Apart

http://www.alistapart.com/

Each week *A List Apart* publishes useful tutorials ("Meet the DOM," "Fear of Style Sheets"), challenging opinion pieces ("The Curse of Information Design," "Sympathy for the Plug-in"), or both. And each week, after reading these articles, ALA readers respond on the site's discussion forum. The site is noncommercial, and you need not reveal your identity or other personal information to participate in the discussion forums.

Astounding Websites

http://www.astoundingweb.org/

Launched by Glenn Davis and maintained by Dave Bastian, this unique discussion community was created to honor the best writing, design, and programming on the Web. Visit this small, friendly forum to discover inspiring commercial and noncommercial sites or participate by reviewing sites you admire. You can also submit your own sites for review in the Site Promotion section.

The Babble List

http://www.babblelist.com/

Maintained by Christopher Schmitt (and resurrected by him in 2001 after a brief hiatus), The Babble List is a well-run general web design mailing list, covering issues of graphic design, information architecture, writing, usability, project management, and related skills. Though the average Babble Lister is a professional with at least two years' experience, the list is beginner-friendly. If you find yourself stuck on a JavaScript or CSS problem or wondering why your site looks great in one browser but poor in another, you can post your message to The Babble List and anticipate useful feedback.

Dreamless

http://www.dreamless.org/

Dreamless is a deep and open community primarily populated by young graphic designers and Flash artists. Though the site's gray-on-gray, Arial-only design gives it a somber appearance, it's anything but dull. Dreamless discussions range from the seriously spiritual to the deliberately silly. The site has a fanatical following and encourages its members to get together at parties in various cities. If you have trouble finding the site's front door, use View Source.

Evolt

http://www.evolt.org/

Evolt, a multi-faceted mailing list, online message board, and member-created publication, provides useful dialog spaces for technically minded web designers and developers worldwide. Accessibility and web standards are hot topics here, and you can learn simply by reading other members' posts. Like all communities mentioned here, Evolt is self-policing; and like all successful communities, it manages the task unobtrusively.

Metafilter

http://www.metafilter.com/

Matt Haughey's noncommercial community site is not about web design or web programming, but many web content creators will be found in its forums. Billing itself as a "community weblog," the occasionally raucous discussion site can help you get a handle on aspects of the Web's emerging culture. This in turn will remind you that the Web is not about HTML tags or graphic design; like Soylent Green, the Web is people.

Redcricket

http://www.redcricket.com/

Dan Beauchamp's personal site includes a web design forum ("Community") that's small, lively, and friendly. HTML questions? JavaScript woes? Redcricket could be the ticket. By maintaining a fairly low profile, Redcricket's forum generally avoids the flame wars and ego trips that sometimes plague other lists and communities. Spend time at the site before you post. Redcricket is a tight community of friends; barging in and loudly demanding attention won't go over well.

Webdesign-l

http://webdesign-l.com/

Stewarded by Steven Champeon, Webdesign-l is a long-running, smartly focused design and development list. Some of the brightest people in the industry participate in this highly respected list. Champeon, a systems guru who technical-edited *Taking Your Talent to the Web* and who co-founded The Web Standards Project, runs a tight ship. As list administrator, he keeps misinformation to a minimum and stops bad behavior before it starts. Beginner questions might be well-received if submitted with restraint. ("Hellllllp! My site is hosed!!!!!!" will probably not generate the kind of feedback you want.) Read the list rules and get used to the general discussion tone before posting to the list.

When All Else Fails

http://www.r35.com/edu/

Consider a class. R35edu offers a curriculum of over 60 courses, covering nearly every facet of web strategy, design, development, commerce, and marketing—all via "a unique distance learning environment that puts you in direct contact with creative innovators and designers from all over the world."

Eye and Brain Candy: Educational and Inspiring Sites

Attempting to figure out web design exclusively from a book is like trying to learn about music without listening to any. Fortunately, the Web is rich in inspiring and educational sites. Following are a few of our favorites, including a couple of our own (cough).

Design, Programming, Content

A List Apart (http://www.alistapart.com/), "for people who make websites. From pixels to prose, coding to content." See previous section for more on this.

Apple Internet Developer (http://developer.apple.com/internet/), launched in 2001, started small, but what it has is choice: brief and pungent tutorials on HTML, online typography, CSS, JavaScript, and the DOM.

Builder (http://www.builder.com/), "solutions for site builders," provides articles and tutorials on graphic design, multimedia, back-end development, and even software ("Fireworks vs. ImageReady"). There is also a discussion board (Builder Buzz), and the site hosts a dandy annual web design conference in New Orleans.

Each month, Digital Web (http://www.digital-web.com/), "the web designer's online magazine of choice," brings you fresh interviews, tutorials, columns, and even classifieds (to help you get your next job). Edited and published by Nick Finck, who also contributes to *A List Apart*.

Web Page Design for Designers (http://wpdfd.com/), published monthly by Joe Gillespie, is "aimed at people...already involved with design and typography for conventional print, [who] want to explore the possibilities of this new electronic medium." In other words, it speaks to the audience of this very book! (We would have titled this book "Web Design for Designers" if Joe hadn't beaten us to the punch, darn him.) The site includes typefaces optimized for the Web, columns on web design and typography, and a solid listing of third-party resources.

The Web Standards Project (http://www.webstandards.org/), co-founded by Glenn Davis, George Olsen, and your humble author, maintains a Resources section for your educational pleasure. Confused about CSS, ECMAScript, and the rest of the alphabet soup? You'll find links to relevant articles here.

Web Techniques (http://www.webtechniques.com/) is a vast, professional publication with an accompanying real-world magazine you can read in the bathtub or carry in your attache case. It covers web technology and business and can help you understand how wireless technology interfaces with web design.

Web Review (http://www.webreview.com/) publishes some of the smartest tutorials we've ever seen on XHTML, JavaScript, and other web technologies and has always been a great friend to web standards. Highly recommended, particularly for those who wish to understand web technologies instead of simply pushing buttons in WYSIWYG editors.

Think of Webmonkey (http://www.webmonkey.com/), originally directed by Jeff "Art & Science of Web Design" Veen, as Builder.com with more attitude. A deep resource dating back to the earliest days of the designed Web, the site sports swell tutorials on HTML, JavaScript, and other technologies, along with columns and articles on streaming media, emerging standards, and the web business. Not updated as often as it used to be, but still a fine smoke.

Webreference (http://www.webreference.com/), a subsidiary of Internet.com (yes, there really *is* an Internet.com), is tailored more to developers than designers but will repay your exploration. Edited by Andy King, the vast site covers everything you could ever want to know on the web technology front. Interviews and discussion forums enhance the site's value.

Webtype (http://www.webtype.org/), dedicated to better online typography, keeps you posted on this vital and sadly under-reported topic. (Sometimes web designers seem more interested in scripting and gimmicks than they are in ensuring that type is legible—let alone attractive and pleasurable to read.) Webtype gives you the lowdown on everything from readability studies and CSS nuances to typographic explorations and downloadable typefaces. Don't miss the survey of fonts installed on PC and Mac users' computers. Founded by the mysterious "Gen," with kibitzing from Dave Bastian, Joe Clark, Julia Hayden, Webmistress Jo, and your humble author.

The World Wide Web Consortium (http://w3.org/), the mother of us all, is the final authority on web standards. Use it to keep track of existing and emerging technologies and to verify the way these technologies *should* work, before running off half-cocked, screaming about aliens jamming the radio transmitter embedded in your skull as part of an evil CIA experiment. Note that W3C articles, while definitive, are among the least easy to read and understand of any we've seen—and that includes VCR manuals written in Japan. You'll do better if you check W3C to see what you should learn about; then read the friendly tutorials at Webmonkey, Builder, or *A List Apart*.

The Big Kahunas

Let us now praise famous art directors:

Adobe (http://www.adobe.com/) not only makes great software for print and web designers, they also run a fine, vast site full of tutorials, columns, and articles on web, print, and motion design. Disclaimer: Your humble author writes a column for this publication.

AIGA (http://www.aiga.org/), the American institute of Graphic Arts, has a long and noble history as a membership organization for designers. But you know that. The site helps you track seminars and conferences and offers a national job bank and member discussion board along with thought-provoking articles ("What is Graphic Design?").

Communication Arts (http://www.commarts.com/) is among the world's most-respected voices for design. Its interactive section includes design technology columns and a Website of the Week. And of course the Communication Arts annuals honor some of the best design and advertising communications in the world.

PDN-Pix (http://www.pdn-pix.com/pix/), the digital arm of Photo District News, provides web design features ("Waiting to Load"), Q&A ("Ask Pix"), reviews of noteworthy sites ("Pix's e-Projects"), and a column by your humble author ("Second Site"). The print magazine will repay your interest; much of this material gets republished on the site along with some web-only content ("Grand Masters of Flash").

Beauty and Inspiration

When grinding out menu bar buttons saps your inspiration, trust well-designed, meaningful sites to restore it. Begin your voyage with sites that deliver compelling, original content (and not in plain brown wrappers):

{fray} (http://www.fray.com/), the ultimate personal storytelling site, was conceived, produced, and art-directed by designer/author Derek Powazek. In addition to showcasing what an imaginative web designer can do with words and pictures, the site functions as an on and offline community. Highly recommended. (Derek Powazek is also the author *of Design For Community,* published by New Riders.)

Glassdog (http://www.glassdog.com/), Lance Arthur's personal magnum opus, is both sarcastic and smooth. As if the site's clever writing and smart scripting were not intimidating enough, Arthur manages to combine clean, spare, easy-to-navigate design with the technical dexterity of a dazzling showoff.

Harrumph! (http://www.harrumph.com/), Heather Champ's charming and witty online diary, sports one of the cleanest web layouts we know. Perhaps this is because Heather has been designing websites since 1995, or perhaps it's because she's got taste. All we know is, every site that uses words should be this easy to read and engaging to look at. Few are.

Media.org (http://www.media.org/), "a collective of artists/architects... fueled by a passion for the Internet medium," was cofounded by Carl Malamud and Webchick in 2000 to debunk web inanities, promote web intelligence, and rescue digital works laid waste by careless businesses. Among the sites they rescued:

Mappa Mundi (http://www.mappa.mundi.net/) a smart, monthly web-only magazine and another Malamud/Webchick production, is perhaps the most intellectual of the noncommercial online 'zines.

Spark Online (http://www.spark-online.com/) is an extremely ambitious monthly online magazine covering media, trends, and society. Like all the others mentioned here, it is essentially a nonprofit labor of love.

The preceding sites show what can be done when original minds combine fresh content with fine style.

Those directly following show what can be accomplished when innovation and skillful graphic design are combined. Indeed, most of the following sites exist solely for that purpose, though a few are also commercial in nature.

Many of the sites listed require Flash and QuickTime, and it helps to have a recent browser and a fast connection.

Amon Tobin Supermodified (http://www.amontobin.com/), previously mentioned in these pages, is an extraordinary music site created in Flash. A cold, high-tech look, with a warmly interactive embrace, the site will reward your patience.

Archinect (http://www.archinect.com/), an ever-changing visual exploration, should be seen and not described.

Assembler (http://www.assembler.org/), Brent Gustaffson's masterpiece of cross-browser DHTML programming has a lovely and understated design sensibility.

Born Magazine (http://www.bornmagazine.com/) is a long-running, ambitious, collaborative work that attempts to continually reinvent the conjunction between word and image. The noncommercial site's tagline is "Design. Literature. Together."

Egomedia (http://www.egomedia.com/) is a design company portfolio with the sensibility of a rock video. Requires Flash.

Lushly designed eneri.net (http://www.eneri.net/) makes no bones about narrowing its audience: "This site targets luxurious people with a fast computer, fast Internet connection, Netscape or IE 4.0 or above, and Shockwave 7 plug-in." For those who meet the requirements, Irene Chan's labor of love offers a beautiful, film-like experience.

Entropy 8 Zuper (http://entropy8zuper.org/) is the site of Auriea Harvey, one of the first web designers to laugh at conventions and bust boundaries. Requires "fast computer, DHTML browser, Flash 5 or better" and "a physical need for wonder and poetry."

Futurefarmers (http://www.futurefarmers.com/), Amy Franceschini's web and multimedia design company, gives the lie to the notion that corporate work must be staid and conservative. Amy is one of the original exponents of fine design on the Web; her early web work is housed permanently at the San Francisco Museum of Modern Art.

Gmunk (http://www.gmunk.com/), a high-density personal site, pushes the envelope every which way. Outrageously high bandwidth, QuickTime movies, layered Photoshop collages rendered in Flash: everything usability experts rail against is practiced here, by a master who can get away with it. Tune in after losing an argument with your information designer or your client.

Interiors (http://www.webproductions.com/photo/) is a dynamic slideshow of digital self-portraits by artist Steve Giovinco. To call the work "disturbing" would be an understatement. It's also quite powerful.

Monocrafts (http://www.yugop.com/) combines powerful visual content with unbelievably innovative interface ideas—extremely inspiring.

One9ine (http://www.one9ine.com/), a web design agency created by designers, not marketers, is gorgeously rich yet entirely functional and easy to navigate. Think the two can't coexist? Look and see.

Once Upon A Forest (http://www.once-upon-a-forest.com/) is an abstract, deliberately cryptic work of genius by Joshua Davis, who also brings us Praystation and Dreamless.

S.M. Moalie's Photomontage (http://www.photomontage.com/) makes us cry. 'Nuff said.

Marc Klein's Pixel Industries (http://www.pixel-industries.com/), well known and widely imitated, is a textbook example of the graphic-design-lead approach to web development. See also Marc's Creative Republic (http://www.creative-republic.com/).

Pixelflo (http://pixelflo.com/), funky and witty, is also a masterpiece of JavaScript programming.

Praystation (http://www.praystation.com/), Joshua Davis's site, is dedicated to exploring and enlarging the boundaries of Flash and interface design. If you are learning Flash and beginning to think you know what it can and can't do, check Praystation. Davis gives away his source code so others can use it in their design projects.

Presstube (http://www.presstube.com/), James Patterson's personal illustration portfolio, reveals mastery of Flash as well as considerable drawing skill.

Projectbox (http://www.projectbox.com/) is an unusually elaborate, strikingly designed illustration and design portfolio site made in Thailand by 22-year-old Krisakorn Tantitemit. The playful and well-crafted interface makes great use of frames and scripting, and the color combinations are uniquely dramatic and pleasing.

Josh Ulm's collaborative Remedi Project (http://www.theremediproject.com/) is a bleeding-edge leading light. Requires a modern browser, a fistful of plug-ins, and a fast connection (or great patience).

Mike Cina's Trueistrue (http://www.trueistrue.com/) is a completely unique, ever-changing, strangely minimalist exploration of line and form.

Volumeone (http://www.volumeone.com/) is Matt Owens's masterpiece. Updated quarterly, the site explores abstract visual issues through Flash and Photoshop.

Yenz: The Secret Garden of Mutabor (http://www.yenz.com/) is a navigable space of large, striking images that load quickly because they are entirely vector-based. Created in Illustrator, Freehand, and Flash 3, the site guides you through one rich image field after another. The effect is both mesmerizing and soothing.

ZX26 (http://www.zx26.com/) is a noncommercial Japanese font site, built entirely with tiny animated GIFs and JavaScript.

Still hungry? The following design community sites showcase some of the newest and funkiest work being done anywhere. In addition, most are lovingly designed and cunningly programmed.

Design is Kinky (http://www.designiskinky.net/), created by Aussies Andrew Johnstone and Jade Palmer, features designer mug shots and hosts interviews with the likes of David Carson (not that there are really any likes of David Carson). For similar material, see Australia In Front (http://www.australianinfront.com.au/).

Kaliber 10000 (http://www.k10k.net/), created by Danish lads Michael Schmidt and Token Nygaard, publishes a special new design project every week and is a superbly designed site in its own right—as you probably gathered from the many times we've mentioned in this book.

Netdiver Net (http://www.netdiver.net/) feeds your eyes with links and your brain with close-up interviews. Got a great site? Netdiver might review it if it meets "chief imagineer" Carole Guevin's criteria: The 'diver seeks impeccable content as well as superb design.

Japan-based Shift (http://www.shift.jp.org/) , the mother of all design portals, has inspired most of the sites in this section. In addition to its online presence, the site generates real-world design products such as the Gasbook series and the IMG SRC 100 book.

Straight outta Luxembourg, Surfstation (http://www.surfstation.lu/) currently features the tiniest type on the Web. Fortunately the site's design news, interviews, and playful collaborative sections are easy and delightful to read.

Three.oh Inspirational Kingdom (http://www.threeoh.com/) brags precision design and special interactive features, as well as advanced and super-funky JavaScript tricks. (For instance, loading an interview or special design feature in a pop-up window causes the original window to be "grayed out" by means of a full-screen layer swap.)

Special mentions:

Joe Jenett's Coolstop (http://www.coolstop.com/v4.5/) was an independent portal to fine design and original content long before there was even a category for such sites, and continues to fulfill its mission with clarity, focus, and integrity. Its spiritual predecessor was Glenn Davis and Teresa Martin's Project Cool, still operational, but not the same since its founders departed.

Notice that nearly every site mentioned is a noncommercial, independent site. Coincidence? Read the Time Life Books.

Believe us when we tell you that the sites listed above are not even a fraction of one percent of the best such sites out there. And there is always room for more, which brings us to our valedictory address:

The Independent Content Producer Refuses to Die!

This book is written for professionals in a competitive market. Consequently, we've spent most of our time talking about job skills—present and future. But designers do not live by bread alone—not even when it's *really good* bread.

We've said it before and we'll say it again: If the Web is fascinating simply as a medium rife with challenges and rich in possibilities, it is even more alluring when you consider its low barrier to entry. This medium does not merely *permit* you to publish your own work, it begs for it.

From a purely selfish point of view, most of today's best-known web designers are famous for their personal sites, not for their commercial projects (though these are of course viewed and respected). Fame may seem a silly thing to seek, but it sure doesn't hurt when you're looking for your next job or your next client or approaching a backer to start your own agency.

The real jazz cats might do studio gigs to put three squares on the table, but dawn always caught them blowing mad bop in crazy uptown clubs. Real web designers jam after hours too—on personal and collaborative content and design sites, online magazines, and experimental spaces.

By creating and maintaining sites that cannot be controlled, compromised, disfigured, or deleted by the indifference or poor judgement of clients or managers, you will always have good work to show for yourself. More importantly, you have the chance to express yourself—to find out what you're made of when no client is paying you and to find out what you really want to say.

If you were a classical composer, you'd have to pay a symphony orchestra just to hear your own music. And if you were a filmmaker, forget about it. But in independent web production, the only questionable part of your budget is how much time you can afford.

No one is in control of this space. No one can tell you how to design it, how much to design it, when to "dial it down." No one will hold your hand and structure it for you. No one will create the content for you. What is in you? What thwarted creative potential is burning to get out, grow, and find its audience?

If you do this well, it will reflect back into the work you do for clients. Not only will this help your career, it will also enrich your life and the lives of others. Creating your content, designing it your way, repositioning yourself from vendor to author, you will have made your mark on the medium and perhaps on your generation.

You will have taken your talent to the Web.

Index

Symbols

A

B

C

D

E

F

G

H

I

J

K

L

M

N

O

P

Q

R

S

T

X-Z